To Svetlana,
my dear wife and best friend ever

Acknowledgments

I want to thank my teachers Georgy Tovstonogov, Mark Rekhels, and Ivan Kokh for sharing their knowledge with me.
I want to thank my wife, Svetlana, for believing in my work.
I want to thank Andy Noble, Sharon Marie Carnicke, Igor Rozinsky, Oscar Dekhtiar, Alex Makhtzier, Alfred Gershfeld, Alex Rivlin, and all my friends who contributed to this project.

Edward Rozinsky

Essential
Stage
Movement

Psycho-physical training for Actors

**This textbook is supported
by the Video Instructor Program on the Internet**

PHYSICAL THEATER
PUBLISHERS

E. Rozinsky
Essential Stage Movement
Psycho-physical training for Actors

ISBN 978-0-578-07436-8

Cover design: Igor Rozinsky
Interior design and illustrations: Edward Rozinsky

Physical Theater Publishers, USA *Miami, Florida*

CONTENTS

PART I   **THE THEORY**

PART II   **THE PRACTICE**

Preliminary exercises

Breathing exercises

Concentration exercises

Warm-up exercises

Concluding exercises

PART III   **THE METHODOLOGY**

INTRODUCTION

Having been studying, practicing, and teaching Performing Arts for the past sixty years and Stage Movement for fifty years, the knowledge obtained directly from my teachers, colleagues, and numerous books blended so much with personal observations, discoveries, and assumptions that it is quite difficult to verify its source. Specific concepts that I learned many years ago seem now like my inventions, and many of my advances sound to me sometimes like textbook proclamations. Serving the Theatre in many different roles, first as a dancer and mime actor, then as a choreographer and director, and finally as an educator and author, learning from some great teachers, and tutoring some celebrated actors led me to some, in my view, reliable conclusions. The fact that I gained all this experience in two culturally dissimilar worlds only persuaded me that the nature of acting is universal – something the great K. Stanislavsky declared long ago.

I began teaching Acting, Directing, and Stage Movement in the US, while toiling with learning a new language and, among other things uncovering equal professional terms, so familiar and so meaningful for me in Russian tongue but sounding ever so dubious in English. Soon I realized that to work successfully in this field, I would have to adjust some of my vocational beliefs to a new environment and a different culture. The texts known in the West as "The Method" and several books by and about Konstantin Stanislavsky that I have read in English did not help me much but produced only more significant confusion instead. As time went on, I realized that Stanislavsky is very much misinterpreted and, in most parts, misunderstood in the West. I often ask myself a question, how could such pedagogues, as Lee Strasberg or Stella Adler brilliant as they were, comprehend Stanislavsky System of Actors Training, for the most part, in absentee? How they managed to grasp it by merely observing its products for two weeks? Finally, one can announce an expert by learning this comprehensive System for several months without even knowing the language, when an average Russian theater artist or pedagogue spends a minimum of four years on discovering just the basics of the Stanislavsky System?

However, changing the status quo has never been even a part of my plans. I just wanted to teach Stage Movement to the future actors and to produce good theater. In doing this, I came across numerous methods, techniques, and systems in movement training in the US that did not impress me much because, in my humble opinion, they all were so detached from any particular acting technique.

I considered myself a practitioner and not a scholar, and I was not intended to spend the remainder of my life, proving what already existed and deemed natural and right to me. Therefore, I based this book on my knowledge of the Stanislavsky System, on the Method of physical training based on this System, and my newly acquired learning of American ethics and aesthetics. I intend to offer a tool to prepare students for acting careers in the area of Stage Movement.

It was in the US that I first heard the declaration, "Art is not Science." This declaration has a lot of sense and is hard to dispute. The problem, however, is that this statement routinely transmitted to the business of teaching the Arts. This formula turned out to be very convenient for individuals who never had a chance or desire to learn a proper method of teaching the arts. Therefore, in the field of Acting, they often confuse the capacity to act with the capability to teach acting. Nevertheless, these two are very different professions. The former is mostly intuitive when the latter is purposeful and meticulous. My deep conviction is that any educational method must be scientific, whether it relates to Mathematics, Astronomy, or Arts.

Useful can only be a theater education built on a set of principles. It should be highly determined, so the skills acquired by it would last. Among many principles of theater education, I value the following the most:

- *Discipline*
- *Commitment*
- *Artistic Taste*
- *Openness*
- *Hard work*
- *Mutual respect*

Regrettably, these and other useful attitudes do not belong to everyone by design. One must perpetually cultivate them in students/actors by developing very particular Faculties, Habits, and Skills that are beneficial for this convoluted, competitive, and rigorous profession. Along with my professional beliefs, I also inherited Stage Movement teaching methods from Russian theater education, and in a shortlist, they are:

- *From simple to complex*
- *Continuity and succession of the process*
- *Frequent change of Given Circumstances and Objectives*
- *Deliberate and repeated changes of Tempo-Rhythm*
- *No demonstration of "how-to" execute a movement*

A group of students must comprehend the material as the class graduates from a unit to semester to a year. We must keep in mind that the Theatre is a collaborative and collective art. Therefore, the ensemble becomes significant only when concepts accomplished collectively and incorporated into everyday existence.

Our Method of teaching Stage Movement stems from the experiments of the pedagogues of 19th century Francois Delsarte and E. Jacques-Dalcroze. Konstantin Stanislavsky himself, creating his program for a well-rounded actor, considered these two great innovators. His request to develop specialized movement training for the actor of Stanislavsky's trend was accomplished later by Muscovite, I. S. Ivanov, and then independently by a professor from Leningrad, Ivan Koch. Working separately and using the assumptions and even some exercises of Delsarte and Dalcroze, both came up with a well-grounded Method that proved to be beneficial for many generations of Russian actors. I studied with and worked under the supervision of Professor I. Koch for some years, further developing his ideas, particularly in the area of Basic Stage Movement and Mime. Since in the US, I have subjected teachings of this Method to numerous changes and adjustments in an attempt to bring to conformity with ethics and aesthetics of American Theater,. The changes were made mainly in the area of the selection of music, poems, and songs incorporated in the exercises. However, I added a good number of new exercises and modified some original ones to adjust this Method to the ever-changing ambiance of theater education.

Besides, I firmly believe that the teaching process is an avenue that runs both ways. I learn something from every student, and in return, I use this new experience to teach the next pupil better.

I completed a good portion of the present text about 30 years ago and proposed it for publishing. Some leading publishing houses politely rejected my proposal, referring to its non-commercial feature. They defined it to be beneficial for teachers as an instructional manual only. Irritated at first, I agreed with them later, for let us be honest: it is impossible to learn a practical subject like Stage Movement by merely reading a book. One may obtain physical skills mainly by practicing the exercises under the instructions of a live teacher. Consequently, until now, this Method was available to my immediate students only.

Recently, it became evident that the traditional ways of passing knowledge are not absolute. The Internet and Online courses are now modern tools in learning numerous subjects. A survey suggests that now young people learn more from video games and the Internet than they do from books. Considering the advancements of modern technology, I realized that a course in Stage Movement could exist in the form of Video Instructor.

Therefore, without compromising my artistic and pedagogical conscience, I have produced a one-semester 30 Lessons course in Essential Stage Movement taught by Video Instructor. This program is available now on the Internet.

However, this textbook would supplement the practical Lessons of the Video Instructor and give those interested in more than just developing their Faculties, Habits, and Skills. It will provide the ability to learn the History, Theory, and Methodology of the Essential Stage Movement.

In this text, we distinguish the following elements:

The goals of the subject or WHY do we teach Stage Movement. The WHAT do we teach or the practical exercises, and the tools of the subject. Finally, the methodological principles and techniques of the subject or HOW do we teach Stage Movement.

It is with great gratitude to my teachers and with an enormous sense of responsibility that I offer this work to the future generations of actors, directors, and pedagogues.

PART I

<u>THE THEORY</u>

CHAPTER ONE

OVERVIEW OF THE HISTORY OF STAGE MOVEMENT

Stage Movement, as an independent subject, is a relatively recent development in theater education. Let us define Stage Movement as specialized training of the body and mind that enables the actor to transform natural or organic movements of the everyday into expressive and meaningful physical actions on stage. Regarding this, K. Stanislavsky wrote, "Before even beginning to create [on stage], one must first bring to order one's muscles so that they would not obstruct the freedom of action."[1]

Let us also distinguish Stage Movement training from Dance exercise, Mime technique, and other stylized, conditional, and symbolic motions.

In the history of Theatre and Acting, from Ancient Greece up until the Nineteenth Century, there is no indication of the existence of any specific physical training for the actor. Nevertheless, we are aware of actor training that was particular in most theater development periods. For instance, in the Theater of Ancient Greece, where performances occurred only once a year during City Dionysia festival, they assigned actors to each participating playwright by a "lot" (or lottery.) We also know that some actors were more skillful than others were due to their experience, abilities, and practices. Therefore, during the preparation of the play period, the playwright worked with the actors, extras, and chorus on the style, characterization, and no doubt on movements to achieve maximum expression. We can assume that throughout six hundred years of Greek theater, generations of actors would improve their skills by learning from each other and practicing their craft. Some of them became famous among contemporaries regards to this training.

In Elizabethan England, theater finally grew to be professional. Out of approximately twenty members of an acting company, there were at all times three to five apprentices who would be trusted to play small parts and who, after five to eight years of continuous training, would become regular members. During the

Renaissance, with minor variations, the training was a part of theater practices in Spain, Italy, France, and other European countries. No question the physical exercise always was an integral element of general acting training. They would expect a skillful actor, among other things, to know how to dance, fence, fall, and realistically portray an assortment of human physical abilities, as well as disabilities.

Acting schools that began to mushroom in the Renaissance Period in many Western European countries paid more attention to the styles, the line of business, and the wearing of a costume than to a general preparation of the actor's body. Besides, most of the actors up until the emergence of Realism would play the same type of roles throughout their entire careers.

It was only in the mid-nineteenth century when the radical change of the political situation in Western Europe shattered many beliefs of humanity that a new era in creative arts, and certainly in theater, started to emerge. The so-called Modern Theatre brought with it many changes and innovations. New Drama demanded new acting styles and gradually elevated the acting as a profession from the level of Craft (akin to silversmith, shoemakers, etc.) to the degree of Art. These changes invited actors to perfect their abilities and not just to acquire, but also to maintain constantly additional skills in Dance, Acrobatics, Voice, Diction, and Movement.

The actor of the Modern Theater period had yet another task to accomplish. The fact that they began translating dramatic works into different languages for producing them in various countries forced actors, among other things, to study outlandish lifestyles, including the physical behavior of different cultures and diverse epochs. In short, there was an increasing necessity in the particular development of the physical apparatus.

History of Theater marks several uncoordinated attempts to concentrate the attention on the physical training of actors. Duke Saxe-Meiningen's troupe during their long rehearsal periods would work on each member's movements bringing it to near perfection. In his Théâtre Libre in Paris, Andre Antoine would reproduce every detail of the reality and apply the same standards to the movement and the speeches of his actors. Max Reinhardt originated a special notebook where he would meticulously record all the details of every move on stage along with other elements in rehearsals to enforce the performance of it by actors every time in the production.

The first known coordinated attempt to create a universal technique in physical education of the actor made by Frenchman François Delsarte (1811– 1871) was around the middle of the Nineteenth Century. Unsatisfied with the existing ways of teaching singing and acting in Paris Conservatory and being a victim of poor instructions himself (Delsarte had lost his voice taking singing classes), he began scrupulous research and managed to collect numerous facts and information on the subject. That led him to start teaching a course in his studio known as Cours d'Esthetique Appliqué.

The innovative method of Delsarte, based on scientific facts of his time, had inspired generations of artists of all kinds – painters, musicians, singers, dancers, and actors. His influence and coercive expertise had spread all over Western and Eastern Europe, and many famous artists claimed François Delsarte as their teacher. His main ideas regarding the actor's movement are as relevant today as they were pioneering and overpowering in his time. Delsarte taught, "Bodily movement produced by emotion, and if the movement was correct and true, the result of the movement left the body in a position which was also expressive of the emotion. However, it would be insincere, false and wrong to 'take a pose."[2]

In his theory and practice, Delsarte went far beyond his time, forewarning the biomechanics of Meyerhold and the Action Analysis of Stanislavsky System. Ted Shawn, known as "Father of American Dance," called him "a true scientist." Regretfully, the Delsarte method did not outlive the Master. During his life, he didn't find the time to systematize and publish his techniques and lessons, so popular with contemporaries. His teachings survived in part due to the efforts of his pupils.

For example, one of his students, an American, Steele Mackaye (1842 – 1894), began to study with Delsarte when the Master was already in semi-retirement and poor health. Mr. Mackaye spent eight months with the teacher, studying daily, and became proficient in Delsarte teachings. While in coaching, he developed his gymnastics system, approved by the Master, known as Harmonical Gymnastics, and designed expressly to train actors physically.

Steele Mackaye returned to America equipped with this great experience, and for the next twenty years "Delsarte" became a household name in theatrical circles and a trend among celebrated people in the country. There were serious plans to start a dramatic school in America based on the theories of François Delsarte. Unfortunately, these were also the years when a gradual emasculation of Delsarte's teachings began. In America, there appeared to be few interested in a deep revision and understanding of his system, and plenty of those eager to cash in by teaching a partial set of exercises to millions of contenders. In the absence of Film, Radio, and TV, the demand for live entertainment at the end of the Nineteenth Century was tremendous.

As a result, there was no shortage of publications concerning the Delsarte system, but they came from the pen of random authors. "The doctrine that [once] was built on a deep philosophical basis, with the scientific consistency, and rich in numerous possibilities regarding applicability in the art, in the third generation was defined as a system of 'aesthetic gymnastics,' with the add-on of 'emancipated dance."[3]

The theory of F. Delsarte also exerted a significant influence upon theatrical pedagogy in Russia at the end of Nineteenth and the beginning of the Twentieth Century. A famous stage pedagogue, art critic, and writer, Prince of Russia, Serge Volkonsky, published his book Expressive Man in 1913, which was a sincere attempt to summarize the principles of the French innovator. His interpretation of Delsarte left an indelible trace on Russian theatrical culture.

Another significant contribution to the development of the actor's physical education in the Nineteenth Century was the work of

Emile Jaques-Dalcroze (1842 – 1950), a Swiss composer, musician, and music educator. He created Eurhythmics, the art of interpreting the rhythm of musical composition in bodily movements, aiming to develop a sense of rhythm and symmetry. His system of musical education, in his own words, called "for a psycho-physical training based on the cult of natural rhythms." The profound influence of Dalcroze on the development of education in Music, Dance, Drama, and Opera is hard to calculate, as it became (whether knowingly or unknowingly) a part of any professional training in modern days.

Although E. Dalcroze created his system of exercises having in mind exclusively musicians, they very soon successfully applied it to the physical education of the actor. Many of his statements directly related to the movement on stage. He writes, "Muscles were made for movement, and rhythm is movement. It is impossible to conceive a rhythm without thinking of a body in motion. To move, a body requires a quantum of space and a quantum of time. The beginning and the end of the movement determine the amount of time and space involved... Neither weakness and stiffness, nor inattention should be permitted to modify the formation of a movement; a properly executed rhythm requires, as a preliminary condition, complete mastery of movements about energy, space, and time."[4]

His Methodological principles are equally significant in any art pedagogy and many great pedagogues of his time and afterward had accepted them. Moreover, indeed, how can anyone be against the following statement? "The best method of teaching is one that offers the pupil a problem which neither his memory nor his instinct for imitation can help him to solve."[5] Or this one: "Nobody can exercise several faculties at the same time before he has acquired, however crudely, at least one faculty."[6]

From the beginning of publishing his works in 1889, the art institutions of most civilized countries in the Western World instantly recognized and widely accepted E. J. Dalcroze. Along with his theoretical declarations, he had developed a series of exercises to drill students in rhythm, sense of space, and awareness. Many practices in the method based on walking. Jaques-Dalcroze assumed this being the natural breakdown of time into equal parts. For example, Dalcroze would improvise on the keyboard and asked the students to walk around the room following the music, responding directly to the beat, and the changes in speed and dynamics. Thus, students would become aware of how they had to adjust the length of their steps and how they needed to control their energy and body weight.

Very resourceful are his exercises where students must react to surprising commands and change the pace of walking while listening to the same music. Developing coordination with the help of special exercises was also a part of his lessons. For instance, students would walk in a specified rhythmical pattern while clapping regular bar time with their hands.

Developing correct breathing was an essential part of the Jaques-Dalcroze system and remains the most comprehensive teaching in this area until today. To develop faculties of the actors, the contemporaries/followers of Jaques-Dalcroze quite often combined his exercises with the exercises of Swedish Gymnastics invented by his compatriot Pehr Henrik Ling earlier in the Nineteenth Century. One of the most significant contributions of Henrik Ling was the invention of Swedish Bench and Swedish Bars. They transformed these two apparatuses later into more sophisticated machinery used currently for gymnastic competitions. Regretfully, these simple apparatuses gradually disappeared from gymnasiums; high-tech machines that, despite their versatility, can hardly replace the minimal initial gear substitute now.

Emile Jaques-Dalcroze increased understanding of the sources of music and movement in the human body. For nearly sixty years, he was an inspiring, imaginative master, whose musicianship and personality helped to shape many outstanding teachers and artists. Beyond the circle of his students and associates, his writings stimulated the broad public due to his Scientific Education ideas. He wrote, "A true pedagogue [in arts] should be at once psychologist, physiologist, and artist."[7]

Further development of Stage Movement as an independent discipline is closely connected with the emergence of a wide variety of acting styles in the Modern Period. Every new tendency or advance in the arts strived to create its unique expression in an attempt to reflect the confusion of its time and explore human fate in the chaos of the novel and complex conditions. The titles of some of these movements were Realism, Naturalism, Purism, Divisionism, etc. The followers of every such "ism" in the arts had to find the means of expression that would help them to prove their point.

Although this tendency regarding exactly the actor's movement was present in most of Western Europe and North America, exceptionally clearly it appeared in Russia at the beginning of the Twentieth Century.

Vsevolod Meyerhold (1874 – 1940), one of the most famous disciples of K. Stanislavsky and actor of the Moscow Art Theatre led by Stanislavsky, broke with his mentor for artistic differences and began his career as a theater director with apparent avant-garde inclinations. To support his unique vision of acting style, he created "biomechanics," a specialized physical training based on the idea that psychological and physiological processes are inextricably linked.

It would be appropriate here to recall that the term "biomechanics" belongs to a distinguished Russian scientist Nikolai Bernstein (1896 – 1966). He was the first to declare that the study of human motion is a unique key to the knowledge of brain activity patterns. Until then, they judged the human movement only in its external appearance. His goal was to discover the mechanism of control over the motion. However, by no means did N. Bernstein influence the study of the acting profession with the help of his method. On the other hand, without detracting from the outstanding contribution of V. Meyerhold in theater arts, we should note that his "biomechanics" not related to the scientific direction, developed by Bernstein.

Meyerhold argued that one could call up emotions in performance using movement and gesture, and he developed a strictly codified system of choreographic sequences (known as études, or "studies") used to express specific emotional and physical scenarios. Meyerhold based his theoretical concept of the "conditional theater" on the symbolic view that art and life are entirely different and should not have to imitate each other.

Nevertheless, "biomechanics" introduced by Meyerhold was a critical step towards developing a system of training that would improve significant faculties, such as balance, strength, coordination, agility, and flexibility.

Another example of a unique approach to the development of the actor's external technique of that period was Alexander Tairov (1885 – 1950). In his Chamber Theater, and later in his school, wishing to give his performers "that free movement, which is so necessary to the actor," Tairov besides the standard at the time classes in plasticity and dance/gymnastics, introduced additional courses in fencing, acrobatics, and juggling. He dreamed of a time when seven or eight years old children would start learning the craft of acting in an independent school. The best of them would become leading artists, and the rest would form, in his word "so-much-needed corps de Theatre."

To create his vision of a "synthetic theater,"[8] an amalgamation of music, design, and movement into a single statement, Alexander Tairov was always in search of a "master actor," an actor who would be able to use "unutilized abilities of the human body." He had a strong belief that drilling an actor in his profession must have the same intensity as a ballet dancer in his. Perhaps he achieved his ideal of physical expression by the actor the closest in his renowned production of "Princess Brambilla."

Still another pupil of K. Stanislavsky that notably contributed to the evolution of Stage Movement was Eugenie Vakhtangov (1883 – 1922). The most critical elements of acting for Vakhtangov have been the sense of rhythm and an expressive movement. He demanded that the actor would subordinate his being, his entire human organism, including the body movements, the movements of thought, and movements of feelings, to a given rhythm. He used to say, "One must take this rhythm inside, then all the physical movements of the body would submit to this rhythm by themselves involuntarily."

Incidentally, Michael Chekhov borrowed for his method the concept of necessity to develop rhythmic expression and plasticity of the body in pupils from his teacher Vakhtangov. In the studio of Moscow Arts Theatre, Chekhov conducted lessons on rhythmic movement and later wrote, "The body in space and the rhythms in time – these are the means of acting expression."[9]

Vakhtangov attributed great importance to the external technique development in the upbringing of actors and thus contributed to the subject of stage movement. In his lecture on the opening day of the Shchukin Studio School, he said, "At school, you should first acquire outer skills – the ability to master your voice and body..." To the development of inner skills, he made only his second point. Such consistency in the setting of goals reflects Vakhtangov's view on the place and the importance of the actor's mastership's outer skills.

It was Vakhtangov who introduced to the Theater such concepts as "sense of the stage," "sense of stage space," "sense of stage environment," "sense of time," "continuous line of movement," and others. As a theorist, Vakhtangov left us remarkably accurate ideas of hard-to-explain concepts such as elasticity and plasticity. As a teacher/educator, Vakhtangov gave the Theater a whole group of like-minded pedagogues trained in his particular theatrical faith.

At various periods, Stage movement disciplines have been taught in the Shchukin Institute of Theatre Arts by famous teachers such as N. G. Kustov, a student of Meyerhold, who taught biomechanics, as V. K. Griner, a pupil of Jaques-Dalcroze, who developed a unique method of teaching rhythm in drama school. Among others, I. S. Ivanov, a movement teacher, published the first textbook on physical training for the actor, and A. B. Nemerovsky, a prominent choreographer of combat scenes and the author of two books on movement for the actor.

K. S. Stanislavsky closely monitored all developments in the field of plasticity and stage movement of the time. Here and there, we find his comments on the work and the discoveries of Delsarte and Dalcroze. The accomplishments of his pupils in this area of theatrical pedagogy also did not escape his attention. In fact, in studios led by Stanislavsky in 20-s and 30-s, his brother, V. S. Alexeev, taught Dalcroze's method. However, the Master had made some significant corrections related to internal justification and comprehension of each movement performed to music. He repeatedly stressed the need to develop a specific discipline that would drill to the highest possible degree of outer skills. However, even though Stanislavsky had introduced some particular physical exercises, his merit in this area was mostly theoretical. Speaking in modern language, he was the consumer and the end-user of physical education for the actor program.

He wrote, "People do not know how to use the physical apparatus given them by nature. Moreover, they cannot even maintain it; they are not able to develop it. Flabby muscles, twisted skeleton, improper breathing – this is the common phenomenon in our lives. The latter are results of incompetent education and incorrect use of our physical apparatus. Not surprisingly, therefore, that the work meant for it by nature performed insufficiently... We need sound, strong, well-developed, well-proportioned bodies, without unnatural excesses."[10]

Fortunately, for us, his students and followers in the second and third generation faithfully fulfilled Stanislavsky's request. Based on the theories and practices of Russian teachers and practitioners of the beginning of the Twentieth Century, a distinct discipline, the Stage Movement began to take shape piece by piece in professional schools.

In 1937, I. S. Ivanov published the first textbook ever on stage movement called "Educating Actor's Movement," summarizing the experience of the pedagogues and theater directors of different trends. In his excellent book, Mr. Ivanov gave an account of the subject's goal and attempted to tie it up with the mainstream contemporary acting techniques. "To teach the creative application of movement is impossible," wrote Ivanov. "We can only educate the psychophysical apparatus in the direction, especially advantageous for the scenic work."[11]

His book intended for the instructors of acting schools became very popular among the students and professional actors. The book offered a particular knowledge of the anatomy and physiology of the human body in connection with theatrical movement applications. However, its significant portion dedicated to the description of numerous physical exercises was aimed at developing various abilities and faculties. The author had used extensive research and knowledge in gymnastics, acrobatics, fencing, wrestling, recreational physical exercising, and even boxing. Many Russian and Western European specialists have developed all these areas of physical training quite well by then.

For many years to come, "Educating Actor's Movement" had been the only source of reference for generations of students, actors, and instructors. The book inspired Ivanov's students and followers to develop the discipline further and one of them, A. B. Nemerovsky later wrote his book "Plastic Expressiveness of Actor,"[12] in which he presented some new exercises and etudes.

It is appropriate to mention here the name of an outstanding Russian pedagogue and researcher P. F. Lesgaft (1837 – 1909), who was a principal scientist in the area of the harmonious development of man through physical exercises. Even though he did not have a direct relationship with theater arts, some of his ideas were very helpful for his contemporaries, theatrical pedagogues. For instance, P. Lesgaft stated that physical exercise has the material (physical) and spiritual (ideal) aspect. He considered the principle of the anticipation of the results of physical actions, or preliminary awareness of what "needs to be done" in the exercise, to be especially important. In particular, he consistently recommended performing tasks "from words," i.e., without a demonstration of the exercise. That would ensure a clear preliminary image of its result and how to achieve the result in the student's mind.

When I. E. Ivanov in Moscow attempted to summarize the experience of movement teachers, Ivan Koch, another movement pedagogue, has emerged in the second-largest city in Russia, St. Petersburg (formerly Leningrad). It is a peculiar fact that these two cities had always been (and still are) rivals in many spheres of life, including the arts. Perhaps it goes back to the times in Russia's history when, in 1712, St. Petersburg became the capital of the country. Then in 1918, after the Revolution, the formal superiority had returned to Moscow. The subject of Theatre Arts is an unconfirmed notion that Muscovites in their approach are more commercial and mechanical than the artists from St. Petersburg. If any of this is true, then it was more apparent in the mid-century than today.

However, the real stimulus for this was that only in 1955, the methodological guidelines of K. S. Stanislavsky became available to the stage movement teachers due to the release of the third volume of his collected works. "Stanislavsky sought to create a special course in stage movement, which would include gymnastics, acrobatics, swordplay, juggling, Rhythmics, etc. all of these specially adapted for actors profession," wrote G. V. Kristy in the Introduction to this book.

Ivan Edmundovich Koch (1901 – 1979) came up with a thoughtful and consistent method of teaching Stage Movement that brought the subject to closer amalgamation with Stanislavsky System of actor training than anybody ever did before.

Ivan Koch was born in a petty-bourgeois family. His father was an architect and had built many significant buildings in St. Petersburg; some of them are still standing tall. When he was young, he became a student of a famous fencing instructor Mr. Ternan, a private school attached to the Corps of Pages. Mr. Ternan gave him the first lesson in 1913. Since then, fencing became Ivan's meaning of life. He managed to win various championships in foil fencing and the swordfight and three times (!) the national championships. Later he became a certified referee in fencing.

In 1933, Mr. Koch began teaching physical education and fencing in the Petrograd (now St. Petersburg) Institute for the Performing Arts. Hence, his association and later obsession with theater arts began. However, he had to move aside his theatrical contribution on the occasion of the so-called "Winter War" between the Soviet Union and Finland, which was a part of World War II. The

Red Army recruited Ivan Koch as a military instructor in hand-to-hand combat or the "dogfight." For 15 to 16 hours per day, Ivan taught Russian soldiers how to use a rifle and bayonet in close combat.

In 1941, when the Nazis occupied eastern parts of Russia, they evacuated the Institute for the Performing Arts to the city of Sverdlovsk. So, Prof. Koch moved there with his wife, Nadezhda Sturova, schooled in the method of Jean-Jacques Dalcroze. Incidentally, her teacher N. V. Romanova was a pupil of Dalcroze. While in Sverdlovsk, Ivan Koch, together with his wife, developed a complete course that combined the exercises in rhythmicity, the techniques of falls and carrying, the routines in stage combat, and speech motor coordination. They named this symbiosis the "Stage Movement."

After the war was over, Ivan Koch returned to Leningrad to resume teaching Stage Movement. By this time, he supplemented his course with the techniques in Period Movement, covering etiquettes of Spain (XVI century) France (XVII-XVIII century) and Russia (XIX century). From 1962 until the end of his life, Prof. I. Koch was the head of the Stage Movement Department of the Leningrad Institute of Theatre, Music, and Cinematography, yet a new name given to the school after the World War II. The department provided such disciplines as Stage Movement, Stage Fencing, Acrobatics, and Dance and later, Mime.

The author of the present book was associated with Ivan Edmundovich Koch from 1972 through 1978, initially as a student in the postgraduate program and then as an Instructor of Stage Movement under the Master. During this time, I wrote and published my first articles on the subject of stage movement. I was also instrumental in establishing the first in Soviet Union professional program to train Mime artists under the auspices of Stage Movement Department for which I created the program and wrote its primary curriculum.

Recognized are the efforts of a famous Polish theater director and pedagogue Jerzy Grotowski (1933 – 1999), to further develop the theory of physical training for the actor. Speaking of the contribution of this unique and innovative artist, we should keep in mind that, for him, the theater arts' most potent stimulus became his one-year apprenticeship with Yuri Zavadsky at the State Institute of Theatre Arts in Moscow in 1955– 56. Prof. Zavadsky is well-known in Russia devotee of his teachers K. Stanislavsky and E. Vakhtangov. Grotowski went his way, which is in the minds of many, a combination of the ideas of Stanislavsky, Meyerhold, Tairov, and Delsarte, but to begin something new, one always has to have a benchmark. For Grotowski, such a starting point was the ambiance of artistic achievements of the 50-s in Russia.

Grotowski's point of view on the physicality of the actor is what Lee Strasberg said about him, "To Grotowski, an actor is a man who works in public with his body, offering it publicly. The work with the actor's instrument consists of physical, figurative, and vocal training to guide him toward the right kind of concentration, to commit him totally, and to achieve a state of trance."[13]

Summing up the history of physical training in Western and Eastern Europe, we would like you to see how this process began in the middle of the Nineteenth Century and by the middle of the Twentieth Century reached the level that was satisfying in many ways. This process did not stop since, and it continues to advance to be on the same level as the ever-growing demand for a more skillful modern actor. The theater increasingly requires the actor to use new means of expressiveness, as every generation invents unique movement styles and patterns, such as French Illusion Mime, a distinctive performing style of Jacques Lecoq, a Break Dance, to name a few.

A single life would not be enough for a theater actor to become proficient in all known styles and patterns. However, what is possible to achieve is a sufficient movement training that would enable the actor to comprehend quickly and with ease any new pattern or any unfamiliar style required by the script, director, or the choreographer.

In North America, stage movement as an independent branch of learning in acting programs began to develop only in the 60-s of the last century when the urgency of such training turned out to be inevitable. A search for a suitable method or technique was on the minds of theater directors, educators, and pedagogues. The first specialists to respond to this need and to fill this gap were dance instructors. There was no shortage of dance teachers of all styles in North America, whether homebred or immigrant. Interesting to notice that in Russia, most of the stage movement instructors came to the theater from athletics, and in America, they came from dance.

However, the Dance was traditionally always a part of actor training, and young aspiring actors are getting the skill either in school or in taking classes on the side. Obviously, in a proper Stage Movement training, there had to be something more than just dance. As there was no comprehensive method known to satisfy the need, many pedagogues began to look into adjacent fields and areas of study, fit to apply to train actors. As a result, there came to light several approaches that are still in use, and some of them, like Alexander Technique, Feldenkrais Method, Laban/Bartenieff Movement Analysis, and Linklater, is considered now "conventional" techniques in American Theater education.

Some students and aspiring teachers went overseas to study with greats like Marcel Marceau, Jacques Lecoq, Jerzy Grotowski, etc. Still, others turned to Eastern culture in search of a "perfect" system to develop the actor's body. From there came such approaches as Yoga, Suzuki Method, and Butoh. Private schools that preach methods and techniques mentioned above have mushroomed in the US and Canada, and soon these approaches made their way to the mainstream of theater and drama departments of Colleges and Universities.

The next stage of this process was the usual attempt of many pedagogues to mix, or somewhat supplement a particular method with the elements of another. All this variety of approaches, combined with many stylized dance techniques, created a colorful picture of physical education for the actor, which is the reality in today's North American theater education.

It seems like it is a typical picture. Remember, "art is not science," right? However, there are two critical problems with most of the methods and techniques employed to develop psycho-physical abilities of the actor. First, none of them is comprehensive, and second, most of them not associated with acting in any way or manner.

One of the main goals of the actor's physical education is to transfer the habits and skills from the training exercises into the stage presentation. Students trained in dance, swordplay, manners, acrobatics, capable of "fighting" on stage, falling and lifting each other, in short, possessing a large complex of necessary skills, more than often, are unable to use these skills in the Acting class. All this supply stays passive until a student/actor learns how to apply one or another skill in the physical portrayal of a character.

A subject called "Stage Movement" or "Movement for Actor" must concentrate its attention on the final goal. It is to develop in the student a string of specific abilities for the acting profession. Besides, this subject should have nothing to do with any known particular style, fashion, or technique. Instead, this discipline must be capable of bringing an individual's physical capacity to such a degree, when this individual can perform virtually any style, fashion, or technique known or novel. The dramatic actor does not have to be a perfect dancer, an accomplished mime, or a skillful juggler. However, he/she must be capable of becoming any of this and do so quickly if his role calls for it.

The subject "Stage Movement" must also provide the actor with an apparent proficiency in how to apply his/her refined by the training abilities to produce unique and electrifying actions on stage. One must practice this in class and not just wish it to happen miraculously all by itself. It means that the exercises in movement class must have a concluding stage when a physical pattern applied in a simple sketch or étude. It also means that a stage movement instructor must possess education in acting methods to implement the basic demands of truthful presentation.

Actor, like any true artist, has an apparatus of the incarnation. The musician has his violin or a flute; the painter has his canvas, and a brush; the poet has words and rhythm. Performer, on the other hand, to express everything and anything that his imagination produces, has only his body. While a dancer depends on his muscles and ligaments, a singer on his vocal cords and diaphragm, the dramatic actor relies on his entire body. It is no secret that the actor's instrument is the most delicate of all. Musician, to protect his tool, would hide his violin in a casing, and the painter would cover his easel with a cloth, but an actor destined to use his instrument not only for the performance but also for sustaining his life. Despite this (or rather owing to this), as Emil Jaques-Dalcroze repeatedly insisted, "the human body is the most expressive instrument."

To maintain and to refine this apparatus actor must know its potentials, consider its weaknesses, and study the laws of controlling it. One can achieve this individually, and the history of theater knows examples of such self-education. However, the best and by far the fastest way to do it is to let a professional teacher train these abilities. A British actor, pedagogue, and author Bella Merlin after her training with Russian teachers in Moscow concluded that only a combination of teachers ("movement, emotion, and acting") could give good quality results.

Undoubtedly, all Theories or Methods, regarding such practical matter as acting are useless for application without the support of a series of exercises. An individual can understand a theoretical concept, but it would not bring him/her closer to the results in our profession. That is what, in our opinion, happened to the Stanislavsky System in North America. It simply dispersed since only a few exercises adopted (or copied) from lore were available to the interpreters of the system. The missing exercises (or missing links, if you wish) are routinely replaced by new ones, created by the interpreters in complete isolation from the original thought and idea, dispatching the method in a completely different direction. At the same time, Stanislavsky's apprentices and collaborators, who continue living and working in the same country and the society as the Master, have managed to develop his discoveries further. Even as Russia's social and political circumstances have changed since then, the fruitful work of Stanislavsky's followers is still in the process.

Recently, several occurrences have assisted in the rehabilitation of the Stanislavsky Method of Physical Actions in the West. Sharon M. Carnicke, in her book "Stanislavsky in Focus," finally voiced the suspicion that perhaps Stanislavsky's work was misunderstood and misrepresented in North America. Jean Benedetti had completed a new translation of some of Stanislavsky's key works and published it with Routledge Publishing. The original translation by Elizabeth Reynolds Hapgood was, in many ways, misleading due to the incorrect interpretation of the main terms of the System. After the collapse of the Soviet Union, some students, pedagogues, and professional actors went to study with Russian masters and came back to tell about it. On the other hand, some professional actors, directors, and pedagogues (including the author of this book) emigrated from Russia eager to share their knowledge with students and colleagues.

"The reason we should still bother with Stanislavsky today," wrote Bella Merlin, "is that maybe it's only now, at the dawn of a new millennium that his ideas are starting to make sense."[13]

Along with renewed information about Stanislavsky comes a growing interest in the news about theater education in general, the organization of theater business, and the essence of theater ethics in Russia.

We hope that this book will further promote the valuable experience accumulated by many generations of artists, scientists, and pedagogues in Eastern Europe in a particular field of Stage Movement.

CHAPTER TWO

MOVEMENT – MANIFESTATION OF ACTION

Since Aristotle, we observe the preoccupation of the critical thought with the leading problem of Literature and Arts – the relationship between Form and Content. As Arts progressed and changed along with the development of civilization, so did the philosophical interpretation of the relationship, control, and subordination between Form and Content.

Aristotle, for instance, believed that imitation involves human experience, and he saw a role for the arts in that sense only. According to Aristotle, the artist has the freedom to imitate aspects of nature but insists on the unity of Form and Content (formal and structural qualities). In short, the Form is what causes something to be the thing it is. Therefore, Aristotle relates Form to something inherent in the object.

Georg Hegel (1770 – 1831) argued as follows: our sensuous appreciation of Art concentrates upon the given "appearance"-- the "form." It is this that holds our attention, and that offers Art its peculiar individuality.[1]

Russian philosopher Plekhanov (1856 – 1918) highlighted the art's meaningfulness by writing that no artwork "may be limited to a form without content" because correspondence of the form to the content determines the artistic value of any work. "The more a form of artwork corresponds to its idea, the more it is successful."[2]

Moreover, the proportion of Form and Content in the mixture created from artwork largely depends on the point of view it looked upon – is it high culture or popular culture?

Let us leave aside the eternal debate about what is more important in the Art, the Form, or its Content. Besides, for various art forms, these terms have different prerequisites. For instance, in Literature, the content is the story, the facts, and the form could be a novel, a poem, or a play script. In Fine Arts, the content is an event, a subject, a story, and the form could be a painting, sculpture, or drawing. In Theatre Arts, the content is a play script, a story, a conflict, and the form may be the genre (tragedy, comedy, drama, etc.) setting, music, acting, etc.

In the present text, our point of interest is the Art of the actor, and we would like to determine what considered its content, and what the form is. The content in the work of actor (in order of significance) is the play script (scenario), the actor's thoughts and visualizations of the story, and the actions, which are determined and carefully selected in collaboration with the theater (TV or film) director. The actor, in partnership with the director, must find a suitable form to deliver the content to his audiences, which would assist him/her in conveying it in the most artistic, convincing, and unique way. Moreover, the form should specify the content, while the content drives the form into existence.

Remarkable is that the tools the actor can use in the creation of a form are all in his/her body: voice, bodily movements, gestures, and facial expression. However, it would be self-delusion to hope that the form would appear on stage by itself because of the truthful experiencing[3] ("perezhivanie" in Russian, Stanislavsky's term). Usually, a high reliance placed on intuition. Some even think that only intuition, and not the mastery of specialized techniques in Speech and Movement, would bring to life the precise and clear form. In stating this, they cite the authority of Stanislavsky, who indeed attached great importance to intuition. However, Stanislavsky never rejected a proper preliminary tuning of the embodiment apparatus so that the intuitively born form becomes most expressive.

Despite the apparent complexity of the concept of intuition, one thing agreed between the modern scientists; in assessing the situation, the individual's previous experience and knowledge are crucial. For us, this means that in addition to life experience, the actor must possess an array of various stage habits and skills that would serve him/her in a particular moment of stage presentation. The future actor should acquire a taste for the vivid physical expression of the life of his character. Moreover, the production, the director, and the actor himself throughout the entire professional career must continuously cultivate this habit under threat of gradually losing interest in physical expression.

Much too often, we come across a theatrical production where the actors rely mostly on the text and insincere ways this text delivered. As a rule, this is an indication of poor stage movement qualification. It results in a low level of psycho-physical qualities and the lack of particular stage habits and skills. The lack of sufficient training makes it extremely difficult to achieve an accurate and expressive form of behavior, even if the rehearsal process is correct.

To create a vivid image using the body, one must prepare his body in advance. The training gives the actor an external technique that enables him to perform any motion with ease and confidence. This external technique is capable of producing superior results in combination with the creative capacity of an individual.

Our observations reveal that young actors regarding moving on stage, as a rule, are inferior to experienced professionals. However, it seems like it is easier to move around for a young person. Experienced actors are considerably more expressive on stage than their youthful counterparts; the youthfulness does not create the quality of stage movement; the external (and inner) technique comes when working on stage, film, or TV.

Does this mean that the young actor should just patiently hang around until the proper skills finally develop? Of course, it does not! It is possible and even necessary to take care of it while in the theatrical school and sometimes perhaps later, in parallel with the first stage of the professional career.

Reduce this mandatory training to the following:
1. The future actor must recognize the capabilities of the extensive use of his body for meaningful stage action. Perhaps, Acting is the only profession where a person is facing a need to learn the facilities of his body particularly.

2. As one can only improve the natural human capabilities with subsequent training, the future actor must develop these capabilities in the right direction.
3. The aspiring actor should bring these capabilities to a level of semi-automatic skills, and some of them even to routine habits. Perfectly shaped permanent physical actions, when transferred to the stage involuntarily, would create superior results in a production.

K. Stanislavsky expressed all the above in one short aphorism: "First perceive, and then discipline thyself."

The result of the actor's work is a determined physical action, externally articulated in motions. Would the audience understand, or would it not the thought communicated by the actor depends entirely on the level of his, the actor's movement refinement. Therefore, the question of the actor's physical preparedness is among the most critical problems of theater education.

In the last years of his life and work, Konstantin Stanislavsky came up with something fundamentally new, something that he called "The Method of Simple Physical Actions." This discovery was unknown in the West until recently, for several apparent reasons. First, it was not widely publicized and known only to a small group of close apprentices and friends of Stanislavsky at the beginning. Second, the so-called "Iron Curtain" that existed between the Soviet Union and the West prevent a free exchange of any information. Third, the West's professionals had been confident they knew already enough about Stanislavsky's System to claim they knew everything.

However, the Master in the Soviet Union's followers picked up by and developed the Method of Simple Physical Actions to a level when no theater, educational institution, or actor could ignore it anymore. It would take another book to describe this system. However, in short, this Method demands from the actor seeking a "small truths" while performing simple physical actions, before searching for "great truth" of essential and profound psychological problems of the role.

"In real life... if a person has to do something," says Stanislavsky, "he goes and does it: undresses, dresses, rearranges things, opens or closes a door, window, reads a book, writes a letter, observes what's going on the outside, listens to what is happening with the neighbors above.

On stage, the person performs the same actions approximately, roughly, not as in real life. We want them to be presented not just precisely as in real life, but even more energetic, brighter, and more expressive."[4]

You should not, says Stanislavsky, "... just come on stage like a human, and not like an actor, without previously justifying your simple physical action with an array of imagination, given circumstances, 'what ifs' and so on."[5]

Therefore, in the end, the importance of simple physical actions is that it makes us justify and fill up this physical action with psychological content using our imagination. It is a trap for the emotion and the imagination, and the secret is that the process is natural and occurs through human psychology laws.

One of the followers of the method, a Russian theater director and pedagogue B. E. Zakhava, explains further, "Physical action arouses all the soulful energy of the creative nature of actor. In a way, it absorbs the emotional life of the actor: his attention, belief, his evaluation of the given circumstances, his attitude, thoughts, and feelings. So, just seeing the actor putting on a coat on stage, we can speculate what is in his soul at that time."[6]

K. Stanislavsky planted the doctrine of the simple physical action at the forefront of his Method as the provocateur of the sense of truth and stage faith, internal action and emotion, and imagination. From this teaching comes a request addressed directly to the actor: to be extremely demanding of himself, and to forbid himself to forgive even a minor inaccuracy or negligence or falsity or assumption in this area.

The importance of working on external technique is doubtless; the actor needs it to acquire the correct ways and habits in the reproduction of these simple physical acts. "Without a consummate mastery of this technique, without an easy skill in this field, the most brilliant ideas of the actor, all his boldest and inspiring inner visions are doomed to failure in advance," wrote Alexander Tairov.[7]

In connection with this, A. Tairov gives the following example described by S. Volkonsky in his book "Animated Man."

An actor on stage declares his love. A sincere and flaming emotion is burning in his heart. However, he cannot control his body. The body left to itself reflects the feeling in its way. His inner romantic excitement incarnates into the intensive trembling of his legs. As a result, the audience laughs: the real emotion of the actor not only did not reach the spectator, but just the opposite, inappropriate trembling of his legs, or wrong form, distorted already the image itself, giving it the features that the actor tried to avoid.

The player must acquire authority over his material; he must recognize it and develop so it would become flexible, reliable, and obedient to his will. The student must prepare himself for an enormous work, for daily training, and should consider the fact that he/she destined to work on the inherited ignorant plasticity - a cranky and ever-changing material.

One of Stanislavsky's assistants in his Opera/Drama Studio recalls the Master as saying, "How terrible must be the suffering of an actor who has great sensations but is unable to express anything because his physical apparatus does not correspond to his feelings. The hands are twisted, the body is clumsy, and the voice has no sound... They are going to laugh at his feelings. Ask your teachers what muscles you should develop and dedicate years to this work. Achieve a state when your muscles would seek the truth of motion by themselves. Develop a muscle regulator in you, so that this inner inspector would control all your movements regardless of your will, and would eliminate all unnecessary stress, leaving only effort necessary to perform this particular action. You cannot even imagine the happiness an actor experiences when the audience understands him. One cannot think of the highest joy. But to experience this, one can, and one must compel oneself to work and more work."[8]

Summarizing the vast experience of many generations of great actors, theater directors, scientists, and pedagogues in the subject of physical expression, we can recognize numerous aspects and qualities of body motion on stage that are and always will be an integral part of the actor's creative process.

Among them are:

Movement on stage is different from movement in everyday life.

Movement on stage is a reflection of the actor's thoughts and ideas at the time of creation.

Movement on stage must contain artistic qualities in it.

Movement on stage should express the unique physical qualities of a portrayed character.

Movement on stage must be economical to save the actor's energy.

Movement on stage is a visual representation of the tempo-rhythm of a character, a scene, and play.

Movement on stage should be a display of human Grace and Sculptureness.

Movement on stage must be void of meaningless gestures.

Movement on stage should create the illusion of habitude related to a character played by the actor.

Movement on stage must look natural in both small and large amplitudes.

Movement on stage demands adjustment to the limited space of a stage, movie, or TV set.

Movement on stage must be brought to a level when the actor finds the body's correct position subconsciously.

Movement on stage must be subservient to the actor's thought and visualization.

But most of all –

Movement on Stage must be the Manifestation of Action.

Somehow or other, one needs to develop all the qualities declared above in the Stage Movement class. This process related to the Methodology of the subject largely depends on the instructor's socio-political views, artistic taste, and the combination of theatrical beliefs he preaches. Also, one can acquire the qualities described above only by developing the psycho-physical capabilities of the body. That is precisely a subject of the next Chapter. Our experience indicates that amalgamating the process of developing the body's abilities and obtaining the necessary qualities of movements with the help of specially selected and thoroughly designed exercises is proven to be rewarding. Besides, these exercises guarantee the best effects of the educational process if arranged in a particular order.

CHAPTER THREE

ANALYSIS OF PSYCHO-PHYSICAL FACULTIES, HABITS AND SKILLS

Physical fitness and expressive body movements have always been a desired part of the acting profession. However, stage movement as a specific and independent subject is a relatively recent development in formal theatrical education.

All the variety and abundance of man's spiritual life ultimately reveals in the movement of his muscles. Actions and deeds externalize in muscular movements while the effort of the respiratory and vocal apparatus muscles create speech. Celebrated Russian Physiologist Ivan Sechenov (1829 – 1905) wrote, "Whether a child laughs at the sight of a toy, or Garibaldi smiles, driven out for his excessive love for the motherland, whether the girl trembles at the first thought of love or Newton creates universal laws and writes them on paper – always the ultimate result is the muscular movement."[1] The image created on stage, and the whole complexity of the life of the human spirit created by him, is also embodied none other than through muscular movement.

If the actor's muscles were underdeveloped and inactive, then the delicate details of his feelings would not reach the audience. Moreover, by the theory of inseparable connection of body and soul, every muscle clamp leads to a mental block, as well as a mental block leads to muscle clamp. The stressed body becomes a hindrance to the completion of organic processes. Likewise, the expressiveness and efficiency of action, the completeness of the external form of embodiment, depends on how good the body prepared.

Stanislavsky always paid a great deal of attention to the development and improvement of the physical apparatus of the embodiment. He strove to make the actor's body responsive to emotional changes with the sensitivity of a barometer.

"The dependence of the physical life of a performing artist from his spiritual life is especially important, particularly in our school of acting," says Stanislavsky. "That is why the artist of our trend must take care not only of the internal apparatus, which creates a process of experiencing but of the outer, corporeal apparatus that accurately portrays the results of creative work of our sense, that is its external form of embodiment."[2]

Ever since the professionals recognized the necessity of specialized body training for the actor, there have been numerous attempts to create a system or a method that would serve as a universal training tool. As a result, there are now dozens of different ways and techniques in existence used by educators to prepare the actor's body for the stage, TV, or film work. Add various combinations of these methods and techniques, and you will get quite a colorful picture.

There are significant differences between these methods and techniques, which we do not intend to discuss here. Instead, we will try to institute essential faculties a stage movement program that maintains to do the job must develop. By faculties, we mean the abilities that a contemporary actor of any trend or style must possess to work in the theater, TV, or film successfully. Every profession on earth requires a specific set of qualities. If an individual wants to succeed in a particular trade, he/she should already have these abilities or develop such in him/herself. It is the same with the acting profession where movement training is just a part of the actor's education.

The exercises might be different. The ways of presenting these exercises might be different. Even the philosophical background of such methods might be diverse, but a human body is continuously built of bones, muscles, ligaments, nerves, etc. Therefore, first, we need to determine what exactly we intend to develop. A human body has limits in developing individual faculties, so we recognize that there must be a limited list of faculties and combinations of these faculties that any stage movement program has to instill. If we all can agree on this inventory, then the next step would be to determine the ways and methods of developing such faculties. However, we must keep in mind that the time to train these qualities is also limited.

Konstantin Stanislavsky once said, "About the art, one should speak and write simple and clear. Obscure words scare a student. They excite the brain and not the heart." We will take this as our guideline. There is a lot of confusion on the subject of what precisely the actor should or should not learn and develop in a movement program. Some are not able to identify skills. Others confuse skills and habits. There is also a popular notion that "Art is not Science" thereby, art does not have to obey any laws or to stick to any criteria. It is true, arts are not comparable to mathematics or physics, but in teaching the arts, there must be an order and a clear objective as in any other field of knowledge.

We will attempt to classify all the psycho-physical capabilities the actor needs to possess and develop for successful and rewarding work in performing arts. "Essential Stage Movement" will use this classification and describe how to deliver all necessary elements to the student. We divide all the knowledge and abilities into the following three categories:

- **FACULTIES**
- **HABITS**
- **SKILLS**

Let us consider the **FACULTIES** as the inherent qualities of the human body. Any healthy individual acquires these qualities throughout the growing to function effectively in everyday life. The degree of development of a particular faculty (or a combination of faculties) varies from one individual to another. In reality, it depends on numerous factors such as the social structure of the society, family upbringing, sex, education, climatic conditions in which the individual raised, as well as current fashion in closing, preference in music and social dance, etc. By the time an individual has entered a stage movement program, he/she already possesses all the Faculties, though developed to various degrees. The higher the advance, the closer the individual is, if you wish, to what some would call talent.

The unique feature of a FACULTY is – once developed, it stays with an individual for the rest of his life. The reason faculties are so stubborn and remain so strong is that we use them continually and apply them perpetually without even knowing it in everyday life.

Let us consider now **HABITS** as learned qualities. Webster's New Collegiate Dictionary defines a habit as "an acquired mode of behavior that has become nearly or completely involuntary." Most professions require specific habits that are beneficial for trade. Acting is not an exception. It requires a person to have multiple particular habits; also, every new role might call for other one or even several specific habits. Thus, the capacity to learn a new habit quickly becomes the essentiality of the acting profession. To make it possible actor must develop the Faculties to the highest probable degree.

Compared with the faculties, the lifespan of the habits is shorter. If not repeated frequently, a habit might fade away. Some of the habits learned in theater school can stay very long and can improve in the course of professional activities. Others, if unused or neglected, would gradually weaken and finally disappear. Another distinction between the Habit and the Faculty is that the habit, in a sense, controlled consciously while the faculty works involuntarily.

SKILLS are specific qualities learned on purpose by the individual. The dictionary description of the skill is "dexterity or coordination, especially in the execution of learned physical tasks." The stage, TV, and film demand many skills from the actor and the skills list is continuously growing with the development of performing arts. It would be fair to say that the more skills an actor possess, the bigger the range of roles he/she can tackle. It is common for the actor to learn new skills for every next character, and so it is difficult, if not impossible, to foresee what skills a professional actor will need next.

Naturally, a stage movement program can develop only some of the skills due to the time limit. Every school determines which skills are most important to cultivate. However, no school or a curriculum can sincerely claim that they develop all the skills the actor needs for a professional career. Fortunately, they do not even have to. What is crucial for the actor is to obtain the capacity to learn a new skill in a short period. Developing Faculties and Habits can enable the actor to do just this.

There is another factor, which affects the quick and steady learning of a new skill. Any physical skill is nothing else but a movement pattern. According to contemporary psychology, the more patterns our mind accumulates, the easier it is to learn a new one.

The lifespan of a Skill is even shorter than that of a Habit. It only lasts while the individual practice it and fades away soon after the repetition stops. Fortunately, the information of this ability remains in our mind for a long time, and should we decide to restore a skill, it will not take as long as it did the first time.

Another distinctive characteristic of a Skill is its unique coloring because any skill incorporates a unique set of previous experiences of the individual multiplied by his/her imagination.

It is important to understand that any habit is a combination of two or more faculties, and any skill is an amalgamation of different faculties and habits. Thus, an individual is quite capable of learning habits and skills even without first improving his faculties. However, in this case, the process of learning will be longer, and the results less impressive. Well, isn't it precisely what we expect from a professional actor? Therefore, the advantage of developing the Faculties before anything else is too apparent.

The following is a list of psycho-physical Faculties, fundamental Habits, and some specific Skills, which in our opinion, are essential for a contemporary acting student to acquire for a career in the performing arts.

FACULTIES:
1. Awareness
2. Balance
3. Coordination
4. Proper Breathing

5. Flexibility and Mobility of Joints
6. Motion memory
7. Rhythmicity
8. Stamina
9. Strength
10. Velocity

Except for Strength, and Flexibility and Mobility of Joints (mostly physical qualities), all faculties listed above are psycho-physical abilities. They are a combination of mental and physical behavior. We have to engage both the mind and the body to develop these faculties productively. More so, all the habits and skills having different faculties as part of their essence inevitably engage a combined effort of body and mind. Therefore, educating one's body, in reality, is educating one's mind. The following definition of each listed faculty to one degree or another will illustrate this statement.

AWARENESS is the ability to apply the mind consciously to an object, sense, or thought. As a psycho-physical quality, it provides the brain with purposeful and selective focusing on a particular object or subject, whether it is outside or inside of the body. Being conscious of delicate deviations in a performance, a knowledgeable actor can apply considerable control over situations on stage. Regarding stage movement training, this faculty is utterly crucial as it takes care of careful consideration of a movement pattern's fine details; it either performed by the student or observed by him.

BALANCE (or equilibrium) is the ability to maintain physical stability by continuously adjusting to changing gravitational and spatial relationships. The three interacting parts of the nervous system that manage this ability are the visual organs, the vestibular apparatus of the ear, and the midbrain. The necessity of performing unusual poses and motions in limited space of the stage, TV, or movie set, and the need to execute it often with reduced support makes the importance of improving this faculty obvious.

COORDINATION is the ability to use more than one set of muscle movements simultaneously. For the actor, this means to coordinate movement patterns performed by separate parts of the body with the voice apparatus. Being responsible for performing intricate movement patterns of different epochs, various age categories, highly stylized movements, etc. the actor has to be prepared to meet endless combinations. It appears as if the mind has to control several movement patterns or several sets of muscles simultaneously, which is virtually impossible. Fortunately, our brain can switch its application from one subject to another almost instantly. So, development of Coordination means enabling the mind to increase the speed of the transitions.

PROPER BREATHING is the ability to maintain rhythmical and continuous breathing in extreme attitudes of the body or unusual motion situations and emotional stress that the acting profession requires more than often. Breathing is the natural act of supplying the body with oxygen and relieving it of carbon dioxide. By learning how to control breathing, the actor learns how to save physical energy and, consequently, become more productive. Proper breathing is related to Stamina and Velocity, the other two essential faculties.

FLEXIBILITY AND MOBILITY OF JOINTS is a quality of being supple and related to the extent of motion that is achievable by a joint or a series of joints. There are certain limitations in the development of Flexibility determined by the structure of the skeleton. However, the achievements of individual acrobats and contortionists make us believe that the human body has no limits. The development of Flexibility is a slow and gradual process of expansion of the range of motion at the joint. Any attempt to speed the process might be harmful and cause injury.

MOTION MEMORY (or Kinesthetic Memory) is the ability to reproduce or remember movements learned and retained, mainly through associative mechanisms. To have a good Motion Memory means to be able to reproduce in the same direction, with the same amplitude, speed, rhythm, succession, and nature once learned movement. It also means the ability to duplicate various motions immediately following a demonstration or even those seen long before. Motion Memory closely connected with and influenced by auditory, visual, and other perceptions.

RHYTHMICITY is the ability of the body to respond rhythmically. Regarding Stage Movement, to act rhythmically means something more than just to have a sense of rhythm. An individual that can sing or play an instrument rhythmically is not necessarily capable of moving his body about rhythmically. To be exact, Rhythmicity is the ability to respond to the inner or outer rhythm with body movements.

STAMINA is the ability to withstand hardship, adversity, or stress. As applied to the movement, it is the ability to distribute the reserve of nervous energy through a time interval, in our trade through a production, rehearsal, or a lesson. The Stamina that is related to the habit called Willpower and developed in combination with other psycho-physical faculties.

STRENGTH is the quality of possessing high physical power. The actor needs Strength to supplement his Stamina and Balance. Also, some special skills and habits demand reasonable Strength. However, the program ought to develop this faculty in the future actors only to a reasonable degree. We have to remember that we train the actor and not the athlete. In our business, overdeveloped Strength often becomes an obstruction to extend other abilities such as Suppleness and Dexterity.

VELOCITY is the ability to perform linear motions with variable speed and rate in a specified direction. The development of this inborn faculty would have to deal with exercising rapidness and slowness in performing different movement patterns. These qualities are essential for the actor to develop, yet we pay more attention to the slowness. The reason is that the high speed of modern life created by competition in every aspect of social existence leaves almost no space for a relaxing pace. The people just do not have enough experience with slow movements. For the future actor, such physical behavior is challenging and in need to exercise.

All the faculties described above are, in fact, essential qualities. It is possible to develop some of them separately, others – only in combination with additional faculties. Faculties eventually become supporters of one or another Habit or Skill in the process of training. In other words, the Habits and Skills built on the foundation of previously developed Faculties. In its turn, practicing a habit or a skill further improves faculties that back them up. That is one of the reasons faculties have a much longer lifespan than habits or skills.

In comparison to faculties, HABITS are abilities that are more complex and demand a various amount of time to acquire. The amount of time needed is in direct relation to the level the associated faculties developed. Also, most Habits listed below have an artistic nature to use by the actor as a material in creating the character. The following is a list of Habits that we believe any stage movement program ought to have.

HABITS:

1. Amplitude of movement
2. Awareness of Space
3. Awareness of Time
4. Concentration
5. Continuous and Halted motion
6. Proper Posture
7. Proper Gait
8. Courage and Decisiveness
9. Dexterity
10. Economy of movement
11. Muscle control
12. Precision of physical act
13. Sculptureness

14. Suppleness
15. Tempo-Rhythm of the physical act
16. Willpower

Amplitude of Movement is the ability to utilize large or small motions with ease when creating different styles of physical behavior. It is common to find this habit underdeveloped in students, especially regarding large amplitudes. The reality of modern social life often requires an individual to hide real emotions and feelings. So-called "good manners" restrict the physical behavior of a contemporary individual in developed countries. Consequently, young people who choose the profession of acting are often habitually limited in their movement expressiveness. Without developing the Amplitude of Movement, the actor will not be able to tackle most of the historical characters and generally would have a problem to be expressive in any role. We must develop this habit purposely to maximize the motion possibilities of the actor's body. Previously developed Motion Memory, Rhythmicity, Coordination, and some other faculties would provide the support.

Awareness of Space is a particular habit, representing the ability to fit physical activity into reduced space without breaking the illusion of reality. It is a vital habit for the actor whose working space is a stage, a TV set, or a Film locality, usually full of subjects and objects, which continuously change positions. Furthermore, it is common in the theater practice to perform the same show on different stages during touring. More so, the conventions of modern theater often put the actor in the circumstances when the physical set is non-existent, and Awareness of space depends solely on the actor's imagination. Sheila Kogan, in her book Step by Step: A Complete Movement Education Curriculum rightly states, "Awareness of space is a set of specific, somewhat mundane skills." The sense of space is a unique habit of a performer acquired by Motion Memory, Coordination, and Awareness.

Awareness of Time is the ability to control stage time (which is virtually different from real life) pertaining to the tempo-rhythm of psycho-physical action. Included in this habit is both the ability either to succumb to the current tempo-rhythm or to challenge the latter with one's own by choice. Stage time depends on "given circumstances" of the play, or a scene, and reflects n the actions of a performer. This habit strongly related to a faculty we call Rhythmicity.

Concentration is the ability to direct attention to a single object for the desired time. This habit itself is a composite of Awareness and Willpower. It is also the capability to switch focus from one object to another instantly. The actor must cultivate this habit to such an extent when the process of turning attention becomes instant, effortless, and natural, thus creating an illusion of reality. There are many distractions during production, the presence of the audience being the strongest. By learning to concentrate on the "physical actions" (Stanislavsky's term) of the character, the actor overcomes this problem.

Continuous and Halted motions are two parts of the ability representing the essence of the actor's body's expressiveness. In real life, no human being intentionally moves either continuous or halted (not to confuse with slower or faster) for any notable length of time. On the contrary, on stage (film, TV), the actor is asked to do so frequently and for substantial periods. This ability should turn into a habit to use it in strictly measured doses at will. Coordination, Motion Memory, Rhythmicity, Balance, and Strength are some faculties that would help to grow this vital habit.

Proper Posture as aesthetic habit, is a conventional notion perpetually changing with the development of the tastes and preferences of the society. What is "proper posture" today did not look the same in the 16th century or 18th century and vice versa. As a functional value, Proper Posture (some would call it neutral) is a balanced position of the body that secures the best conditions for breathing and minimizes muscle tension. According to the modem notion of beauty and harmony, the aesthetic value of it is in carrying the body with poise and grace. The actor must make a habit of positioning his feet, neck, spinal column, legs, and arms with ease to reflect a Proper Posture.

Proper Gait is akin to Proper Posture regarding its conventionality. Because every individual has a unique background in developing his walking habits and that most parents and schools are no more concerned with the manner young people walk, the development of Proper Gait becomes a significant part of the actor's movement education. Even though our society is overly concerned with self-image, for the actor, it becomes an artistic value. It is a known fact that the stage and camera "magnify" any imperfection in motion. Bad habits in walking might become such a substantial issue on stage that it would take the attention of the spectator away from the creative features. Drill both Proper Posture and Proper Gait continuously in Stage Movement program. Many of the faculties and habits described in this chapter also actively support these habits.

Courage and Decisiveness. Webster's Collegiate Dictionary defines courage as "mental and moral strength to venture, persevere, and withstand danger, fear, or difficulty." Indecisive, weak individuals can easily give up in ever-changing and challenging circumstances of stage performance. More so, theater and film work sometimes demands to perform dangerous movement patterns, such as acrobatic stunts, jumps, scenes with wild animals, scenes involving dangerous weapons, etc. In situations like this, courage would be a desirable skill. Even the decision to take on a complex and uncommon role is hard to make without trained courage. Related to Willpower, Courage includes a combination of many faculties. An individual who has his Balance, Coordination, Strength, Flexibility, and Stamina developed to the degree of self-confidence would have no problem building Courage and Decisiveness into his habit.

Dexterity is an intricate and multi-faceted psycho-physical quality. We define it as dexterity in using the body or parts of the body "to the fitting of our movements to the arising problems."[3] In everyday life, one can observe dexterous people everywhere: in the workplace, on the street, at the stadium, etc. We also consider dexterous those who move with readiness and grace. An individual found a Dexterous is a compliment to a highly developed combination of the following faculties: Balance, Coordination, Rhythmicity, Strength, Mobility of joints, and Velocity. Athletes must be dexterous too. However, there is a difference between the dexterity of an athlete and the dexterity of an actor. We define the actor's dexterity as the ability to perform desirable movements swiftly and precisely in the "given circumstances"[4] of the performance, based on a correct evaluation of the stage situation. Everyday experience suggests that Dexterity is not innate quality and liable for improvement. Dexterity is obtainable and does not require any specific characteristics of a human body.

Economy of Movement is the ability to minimize the effort consciously in performing a motion. We know that various individuals use different degrees of energy to perform certain physical activities. The more the effort, the sooner the individual gets exhausted. The actor must acquire a habit to find the most economical way of performing a physical act. One can achieve this essential habit with special exercises utilizing Balance, Motion Memory, Stamina, Strength, Awareness, as well as other faculties.

Muscle Control is the ability to control all the voluntary movements that form a physical activity and turn them into automatic or semi-automatic. According to Stanislavsky, these thoroughly selected and properly organized movements would bring to life involuntary actions and even emotions, thus making the stage appearance vivid and realistic. Muscle control becomes a habit upon specialized training using vastly developed Motion memory and Awareness.

Precision of Physical act is a quality related to the Muscle Control but singled out as a specific habit due to its immediate importance for the actor. We believe that any physical action on stage must be definite and clear as it represents an exact and precise thought or intention. It must have all the following characteristics: the beginning, the progression, the climax, and the end. There should be no confusion in the spectator's mind as to where one physical act ends, and the next physical action begins. Developed Balance, Awareness, Motion memory, Coordination, and Rhythmicity would serve as a sound basis for training Precision of Physical act to make it a steady habit.

Sculptureness considered the highest demonstration of the physical form of the body. Manifested in the precise muscle tension (as Stanislavsky put it "no more, no less"), this quality, when comprehended, makes the actor look graceful and organic throughout his/her stage existence.

Suppleness is the ability to perform bending and twisting motions with ease and grace. Related to Dexterity, it is a physical quality based on Flexibility and mobility of joints and Rhythmicity. Suppleness becomes an artistic habit when determined by the performance of motivated, thoroughly selected movements while creating a character.

Tempo-Rhythm of the Physical Act. K. Stanislavsky introduced this term to define the intensity of the actor's inner or emotional life in the role. He wrote, "Every human passion, or state, or emotion has its own Tempo-Rhythm. Every minute of existence inside and outside of us, there exists one or another Tempo-Rhythm."[5]

Tempo-Rhythm of Physical Act is the ability to perform a physical action at a given pace, during a given time, within a given space. According to Stanislavsky, precisely as any real-life emotion expresses itself in a certain Tempo-Rhythm of physical behavior, the properly built Tempo-Rhythm of physical action on stage will undeniably bring corresponding emotion. Base the drilling of this habit on previously developed Coordination, Rhythmicity, Velocity, and Awareness.

Willpower is an essential quality of human consciousness and is an integral part of any psycho-physical act. Some of the faculties that form Willpower are -- Courage and Decisiveness, Stamina, and Concentration. Another definition of Willpower is a regulator of human impulses and actions. Developed to the level of a habit, Will Power becomes one of the most desired qualities of the professional actor.

Finally, we will define SKILLS as unique capabilities the actor should possess during his professional training to expand his/her repertoire, thus becoming versatile and employable. A student can successfully learn these skills by making use of the arsenal of developed faculties and habits.

In comparison to faculties and habits, skills have distinct artistic characteristics and values as they include creative elements. The professional actor must own an assortment of skills just to begin his/her career. However, it is unreasonable to attempt to teach the student all the possible skills. Firstly, the time for initial training is limited. Secondly, why waste time on a skill that the actors might never need? Instead, the actor should be able and even eager to learn any new skill or recall a forgotten one if a particular role demands it. It would be appropriate to begin working on skills only after robust faculties and steady habits already developed.

Below are both the list and definition of several movement skills, which in our opinion, are the most valuable and widely used. These skills should be a part of any respectful program of a professional acting school.

SKILLS:

1. *Acrobatics*
2. *Unarmed stage combat*
3. *Illusion Mime techniques*
4. *Period movement and Period manners*
5. *Stage falls*
6. *Stage lifts and carries*

7. *Armed stage combat*

There are also special skills in different styles of Dance, which are equally crucial for the actor, but we left them off intentionally as it would be the dance program's subject. However, we firmly believe that the actor's dance program must be specially designed and limited in scope to preserve the sincerity and spontaneity of the actor's physical behavior. Regardless of widespread opinion, just any dance class is not necessarily beneficial for a future dramatic actor.

Acrobatics is a set of skills that is very functional for the actor, especially in the theater, where the use of a stunt person is not an option. However, these skills must be limited to the most common techniques, such as tumbles, cartwheels, hand and shoulder stands, etc. The essential purpose of acrobatics is that it helps to develop Courage and Decisiveness in students. Acrobatic skills also serve as a preparation for more complex and artistic skills such as Stage falls and Stage combat.

Unarmed Stage Combat is a group of sophisticated techniques in stage violence. It ranges from simple stunt such as the slap in a face, pushing, and pulling the hair to very advanced techniques creating an illusion of a fistfight, various kicks, and even a mass brawl. The essential quality of stage combat techniques is that once being comprehended, they are mostly harmless. Using acrobatics as groundwork, Unarmed Stage Combat also employs many faculties and habits developed previously in Stage Movement class.

Illusion Mime Technique is a very particular skill. One should present it to the dramatic actor in moderate doses due to the highly stylized movements it incorporates. Just like it is with the Dance, if overdone, it might affect the physical behavior of the actor and cause some mannerism in his/her movement. Teachers and instructors must remember that the actor should be able to create any stylized motion when the role demands it. Still, we do not believe any director wants Hamlet, or Cyrano de Bergerac, or Willy Loman to look like a mime or a dancer. However, mime techniques allow the student to develop and improve his faculties and habits further using a different material. Besides, mime techniques widely used in contemporary theater, TV, and film as a genre, so the producers and directors much appreciate actors who have these skills. Alternatively, nothing wrong if an aspiring dramatic actor upon studying mime chooses it as an art form he/she wants to pursue. Having all the previous training in acting, dance, and stage movement, an individual might be very successful in this field.

Period movement and period manners is a whole group of skills enabling the actor to perform the physical behavior of people who lived in different epochs, in various countries. Combine teaching these skills by offering the students basic knowledge of habits and ways of the corresponding periods. This information, along with a visual demonstration and imagination, would help the actor create skills appropriate for a particular era of history. Nevertheless, see that the scope of such skills was carefully planned and limited to only those periods and countries, represented by a significant number of dramatic and other literary works.

Stage Falls is a series of unique skills to enable the actor to perform various falls and tumbles realistically and with a high degree of safety. Based on previously comprehended Faculties, Habits, and Skills, the actor can create a truthful and emotional action of the fall. On the other hand, brave but an untrained actor might easily be injured and even ruin the entire production created by the effort of many people. Stage falls can be offered only to trained students because a negative experience, if it occurs, would reduce the courage and self-confidence to the point when the actor would never be able to perform this or similar technique. Considering the abundance of violence in current TV shows and movies as well as the growing popularity of Physical Theatre, this skill becomes worth acquiring.

Stage Lifts and Carries is another group of skills often used in stage and film productions. There are particular techniques of carrying a "dead" body, or a wounded "friend," or an "enemy" in different combinations such as "two carry one," "three carry one," etc. The goal is to learn unique ways to minimize muscle effort and maximize artistic expression. These techniques are coincidentally perfect exercises in developing Coordination, Awareness, Tempo-rhythm of the physical act, Strength, and other faculties and habits. They also are an excellent source to train essential physical interaction on stage.

Armed Stage Combat is yet another intricate group of skills, which the students advanced in other skills and habits can acquire. Just as no teacher would teach student calculus without first introducing them to arithmetic, no teacher should teach Armed Combat to beginners. Due to the extreme danger that this class presents to students' safety, they offer these skills only to a group of people prepared for such training physically and psychologically. When teaching students armed combat, there should be no protective or safety gear since the actor will not be able to use them on stage or in front of the camera as well. Although we tend to employ only special practicing weapons in the process, even those might be unsafe or even fatal if untrained or unprepared individuals are involved. However, a consistent and well-organized movement program can benefit from teaching Armed Stage Combat to its students. There are many elements of acting and self-control discipline present in it. Besides, the Armed Stage Combat course develops most of the Faculties, Habits, and Skills even further.

* * *

Yet again, the list of skills does not end here, and some teachers might find other skills to be of importance to the actor. However, the time limitations of any reasonable stage movement curriculum would force one to reduce the list of skills to those vital for the acting profession.

Now that all the Faculties, Habits, and Skills are defined, our next step is to decide what the best way to develop them. In other words, we have to choose from the known or create new exercises that would do the job sooner and better. There are numerous exercises designed by different people, in various periods of history and with diverse objectives. In selecting exercises for the stage movement program, one should always remember that our goal is to develop an artist, a creator, and not an athlete, not a bodybuilder, not even a dancer or mime. We are responsible for developing the actor's body and mind so that the individual trained in Stage Movement program would be able to take on any role, confident that he/she is equipped with all the necessary Faculties, Habits, and Skills to create a character.

PART II

THE PRACTICE

CHAPTER FOUR

OPENING AND CONCLUDING EXERCISES

Generations of practitioners involved with various kinds of physical training have determined that the optimal length of a lesson is about one hour and a quarter to one hour and a half.

Longer classes than that have a potential for tiring or annoying students, thus generating negative emotions. Besides, lessons that last less than an hour and a half, lack sufficient working time. We must consider here that any physical training class must include a Warm-up and a Concluding part in it. Just these two combined routinely would take about 15 minutes. We must also keep in mind that Stage Movement training is not a recreational workout but intended for future artists and not for athletes. Therefore, the negative sensations such as fatigue, pain, monotony, etc. might be very damaging for our students. However, the critical qualities such as strength, stamina, and self-control we still must develop in our students, and we have to do this in a manner closely associated with the acting profession. The content of this particular chapter and other chapters in our textbook will illustrate precisely how one can achieve it.

As the standard running time of a lesson in North American theater education is one hour and fifteen minutes, we presented all the exercises in this book with this length of class in mind. We recommend that the stage movement class be held two or three times a week evenly spread throughout a week. That would allow the student's mind and body to absorb the information on one hand and prevent the class from becoming a meaningless routine. However, the realities of school scheduling and daily life often force us to compromise our principles. The instructor (student) would have to establish the program's length and intensity individually.

As with any physical conditioning subject, stage movement class requires warming up the muscles and stretching ligaments before any further exercise. The cardiovascular and respiratory systems also have to be prepared for the necessary strenuous activities of the class. The simple general physical exercises described below are the first in a line of many others summoned to stimulate the student both physiologically and emotionally. They include some elements of motor coordination that make them relatively challenging, and the objectives induce the desire to perform them correctly. These last two aspects would undoubtedly call for student's concentration right from the beginning.

Preliminary Exercises

The exercises of this chapter borrowed mostly from athletics, specifically from gymnastics and acrobatics. We offer this group of exercises before any other activities, so we call them preliminary. We strongly advise the instructor to begin each lesson with a mixture of these exercises. The duration of this part of the class may vary and should last anything from seven to twelve minutes. Included in this part should be the warm-up exercises, with an assortment of them planned for each lesson. However, the preliminary part of a class would be longer at the beginning of the program, while the students familiarize themselves with the routines and comprehend the unknown exercises. The duration of this part should gradually decrease toward the middle of the semester and remain the same afterward. As the tasks become familiar, the need to explain them fades away. From then on, have the students perform them one after another as a continuous chain. It will save valuable time and perhaps would allow for more repetitions of the Preliminary exercises in the same period.

We highly recommend performing the Preliminary Exercises, as well as most of the exercises in the Essential Stage Movement program, with live music (piano player.) If this is not possible, have someone count rhythmically for you or use a metronome. It is crucial to perform all the movements precisely with the tempo and the rhythm of musical accompaniment. Musical selections that accompany the exercises should be simple and clear. The accompanist should maintain a particular tempo and rhythm throughout the exercise, at least at the beginning of the semester. Later in the program, the pace and the rhythm can fluctuate; finally, the accompanist can even change the style of the music for some exercises. Because preliminary exercises do not contain any semantics or emotional significance, the musical accompaniment to substitute for that and to create a cheering sensation in students must have some expressive element.

Soon in the process, each student would develop his/her way to perform the preliminary exercises that might be slightly different from others. It is perfectly alright since the goal of this group of practices is not to create a uniformed choreography but to encourage the students to put maximum energy in the performance of the exercises. After all, we are training future artists and not corps de ballet dancers.

It is usual for the students to experience some soreness during and especially after the execution of these exercises at the beginning; it indicates the fact that certain groups of muscles and ligaments are not functioning correctly, or that the body is out of shape. Performing exercises of this chapter pay a great deal of attention to the strengthening of the abdomen and back muscles. These muscles increasingly generate support of breathing apparatus, which is essential for the actor assisting the singing and speaking on stage.

As soon as the preliminary exercises absorbed, perform them as a sequence; one exercise should follow another in an established order and without any (or with short) pauses. The effect of such training will be fundamental and will help to develop Muscle Memory in students. An energetic tempo-rhythm of the Warm-Up set would save time and make this part of the lesson a bit more exciting. To accommodate the continuity of warm-up exercises, offer them in such an order that makes the transition from one to another convenient and swift.

Included in this chapter are the following groups of exercises, each group carrying distinct objective:

Opening exercises

Breathing exercises
Concentration exercises
Warm-up exercises
Lunging exercises
Exercises in Squatting
Concluding Exercises

Opening Exercises[1]

Presented below is a collection of exercises that include several natural organic movements of every day, such as walking, running, and skipping. To start, perform each of them separately then combine them in one complex exercise. After that, offer this combination at the beginning of each class as an Opening exercise.

Exercise 1 WALKING

Music is improvisation 4/4-time,[2] March.

Form a line upstage in order of height with the tallest person on the right. Make sure the distance between you and your partners is about six inches; arms down along your body.

Put your heels together and the toes slightly apart. Keep your body upright, shoulders relaxed. To make sure your shoulders relaxed, perform the following test -- lift your shoulders, then free your muscles and drop arms down. Try to memorize the state of your muscles at this moment and check it periodically in the future. Keep your chin slightly up and look straight ahead. Let us call the position you are in right now The Regular Stance (See Figure 1.)

Figure 1

Make sure you begin walking with your left foot and walk forward in sync with the music. Make eight regular steps forward, then turn left and continue walking one following another around the room. When turning left, make sure you do not stop walking; do not pull your feet together, or change the walking pattern. That means, continue to walk forward with your left foot on Downbeat[3] and maintain your body's upright position. That would allow you to breathe freely. Walk with simple steps using your everyday walking skill and move your arms only to maintain the balance. Keep breathing through the entire exercise; inhale for four quarters of music (or for the duration of four steps) and exhale for the next four quarters.

Now, repeat the exercise and, while walking around the room, gradually shape a circle. Try to accomplish this task as quickly as possible, but without displaying any disorder. Students at the head of the line should make bigger steps, trying to catch up with one at the end. Students walking at the end of the line, on the contrary, must take shorter strides to allow the latter to catch up with them. Once you create a circle, continue walking and make your circle as big as the room permits. It would allow maximum space for exercising. Continue walking forward, maintaining the circle, and equal distances between you and the person in front of you.

Methodological guidelines: It is customary that the tasks described above would not be difficult to accomplish from the first attempt. Depending on the abilities of the group, offer the exercise in a step-by-step manner. The instructor should also remember that this is the first exercise of the program and present the "rules of the game" quite clearly already in this seemingly simple exercise. The students must listen to the task's explanation first and then begin the execution at the command of the instructor.

Every command must consist of two words or two beats. The first is to mobilize the students, and the second is to make them start the exercise on time. Deliver these two beats, or two words, clearly and forcefully. A meager or indefinite command most likely would cause hesitation and confusion in the execution of the exercise. Also, voice these two parts in a definite tempo-rhythm, the one you want the following exercise performed. Your command would equally pertain to the accompanist. For Exercise 1, we suggest using a simple command, "Forward – March!"

The instructor should anticipate some errors in the execution of this seemingly simple exercise. For instance, there often will be a problem to make a left turn without hesitation or interruption. If this occurs, the instructor should stop the exercise right there and explain the task again. Sometimes the students tend to pull feet together before making the turn, which drives them out of the rhythm. It would also take a while to make them assemble a circle and to maintain equal distances while walking. Concerning the latter, the instructor should explain that this is the matter of the entire company; each member must see that the gap in front is large enough to continue the exercise, and it is about the same as other distances. Eliminate immediately common blunder such as turning around to check the distance, or trying to help other members to perform the task either with gestures or with words.

The instructor should explain that the task is simple enough to accomplish without noticeable communication; continue practicing this exercise in the single lesson until all the following objectives achieved:

a/ Walking in sync with the music
b/ Maintaining the posture
c/ Breathing rhythmically
d/ Maintaining the distance
e/ Minimizing the effort

Conduct the final version of the exercise "Walking" for the duration of eight bars[4] of music, or thirty-two steps.

Exercise 2 WALKING ON TIPTOES

Music is improvisation 4/4-time. The tempo is the same as in Exercise 1, but with a different style of music. It is now staccato in high-pitched chords to imitate walking on tiptoes.

Formation – a circle.

Begin with the left foot and walk in a circle in sync with music on tiptoes. Keep your body upright, shoulders relaxed, and chin slightly up. Maintain proper distance between you and a person in front of you and keep breathing rhythmically in a similar to the previous exercise way. Inhale for the duration of four steps, exhale for another four steps.

Methodological guidelines: As before, it is crucial to maintain the initial size of the circle, as the students in the process of walking tend to move closer to the center of the room, thus making the circle smaller and the distances shorter. The instructor should sporadically remind the students about it while they perform the exercise. The objectives of this exercise are similar to those of the previous; implement them strictly. Walking on tiptoes is unusual for a beginner, so some students would get tired and switch to regular walks. The instructor should encourage such students to perform the task accurately.

The duration of this exercise is also eight bars of music.

Exercise 3 WALKING ON TIPTOES, KNEES UP

Music is improvisation 4/4-time. The tempo is a bit slower than in the previous exercise to accommodate larger amplitudes of motion; the style of music changes again to imitate the physical effort. It is still staccato but more massive with a stress on every quarter.

Keep walking on tiptoes around the circle and reach for your chest with your knee with each step. Do not tilt the upper body forward to meet the knee. Instead, keep your body upright. Move your arms just enough to maintain the balance.

Also, do not forget to maintain rhythmical breathing during the entire exercise, inhaling for four steps, and exhaling for the next four steps. Never stop breathing for a moment.

Repeat the exercise for at least the duration of eight bars of music.

Methodological guidelines: Keep the objectives the same as in previous exercises; however, pay special attention to the breathing, as this exercise is more physically challenging, and the students often tend to hold their breath to concentrate on the task.

Exercise 4 SKIPPING

Music is improvisation 4/4-time. The tempo is a bit slower than in the previous exercise, and the rhythmical pattern for this exercise is as follows:

Listen to this rhythmical pattern and note the specific beat. Begin with your left foot and move forward by skipping; lift your knee to the chest with each such skip. Swing your straight arms from the shoulders joint with each step up to a horizontal position. It would help you to skip more dynamically and maintain balance at the same time. Make sure your right knee goes up while the left arm goes forward and vice versa.

If you perform this correctly, your entire body will fly up in the air. Do not resist the momentum, and make sure you hop up on the downbeat. Do not forget to breathe rhythmically. In this exercise, inhale for two quarters (or two skips) and exhale for two quarters. That is because your body needs more oxygen with vigorous motion in this exercise. As a result, your breathing will be more frequent. The musical pattern will help you to synchronize your moves precisely with the rhythm.

Methodological guidelines: The command to begin this exercise could be "Forward... Skip!" The requirements for it are the same as in previous exercises. Repeat "Skipping" for the duration of eight bars.

Exercise 5 RUNNING

Running is going to be used in our program frequently; we recommend paying particular attention to the technique. Running in combination with some other exercises is an excellent way to develop correct breathing. However, as natural and familiar to people this activity is, many perform it incorrectly. Common mistakes often are -- overstraining of legs' and arms' muscles and improper head and upper-body position. These errors usually produce incorrect breathing. Also, excessive jumping and swinging of the body typically cause loss of energy.

Music is improvisation 4/4-time, lively tempo, each quarter stressed, musical articulation is staccato.

Figure 2

The beginning position is standing in the spot, feet slightly apart (for better balance). Bend your elbows, so your forearms are in a horizontal position in front of your body. Collect fingers a little (but do not squeeze) into a fist. Move your arms forward and backward across your body as if you are running and repeat it several times (See Figure 2).
Now repeat this exercise and run on the spot at the same time.

Begin with your left foot and run around the room in a circle formation; run in accord with the music. Keep moving your arms as in preliminary exercise. When running, place your feet along one line, touch the floor first with your heel, and then with the sole of your foot. With each step, lift your knee in front of your body a little and let the other leg swing freely back and upwards. Do not force your legs to swing higher than needed to provide your body with enough momentum to move forward. When running, tilt your body slightly forward as if leaning on a cushion of air. Performing all the rules accurately would create a dynamic and definite forward motion.

Just like you did in previous exercises, maintain the distance between you and a partner in front of you. That would harmonize your motions with the rest of the company.

Now, to the technique you learn from above, add the correct breathing; it is a crucial element of running. A common mistake is to hold the breath and occasionally make a quick inhale/exhale action. To avoid this mistake and acquire a proper breathing habit, make sure you gradually inhale for four steps, and exhale continuously for the next four steps. Note, inhale through your nose and exhale both through your nose and slightly open mouth. Have your neck and head in line with the spinal column to provide free breathing.

Methodological guideline: Make the students repeat all five previous exercises separately and in various combinations in several consecutive lessons. Continue correcting the errors during the training and between the repetitions, until everyone performs all the tasks satisfactory. Try to obtain a semi-automatic performance.

Explain to the students that the process of perfecting the technique of these simple exercises is necessary and that it is no use moving further until everyone executes the task correctly. The chances are, if you do not do it now, some of them might develop a bad habit, which would be hard to retrain later.

Various groups would require a different amount of repetitions, but with persistence and concentration, they would accomplish it in a relatively short period.

Maintain the duration of the running exercise about 30 to 40 seconds at a time. Each time concentrate your attention on one particular element and correct other mistakes on the next repetition. We stated it before, and it is appropriate to pass this information to the students: the human brain designed to focus only on one problem at a time. However, we can switch our attention from one subject to another, thus creating an illusion of controlling several tasks simultaneously. One of the movement training objectives is precisely this: to teach the brain switching from one subject to another instantaneously.

Exercise 6 (**Complex**) WALKING, WALKING ON TIP-TOES,
WALKING ON TIP-TOES KNEES UP,
SKIPPING, RUNNING, WALKING

A combination of all the previous tasks is a composite exercise that we will call from now on the Opening Exercise. All modes of movements described above included in this exercise in the same order as presented initially.

Music – see Appendix 1. The transitions from one part to the next are gradual to allow the students to follow them naturally.
Formation – start in a straight line, then form a circle.

Begin the exercise with the left foot, walk forward (as in Exercise 1) shaping a circle, then walk on tip-toes, then walk on tip-toes lifting your knees, then skip, then run, and finally walk with regular steps again and stop at the end of the musical piece. Perform this combination of different movements without a break, changing from one mode of motion to the next seamlessly.

When performing the Opening Exercise, do not forget the requirements for each of the component movements. Make sure you follow the music to the point that the transition from one mode of motion to the next performed flawlessly. It means that you have to land with your left foot on the bar's downbeat from the first step to the end. At the end of the Opening Exercise, the music would come gradually to a halt. You must catch the tip that the accompanist would give you and to stop along with the music. For the final two quarters (or two chords) of the music, make your last step forward with your left foot and bring your right foot together with the left. Your final position must be the Regular Stance or the same pose you began the Opening Exercise, i.e., heels together, toes slightly apart.

Methodological guidelines: When the entire Opening Exercise first performed, the instructor should prompt the transition to the next mode of movement. As soon as everyone in the group makes all the shifts correctly (perhaps in the following lesson), the instructor should announce that there will be no additional commands. As the students memorized the order of the exercise's components, they should perform them, making the transitions by following the music. By this time in the program, the students must easily recognize the different music nuances that suggest specific modes of movement.

However, be ready to prompt the next mode in case of confusion. After the Opening Exercise comprehended, make the students perform it as one continuous routine at the beginning of each lesson until another opening routine would substitute it.

It is imperative, yet at this early stage, to make the students acquire a habit of emphasizing the beginning and the end of a movement with absolute clarity. This performance quality is essential on stage as the actor regularly uses gestures and body movements to make a clear point, akin to the clear speech with all the punctuation marks. The Opening Exercise is an excellent opportunity to begin practicing this habit.

The instructor should make sure that the exercise begins from a complete stillness and finishes with an absolute standstill. The students must make it a habit of remaining motionless for a few seconds after they finish the exercise. Later in the program, reinforce this habit by applying it to nearly all the exercises.

Let us compare that to a dot at the end of the phrase. The instructor should see that all the students stop moving with the musical piece's last sound. Usually, it takes several repetitions to achieve this seemingly simple goal, but the instructor should be persistent. However, it is not necessary to repeat the entire Opening Exercise several times to practice the final steps and the halt. Make the group walk only the final four (eight) bars, after which the music should suggest the end and stop. The accompanist may exaggerate and accentuate (at least in the several lessons) the last two quarters. Remind the students to execute the final step at the end of the music with the right foot placed next to the left, heels together, toes apart.

An instructor needs to find proper time during the execution of the Opening Exercise to remind of continuous and rhythmic breathing. One should insist on having all established objectives for each of the Opening Exists' components permanently implanted in its fabric. Usually, it cannot be accomplished in one or several lessons. However, as this exercise repeated in many following classes, and most of the tasks automatically executed, the necessity to remind these things would fade away.

Modify the Opening Exercise as soon as it becomes a routine. One way to do so is to change the tempos of different parts; another is to change the duration of various components. For instance, the walking part can be longer in one lesson and shorter in the next, etc. That would challenge the students and test their attention. Gradually, it would teach them to be alert at all times, as the sudden change of circumstances is a norm in the theater. Besides, this technique helps to break the routine in the exercise repeatedly practiced in every lesson. Remember, the monotony is perhaps the actor's worst enemy.

Note: Opening Exercise develops such faculties as Balance, Coordination, Rhythmicity, Velocity, Awareness, and Correct breathing. It also drills such habits as Economy of Movement, and Awareness of Space.

Breathing exercises

In addition to the techniques concerning correct breathing described above, the following exercises specially designed to improve proper breathing skills in students. However, we do not consider the Breathing as solely objective of stage movement class. We believe a vocal instructor must develop it further in the Speech class. Nevertheless, considering the importance of correct breathing for an actor, we will concentrate our effort on regulating breathing immediately after strenuous physical activity. The profession often demands the actor speak or sing right after intensive physical effort and often even in the process of it. The student must learn how to calm down breathing while speaking or singing, within a short time. To train this skill, the instructor should expose the students to an intensive physical routine followed by a particular text's rhythmic articulation. There are yet some other exercises introduced later in the program that mixes vocal passages and energetic movements.

Exercise 7 RUNNING, WALKING, COUNTING OUT ALOUD

Music is improvisation 4/4-time, plain quarters; tempo moderate. Formation – a circle.

Run for 30 to 40 seconds (tempo 120–130 by a metronome), then gradually switch to walking mode; walk for another 40 to 50 seconds and stop. The walking time should be a bit longer than the running time. After you finish, take a deep breath and begin counting audibly in sync with the music. Exhale while pronouncing the first three words and take a deep breath on every measure's fourth beat.

Example:

1st quarter	2nd quarter	3rd quarter	4th quarter
One	*Two*	*Three*	*(inhale)*
Four	*Five*	*Six*	*(inhale)*

Continue counting for the duration of four or eight bars of music and try to calm down breathing to normal as soon as you can. Make sure you articulate each word. Pronounce the numbers consisting of two or more syllables still for one quarter of music.

Methodological guidelines: Shortness of breath would usually cause inaudible speech. The instructor should watch that every student makes an effort to speak up and make the words clear. Later in the program, one may vary the intensity of the speech and suggest pronouncing the numbers a bit louder, then a bit softer. This way, one can test the success in developing a good habit.

Exercise 8 RUNNING, COUNTING OUT ALOUD

Music is the same as in the previous exercise.
Formation – a circle.

This exercise is similar to the previous only this time omit the walking part. Run for 30 to 40 seconds, stop abruptly, and right away begin counting. Continue counting for the duration of four to eight bars of music.

Note: The instructor should stop the running anytime the load on the cardiovascular system is visibly sufficient. Use a sharp command, "Stop!" for this. Offer the current exercise only after the previous variation practiced in four or five consecutive lessons. Make sure the students maintain proper breathing during the running, as explained before in the Opening Exercise. If the students still lacking the skill or ignoring the rules, they might be entirely out of breath, hence reciting a text might be even harmful.

Exercise 9 RUNNING, RECITING LOGICAL TEXT

Music is the same as in the previous exercise.
Formation – a circle.

Run for about a minute around the circle, stop abruptly, and recite multiplication tables for "two" in such a way that you pronounce the words in the first three quarters of a bar and take a breath for the fourth quarter.

Example:

1st quarter	2nd quarter	3rd quarter	4th quarter
Two	*times One*	*is Two*	*(inhale)*
Two	*times Two*	*is Four*	*(inhale)*

Repeat the exercise for the duration of four to eight bars of music.

Methodological guidelines: Before introducing multiplication tables into the exercise, the instructor should teach the students how to organize the words and to coordinate the text with the music. Again, if possible, do it without demonstration and rehearse along with the music while standing in the spot; this way, the students would not be confused with recitation after running.

Repeat the exercise in several lessons, and then begin gradually reducing the time needed to calm the breathing.

See that the students inhale at the end of each bar quickly but not frantically. Lungs filled naturally would help to produce a good sound. Besides, we do not want the actor to show the struggle to catch a breath, or as an old saying goes, "never let them see you sweat."

Exercise 10 RUNNING, RECITING LOGICAL TEXT (2nd version)

Music is the same as in the previous exercise.
Formation – a circle.

The difference between the present and the previous variation of the exercise is that after running, you should stop, and recite the multiplication table for five, or for six, which have the numbers consisting of two words, for instance, "twenty-five." Pronounce these numbers for the last two quarters of a bar instead of one.

Example:

1st quarter	2nd quarter	3rd quarter	4th quarter
Six times	*Four*	*is Twenty*	*Four (inhale), or*
Seven times	*Five*	*is Thirty*	*Five (inhale)*

In this situation, you would have to inhale between the last crotchet of the bar and the first crotchet of the next bar; obviously, you would have less time.

Methodological guidelines: The instructor can gradually reduce the tempo of the reciting in the process and then increase it toward the end. The accompanist also can make such changes; however, he/she should know how to do it properly. Do it unexpectedly and gradually, in such a manner that it would not confuse the students.

After the initial exercise performed successfully, we recommend gradually extend the running time in the following lessons up to 1.5 minutes, and little by little increase the tempo of running.

Note: Include breathing exercises in training from the very first class and continue throughout the program until proper breathing becomes a solid Habit. In addition to Proper Breathing, the exercises of this kind develop Rhythmicity.

Exercise 11 RUNNING, RECITING IMAGINATIVE TEXT

Music for reciting is improvisation 4/4-time, basic quarters; moderate tempo.
Formation – a circle.

As in previous breathing exercise, run for thirty seconds to a minute, stop abruptly and recite the following nursery rhyme:

Humpty-Dumpty sat on a wall.

Humpty-Dumpty had a great fall.
All the king's horses and all the king's men
Couldn't put Humpty together again!

When reciting, break the lines to accommodate the 4/4-time musical accompaniment as shown below:

Example:

1st quarter	2nd quarter	3rd quarter	4th quarter
Humpty	*Dumpty*	*sat*	*on a wall,* etc.

In this exercise, inhale between the lines, or between the bars of the music.

Methodological guidelines: Apply the same tactics as in previous breathing exercises.

We will use this nursery rhyme as a component in several other exercises of the Essential Stage Movement. When it appears for the first time, make sure they learn the lines and memorize them before incorporating it into the training. If the majority of the company does not know the rhyme, the instructor should recite it several times. Have a student who knows the poem recite it for the group. It would make the process livelier. Also, use a blackboard or a poster to present the lines. Make the group recite the rhyme once or twice, or until everybody memorizes the lines.

It is a proper occasion to tell the students that the ability to memorize the text quickly is one of the essential skills of the actor, required in the future professional setting.

Concentration Exercises

After simple physical warm-up exercises, there comes the turn for more complicated, psycho-physical ones. The purpose is to raise the students' level of attention and concentration in a transitional phase of the lesson. Consider the fact that students come to class bringing with them the happenings of their daily lives, such as various trials, and worries, impressions of previous lessons, etc. Therefore, focusing their attention right at the beginning is beneficial.

Offer these exercises next after the warm-up part of the lesson. The objective of the following selection is to develop further Concentration and Coordination skills.

Exercise 12 THREE STEPS FORWARD, ONE STEP BACKWARD

Music is improvisation 4/4-time, slow tempo; plain chords.
Formation – a circle.

Begin with the right foot and walk in a circle with simple steps. Move in quarters and make three steps forward and one step backward without any break, walk in sync with the music. Repeat the sequence four times and stop; turn around and repeat the exercise one more time, but begin this time with your left foot.

Methodological guidelines: A common mistake in this exercise occurs when a student merely extends the foot backward instead of making a full step for the fourth quarter. That would make him continue the next sequence with the left foot because the bodyweight is on the right. That would break the pattern. The instructor should use such an occasion as an opportunity to explain the difference between "step back" and "extend foot backward." We call a step, a move that shifts the weight of the body on the foot that executes the action. It is appropriate at this point to demonstrate "how not to" do this movement.

By this time in the program, the students must attain proficiency in maintaining equal distances between participants while moving in the circle. This skill would come very handy for this particular exercise because if anyone makes an error, it can cause stepping on each other's heels or toes. If this skill is not sufficient yet, this exercise is an excellent tool to drill it further.

In subsequent repetitions of this (and similar) exercise, the instructor should vary the tempo of the music. However, the instructor should tip the students off before the exercise begins that this can happen. The accompanist should tease the students gradually accelerating or decelerating the tempo.

Exercise 13 TWO STEPS FORWARD, STEP BACKWARD

Music is improvisation ¾-time, moderate tempo, with stress on every first beat.
Formation – a circle.

Start with your right foot and walk in a circle. Make two steps forward, then a step backward. Notice, this exercise's rhythm is ¾-time, which means there are only three quarters in a bar. Realize, it means that every new sequence, you have to start with a different foot. So, if you begin the first sequence with the right foot on the downbeat, you would have to continue the next one with the left foot on the downbeat beat.

Methodological guidelines: The order of learning and further progress of this exercise is similar to the previous one.

Exercise 14 THREE STEPS FORWARD, ONE STEP SIDEWAYS, ONE
         STEP BACKWARD

Music is improvisation 5/4-time, slow.
Formation – a circle.

Begin with the right foot and take three steps forward, then a step sideways, then a step backward. Since music is 5/4-time, there are five quarters in one bar. Accordingly, there must be five steps in each sequence. Notice, the number of steps is odd. So, be aware, and as you begin the first sequence with your right foot, start the next one with the left. Make sure you make a full step sideways and backward. Remember, it means shifting the weight of your body on that foot. It is essential to keep walking continuously. Make one full step for every quarter of the music.

Methodological guidelines: Students sometimes try to guess beforehand which side to make a sideways step. Some might even ask the instructor about it. The instructor should encourage the students to begin the exercise without much thinking about it; when the time comes to the sideways or backward step, to make it with the alternative foot.

Another probable complication is changing the formation. Have every student move close to a person in front and put the right hand on his/her shoulder. The first (the tallest) student should stay in place. As a result, you would have a formation we call a "chain." Make the group repeat this exercise in a chain formation, still moving in a circle. Every student must coordinate his or her movements with the rest of the group. If the exercise performed satisfactory, repeat it at an increased tempo.

To make this exercise even more complicated, in the following class, ask the students to get even closer to each other by holding both elbows of a person in front. Make sure the students maintain the "chain" during the entire exercise. For that, the students must coordinate the amplitude of their motions with the steps of the partners.

When this complication eliminated, perhaps in the following lesson, suggest executing the exercise in a "chain" and then, in the process, giving a command such as, "continue exercise, get your hands down!" After the group performs several sequences with hands off the elbows, instruct "grab the elbows again!" Most likely, the students will not be able to do so, because of the changed distance between them. Stop the exercise and explain that to the students. Repeat the exercise until performed sufficiently. Use the same technique with other similar concentration exercises.

Note: This exercise is an excellent tool to train such faculties as Awareness and Coordination, and such habits as Muscle Control, Concentration, and Awareness of Space. It also develops an essential skill – Interaction with a partner.

Exercise 15 FOUR STEPS FORWARD, TWO STEPS BACKWARD, STEP ACROSS, TURN AROUND

Music is improvisation 4/4-time, tempo moderate.
Formation – a circle.

Begin with the right foot, and take four steps forward, then two steps backward. Next quarter, make a step with your right foot in front and across your left foot. Finally, for the last quarter of sequence, rise on the toes of both feet, turn around and place heels on the floor—all in one motion. Notice, the sequence in this exercise takes eight quarters or two bars of music. After finishing the first sequence, continue the exercise and repeat it four times, moving in opposite directions.

Methodological guidelines: Sometimes, students are confused about how they should turn on the last quarter of the sequence. Explain that since the right foot is in front of the left, it is only logical to make the about-turn over the left shoulder. Use the "how not to" demonstrate the nuisance of doing it the other way.
    In the following lessons, suggest starting this exercise with the left foot and, accordingly, rearrange all the motions.
    After both versions of the exercise performed satisfactory, offer a combination of two. Offer to begin the first sequence with the right foot and, after the about-turn, repeat the exercise, but to begin it with the left foot. Repeat the sequence four to six times in a single lesson or until performed correctly by the entire group.

Note: In addition to the qualities developed in the previous concentration exercises, this also improves the Balance.

Exercise 16 JUMP FEET APART, JUMP TWICE FEET TOGETHER

Music is improvisation 2/4-time in the following pattern:

Formation – a circle.

Listen to the music for several sequences. Notice that in this rhythmical pattern, some notes are quarter-notes, and others are eighth-notes.

Beginning position is the regular stance, i.e., heels together, toes slightly apart.

Begin the exercise and jump forward feet apart for the quarter-note; for the following two eighth-notes, make two small jumps forward, keeping your feet together. Repeat the same steps three times, moving in a circle. For the last bar (which consists of only two quarter-notes,) jump forward feet apart and then jump forward feet together. That would constitute the sequence. Repeat it four times.

Now, go over the exercise again. This time, on the last jump, turn around over your right shoulder and land precisely at the last quarter of the pattern. Then continue and repeat the exercise in the opposite direction. Perform the sequence four times in succession.

Methodological guidelines: Most likely, performing this exercise, the students will make a lot of noise jumping around. The instructor should explain that the actor must make it a habit of moving about the stage with minimal noise. They should avoid as much as possible any interference with the sounds on stage. These could be voices of the actors, music, silence, sound effect, etc. Besides, many theaters still have stages built like a drum. They are hollow inside and covered with wooden boards, so when actors move around any sound multiples. The ability to move silently about the stage is the first sign of the actor's Dexterity. Therefore, from that day forward, have your students always remember this rule, and continuously remind them to keep the noises associated with moving around suppressed.

Combine this exercise with others, described before, to create new challenges. For instance, perform one sequence (2 bars) from Exercise 15, then continue and complete one sequence (4 bars) from Exercise 16.

Note: The Concentration Exercises effectively develop a wide variety of faculties and habits, such as Awareness, Coordination, Sense of Space, and Motion memory. However, we recommend using only one of these exercises in a single lesson. More than one or too many repetitions of one might have a negative effect and even reduce the ability to concentrate on the following exercises of the class. None of these exercises include elements of acting. Therefore, focus on the precision of performance. The actor must learn that no motion on stage can afford to appear approximate or indefinite.

When increasing the tempo of an exercise, demand that the students preserve a natural and graceful performance. Make sure your students on the fabric of these simple exercises already begin discovering the first attributes of artistry in body movements. Also, the instructor needs to understand that the Concentration Exercises described above are effective only until the student performs the pattern semi-automatically. After this level attained, further repetitions are pointless. To continue extracting benefits, the instructor must either add a new complication to the exercise or replace it with a new one. We challenge the instructor to create further complications, and even new exercises using the techniques and methodology described in this chapter.

Warm-up Exercises
Collection I, Exercises on the Floor

Methodological guidelines: Warm-up exercises can be performed either in a circle formation with students facing the center or in a free formation with students facing the instructor. The exercises described below designed to stretch and warm various parts of the body up. Out of all the exercises described, the instructor should choose a set that would take 8 to 15 minutes of a single lesson. Arrange the exercises so that the warm-up would begin with legs and move successively to the upper parts of the body.

It is imperative to achieve continuity in the warm-up part of the lesson. With this in mind, the instructor should arrange the exercises in such a way that the time needed to change beginning positions would be minimal. For instance, make the students perform first all exercises that require standing position, and once they are sitting on the floor, offer the ones requiring a sitting attitude.

At the beginning of the program (semester), you will need to pause after each exercise to explain the next one. However, as the study progresses make the explanations increasingly shorter to the point when the only announcement of the title needed.

While the students perform the Warm-up exercises, the instructor should move about the room and correct individual errors in the performance without interrupting the process.

Do it either by comment or by touching and even gently pressing parts of the student's body to a proper position.

Conduct the warm-up part in such a way that very early in the program, the students would physically feel the benefits of stretching and warming up before the major of the lesson begins.

Exercise 17 SQUATTING
Music is improvisation 4/4-time, tempo adagio.

Put your heels together, toes slightly apart (Regular Stance). Place hands on your hips. During the following exercise, keep your chin slightly up and breathe rhythmically. Inhale for four quarters (first half of the exercise) and exhale for the next four quarters (second half). Exhale forcefully just before the exercise is about to begin. It would allow you to inhale at the beginning of the exercise. Keep your spinal column vertical during the entire exercise.

On the first quarter of the bar, gently but swiftly lift your heels off the ground. Then, on the second, third, and fourth quarters gradually bend your knees away from each other and sink all the way, until you sit on your heels. The second half of the exercise - lift your body gradually up for the first, second, and third quarters of the bar until you are on your toes. Finally, for the fourth quarter, gently lower your heels and return to the beginning position. Notice, the entire exercise takes two bars of music or eight quarters. Continue exercise right away by lifting your body.

Repeat the exercise four times and see that your shoulders and neck muscles are relaxed and that your spinal column is vertical.

Methodological guidelines: The instructor should see that the exercise performed continuously and following the music, which requires a maximal muscle strain. The instinct to minimize the effort would make the students squat down rather quickly, so they can relax before getting up. Explain that the goal of this exercise is definitely to develop the strength of leg muscles.

The exercise also drills Balance and Correct Breathing. As the program progresses, increase the number of repetitions to six or eight times in a single lesson.

Exercise 18 SQUATTING, KNEES TOGETHER
Music is improvisation 4/4-time, tempo adagio.

The beginning position is standing with heels and toes together, your hands on hips.

The technique is the same as in the previous exercise only keep your knees and toes together while squatting down and getting up. Be prepared; this exercise would challenge your balance skill.

Methodological guidelines: Offer this exercise later in the program as a part of a Warm-up section to substitute the previous version of squatting.

Exercise 19 SQUATTING, HEELS ON THE FLOOR
Music is the same as in the previous exercise.

The beginning position -- heels and toes together, your hands on hips.

Unlike the previous two exercises, begin squatting down right away, i.e., in the first quarter of the music, and continue moving down gradually for the second, third, and fourth quarters. Keep your knees together and heels planted on the floor all along. To accommodate this task yet maintain the balance, you would need to tilt the upper body simultaneously forward and extend your arms forward.

For the next bar of music, gradually lift the body and place your hands on hips. Inhale on the first half of the exercise and exhale during the second half.

Methodological guidelines: This exercise would present a challenge for most of the students. However, introduced in the middle of the program would require several attempts to execute it properly; be persistent until everyone would do it right. We do not recommend interrupting the exercise in case one or two students cannot complete it. Their apparent failure would coerce them to do their best and to pull alongside the group.

Note: This exercise develops such faculties as Flexibility and Mobility of Joints, Strength, and Balance.

Exercise 20 BENDING FORWARD
Music is improvisation 4/4-time, moderate tempo.

The beginning position -- heels together, toes slightly apart, hands on the back of the neck, and elbows apart (See Figure 3).

Figure 3

For the first four quarters of the music, gradually bend the upper body forward to a horizontal position, simultaneously stretch your arms forward palms down, and look onward. For the next four quarters, gradually unbend and simultaneously bring your hands back to the beginning position. Inhale during the first half of the exercise and exhale for the second half.

Repeat exercise four times in a single lesson.

Methodological guidelines: As with other exercises of this group, begin with four repetitions in a single lesson, and gradually increase the number of repetitions as the program progresses.

Note: This exercise develops such faculties as *Flexibility* and *Mobility of Joints* and *Rhythmicity*.

Exercise 21 ROTATING UPPER BODY

Music is improvisation ¾-time, moderate tempo.
The beginning position is the same as in the previous exercise.

Keep upright position and gradually rotate upper body along with your head to the right; simultaneously open your arms out to the sides, palms up. Take four bars of music to do this part. Make sure you reach the limit of rotation by the end of the fourth bar. Then, gradually return to the beginning position for the next four bars of the music. Maintain the position of your feet throughout the exercise.

Now, repeat the exercise in reverse: turn your upper body along with your head to the left. Repeat the entire exercise four times.

Breathe rhythmically -- inhale for the first half of the exercise and exhale for the second.

Note: This exercise develops Flexibility and Mobility of Joints, Correct breathing, and Muscle control.

Exercise 22 BENDING OVER
Music is improvisation ¾-time, tempo moderate.

The beginning position is heels together, toes apart, arms stretched up, onward.

Take four bars of the music to bend the upper body over gradually. Reach the floor with the tips of your fingers for the last quarter. Unbend and bring your body and arms to the beginning position for the next four bars. Inhale for the first half of the exercise and exhale for the rest of it. Make sure you execute the exercise without pausing; instead, distribute all the movements evenly throughout the exercise. It is also essential to keep your knees straight continuously. Repeat the exercise four times.

Methodological guidelines: Encourage students to make an effort and touch the floor with tips of the fingers while keeping their knees straight. Expect some students unable to do this right away. Do not force them; instead, encourage them to attain the results gradually in several lessons. Continue to remind them to stretch as far as they can until they succeed.

We recommend doubling the number of repetitions in a lesson as the program progresses.

Note: The exercise develops Correct Breathing, Willpower, and Flexibility, and Mobility of Joints.

Exercise 23 BENDING BACKWARD
Music is improvisation 4/4-time, slow.

The beginning position is heels together, toes slightly apart, hands on the back of your neck, and elbows apart.
Bend upper body at the small of the back backward and tilt your head back; simultaneously open your arms out to the sides, palms up. Distribute the movements gradually for the four quarters of the music. Then, unbend and return to the beginning position for the next four quarters. Inhale when bending backward and exhale for the second half of the exercise. Keep your knees straight at all times. Make sure you bend as far as you can, even if it hurts a bit.
Repeat this exercise four times continuously.

Methodological guidelines: As with the previous exercises of this group, gradually increase the load from one lesson to the next. See that the students stretch enough to acquire larger amplitudes of motion. A common mistake is bending at the shoulder blades. It is usually an attempt to minimize the pain this exercise may cause. Remind the students to bend at the small of the back as far as possible, so their flexibility at the waist would gradually expand.

Note: This exercise develops Flexibility and Mobility of Joints, Willpower, and Correct breathing.

Exercise 24 BENDING SIDEWAYS
Music is improvisation ¾-time.
The beginning position is heels together, toes apart, your hands on hips. Bend your torso in the plain of your body gradually to the right as far as you can; simultaneously stretch left arm up, make a fist, and tilt it along with a torso. Take four bars of the music to complete this half of the exercise. For the next four bars, unbend and bring the left hand back on your thigh. Repeat the same in reverse. Keep your knees together and straight. Breathe rhythmically, i.e., inhale during the first half of the exercise and exhale for the second half.
Note: This exercise helps to develop Correct Breathing, Willpower, and Flexibility, and Mobility of Joints.

Exercise 25 BEND-UNBEND LEGS

Music is improvisation 4/4-time, first three quarters stressed, last regular.

Figure 4a

The beginning position is sitting on the floor, legs together and stretched, toes pointed. Put the palms of your hands on the floor behind your back liberally; lean on your hands. Keep your spinal column straight (not collapsed), chin slightly up (See Figure 4a.) Bend your legs sharply and bring your knees to the chest for the first quarter. Stretch your legs sharply up (45°) for the second quarter.

Bend your legs again, bring knees to the chest for the third quarter, and, finally, stretch your legs to put them down on the floor for the fourth quarter. Breathe rhythmically, inhale for the first two quarters, and exhale for the next two quarters of the music. Repeat the sequence four times. Make sure your toes pointed at all times and knees completely straight when stretching legs. Do not collapse your back through the entire exercise.

Repeat the sequence four times in a single lesson.

Methodological guidelines: There is often a tendency to drop the legs on the floor with the last movement. It stems from the desire to ease the stress on the abdomen muscles that accumulates during the exercise. The students tend to relax the muscles as soon as they can. The instructor should request to eliminate the noise when lowering the legs to the floor. That would also protect the heels from possible harm.

Note: This exercise develops Strength (especially abdomen muscles), Flexibility and Mobility of Joints, Rhythmicity, and the physical act's Precision.

Exercise 26 BODY ARCHING
Music is improvisation ¾-time, slow waltz.

The beginning position is the same as in the previous exercise.

Lift your body off the floor gradually and continue moving your abdomen up as high as you can. Lean your neck backward simultaneously. Perform this part of the exercise in four bars of the music. For the next four bars, gradually lower your body to the beginning position. Inhale during the first half of the exercise and exhale for the second half. Perform the exercise continuously without any pause. Repeat this exercise four times.

Note: This exercise develops Strength, Flexibility, and Rhythmicity.

Exercise 27 LIE DOWN, SIT UP
Music is improvisation 4/4-time, moderate tempo.

The beginning position is sitting on the floor, stretched legs together, toes pointed, and arms crossed on your chest and spinal column upright.

Take four quarters to lie down gradually on your back; gently place your head on the floor at the end. For the next four quarters, lift your upper body gradually off the ground and sit up. Try to touch the floor with the back of your head precisely in the fourth quarter; finish in the beginning position in the fourth quarter to express the end of the exercise. Inhale when you begin the exercise and exhale towards the end of it.

Repeat this exercise four times.

Methodological guidelines: As with other exercises of this group, increase the capacity later in the program by adding two or more repetitions. To make this exercise even more physically challenging, suggest performing it with your hands on the back of the neck. Do it only after considerable progress visible. That would develop muscle strength further.

Note: This exercise develops Strength, Rhythmicity, and Willpower.

Exercise 28 LEGS APART, LEGS TOGETHER
Music is improvisation 4/4-time, adagio.

Figure 4b

The beginning position is sitting on the floor legs together; toes pointed; place palms of your hands on the floor behind your back and apart. Lean on your hands, keep your upper body straight, and chin slightly up (See Figure 4a).

Lift your stretched right leg off the floor, and gradually shift it to the right as far as you can, then place it on the floor. Sustain the rest of your body, and take four quarters for this part of the exercise. Then, for the next four quarters, lift the right leg again and bring it gradually back to the beginning position (See Figure 4b).

Continue the exercise and repeat the same with your left leg. Remember to keep your toes pointed at all times.

Then, lift both legs off the floor and move them wide apart. Lower your legs on the floor in the fourth quarter of the bar; lift them again and place your legs together on the floor for the next fourth quarters (See

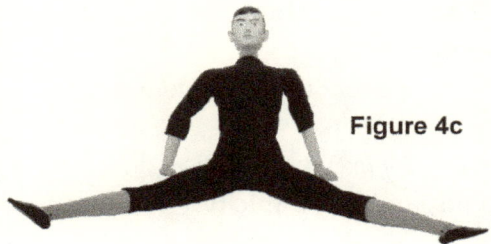

Figure 4c

Figure 4c.) Repeat this part of the exercise twice.

To sum up, you should execute the pattern once with your right leg, then once with your left, and then twice with both legs. See that your legs stretched and toes pointed all time. Breathe rhythmically, inhale for the four quarters, and exhale for the next four quarters. Repeat the entire combination two times.

Methodological guidelines: Anticipate the students impulsively trying to ease the tension on the abdomen muscles by leaning on their elbows instead of hands. The instructor should gently point out on this and insist on the proper execution.

In the following several lessons, repeat the entire pattern two times only. However, as the strength of the abdomen muscles improves, increase the number of repetitions to three and even four times in a single lesson.

Note: This exercise is sufficient to train Strength, Stamina, Rhythmicity, Flexibility, and Willpower.

Exercise 29 BODY ARCHING
Music is improvisation ¾-time, slow waltz.

The beginning position is lying on your stomach; legs together and hands on the back of your neck. Gradually lift your head and shoulders; simultaneously lift your stretched legs off the floor and arch the body. Take four bars of music for this. For the next four bars, slowly lower your legs and shoulders and return to the beginning position. Make sure that you do not bend your knees in the process. Inhale when arching up and exhale when returning to the beginning position.

Repeat the exercise four times.

Note: This exercise develops Strength, Flexibility, Mobility of Joints, and Rhythmicity.

Exercise 30 SPRING (sitting position)
Music is improvisation ¾-time, the first three quarters stressed, the fourth quarter – regular.

The beginning position is sitting on the floor with legs stretched wide apart, with palms on your knees and spinal column upright.

First variation:

Bend forward three times energetically, once for each downbeat and try to reach the toes with the tips of your fingers; spring back a little after each bend; return to the beginning position in the fourth bar of music. Note, breathing in this exercise is different. Unlike you did in most of the exercises of this group, exhale for the first three bars, and inhale when returning to the beginning position. To accommodate this, you must take a deep breath just before the exercise begins. Repeat exercise minimum four times.

Second variation:

Perform the same as above, only on the hard beat of the fourth bar, while returning to upright position clap your hands above your head. Repeat this exercise six to eight times continuously.

Third variation:

Bend three times forward and try to reach for the toes of your right foot with the left hand (stretch right hand backward), then unbend and sit straight in the beginning position; now bend forward three times and touch the toes of your left foot with the right hand, then unbend and sit straight. Control your breathing the same way you did in the previous variations of this exercise.

Methodological guidelines: Introduce the first version of the exercise and repeat it in five or six consecutive lessons. Later in the program, substitute it with the second and then the third version.

Note: This exercise develops Flexibility, Rhythmicity, Strength, and Correct Breathing.

Exercise 31 PUSH-UPS
Music is improvisation 2/4-time, slow tempo.

The beginning position is lying on your stomach. Place the palms of your hands on the floor under your shoulders and lift your body. Have your body supported only by stretched hands and the toes of your legs. Make sure your body is not sagging.

Gradually bend your arms and lower your body to the first bar; then, by force of arms, lift your body for the next bar and return to the beginning position; inhale while going down and exhaling on your way up.

Repeat exercise at least four times.

Methodological guidelines: As the training advance, increase the number of repetitions. However, do not compel anyone, instead suggest it to those who want or can do it, as Push-Ups is a very strenuous exercise. Remember that we are training actors and not competitive athletes or bodybuilders. Also, allow female students to do fewer repetitions.

Note: This exercise develops Strength, Stamina, Rhythmicity, and Willpower.

Exercise 32 SPRING (standing position)
Music is improvisation ¾-time with a stress on the downbeat of the first three bars and a soft, slightly delayed (*Ritenuto*) fourth bar.

The beginning position is standing heels together, toes slightly apart, and arms stretched up with palms facing forward.

On the downbeat of the first, second, and third bars, actively bend over at the small of your back, trying to reach the floor. After each bending, bounce spring-like a little up; for the fourth bar, unbend back to the beginning position. Keep your knees straight at all times. Unlike many other warm-up exercises, exhale while bending forward and inhale while returning to the beginning position.

Repeat exercise four to eight times.

Methodological guidelines: After performing the "spring" in several consecutive classes, vary it slightly by gradually increasing the tempo of the music. Also, introduce clapping hands above your head when returning to the beginning position on the fourth bar's downbeat. In the beginning, suggest clapping hands once, then in the following lesson twice, and later even three times.

We recommend using this exercise after the warm-up part of the lesson, followed by 30 to 40 seconds of running, then walking.

Note: This exercise develops Rhythmicity, Flexibility, and Mobility of Joints, Amplitude of movement, Velocity, and Correct breathing.

Collection II, Exercises on the floor

Note: This set of Warm-Up exercises is more complicated than the previous one. Introduce it in the second half of the semester.

Exercise 33 STRAINED BACKWARD BEND
Music is improvisation 4/4-time, slow, and legato.
The formation is a circle.

The beginning position is standing on left foot, right foot extended back with the toes touching the floor, hands on the back of the neck.

Gradually bend your neck and tilt your head and upper body backward; simultaneously open your arms out to the sides, inhale; then, unbend and return to the beginning position, exhale. Go over the exercise four times, then switch legs' pose and repeat it four more times.

Exercise 34 BEND FORWARD, TWIST BODY
Music is improvisation ¾-time, medium tempo.

The beginning position is standing feet wide apart, hands out to the sides.

Bend forward and twist the upper body at the same time, trying to reach the toes of your right foot with your left hand; extend your right hand up. Take four bars of music to do this. For the next four bars, unbend and return to the beginning position. Repeat the exercise in reverse; breathe rhythmically. Repeat the exercise minimum four times to each side.

Exercise 35 BENDING FORWARD, STRETCHING ARMS
Music is improvisation 4/4-time.
		The beginning position is standing feet shoulder-width, hands on the back of the neck.

		Gradually bend the upper body forward to a horizontal position. Simultaneously stretch arms forward and flex hands upward palms frontward; tilt your head up substantially so you can see the ceiling; inhale. Take one bar (four quarters) of the music for this then gradually return to the beginning position for the next bar of music. Repeat the exercise four to six times.

Exercise 36 BODY AND FISTS TWISTS
Music is improvisation ¾-time with a stress on the first quarter.

The beginning position is standing feet apart; arms out to the sides, fists clenched (see Figure 4d.)
		Gradually turn upper body along with extended arms to the right; simultaneously

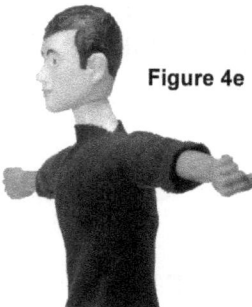

Figure 4d

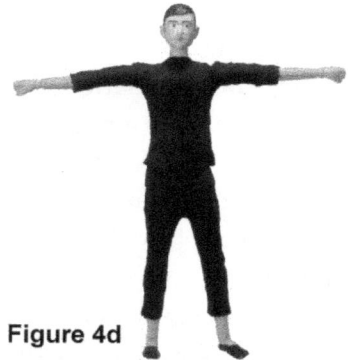

Figure 4e

Figure 4f

twist both fists clockwise as far as you can (see Figure 4e.) Take four bars of music for this. Gradually return to the beginning position for the next four bars of music; now, twist upper body to the left; simultaneously rotate your fists counterclockwise (see Figure 4f); then return to the beginning position. Keep your feet firmly on the floor and see that your shoulders are relaxed. Repeat the exercise four times in each direction.

Exercise 37 ARCH BODY, LIFT LEGS
Music is improvisation 4/4-time.

The beginning position is sitting on the floor, palms behind on the ground, legs together (see Figure 4a).

Lift your pelvis by arching the body; simultaneously lift your stretched right leg (45°) and point the toe; tilt your head back, inhale. Take four quarters of the music for this part; now, gradually return to the beginning position, exhale. Repeat the exercise lifting your left leg. Make sure the supporting leg is also straight with the toe pointed at all times. Repeat the entire exercise four times.

Exercise 38 "LOOPHOLE"
Music is a waltz, medium tempo.

The beginning position is standing on your spread knees facing the center of the circle (or forward) and hands placed in front of you on the ground; tilt head up, stare onward (See Figure 5.)

Imagine a fence in front of you with a

Figure 5

"loophole" about one foot high under it. Keep your hands and knees fixed on the floor and "squeeze" your head and then your body under the "fence." To do it properly, you would have to bend your arms. Take four bars of music for that; then, pull your body back and return

to the beginning position; breathe rhythmically. Repeat the exercise four times.

Methodological guidelines: Performed correctly, this is an excellent exercise to develop the Flexibility of Joints. Make sure the students first bend their arms then extend their bodies forward all away until their arms are straight. To be able to execute the exercise correctly, the students must also arch their backs.

Exercise 39 LEGS LIFTS
Music is improvisation ¾-time, slow tempo, every first beat stressed.

The beginning position is sitting on the floor, stretched legs together, hands on the back of the neck, spinal column straight.

Bend your legs sharply and bring your knees to the chest on the first bar. Stretch your legs sharply up (45°) on the second bar; bend your legs again, bring knees to the chest on the third bar, and, finally, stretch your legs and put them down for the fourth bar. Thus, the entire exercise takes four bars of the music. Keep the toes pointed at all times. Breathe rhythmically and repeat the exercise four to eight times.

Exercise 40 BODY LIFTS WITH TWIST
Music is improvisation ¾-time, Adagio.

The beginning position is sitting on the floor, leaning on your hands placed on the floor behind; stretched legs wide apart (see Figure 4c).

Gradually lift your body; simultaneously lift your right arm and twist body to the left, tilting your arm over the head. Take four bars of music for this. Gradually, return to the beginning position for the next four bars of the music. Repeat the exercise in reverse and twist your body to the right with the left arm tilting over your head. Both feet and one of the hands remain on the ground for support. Repeat the exercise four to eight times.

Exercise 41 SIT-UPS
Music is the same as above.

The beginning position is sitting on the floor, straight legs together, hands stretched up, and palms frontward.

Gradually lie down on your back and gently place arms on the floor behind your head, inhale. Now, continuously sit up and return to the beginning position; try not to help yourself up by swinging your hands.

Collection III, Exercises with an ordinary chair

For best results, introduce exercises with the ordinary chair in the second half of the program to replace the warm-up exercises on the floor. By this time, the previous exercises should become a monotonous, so a new collection would stimulate the interest in a warm-up part of the lesson. Also, the process of learning the new set of exercises would provoke the imagination. We are offering here only a limited choice of exercises with the ordinary chair. However, a teacher can create his or her new exercises additionally.

Our society is obsessed with physical fitness, so the always-accommodating market offers a wide variety of apparatuses to satisfy popular demand. It seems like practically every day there is a new device on the market. The good thing is -- such devices promote physical exercise. However, our own experience demonstrates that a smart set of simple exercises on the floor always was, and still is, the best way to develop most of the physical abilities. No matter how sophisticated an apparatus is, its user still faces a major physiological problem -- overcoming natural resistance to engage in physical activity. In other words, easy as it seems, no apparatus would do the hard work for the person in training.

Fortunately, in our line of business, the student has a worthy purpose of taking on this challenge. It is to make a physical instrument capable of responding to any thought or idea created by the imagination.

To diversify the strenuous physical training and to make it more attractive for the public, pedagogues of the Nineteenth century created simple gymnastic apparatuses. These devices became very popular in gymnasiums all over the world and remained popular until the middle of the Twentieth century. Unfortunately, they do not exist anymore. We are talking here about two versatile apparatuses: the Swedish Wall, and the Gym Bench. These apparatuses were very

helpful in developing many physical faculties and habits effectively and were comfortable for the simultaneous use by several students. However, they replaced them with individual machines that make you think that they, the devices, would do all the hard work for you.

Therefore, the exercises with an ordinary chair (easily obtainable) are just another means to train the physical abilities without becoming dependent on convoluted and cumbersome machines. For this collection of exercises, use a simple but sturdy wooden chair; preferably with a straight back, plain seat, and no armrests (see Figure 6.) The weight of the chair should not exceed 20 pounds. Besides other essential qualities, the exercises with an ordinary chair are excellent to develop the Balance.

Figure 6

Exercise 42 BACKWARD BENDS
Music that has a distinct rhythm (improvisation 4/4-time or ¾-time, slow and continuous) is an essential partner in all exercises with a chair.

Figure 7a

Figure 7b

The beginning position is sitting on the chair with the

back leaning against the chair' back, feet on the ground, knees together, and hands resting on your knees (See Figure 7a.)

Remain seated and gradually lift your straight arms; simultaneously arch your upper body and tilt your neck back. Take four quarters for this half of the exercise (see Figure 7b); now, for the next four quarters of the music, gradually return to the beginning position; inhale for the first half and exhale for the second half of the exercise. Repeat exercise four to six times.

Exercise 43 SIDEWAYS BENDS

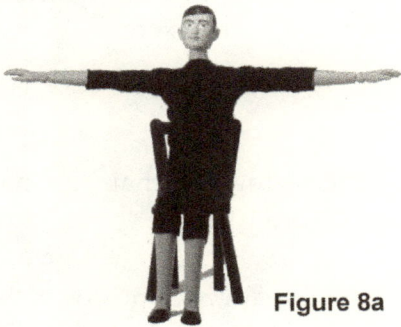

Figure 8a

Figure 8b

The beginning position is sitting on the chair, feet on the ground, knees together, and arms out to the sides (see Figure 8a).

Gradually tilt the upper body to the right and reach the ground with your right hand (see Figure 8b). Take four quarters of the music for this. For the next four quarters, unbend and return to the beginning position. Repeat the exercise in reverse, or tilting to the left. As usually, inhale during the first half and exhale during the second half of the exercise. See that you do not lean forward in the process.

Figure 9a

Figure 9b

Repeat the cycle four times.

Exercise 44 FORWARD BENDS

The beginning position is sitting on the chair with your back upright.

Clasp the front legs of the chair with your legs from outside, extend your hands up, palms forward (see Figure 9a).

Gradually bend forward, reach the ground with your hands, then unbend, and return to the beginning position (see Figure 9b). The entire exercise should take two bars of music or eight quarters; inhale for the first half, and exhale by the end of the exercise. Repeat exercise four to six times.

Exercise 45 LEG OVER SEAT

The beginning position is standing facing the chair, a small step away from it, put hands on hips (see Figure 10a).

Begin with your straight right leg and carry it once over the seat of the chair from left to right; bring it down next to the left foot in the fourth quarter of music (see Figure 10b). Now, carry the same leg over the seat, but from right to left and bring it down next to the left foot. The whole cycle must take two bars of music. Repeat the sequence with your left foot. The challenge in this exercise is keeping the balance.

Repeat the exercise minimum four times with each foot.

Figure 10a

Figure 10b

Methodological guidelines: The instructor should see that students carry their legs gradually and smoothly without touching the seat of the chair. When the exercise performed sufficiently in several lessons, suggest moving legs over the back of the chair. For this variation, the student must face the back of the chair. See that both legs are straight in the process of the execution.

Exercise 46 CHAIR LIFTS

The beginning position is standing behind the chair; put feet shoulder-width, bend forward, and hold the back of the chair with your straight arms (see Figure 11a).

Figuer 11a

Gradually lift the chair in straight arms, and continue moving it over your head until the edge of the seat touches your back; for that, you would have to bend your arms (see Figure 11b); perform it slowly in four quarters of music. Now, for the second half of the exercise, bring the chair back to the beginning position straightening your arms in the process; take four quarters for this part as well. Make sure you breathe continuously.

Figure 11b

Repeat exercise four to eight times.

Methodological guidelines: Since all chairs are different, the instructor must choose a proper chair. Do this to avoid any injuries. For this particular exercise, we recommend testing the chair and finding the best-balanced handling position before offering it to the students. If mishandled, the chair might drop and harm a student.

Note: This exercise develops Strength, Flexibility, and Balance.

Exercise 47 BEND, UNBEND LEGS

The beginning position is sitting on the chair with your right flank to the back of the chair; upper body upright; hold the top of the chairs back with your right hand, and the seat with your left hand; legs half-extended, feet on the ground (see Figure 12a).

Figure 12a

Note: Make sure you sit in the center of the seat to avoid capsizing off the chair.

Figure 12b

Perform the following four movements, one for each quarter of music:

One – bend both legs and bring knees to the abdomen (see Fig. 12b);

Two – stretch legs forward and up (45°) (see Figure 12c);

Three – bend your legs again and bring knees to the abdomen;

Four – put your feet on the ground to the beginning position.

Figure 12c

Figure 13a

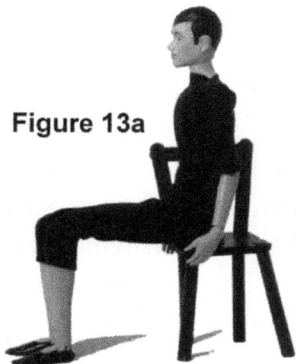

Repeat exercise four times, then switch the position and sit with your left shoulder to the back of the chair; repeat it four more times.

Methodological guidelines: After drilling the exercise in several lessons, make it more challenging by suggesting performing it with arms crossed on the chest. This variation of the exercise, besides other abilities, would actively train the Balance.

Exercise 48 SIT-UPS

The beginning position is the same as in the previous exercise, except this time, sitting on the edge of the seat (see Figure 13a).

Grab the chair with both hands next to your hips and hold tightly to the chair; gradually tilt backward, lie down on the seat and tilt your neck back as if trying to reach the floor with your head (see

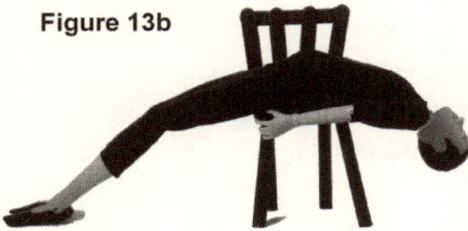

Figure 13b

Figure 13b). Take four quarters of the music to do this. Now, gradually sit up and return to the beginning position for the next four quarters. Repeat exercise four to eight times.

Exercise 49 STEP UP, STEP DOWN

Figure 14a

Figure 14b

Figure 14c

Music is improvisation ¾-time, slow waltz.

The beginning position is standing in front of the chair and facing it, hands along your body (see Figure 14a).

On the first bar, perform the following: step on the seat with your right foot (see Figure 14b), lift your body, and pull your left foot next to the right (see Figure 14c). The second half of the exercise is -- step down with the right foot, and then bring your left foot next to the right; do it for another bar of the music. Notice, the entire sequence takes only two bars of the music. Repeat exercise four times, and then continue and do it four more times with your left foot up on the seat. After this, sit down on the chair and recite Multiplication Tables for "two."

Exercise 50 THE ARM AND LEG LIFTS

The beginning position is kneeling on the front edge of the seat facing the chair; hold the top of the chair's back with your hands (arms half-bent); spinal column upright (see Figure 15).

Figure 15

First version

Slightly lower your upper body; simultaneously stretch the right arm forward and up and left leg backward and upward. Keep your head up and stare ahead. Take four quarters of music to execute this half of the exercise. For the next four quarters, gradually return to the beginning position. Repeat the exercise in reverse and stretch your left arm and right leg; maintain the balance, and breathe rhythmically. Repeat the whole cycle four times.

Second version

Same exercise as the previous, but stretch simultaneously right leg and right arm, and then left leg and left arm.

Note: This is an excellent exercise to develop the Balance, among other qualities.

Exercise 51 STEP OVER SEAT

The beginning position is standing and facing the side of the chair; bend forward, and grab the seat with one hand, and the back of the chair with another; feet together.

Hold the chair at all times, begin with your right foot, step over the chair's seat on the other side of it, then step over with your left foot, and place it next to the right. Take four quarters of music for that – two for the right foot and another two for the left. Now, for the next four quarters, return to the beginning position bringing your right and then left foot. Try not to touch the chair with your feet. Repeat exercise four to eight times in a single class. Breathe regularly and rhythmically.

Methodological guidelines: Among other faculties and skills, this exercise helps to develop Dexterity to a great extent. Make sure the students do not move the chair to accommodate the motions and hold to the chair at all times. Continue to train Rhythmicity and Tempo-rhythm of Physical Act even in extreme situations, which exercises of this kind present to students.

Exercise 52 JUMP OVER THE CHAIR
Music is improvisation 4/4-time plain chords, slow and definite.

The beginning position is standing to face the side of the chair about one foot away, with hands down.
To get ready for the jump, bend your knees slightly and, at the same time, swing your arms back (see Figure 16). Now swing your arms up and jump over the seat on the other side of the chair. Land on both feet on the downbeat of the music; to accomplish this task, you must begin the preparatory motion (or pickup motion) a bit before the

Figure 16

music starts. Now, gain your balance for the second quarter, then with a small jump make an about-turn on the third quarter, and pause/prepare for the next jump for the fourth crotchet. Perform another jump over the chair and land on the other side. Repeat the entire sequence four to eight times in a single lesson.

Methodological   guidelines: Such qualities as Dexterity, Courage, and Decisiveness developed to a suitable degree by this time in the program would help to perform this exercise safely. If the group is not ready for this (in the instructor's opinion), it is better to delay or even skip the exercise by any means.

However, it is an excellent exercise to develop further the qualities mentioned above. To make the exercise even more complicated, increase the tempo in the following lessons.

Exercises in Lunging

The following collection of exercises intensively drills such abilities as Strength, Flexibility, and Mobility of joints. Combined with other body motions, they serve as excellent training for overall body conditioning and significantly increase the cardiovascular and respiratory system load. We recommended including these exercises in the warm-up part of the lesson towards the end of the semester. Notice, there is a distinctive difference between a "step forward" and a "lunge forward" that the students must understand before these exercises offered. The lunge is, in essence, a sizeable step forward culminated in a position, in which the front leg bent, and the back leg stretched with only the toes of it on the ground; the weight of the body is mostly on the front foot, and the back foot serves as a support.

Exercise 53 LUNGES FORWARD

Music is improvisation 4/4-time, slow with sharp chords.
The Formation is a circle.

The beginning position is a regular stance, your hands on hips, right flank towards the center.

Lunge forward with your right foot for the first quarter of the bar; for the second quarter, stand up and bring your left foot next to the right to the beginning position. Repeat the exercise with the left foot. While lunging, keep the upper body straight. Try to get a maximum extension when lunging, but see that you do not sink. That might prevent you from standing up in time. Inhale for two quarters, or during the first half of the exercise, exhale for the second half.

Repeat the sequence minimum eight times, moving in a circle.

Methodological guidelines: Perform the lunging in quantities, carefully determined by the instructor, as it is a strenuous exercise. Offered usually at the beginning of the lesson, it should not tire the students, but rather condition the skeletal muscles. Increase the number of lunges gradually for up to sixteen in the subsequent lessons if the students demonstrate enough strength and energy.

Note: This exercise develops Strength, Flexibility, and mobility of Joints, and Balance.

Exercise 54 LUNGING, MOVING ARMS AND BODY
Music is improvisation 4/4-time.
The Formation is a circle.

The beginning position is standing with heels together, with your flank toward the center, arms along the body.

Maintain the circle formation and lunge forward with your right foot for the first quarter, simultaneously extend your arms out to the sides. On the second quarter bend forward, place your chest on the knee and your palms on the floor; for the third quarter, unbend, extend arms out to the sides; for the fourth quarter, bring left foot next to the right foot and get back to the beginning position. After that, continue the exercise with the left foot. Repeat it four times alternating feet, then turn around quickly and repeat it four more times, moving in a circle in the opposite direction. Maintain the balance and perform the exercise in sync with the music.

Note: This exercise develops Balance, Flexibility, and Strength.

Exercise 55 LUNGING SIDEWAYS
Music is improvisation 4/4-time.
The Formation is a circle.

The beginning position is a regular stance, facing the center.

Lunge with your right foot to the right; at the same time, put your arms out to the sides, palms down. For the second quarter of the bar, bend over and touch the ground with your palms. For the third quarter, unbend and put your arms out to the sides and for the fourth quarter, bring your left foot together with the right and return to the beginning position. Repeat this exercise four times, moving in a circle to the right, then reverse and repeat it four times in the opposite direction. Breathe rhythmically, inhale for the first two quarters and exhale for the next two quarters.

Note: This exercise develops Balance, Flexibility, and Strength.

Exercise 56 LUNGING, TWISTING BODY
Music and Formation are the same as in the previous exercise.

The beginning position is standing with a left shoulder to the center of the circle, feet together; place your hands on your shoulders, elbows apart; chin slightly up.

Lunge forward with your right foot on the first quarter of the bar; simultaneously twist your upper body to the right. Lunge forward with the left foot on the next quarter; twist your body to the left. In other words, perform a lunge for each quarter of the music and twist your body towards lunging foot. Keep the upper body upright and breathe rhythmically; alternate inhale and exhale with each lunge.

Repeat the exercise eight times, moving in a circle.

Methodological guidelines: This exercise is quite demanding, and it activates the cardiovascular and respiratory system considerably. Thus, use it as the concluding exercise of the entire lesson, perhaps followed by walking and running.

Exercise 57 PICKING APPLES
Music and Formation are the same as in the previous exercise.

The beginning position is standing feet together, hands along the body.

Imagine that you are in the apple orchard full of trees, and the branches are just above your head; all you have to do is to reach for an apple, pull it out and throw it on the ground. Consider it a competition between the pickers to collect more apples in a given time. The "judges" would count the apples later. However, they would select the winner based on the performance of the task, i.e., on keeping in sync with the music and executing lunging gracefully.

For the first quarter of the bar lunge forward with your right foot, for the second quarter, grab an apple with your left hand, on the third quarter twist the apple, and for the fourth quarter, throw it on the ground. Then, lunge forward with your left foot, reach for an apple with your right hand, twist the apple and throw it down. Repeat the entire sequence eight times. Notice, you must lunge forward as far as you can and reach for an apple as high as you can.

Breathe rhythmically, inhale in the first and second quarters and exhale in the third and fourth quarters.

Methodological guidelines: Note that some given circumstances are already incorporated in this exercise, challenging the students to use their imagination. This exercise also involves "imaginary objects." It is natural for the students to become animated in the process. Still, the instructor should watch mostly for the proper execution of the movements and should correct the errors if necessary.

Offer this exercise in the last quarter of the program, or when other imaginative exercises and exercises with given circumstances from different chapters of the textbook are offered.

Note: The exercise develops Strength, Flexibility, and Balance along with Concentration and Tempo-Rhythm of Physical Act.

Exercises in Squatting

This small collection of exercises would help the instructor diversify the warm-up part of the lesson and develop muscle strength and other qualities even further. Include it in the warm-up section towards the end of the program.

Exercise 58 SQUAT WALK
Music is improvisation 2/4 time.
The Formation is a circle.

The beginning position is squatting down, a shoulder toward the center of the circle, your hands resting on knees.

Walk forward in a circle and make eight steps remaining in the squat position; to help yourself, bounce with each step; take one quarter of the music for each step. Then, stand up and walk forward with regular steps for the next eight quarters to relax your leg muscles. Repeat the entire exercise at least four times.

Exercise 59 SIDEWAYS SQUAT WALK
Music and Formation are the same as in the previous exercise.

The beginning position is the same as in the previous exercise, but facing the center of the circle.

Maintain the squat-down position and walk with the right foot, followed by left. Make eight such steps; bounce with each step to help you move freely. Stand up and continue walking with regular steps in the same direction to relax your muscles. Repeat the exercise in reverse.

Exercise 60 SQUAT JUMPS
Music is improvisation 2/4-time, lively.
The Formation is a circle.

The beginning position is squatting down, right shoulder toward the center, your hands resting on knees.

Move forward by taking small jumps for each quarter-note of the musical accompaniment. After eight jumps, stand up and walk eight steps in the same tempo. Maintain the shape and size of the circle; also maintain the distance between yourself and your partners. Repeat exercise two to four times in a single lesson.

Note: After exercising in squatting, it is beneficial to run for a short period, gradually slowing the tempo and bringing it to a stop.

Exercise 61 DOWNSTAIRS, UPSTAIRS
Music is a March.
Formation – a circle.

The beginning position is standing with your shoulder toward the center of the circle, hands free along the body.

Imagine that there is a staircase going down in front of you. Walk forward, and with each step, descend your upright body down a bit. Make four such steps, one step for each quarter of music. Try to distribute your movements so that with the last step, you finish in a squat position.

For the second part of the exercise, remain in the squat position, walk forward four more steps. Remember, to be able to do this, bounce a bit with each step.

The third part of the exercise is walking four steps "upstairs," i.e., elevating your body a bit with each step.

Stand up and make four regular steps forward to relax your leg muscles for the final part of the exercise. Maintain an upright position of your body at all times. Perform the task four times, then stop, make an about-turn, and repeat it four more times.

Note: This exercise actively develops Strength and Flexibility.

Concluding Exercises

It is beneficial for the students to perform a short but rigorous exercise at the end of each class, immediately followed by another one that would calm down the entire body system. The Concluding Exercises intend to reduce the high level of concentration imposed during the class and boost the students' sense of satisfaction. It is yet another opportunity for the pupil to concentrate solely on proper breathing. This kind of exercise should last no more than two minutes. They are usually a combination of fast walking, running, jumping, and crawling.

After a minute or so of intense movements, stop the group and make them recite a text, such as sequential numbers. It is enough for the beginning of the program. However, towards the middle of the program, recitation of a logical text, such as Multiplication Tables, is appropriate. Switch to the recital of a poem or to singing a song towards the end of the semester. That would constitute the end of a lesson, a kind of closure, and should be akin to a ritual. It also brings class a bit closer to a stage performance.

Recital at the end of the class might begin in a natural tone. However, after the breathing restored, command the students to lower their voices, then recite the last two or three lines in a loud, self-confident voice. Concluding a class in such a way would raise the energy and bring a sense of satisfaction with the work done. After this simple pedagogical technique, students would leave the class in a happy and elevated mood, as if they just concluded a successful presentation.

Exercise 62 JUMPING "CHAIN"
Music is improvisation 2/4-time.
Formation – a "chain."

First version

The beginning position is a "chain," i.e., standing in a file one behind another. Put your right hand on the right shoulder of the person in front of you; bend your left leg, and clasp your ankle with your left hand behind your back. The first in the chain must put his right hand on the hip.

Move forward by jumping for each quarter of music on the right foot; Move in a circle and do not break the "chain." After eight (or sixteen) jumps, making no pose, continue by walking forward eight (or sixteen) steps. Then stop, place left hand on the shoulder in front of you, grab your bent right leg with your right hand, and repeat the exercise in reverse, i.e., jumping on the left foot.

Second version

Formation and beginning position is similar to that of the previous exercise, only this time bend your right leg, and clasp the right foot of a person in front of you with your right hand. The leader of the formation should keep both hands on hips; the last one in the chain keeps his clamped leg bent and jumps on one foot. After eight or sixteen jumps, stop, make an about-turn, and repeat the exercise in reverse.

Note: Along with other essential qualities, this exercise helps to develop Awareness, Coordination, and Balance.

Exercise 63 STAGE SCENERY

Methodological guidelines: The following exercise, in addition to common objectives of the previous Concluding Exercises, also serves to develop some specific stage skills. Before introducing it, the instructor should tell the students that there are many peculiar objects on stage, which the actor must avoid touching during the performance. These are made of fabric, cardboard, or foam, or other delicate materials to imitate the real objects or create an illusion of interior or exterior. It is easy to destroy the theatrical illusion by merely touching such things on stage. An actor must possess an adequate degree of dexterity to be able to move about stage packed with such things, especially if space is limited. In other words, the actor must obtain the Sense of Space, quick reaction, and a high degree of Stage Attention to maneuver amidst these items on stage. There is a fair grain of truth in the old joke – all the performers must learn to act on stage is "to memorize the lines and miss the furniture."

First version
Music is improvisation 4/4-time.
        Formation – two lines, all students are facing forward. The participants in the rear line stand right behind a partner in the front line. The distance between students standing in line is three feet.
        Let us agree that a person in the front line represents "scenery," which cannot be touched; students in the second line represent "actors."
        Both "actors" and "scenery" should begin with the right foot and walk forward, taking eight steps in quarter-notes. After this, for the next two bars of music, the "scenery" freezes, and each "actor" circumnavigates a partner in front. You should pass your partner on the right side and make a one-and-a-half circle, so you finish in front of him/her. Next, switch roles, so the "actors" become "scenery" and

vice versa. Repeat the exercise and make sure the "actors" arrive in front of "scenery" without ever touching it. Repeat exercise four times.

*

Next time the exercise performed, walk forward eight steps, then "scenery" stops, and "actors" run around making two full circles for the next two bars of music. At the end of the fourth bar, everyone promptly turns about-face over the right shoulder, and the exercise continues in the opposite direction, while the participants switch roles. Repeat the exercise four times.

Second version
Music and Formation are the same as in the previous exercise.

The technique is the same as in the previous exercise. Only this time, the "actor" should circle the partner two and a half times around and position him/herself in front of him, thus taking on a role of "scenery." Repeat the exercise four times.

There is a hint -- to decrease the momentum timely, bend your knees slightly when running.

Third version
As before, everyone walks eight steps forward in quarters, and then the "scenery" continues moving forward but slowly, walking in half-notes. The "actors" must circumnavigate the moving "scenery," making one and a half circles. Finish in front, thus becoming the "scenery." Repeat the exercise four times.

In the next class, when you repeat this exercise, make the "actors" run two and a half circles.

Fourth version
In this version of the exercise, the students representing "scenery" would not just stop after eight steps, but freeze in a pose,

which would make the "actor's" task even more difficult. Vary the attitude with each repetition.

Fifth version

The beginning of this exercise is similar to the previous versions, only the students representing "scenery" instead of the last step jump feet apart. The "actors" crawl between the legs and run a full circle to make it on time in front of their respective partners. Take two bars for that. Execute all movements in the second part, still within two bars of music, and do not ever touch the "scenery."

Repeat the exercise four times in a single lesson, switching the roles.

Sixth version

Same as before, only after you crawl between the legs get up, circumnavigate your partner to the right making one half-circle, then crawl again between legs, and stand up in front to become the "scenery."

Methodological guidelines: See that all the students who play "actor" would circumnavigate in the same direction to avoid a collision.

Follow each version of the exercise "Stage Scenery" with 30 to 40 seconds running in a circle; stop and recite logical text standing in place.

CHAPTER FIVE

IMPROVEMENT OF RHYTHMICITY

As we established previously, Rhythmicity is the human body's ability to respond rhythmically. Concerning the subject of Stage Movement, it means reacting to the stimulus, originated either inside of the individual, or outside; it means acting with the entire body.

In our opinion, Rhythmicity is of such importance for the actor that the development of this faculty should be one of the primary goals of the stage movement program. Without obtaining this faculty in the highest degree, the concept of tempo-rhythm would remain as something abstract for the actor.

Ideally, the Rhythmics should be available as a distinctive course in acting schools; it definitely must be a part of any Stage Movement program. Develop Rhythmicity purposely; it is hardly something to put away to chance. Webster's Collegiate Dictionary defines Rhythmicity as "the state of being rhythmic or responding rhythmically." Although most human beings do possess this quality to some extent, we are poised to make this psycho-physical faculty much more sophisticated in Essential Stage Movement training. We are seeking to bring this body and mind ability to the level when it responds selectively and consciously to any nuances of the environment. The rhythm in all its variations is just one of them.

It would be virtually impossible for a student without a sufficient level of Rhythmicity, to grasp such complex perception of Konstantin Stanislavsky as the Tempo-rhythm of a Physical action, or the Tempo-rhythm of a scene, or play. However, once acquired, the prominent Rhythmicity level would assist the student in the timely progress in such subjects as Period Movement, Dance, Speech, Voice, and Acting. Each of these subjects, using its specific material, in return, would develop Rhythmicity even further.

It is essential to introduce the students to the musical terminology as early as possible in the stage movement program. This way, a mutual vocabulary may be established and used at the onset. Theater students must be familiar with basic terms such as the time signature, bar, length, pace, tempo, beat, the timing of the sound, and so forth. They have to learn simple definitions of words like "stress" and "nuance" and some other essential musical notions. [1]

After basic terminology comprehended, the students may start learning how to distinguish and respond to musical sounds and rhythms with their bodies. We strongly believe that there is no better and faster way to improve Rhythmicity then using live accompaniment for physical exercises in a movement class — actually, the exercises described in this chapter explicitly designed to perform them with live music.

The accompanist's (pianist) responsibility is to present apparent rhythm and appropriate tempo for the exercises. At the same time, it is equally important to convey an emotional message through live music. The accompanist should be able to change the style and the characteristic of music when needed at the instructor's request. Therefore, the pianist must be an adequately skilled musician capable of presenting colorful and diverse music, as well as one familiar with the dynamics and specifics of body movements. It is similar to a dance accompanist, except that in stage movement class, the means of expression are movements of the everyday.

Some of the exercises included in this chapter borrowed from Emile Jaques-Dalcroze's System and used by several Russian pedagogues over many years. Others are specially developed for the Essential Stage Movement by the author of this book. Incidentally, Konstantin Stanislavsky, without a doubt, was familiar with the Eurhythmics of Dalcroze. He even recommended it for the program in his school, and his brother Vladimir Stanislavsky taught these exercises.

Since the exercises in Rhythmicity introduced, the students must understand several things from the outset. The training consists of responding to a musical pattern with regular body movements. The instructor should explain that a musical pattern consists of sounds and pauses, and each sound or pause has a certain length. In standard music notation, a single sound written as a note. There are whole notes, half-notes, quarter-notes, and so forth. So, for example, if a sound that lasts four seconds is whole-note, then a half-note is a sound, which lasts two seconds, and a quarter-note is a sound that lasts only one second.

Repeat some exercises of this chapter in several lessons, but perform others, like the exercise below, just once.

Exercise 64 QUARTERS, HALVES, WHOLE NOTES
Music is improvisation 4/4-time, simple chords.

Listen to the sound of quarter-chords played at a speed of 60 per minute.

1. Mark each quarter by clapping your hands in sync with the music.

2. Mark only the half notes, i.e., clap your hands only on the first chord and on the third chord in each bar.

3. Mark only the whole-notes. In this case, clap your hands on the first chord and rest for the next three sounds.

4. Perform this exercise in the following order: In the first bar mark all four quarters, in the second mark only two half-notes, and then in the next two bars mark only whole-notes. Repeat this sequence four times.

*

Repeat the exercise described above again. This time vocalize "La-La-La" along with clapping hands and make the sound "a-a-a" last until your next clap. Please do it for quarter-notes, half-notes, and whole-notes. Repeat this exercise four times.

Methodological guidelines: Everyone in the class must understand and perform this simple exercise. Sometimes students, trying to conceal the lack of comprehension of the task, would mechanically follow other students; or skip clapping or singing. The instructor should expose such occurrences and point out the errors.

Make one or several such students repeat every exercise in the order described above four times, and then, if necessary, repeat it by the entire group.

Exercise 65 FOUR QUARTERS, TWO HALVES
Music is improvisation in the following rhythmical pattern:

Formation – a circle, left shoulder towards the center.

Listen to this pattern several times, and then replicate it by clapping your hands along with the music.

Now, reproduce this pattern by stamping your feet; make sure you alternate the feet.

Now, produce the pattern by walking forward in a circle in time with the music. Begin walking with your right foot and swap feet. Repeat the pattern four times and stop.

Now, reproduce the same pattern but walk backward.

Methodological guidelines: While the exercise seems easy to perform, it is essential to go through all the stages in the order described above and to move to the next level only after the previous completed sufficiently.

Common mistake students make in this exercise is pulling feet together when making half-note steps. Try not to leave it undetected before it becomes a habit. See also that the students maintain equal distances and keep the initial size of the circle. By imposing these items, you would drill an additional skill called Sense of Space. Besides, by controlling different elements at the same time, the students learn how to switch their attention quickly from one to another. Incidentally, this is one of the primary objectives of the entire training.

Increasing the tempo after major requirements accomplished would challenge students further.

Exercise ***66*** TWO HALVES, FOUR QUARTERS, WHOLE NOTE, TWO HALVES
Music is improvisation in the following pattern played in chords:

Formation – a circle.

Listen to the pattern several times, and then vocalize it (la-la-la) along with the music.
Reproduce the pattern by clapping your hands.
Now, replicate the pattern along with music by walking forward in a circle. Repeat the exercise four times.
Now, perform the pattern by walking backward. Repeat it four times and stop.

Methodological guidelines: In exercises of this kind, use your judgment as to how many repetitions needed. The main criterion is to repeat the exercise until everyone in the group performs it correctly. However, if necessary, go back to earlier stages of exercise.
Walking backward requires more concentration than walking forward as it is not an ordinary action for a human. Therefore, some errors in this exercise are quite reasonable. Also, the students would tend to look over their shoulders to make sure there are no obstacles in their path. If you observe this, make a point that actors always have to trust each other. In this case, it is safe to walk backward if everyone in the group would maintain the distance between him/herself and a person in front. Developing confidence in the partner already in a class situation is a good start to build an Ensemble later in a stage presentation.

However, when creating additional tasks and obstacles in the exercise, the instructor should always keep in mind the main objective of the exercise. In this particular one, it is the correct performance of the rhythmical pattern that the students must achieve in the shortest possible time.

One of the complications to use in this and similar exercises is the changing of tempo while the practice is in progress. However, the instructor should warn pupils about this feature in the early stages of training. When the exercises of this kind performed satisfactorily in all possible variations, abandon it and offer a new pattern. We recommend practicing such exercises for no more than three to four minutes in a single lesson. If some of the variations did not fit in this timeframe, continue developing the exercise in the next class.

Exercise 67 FOUR QUARTERS, EIGHT EIGHTS

Before introducing this exercise, the instructor should bring to the students the fact that there are sounds in music that are shorter than a quarter-note. For example, there are eighth, sixteenth, and thirty-second-notes. These notes sound correspondingly 1/8, 1/16, and 1/32 the time of a whole-note. They should also understand that two eight notes played one after another last as long as one quarter-note, or two sixteen notes, when played one after another, last as long as eight-notes, etcetera.

Notes that are shorter than eighths not suggested for imitation in such exercises because they are too quick to express with body motions. However, it is appropriate to articulate notes shorter than a quarter with light passing steps when imitating them by walking.

Music is improvisation in the following pattern:

Formation – a circle.

As it is usual for these kinds of exercises, listen to the music first, then duplicate the pattern by clapping hands, and then repeat it by stamping your feet on the spot. Finally, imitate the pattern by moving forward in a circle formation. Do not forget to perform eighth-notes by running instead of walking.

Repeat exercise four or six times.

Exercise 68 FOUR QUARTERS, EIGHT EIGHTS, TWO HALVES, WHOLE

Music is improvisation in the following pattern:

Formation – a circle.

The technique and the order of presentation of the pattern are similar to the previous exercises, though there is one important transition you must be aware of. When the rhythm changes from eighth-notes to half-notes, make sure you control your body's momentum to accommodate the slower motions. Try not to lose your balance and to make the changing of the tempo of movement natural.

Begin with the right foot and repeat the entire pattern four times in a row. Notice, as the pattern consists of the odd number of sounds, you would have to start every next pattern with a different foot. In other words, as you begin the exercise with your right foot, continue the next repetition with the left.

Exercise 69 FOUR QUARTERS, DOTTED QUARTER, EIGHT, HALF, FOUR QUARTERS, FOUR EIGHTS, AND TWO QUARTERS

Explain that in music notation, there is such a peculiarity as a note with a dot next to it. If there were a blackboard in the room, it would be appropriate to demonstrate this and other patterns graphically. One can also use for this purpose a chart, prepared beforehand. The dot next to the note adds half as much time to the duration of the sound. For example, if the basic note is a quarter, the corresponding dotted quarter-note lasts one quarter plus one eighth of a quarter.

Music is improvisation in the following rhythm:

Formation – a circle.

The technique and the order of reproducing this pattern are the same as in the previous exercises. Pay special attention to the second bar, which consists of the quarter with a dot note, the eighth-note, and one half-note. The number of repetitions and complications is also similar.

Exercise 70 FOUR EIGHTS, ONE QUARTER, TWO QUARTERS, TWO EIGHTS

Before practicing the next exercise, one must introduce the concept of a time signature. The time signature is a notational convention used in Western musical notation to specify how many beats are in each unit. The unit in music called a "bar" or "measure." For instance, 4/4-time means that there are four quarters in a bar, or ¾-time implies that there are three quarters in a bar, or 6/8-time means that there are six eighths in a bar. Until now, we introduced only a 4/4-time signature. The following exercise represents a different time signature, which is a 6/8-time.

Music is improvisation in the following pattern:

Formation – a circle.

Listen carefully to this pattern several times; then imitate the pattern clapping your hands once for each sound; then repeat the same pattern by stomping your feet on the spot. Finally, duplicate the pattern by walking in a circle. Remember to perform eighth-notes by running gently, as these sounds are too short to try imitating them with regular steps. Repeat the final exercise four times.

Methodological guidelines: The concept of the time signature might produce some confusion at the beginning. The instructor should suggest counting the eighth-notes loud (from one to six) while at the same time, clapping hands duplicating the pattern. Incidentally, the same technique applies to the previous and following exercises of this chapter. After a new pattern understood, repeat it with a fluctuating tempo. It would bring complications to the process of performance.

To train the Rhythmicity further, the instructor can create many other similar exercises. However, it is essential to present a challenge with every new task.

Exercise 71 ECHO

This exercise is more complicated than the previous one. Offer it to students only after the adequate performance of all the earlier tasks by the entire group.

"Echo" resembles the game "follow the leader." In this exercise, the role of the "leader" given to the accompanist, and the students are the "followers."

Music is improvisation 4/4-time, performed one bar at a time, and paused after each sample had the same duration as the sample.

Formation – a circle, shoulder toward the center.

Stage 1

The beginning position is a regular stance, heels together and toes slightly apart.

The pianist will play one bar of the music with a clear rhythmical pattern. Listen to the pattern, and after it stops, replicate it right away by walking forward in a circle. After you finish, stop and listen to the next pattern. Notice, there will be no music while you repeat the pattern. Repeat this following pattern and halt again, and so forth. In replicating a pattern, you must preserve the tempo and the rhythm of it. Be alert -- all the patterns are going to be different.

Attention, the following task is crucial: finishing a pattern, bring the weight of your body on the foot that made the last step; stay in this position until you have to perform the next pattern. Keep your other foot extended behind, and ready to begin the following pattern. Remember, a "step" is placing a foot down and shifting the weight of your body to it.

Methodological guidelines: As the students are still adjusting to the rules of the game, the tempo of the patterns should be moderate, and the samples uncomplicated. However, as soon as they consent to it, decrease or increase the pace at your will, and create additional challenges.

Make sure the students follow the specific direction described above and finish each pattern with the weight of the body on the front foot. That would assist in starting every new pattern with the same foot by the entire company. A common mistake at the beginning is to pull feet together at the end of the pattern. The position in which the students should stand listening to the next pattern must be balanced, so the foot behind must firmly touch the ground to maintain the balance; for the same reason, do not allow students to stand on one foot only.

Practicing exercises in a circle formation, always remind the students to maintain the distance and the shape of the circle.

The instructor should limit each "echo" exercise to eight or ten patterns at a time. Change the direction of moving around the circle after each chain of echoes. However, if one or several students make an error in replicating a pattern, the accompanist should repeat the same pattern to give them a chance to correct the mistake.

Below are some examples of the ECHO patterns for the pianist.

Stage 2

We recommend moving to this stage of the Echo exercise only after many various patterns described in the previous chapter drilled in several consecutive lessons. Stage 1 was, in essence, the next level in developing Rhythmicity.

Therefore, beginning from Stage 2, the students must replicate not only a rhythmical pattern but also all various qualities that the music presents. The instructor should explain that, for instance, the Dynamics are the various sound levels in music, such as Piano, Pianissimo, Forte, Fortissimo, and so forth. 1

The accompanist plays one-bar patterns as in the previous stage of the exercise, but these patterns now will express more than just the rhythm and the tempo. If, for instance, you detect some sounds played quietly, so must be your replication. In other words, you have to recreate the dynamics of this sample as precisely as possible to the initial. Remember, the level of intensity will vary from one pattern to another. It will be not just loud or soft, but anything in between. Your objective is to notice the peculiarity and to express it with your steps.

Practice this stage of the Echo exercise in several consecutive classes.

Stage 3

This final stage of the "ECHO" exercise incorporates the two previous stages plus the sound qualities called Legato and Staccato. In musical notation, the Italian word legato (literally meaning, "tied together") indicates that musical notes played or sung smoothly and attached. That also means there should be no intervening silence from one note to another. Legato and staccato are kinds of articulation. Staccato is a form of musical articulation, signifying an independent sound, which is short and detached.

From now on, each one-bar pattern would contain as many qualities as possible, and you must detect them all to reproduce with your steps.

Methodological guidelines: One should take into account that human feet are not a musical instrument. However, with rigorous practice and diligence, the results in expressing the rhythm and various nuances of a pattern may become quite amazing.
Undoubtedly, the effectiveness and the emotionality of this drill largely depend on the skills and creativity of the accompanist. The musician should always start a chain of echoes with simple patterns and gradually move toward more complex and artistic ones. The students would never get bored with these exercises if the music has an emotional quality to it. As a result of this drill, the student should acquire a sensation of creating sounds with his own body.

The Echo exercise can become more complicated later in the program by making a sample consisting of two or even four music bars at a time. However, coordinate those changes with your accompanist first.

The next level in training the Rhythmicity could become "echoes" in 6/8-time.

Note: This exercise is an excellent training of Rhythmicity, but some other critical psycho-physical qualities, such as Concentration, Balance, and Coordination, are progressing with it. We highly recommend including the exercises of this kind in most lessons of the program after they introduced.

Exercise 72 CONDUCTING MARCH

Conducting is a series of intricate exercises intended to develop Rhythmicity along with other essential faculties and habits such as Coordination, Motion memory, Amplitude of Movement, Awareness of space, Concentration, and Tempo-rhythm of the Physical action.

Methodological guidelines: Introducing this group of exercises, the instructor should explain that in music, there are two distinct kinds of beats or pulses – a downbeat and an upbeat. Each bar, as a rule, starts with a downbeat and ends with an upbeat. The syllables "up" and "down" describe the gestures of a conductor, whose preparatory upbeat is of even greater importance to musicians than the downbeat.

In the March time music (2/4 time), there are two downbeats in a single measure and two weak bits as well. The downbeat and upbeat rotate. An upbeat is a beat that occurs just before a downbeat in conducting.

Music is improvisation 2/4-time.
Formation – a crowd.

Figure 17a

Imagine that you are the

Figure 17b

conductor of a marching band and that you are rehearsing a March in preparation for a football game. You are facing a "band" of musicians, who play all kinds of instruments, and you want them to play unified and in agreement; for that, they must obey your gestures.

In conducting business, the first thing a conductor should do is make sure that everybody is ready to begin playing. For that, raise the palms of your hands at a chest level, palms facing the band, so the musicians would concentrate their attention on your hands (see Figure 17a).

Next is the preparatory motion, or the upbeat. Uplift your palms at your face level with a decisive, but soft motion (see Figure 17b), and then downshift the hands in front of your body with a quick and robust move. Clench your fists at the same time. The last movement of yours would indicate the downbeat of the music – perform it in an authoritative mode (see Figure 17c).

Continue conducting and move your hands up and down in vertical line and in time with the music. Keep stressing the downbeat movement and alleviate the upbeat. See that you make fists with the downbeat motion and open your palms when moving hands up.

Figure 17 c   Please conduct sixteen or thirty-two bars of music.

Stage 2
Music is the same as in Stage 1.
Formation – a circle, stand with your shoulder toward the center.

Begin with your right foot and walk around the circle in time with the music; at the same time, conduct March. Remember, the downbeat must coincide with your first step, or with the movement of your right foot during the entire exercise. Repeat the exercise, marching for sixteen or thirty-two bars. Stop, make an about-turn, and continue moving in the same direction but backward; begin with your right foot again. As before, the downbeat must coincide with the steps of your right foot. Repeat this exercise for sixteen bars of music.

Stage 3
Music is the same as in the previous exercise.
Formation – a crowd.

One of the students faces the "band," i.e., the rest of the group. This student would play the role of the conductor.

The conductor will conduct the band and perform steps in different directions but in time with the music. The group members would duplicate the conductor's moves as a mirror reflection; also, the band should imagine that they are attached to the conductor with an invisible pole. Thus, they would have to follow the conductor in all different directions. For example, if the conductor stands on the spot, so does the band; if the conductor walks backward, the group walks forward; if the conductor walks in place, so does the band. When the conductor walks forward, the band moves backward, and so on.

The conductor must conduct a 2/4-time rhythm and invent various movements.

Stage 4
Music and Formation are the same as in the previous exercise.

One of the students faces the band, conducts the March, and improvises the moves. In addition to duplicating the conductor, the members of the band should mimic "playing" different instruments. Surely, the "musicians" must perform their motions in time with the music as well.

Stage 5
In this version of the exercise, the conductor must add sideways steps to his improvisational movements; the band must follow the conductor in any direction he/she chooses to walk.

Methodological guidelines: Switch players for every new repetition and let another student play the conductor role. Notice, this exercise contains some simplistic given circumstances and even different characters. The instructor should present it as a game and make sure the students get involved.

However, most importantly, to make sure every conductor performs the movements correctly. The hands must move up and down in the body's plane, fists clenched on the downbeat and palms open on the upbeat, downbeat movement is strong and determined, upbeat is easy and swift.

As to the command to begin the exercise, each one should consist of two words. We recommend the following -- "ready?... begin!" Explain to the students that after the second command, the conductor will perform the upbeat movement, i.e., to let the band know when the music begins. The two-word command given by the instructor implies the suggested tempo for both the conductor and accompanist.

In Stage 4, it would be appropriate to explain sideways steps before using them in the exercise. Practice sideways steps first to the right, then to the left. Step sideways for a downbeat and put the other foot together on the downbeat.

Before practicing Stage 5, make the students choose an instrument from the marching band variety. Encourage the students to select different instruments then arrange the "musicians" in groups accordingly. That can also have cognitive importance, as the students learn the structure of the marching band.

Present the five stages of this exercise in three or four consecutive lessons and practiced in the following sessions.

Exercise 73 CONDUCTING THE WALTZ

Note: Waltz as a musical form has three quarters in each bar, and only the first quarter is downbeat.

Music is improvisation ¾-time, slow waltz.

Stage I
Formation – a crowd.

The beginning position is Regular Stance; both hands palms outward on the chest level.

Gently lift your palms as a preparatory gesture or upbeat, then, clench fists and lower hands down in front of your body with dynamic motion. This motion indicates the downbeat of the music. For the second quarter of the bar, draw your hands apart on the abdomen level and open fists at the same time. For the third quarter, bring both hands the shortest way to the beginning position. As a result, hands would "draw" a triangle in the air. The last two movements must be soft but quick. Notice, although the beginning position for your hands is at the chest level, move your hands so that the peak of the "triangle" is slightly above your head. This way, your downbeat would be more expressive.

Please conduct waltz for eight or sixteen bars of music.

Stage 2
Formation – a circle.

The beginning position is stand heels together toes apart, put hands on hips, left shoulder toward the center of the circle. Walk forward in a circle in ¾-time. Stomp your foot on every bar's downbeat, and execute the next two steps softly. Notice, every next bar you would stomp with the other foot. Maintain the distance between you and your partner in front of you.

Repeat the exercise for the duration of eight or sixteen bars.

Stage 3
Formation – a circle.

This stage is a combination of Stage 1 and Stage 2. Walk around the circle, stamp your foot on the downbeat, and conduct the

¾-time with your hands. Remember, the downbeat must be matched by movement of your hands and stomping. Control your movements as well as the distance.

Note: The final stage of this exercise develops Motor Coordination along with Rhythmicity.

Exercise 74 CONDUCTING 4/4-TIME

In 4/4-time music, there are four quarters in each bar; usually, only the first quarter, the downbeat, is stressed. The three other beats not emphasized.

Music is improvisation 4/4-time.

Stage 1
Formation – a crowd.

The beginning position is the same as in the previous exercises.

Begin with the upbeat motion and gently raise both hands slightly above your head; next, clench your fists and energetically bring your hands down to indicate the downbeat. For the second quarter, draw your hands apart and open fists; for the third quarter, bring hands back together on the level of your abdomen; for the fourth quarter, raise hands slightly above your head, palms outwards. Remember, only the first motion is firm and definite; the other three are soft but swift.

Repeat this exercise for the duration of eight bars of music.

Stage 2
Formation – a circle.

The beginning position is a regular stance, shoulder toward the center of the circle, hands on your hips. Walk forward, stomping your foot on each downbeat of a measure. Stop, then walk backward and stomp for each downbeat of the music.

Stage 3
Formation – a circle.

Begin with your right foot, walk forward in a circle, and conduct 4/4-time music at the same time; mark each downbeat with a loud stomp. Besides conducting, maintain the size of the circle and the distance between you and the person in front of you. Repeat the exercise for the duration of eight bars of music. Stop, make an about-turn, and repeat this exercise for the length of eight bars, this time walking backward.

Stage 4
Formation – a circle.
Music is 4/4 improvisation.

The beginning position is a regular stance, your hands on hips, left shoulder toward the center of the circle.

Begin with your right foot, walk forward for one bar only, i.e., four quarters, or four steps, accentuating the downbeat. After that, quickly turn about-face over your left shoulder for the last quarter of the bar, and continue walking in the same direction, only backward. Make four steps backward and make an about-turn over your left shoulder again. Continue the exercise and turn about-face at the end of each bar. Repeat it for the duration of eight bars of music.

Now, position your hands for conducting. Conduct 4/4-time music in combination with the walking pattern you just learned, i.e., walk four steps forward, and then make an about-face turn and walk four steps backward. Remember to walk in the same direction in a circle. Repeat the exercise eight times.

Stage 5
Formation – a crowd.

A student who plays the role of the conductor positions him/herself in front of the "band." The rest of the students choose "instruments" they wish to play in the following exercise. The conductor would lead the band by performing different steps, and the band would mirror the conductor and maintain the distance between themselves and the conductor (see Exercise 72, Stage 3).

Now, the conductor would conduct 4/4-time music and improvise the steps; one may walk forward, or backward, sideways to the right or left, facing the band or even with the back to the group. The members of the band should follow the conductor and maintain the distance. The only thing the band cannot do is to turn back to the conductor because, in this case, they will not be able to see what to do next.

The conductor should begin the exercise facing the band, and for one or two bars stand in the spot; after that, the improvisation might begin. Repeat the exercise with each conductor for the duration of at least sixteen bars of 4/4-time music.

Methodological guidelines: The instructor should see that every student performs the conducting techniques correctly and in time with the music. Make sure the conductor accentuates the downbeat movement differently from the other three actions by intensity.

Keep reminding the students about the distances between the participants and the shape of the circle. It is imperative to control all the tasks, especially with the introduction of the about-turn maneuver.

When every student in the class performs the exercise satisfactorily, the instructor might turn it into a skit by introducing uncomplicated given circumstances. For instance, the "marching band" is in a corrupt mood because their team is losing the game. So, the conductor wants to cheer them up while conducting. That would make each performer find his/her adjustments to the movements. However, the circumstances should not supersede the primary goal - performing all the moves correctly and in time with the music.

If the conductor changes the direction and the mode of walking, he/she must do it so that the band understands the intention. Catching the musicians by surprise is not the objective of the conductor.

With every repetition, have another student play the Conductor, but no more than three or four conductors in a lesson.

Exercises 75 CONDUCTING CHOIR, 2/4-TIME
Music is "Oh, Susanna" (see Appendix 2).
Formation – a crowd.

Stage 1

Listen to the music several times and memorize the tune.

Learn the lyrics and sing it along with the music several times (view lyrics in Exercise 107, Stage 7).

One of the students positioned in front of the group as the conductor. The rest of the company plays the "choir." The conductor would conduct the "choir" in this 2/4-time song. Before the music begins, the conductor should establish eye contact with the choir to make sure everyone is ready to start. Then, the conductor should position his/her hands in front of the chest, inviting everyone to pay attention. Then the conductor should turn towards the accompanist and begin conducting. In this exercise, the conductor, and not the instructor, establishes the tempo. The two movements, up and down, would do the job. Following this command, the accompanist begins the Introduction.

In this case, the Introduction is four bars of music. Within this period, the conductor needs to synchronize the tempo of the song with the accompanist by continuing down- and upbeat motions.

Now, for the choir to begin singing on time, the conductor must turn towards the choir a bit before this moment and, with the help of eye expression, hand movements and, perhaps, the entire body, give them a sign to begin singing. For this purpose, indicate the upbeat clearly, to make the choir start the song with the music. Incidentally, the upbeat movement is the time for the singers to take a breath. Then, the choir sings the verse and chorus of the song while the conductor maintains his gestures continuously to keep the rhythm.

Repeat the exercise several times with a different student acting as the conductor each time.

Methodological guidelines: Make sure your "conductors" move their hands continuously and assuredly through the entire exercise. A common mistake is the tendency to interrupt the movements when switching from conducting the accompanist to conducting the choir.

In several following lessons after this exercise introduced, give each student a chance to act as a conductor. Sometimes, it is better to stop the exercise and point on errors instead of wasting time and going through the sixteen bars of the piece.

The instructor should disallow any verbal communication between the conductor and the choir. That would leave the performers only one chance -- expressing themselves using persuasive gestures only. As an element of role-playing is introduced, get ready to detect and ban any attempt to "play a conductor in general." It usually happens when a student lacks or does not believe in a precise objective. Moreover, the goal is to make the accompanist and the choir sing simultaneously, maintaining tempo and rhythm throughout the piece. Also, the conductor should remember that he is responsible for the quality of his choir's performance.

By believing in given circumstances and having the objective and will to accomplish it, the student would rid himself of the pressure to play a character, quit overacting, or utilize any cliché.

Stage 2

In this stage, the conductor may improvise the tempo of the song at will. To make your choir follow you when modifying the pace, make these changes gradual, and make sure your gestures are definite. Remember, neither the accompanist or the choir knows your intention. The conductor's goal is not to confuse the accompanist or the choir. The goal is to make them follow the transformations. So, avoid sudden changes, especially adjustments immediately after the Introduction. Try not to change the tempo too often. Let the choir sing at the same pace for at least four bars before any changes. Also, stick to the logic of music and lyrics, when increasing or decreasing the tempo.

Have a plan on how you are going to interpret and to conclude the song.

Stage 3

The conductor may now improvise the dynamics of the music. That means the conductor at his/her choice can make the choir and the accompanist perform the song either Piano or Pianissimo, Forte, or Fortissimo. To achieve this effect, one should make the amplitude of motions smaller for softer singing desired and bigger for louder sound. Try to find the proper degree of your gestures to express your interpretation of the song and make them clear enough for the group to understand and to obey your intentions.

Repeat the song several times in a single lesson, alternating conductors.

Stage 4

At this level, combine the two previous stages; you may improvise not just the tempo of the song, but also the dynamics. Remember, most significant is to sustain the continuity of the song and to deliver its meaning to the listeners.

Methodological guidelines: Practice the song with different conductors; encourage the students to create an original interpretation of the song. However, let them know that the quality of the singing is primary, and the amount of transformation is secondary. That would also mobilize the group, as a common goal becomes an essential part of the exercise.

As the exercise repeated several times in a lesson, do not overdo this. After a while, it becomes monotonous, which is an undesirable effect.

Stage 5, Final
The formation is two equal groups facing the conductor and positioned several feet apart.

The conductor now has a choice - to make the entire choir sing together, or to have only one group singing while another keeps silence. So, if you wish only the right group to sing, you should conduct it only with your right arm. Conduct the left group with your left arm only. Conduct the entire choir with both arms. You can shift from one group to another at your will.

However, make sure the resting hand remains visible in front of your chest with palm opened. It would retain the attention of a group that is not singing at this time. Use your entire body, and even the facial expression if needed to help the singers understand your intentions.

It is essential to let the choir know about your intended changes a bit earlier. You may hint on the singers by merely glancing in the direction of the group. You can also turn your body toward the group that you want to sing next. However, you need to do this before making the change. With all these transitions, make sure you sustain your conductor's gestures; interruption of any kind would surely confuse your singers and the accompanist.

Methodological guidelines: Towards the end of the program, suggest mixing all the previous stages of this exercise and trying different variations. Judge the success of the student/conductor by the smooth and meaningful performance of the song.

Include the Final Stage of this exercise in the test class.

Note, this exercise designed to develop Rhythmicity. It is also an excellent tool to improve the Tempo-rhythm of the physical act, Willpower, Attentiveness, and to gain a skill known as Communication with a partner.

Exercise 76 CONDUCTING CHOIR, 4/4-TIME
Music is the song "Mary Had a Little Lamb" (see Appendix. 3.)

To begin with, learn the tune and the lyrics of this song (see Exercise 105, Stage 3.)

Methodological guidelines: This exercise is similar to the previous one. Using the skill learned in Exercise 74, move successively through all the stages of the previous exercise. Then have the students perform the final stage, using different combinations of tempos and dynamics to create an original interpretation of the song. The conductor's movements in this exercise are more complex than in the previous ones, which make it more challenging.

Exercise 77 CONDUCTING CHOIR, ¾-TIME

Music is the song "How much is that Doggie in the Window" (see Appendix. 4.)

This exercise is similar to the previous two. Learn it by following successively all the stages presented and explained above. Before you begin Stage 1 of the exercise, learn the tune and the lyrics of this song.

> *How much is that doggie in the window?*
> *The one with the waggle tail,*
> *How much is that doggie in the window?*
> *I do hope that doggie's for sale.*

Methodological guidelines: After all the exercises that include conducting comprehended, the instructor may incorporate one or another, or even all of them in a single lesson. However, this block of the class should not be too long and should correlate with other parts of the class.

The exercises that improve Rhythmicity must be a part of each lesson through the entire program. However, we strongly advise to practice them for no longer than six to eight minutes in a single lesson or until the emotional appeal begins to fade. If the exercise has several stages, it would be smart to practice one stage at a time in a single lesson, and then move to the next segment of the class. Then, in the following class, repeat that stage once and move to the next stage, and so forth until the final stage of the exercise contained. Avoid mechanical repetitions. Achieving a perfect performance ready for public display is not the objective. As a rule, the process is more important than a spectacular demonstration.

It is the signs of improvement of a particular faculty or habit we are looking for in a training program. For that reason, use precious time for a better purpose rather than spending it to polish a particular exercise. However, to avoid disappointment and uncertainty in students, never drop a task before a positive result achieved.

In exercises of this chapter, the student needs to achieve a level of bodily expression, which encompasses all the delicate nuances suggested by a specific piece of music. The piano player must be proficient enough to improvise within a given rhythmical pattern and switch rhythms, tempos, and dynamics without breaking the music's logic. A skillful and artistic piano player would help you in the development of Rhythmicity. The improvement of Rhythmicity started in this chapter would continue with the help of various exercises of other sections of the Essential Stage Movement.

The knowledge and the skills developed with the help of this chapter's exercises would be most beneficial for the students. They would use them successfully in performing other exercises described in this textbook, and they would find them undeniably valuable in the future professional life in general.

CHAPTER SIX

IMPROVEMENT OF POSTURE AND GAIT

The mission to improve Posture and Gait has given significant consideration in the Essential Stage Movement program. There are two main reasons for this. One is to train proper breathing, and another is to attain gracefulness in students' appearance. Both are of great importance to the actor.

Unfortunately, in modern society, very little, if any, attention paid to the education of young people regarding proper posture and gait. When a teenager decides to become an actor, he/she already possesses pretty heavy faulty habits in walking and physical demeanor. We know that many different circumstances affect the shaping of Posture and Gait of a child since he begins to walk. Among others are climate, upbringing, physical activities, tastes, family traditions, clothing, physical injuries, illnesses, and so forth.

Motions like walking and body bearing become steady habits, which are extremely difficult to change because they inevitably constantly repeated through life day after day, year after year. Sometimes, these habits are so stubborn that to change them, it is not enough to understand them or to have someone point out to them. The solution is – get rid of a bad habit, obtain a better one instead. The experience proves one can accomplish this only with training that is both methodologically reliable and supported by continuous individual work of the trainee.

In any theatrical school, this training must begin from the very first lesson in a stage movement program and last for at least one semester. The goal of the drill is not to attain a particular fashionable posture or gait, but to acquire natural and practical habits instead. Stanislavsky wrote, "Stage gait must be one created by nature, according to all its decrees. In it is its main complexity."[1]

Regarding the improvement of posture, the objective is to provide the body with the best breathing conditions by positioning one's spinal column, shoulder blades, neck, and head naturally.

The goal in the development of gait is to make one's body move smoothly and continuously with grace and ease. As a reward, one discovers how to conserve energy while walking; something the actor would need for endless rehearsals and tiresome performances.

A professional instructor must possess at least two essential skills. First is an eye enabling him/her to detect the blunders in posture and gait; second is the knowledge to correct bad habits in posture and gait. Fortunately, the departures from the norm, in most cases, are common. Nearly all people living in developed countries make similar mistakes in physical demeanor and walking. To get inspired to make any changes, the individual should first know about it.

An experienced movement instructor is capable of noticing any deviation from the norm in posture and gait and pointing them out to a student. However, sometimes, it is not easy to commit an individual to work on improvements. The abundance of modern digital technology offers another way to demonstrate incorrectness in posture and gait. Just have someone secretly videotape the student walking, standing, and changing stances. By examining this documentary, a student would find out a lot about his mistakes and be encouraged to eliminate them.

After admitting the fact, it is essential to understand what precisely the correct posture and gait is.
When yet this becomes clear, the student must continuously begin working on the posture and gait constantly and everywhere – in class, at home, at the party, in the streets, and so forth. We must not deceive ourselves that a habit acquired during all previous life can change in several hours of training.

All our experience demonstrates that only those who are determined to change an old habit would succeed within one year, perhaps even faster. It is only with the full cooperation from the student that this goal becomes reachable. Taking classes in ballet also considered an excellent tool to improve posture and gait.

Here are some typical irregularities in posture: one shoulder is higher than the other, the arched back, the elevated shoulders, and shoulder blades are pulled together. Some of the common abnormalities in gait are in-toeing, leaping, swinging, the half-bended knees, the parallel feet, the crossing of feet, bouncing, and so forth. In the book "Rabota aktera nad soboij" ("Actor's prepares") Konstantin Stanislavsky writes, "One must walk so that the body would float horizontally, without visible vertical descent and ascent." [2]

This chapter presents exercises specially designed to reveal the common faults in Posture and Gait and to improve good manners. The reason these two entities combined in the same chapter is that they are closely correlated.

Exercise 79 REGULAR WALK

Music is improvisation 4/4-time, moderate tempo, and legato.
Formation – a crowd.

Stage 1

Position your right foot in front of the left in one line so that the heel touches the toe (see Figure 18a). Now, open your toes at approximately 15° to 20°. Notice that this position of your feet provides you with sufficient balance (see Figure 18b).

Walk forward without the music at your own pace. Place your heels on the ground first, followed by the rest of your foot. Place heels in one straight line and make sure you maintain the accepted angle. Remember, "step forward" means shifting the weight of your body on the front foot.

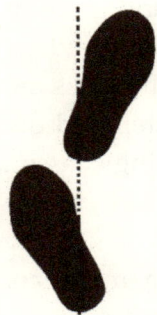

Figure 18a

This one time only, you may look at your feet while walking to make sure the position and movements are correct. In the following lessons, when walking, always stare forward. Practice for a while, and then stop.

Figure 18b

Now, in the established above mode, repeat the exercise and walk forward in time with the music. Walk forward for four bars of the music; take a step for each quarter. Stop, make an about-turn, and repeat the exercise one more time. Keep your upper body erect, shoulders relaxed and open chest while walking. From now on, without ever looking down, try to position your feet correctly, i.e., heels in one straight line, and toes slightly apart.

Now, bend arms behind your back and grab forearms with your hands. This maneuver would force you to align your back. Lift your chin slightly and straighten your legs. The posture you gain as a result is the one you want to own. Now, carefully disconnect your arms and bring them down but preserve the position attained. We recommend doing this maneuver quite often until you acquire a steady habit in the correct posture.

Now, repeat the exercise and try to control both -- your gait and posture at the same time. Remember, the human brain can only perform one task at a time. So when we attempt to monitor two or more tasks simultaneously, in reality, we only switch our attention from one item to another.

Now, take upon yourself yet another task – try to walk continuously and to control all the previous objectives. Repeat the exercises for the duration of four bars or sixteen steps.

However, that is not all; in addition to the tasks you already accomplished, take into account the following rules to create natural and graceful posture and gait. Try to remember them all and to carry them out in your next repetitions of the walking exercise. Moreover, the rules are - avoid swaying your body; avoid bouncing with every step and breathe rhythmically. Repeat the exercise several times in a single lesson.

Methodological guidelines: It would take numerous repetitions in many consecutive lessons to learn to control all these things at once. The instructor must be patient and include these features one at a time. The final goal of this drill is to achieve such results when the students would carry out all the rules without any effort, occasionally checking one of them or another. In other words, eventually, the students must execute this intricate physical act semi-automatically. Many different exercises in our Program include walking. Practicing would gradually turn into a good habit of the everyday walk.

In the long process of drilling this habit, the instructor should continually remind of one rule or another, as it falls out of the students' site. Most likely, some students would require special attention and additional prompting. However, to accelerate the process significantly, the instructor should encourage the students to continue working outside of the class. They should make it a task to control their posture and gait whenever they walk on the street, at home, or in a shopping mall. If practicing in class only, this habit would take much longer to acquire.

Stage 2
Formation – a crowd is facing upstage.

Begin with your right foot and walk backward in time with the music. To walk backward correctly, touch the floor with your toe first, and then with the rest of your foot. Nevertheless, as in walking forward, continue placing your heels on a straight line. Maintain the same features as in walking forward: walk continuously, avoid swaying, avoid bouncing, and breathe evenly.

Repeat the exercise several times.

Stage 3
Begin with your right foot and walk forward. On the command of the instructor, switch the direction and walk backward. Be alert -- the command would come unexpectedly. Make the transition effortless and maintain the pace of the walk. Note, before you begin moving backward, complete the previous step forward. In other words, bring the weight of your body on the front foot. Repeat the exercise for the duration of eight or sixteen bars of music.

Now, begin to walk backward, switch the direction, and walk forward on the instructor's command. It is a reverse exercise and the rule is the same – complete your last step backward before you begin walking forward.

Repeat the transitions from walking forward to walking backward and vice versa several times in a single lesson and maintain correct posture and proper gait.

Methodological guidelines: Changing the mode of walking from one way to another would gradually become a routine in many different exercises of this program. It is essential to achieve the proper performance of this transition from the beginning so one can use this technique semi-automatically in combination with other tasks in the future. Common mistake students make -- pulling feet together before changing the direction of walking. That would result in breaking the pace and switching the feet. Remind the students to continue walking with the right foot on the downbeat throughout the exercise, even if they change the direction.

Give the unexpected command to change the mode of walking at a proper moment in the exercise to enable the students to make a smooth transition. The call must come at the end of a bar (precisely on the last beat of a bar) to allow students to complete this final step and to begin the next step in the opposite direction. The command should be clear and firm, such as "Forward!" or "Backward!"

While working on the transitions, never let the main goal slip out of your mind: they must perpetually maintain correct posture and proper gait.

Keep practicing this exercise in several consecutive lessons until the students would perform the pattern semi-automatically.

Stage 4
Music is improvisation 4/4-time with the stress in the first and the third quarter in each measure.

Begin with the right foot and walk forward/backward in half-notes, i.e., make steps on the first and third quarters of a bar. It means that you would walk twice slower than in the previous exercise.

Maintain all the rules of correct posture and gait even though the circumstances have changed. While walking in halves, make sure you preserve continuity in your motions. See that the transitions from one mode of walking to another are also smooth. Remember; do not panic on the command to change direction. You must first complete the step, and only after that, continue walking in the opposite direction.

Now, walk forward in quarter-notes for two bars of music and then switch to halves and walk forward for the next two bars. Practice this exercise alternating the direction and the rhythm of walking.

Now, repeat the exercise, but expect this time, the instructor announcing all the transitions without warning.

Methodological guidelines: It is evident that measured walk requires more concentration to maintain the balance. People in modern society have very little (if any) experience in walking slow. Our life's tempo is much faster than it was, let say one hundred or three hundred years ago. However, an actor must be able to portray a character from such periods naturally.

As usual, require switching from one speed to another with the last step so that the next step already performed in the new style.

Stage 5
Music is improvisation 4/4-time with a stress on the first beat.

Begin with your right foot and walk forward in whole notes. That means you have to take a step only on the first beat of each bar. Maintaining the continuity of the walking and the balance would require even more concentration.

Now, walk in the whole notes backward. Then, begin with your right foot, walk forward in the whole notes; and prepare to change the direction on the instructor's command.

Because you already practiced walking in quarters, in halves, and whole notes, prepare for unexpected changes from one of these modes to the other; also, be prepared to switch the direction of walking. Repeat the exercise several times in a single lesson.

Methodological guidelines: Continue correcting a common mistake when students try to maintain the flow of walking, extending a foot forward (or backward) instead of taking a step. If this occurs, the instructor should stop the exercise and explain that slow walking is still making steps, and then gradually shift the weight of the body on foot, which took a step. Remind the students that they must keep both feet on the floor as long as they can, to maintain the balance in the best way, and to take the next step only at the last moment. However, at this particular moment, make sure the other foot is free of weight to make the step.

The instructor should inform the students that moving about slowly is unusual for modern humans, which is why we are not skillful in it. Nevertheless, the actor needs this skill; it might be useful in stylized movements, such as dance and mime, and it definitely would come in handy in period plays. On the other hand, by practicing these styles, one can develop the ability to move slowly and gracefully further.

Offer exercises in regular walk many times in consecutive classes and in a variety of combinations of rhythms and modes of walking. Doing this, remember that the main goal is to develop correct posture and correct gait. When the time comes to drop these exercises, drill the skill with tasks from other chapters that include walking.

Exercise 80 REGULAR WALK WITH ARMS' POSITIONS

Music is improvisation 4/4-time, continuous, moderate tempo.
Formation – a crowd.

It is beneficial to know which arm positions for both men and women we consider as essential in modern society. They are the following: arms free and hanging along the body, arms crossed on the chest, arms resting on hips, and arms folded behind the back. These positions are common and do not need any particular explanation or demonstration. We are going to utilize these positions in the exercise that follows.

The beginning position is the regular stance.

Begin with your right foot and walk forward in quarters. While walking, change the positions of your arms in the following order. First - free, and then cross them on the chest, put them on hips, and finally, fold arms behind your back. Switch one position to another after every bar of the music (or after every four steps). Maintain correct posture and gate continuously, even though you ought to concentrate on your posture, gait, and changing arms' attitudes.

Repeat the exercise for the duration of four bars, stop, turn around, and do it again; now, repeat the exercise by walking backward.

Repeat the same exercise. Now, the instructor announces the changes of the arms' positions and style of the walking. Be aware, because the order of arms attitudes would depend on the instructor. Repeat the exercise several times in a single lesson.

Methodological guidelines: This exercise is just another way of drilling the correct posture and gait by using the arms' positions as an additional complication. The commands for the changes might sound like "arms free," "cross on chest," "hands on hips," and "hands behind back." Give a command at the end of a bar of music. Later in training, you may announce it at any time in the exercise.

An excellent tool to further train the posture and gait is changing the tempo of walking. At first one can give a warning, but soon let the accompanist improvise it. However, the pianist should make these transitions gradually. Practice the exercise several times in several consecutive lessons and include many different combinations of directions of walking, tempos, and arms attitudes; do not overdo with the surprised commands. The main goal is still to train the correct Posture and Gait.

Exercise 81 REGULAR WALK IN A CURVE
Music is the same as in the previous exercise.
Formation – a crowd.

The next variation of walking is walking in a curve. When you hear a command "right curve" or "left curve," continue walking forward, gradually turning in a right (or a left) curve until you complete 180°-turn. You should complete this turn in four steps and continue moving forward in the opposite direction. This change of mode should not affect your posture or gait.

Repeat the initial exercise and walk forward in quarters. Be prepared for the surprise commands, including walking in a curve, among others.

Now, walk forward in half-notes and obey the instructor's commands regarding the right or left curve.

Methodological guidelines: Add this new mode of walking to your arsenal of sudden changes and keep drilling the correct posture and gait. We recommend practicing exercises in walking no more than eight to ten minutes in a single lesson, because generally speaking, they are tedious. If you notice that the interest to an exercise is decreasing, put an end to it and move to the next planned theme of the lesson.

Exercise 82 WALK, COUNT OBJECTS
Music is the same, as in the previous exercise.
Formation – a crowd.

Begin with your right foot and walk forward (backward) in quarters. As you walk, count how many light bulbs (or chairs, or any other multiple objects) are in the classroom. Remember, in this exercise, the accurate inventory is just as important as the correct posture and gait.

Now, walk forward and backward, improvise the curve turns and arms positions, and simultaneously count items in your classroom. While moving around the classroom, avoid collisions with your classmates. Perform this exercise for the duration of thirty-two bars of music. After the exercise is over, you may stop and check the accuracy of your inventory.

The next stage of this exercise is to walk around the room, improvising different transitions. At the same time, count in the mind's eye objects in your bedroom (e.g., light bulbs, pictures, vases, etc.) This exercise would involve your active imagination as well as the control of your movements.

Methodological guidelines: According to contemporary psychology, the human mind can concentrate only on one subject at a time. For example, in exercises described above, one can control either gait, or posture, or focus on counting objects, or observing objects, and so forth. Unfortunately, a human being cannot distribute the attention between two or more subjects simultaneously. Nevertheless, humans are usually capable of performing several tasks at the same time. A good example is driving a car. It is usual to observe a driver who controls the wheel with hands, pushes the gas pedal with the foot, listens to music on the radio, and talks to a passenger, all at the same time. That becomes possible because, after many repetitions, one can perform certain physical acts automatically or semi-automatically. It is also true that our mind, at any given moment, chooses a particular object needed critical care. As a rule, it is the most significant for a person object in a given period. The mind continues to control the other tasks but only occasionally, from time to time. In our example above, a slight change in traffic conditions makes driver terminate the conversation in the middle of a sentence to concentrate on the driving.

The actions performed automatically we call habits. The actions performed semi-automatically we call skills. However, even strong habits and steady skills need to be increased from time to time, especially when new or unexpected circumstances emerge. It is due to the natural ability of the mind to switch attention swiftly from one item to another that we are capable of doing this. The faster our mind makes this transition, the better our reaction to changes. In the end, when developed to a high level, this ability creates an impression that several things controlled simultaneously.

The exercises described in this chapter are crafted precisely to drill the capacity to switch attention from one object to another practically instantly. We use physical exercises to train the nervous system. Both the science and the practice demonstrate that this is entirely possible.

Graceful gait and correct, attractive posture must become essential habits to serve the actor. It is not easy to change bad habits obtained previously and to cultivate new, a fine one. However, hard work and awareness of the importance of improvement will do the job.

Exercise 83 HALTED WALK
Music is improvisation 4/4-time with stress on every 1st and 3rd quarter.
Formation – a crowd.

Begin with your right foot and walk forward in halves; freeze after each step. Notice, this manner of walking is contrary to a continuous walk. Try to attain full stillness after each step, but make sure to eliminate the muscle tension. This style of walking should not influence your posture or balance. When taking a step, plant your front foot firmly and bring the weight of your body on this foot right away. Make sure you position your heels on one straight line and your toes slightly open, as usual. Repeat the exercise for the duration of sixteen bars of music.

Now, move in whole-notes halted, i.e., take a step only for the first quarter of each bar, and stay motionless for the rest of the bar.

Next, walk forward with halted steps in quarter-notes; maintain correct posture and the position of your feet.

Walk backward with halted steps; first in halves, then in whole-notes, and then in quarters, sustain the same rules as in walking forward.

Methodological guidelines: The Halting walk is yet another kind of motion, which is peculiar for humans. It is quite seldom that we move this way in real life. However, in the acting profession, this skill is essential, especially in stylized movements. Nevertheless, a pose between the motions should be natural, graceful, and sculptural.

Practice halted walk in different combinations continuously and include it in every potential exercise later in the program.

Exercise 84 WALKING, CHANGING MODE
Music is improvisation 4/4-time, moderate tempo, in the following pattern:

Begin with the right foot and walk forward four steps in quarters, then two steps in halves; perform all steps continuously; on the command of the instructor change the direction, but continue walking in the same pattern.

Repeat the exercise and be alert -- this time, an unexpected command may include left or right curves — no matter what, maintain the rhythmical pattern and walk continuously.

Now, walk forward in this pattern but with halted steps; obey various commands of the instructor; inspect your posture and gait whenever it is possible. Repeat the exercise several times.

Now, repeat the exercise and improvise the directions you walk and the positions of your arms. Perform this for the duration of thirty-two bars of music.

Repeat it, but be alert. In addition to the changes you have in mind, the piano-player would improvise the pace of the music.

Methodological guidelines: After the exercise is over, make comments regarding individual errors in posture, gait, transitions, and the rhythmical pattern's execution.

Exercise 85 WALK, OBSERVE PARTNERS
Music is the same pattern, as in previous exercises.
Formation – a crowd.

Secretly choose a classmate whom you would observe during the execution of the following exercise.

Begin with the right foot and walk continuously in the rhythmical pattern improvising the direction of walking, changing the positions of your arms, and the path of the curves. At the same time, observe the person you choose and try to memorize as many details about this person as the time permits. The exercise would last only thirty-two bars.

When exercise ends, you would turn your back to the group and name the person you have observed. Then, you would give all the details you managed to memorize for the rest of the group to judge the accuracy of your observations.

Repeat the exercise several times and have a different student describe the subject of their observation after every repetition.

Methodological guidelines: While the students occupied with their objective, the instructor should observe the group and note the errors made by them in performing the exercise. After the exercise is over, the instructor should point out these errors. Note, if a student could remember only a few details, he/she had been too busy controlling his movements. It means he/she did not yet reach the desired level of automatism.

Also, it makes no sense to repeat this exercise more than twice in a single lesson. Students might take advantage of a pause between repetitions and observe the chosen subject in advance. However, repeat the exercise in the next class offer other individuals to perform the task. Exercises of this kind are an excellent tool to train not just Posture and Gait but also Stage Attention and Memory.

Exercise 86 WALK, OBSERVE IMAGINARY OBJECTS
Formation – a crowd.

Music is improvisation 4/4-time in the following pattern:

Imagine yourself visiting a museum of Fine Arts or an Art Gallery; also imagine that your classroom is one of the rooms of this museum. Imagine that your classmates are strangers and visitors to this museum just like you.

Begin with the right foot and walk continuously in the following pattern: four steps in quarter-notes, two steps in half-notes, and two steps in whole-notes. Notice, the sequence consists of four bars of music. Improvise directions and curves, and "observe" pictures and "sculptures" in the museum. Everything is the art object in this hall; even floor work and ceiling could also be of artistic interest. Act as if you are in the museum, but avoid playing any particular character; also, do not pretend you are enjoying or disliking the art. Just take the objects in the classroom as pieces of art. Besides, this is not your objective. The objective is to observe the art items that you see, perhaps for the first time. You might want to incorporate the things existing in this room: the chairs, the posters on the wall, the piano, even the electric switch. There is plenty to observe and to decide for yourself whether it is of any interest to you.

Carry out this exercise again. This time try to justify every transition from one mode of motion to the next. For instance, you might explain your four steps backward as an attempt to see the entire picture from afar, or your two steps forward in halves as an attempt to read the artist's name in the lower corner of the picture, etc. Be prepared to answer any question asked by the instructor after the exercise is over. For instance, why you changed the direction of movement or the mode of walking?

Methodological guidelines: This exercise suggests some acting, so the instructor should be vigilant and ready to prevent any attempt to overact or to use any clichés. In tasks of this kind, the instructor should look for a sincere belief in given circumstances and for believable action, which in this exercise is -- "to observe the art" created by student's imagination. In case these elements are not considered, the student most likely would pretend to be interested, or pretend to observe the art, et cetera. Stanislavsky calls this occurrence the "Magic If." To begin believing in the given circumstances, the student should ask himself, "What if I am a visitor in a museum," or "What if the things around me are pieces of art," et cetera.

Of course, every participant would have something different in mind, even though the circumstances are the same for everyone. Visualizations depend on one's personal experience. However, the most important thing is that the student actively uses his/her imagination. It would take most of the attention, living very little time to control the Gait and Posture. It is quite all right because by this time, provided the learning process was correct, they should have these skills developed to the level of semi-automatism.

The instructor should explain that trying to pretend to observe the art instead of honestly believing in given circumstances would take about as much of the student's attention. Therefore, it pays to do it the right way. Here lies the difference between the Art of Representation and Art of Experiencing, the two different approaches to stage presentation, acknowledged by Konstantin Stanislavsky.[3] It is easy to detect the difference. Those students who tend to pretend would probably exaggerate the movements and gestures showing off his extreme interest (or indifference) in the subjects. Such a performer would perhaps use all kinds of clichés to convince the observer in the significance of the action.

However, observing the imaginary object does not mean that the actor should hallucinate or try to see something that is not there. It would be wrong to attempt to visualize "The prodigal son" by Rembrandt on the wall or try to see Rodin's "Eternal Spring" in place of a classroom chair. However, one can observe the classroom wall "as if" it is a real piece of art, or the chair in the room "as if" it is a fantastic sculpture. It is with the help of imagination that the actor becomes interested in observing ordinary subjects or objects. Consider this exercise as a skit with Given Circumstances and Physical Action.

Nevertheless, the most important for the stage movement instructor is to keep in mind that this exercise is to drill correct posture and gait in students and to utilize the acting techniques with great caution and in limited doses.

Exercise 87 "HAMLET"

Formation for all stages of exercise "Hamlet" is a crowd.

Methodological guidelines: The title of this exercise inspired by the Shakespeare's "Hamlet." The music for the final stage of the exercise is created mainly with the idea to express emotional impressions related to the particular scene of the Shakespearian play. The exercise intended to allow the students to utilize their habits in Posture and Gait in given circumstances of a skit. Make sure these habits developed to the level of semi-automatic by this time in the program.

This exercise consists of seven stages; offer them in the order they described. This work would take quite a few successive lessons before the final stage introduced.

Announce the title of this exercise only before introducing its Final Stage. It would prevent the attempts to portray a familiar character right from the beginning when particular given circumstances and actions are yet unknown to the students.

Stage 1
Music – see Appendix 5.

Listen to the music. Note that it is in 6/4-time with a stress on the first, third, and the fifth quarter of the bar. Now, listen to music again and count aloud the six quarters in each bar.

Now, count quarters and clap your hands on the first, third, and fifth quarter.

Now, start with the right foot and walk continuously in half-notes, intentionally making steps only on stressed quarters. Practice the exercise several times, walking forward and backward, and monitor your gait and posture.

Stage 2
Music – see Appendix 6.

Listen to the new musical sample. Notice that the time signature is still 6/4-time, but the stress is now on the first and the fourth quarters. Standing in place, count the quarters aloud and clap your hands in the first and the fourth quarter only.

Now, walk forward with halted steps on the first and the fourth quarter only; stay still between the steps.

Make sure the transitions between immobile positions and dynamic motions are smooth and natural. To justify such movements and transitions, consider the following given circumstances - you are walking in the dark forest and stop after each step to listen to any possible threatening noise.

Methodological guidelines: Move to the next stage of the exercise only after you observe previous stages performed adequately. However, spend no more than 5 minutes of a single lesson to practice these patterns.

Stage 3
Music – see Appendix 7.

Listen to the music first, and note, this piece is also in 6/4-time, but it has a peculiar feature. First and third bars have the stress on the first, third, and fifth quarter, while in the second and fourth bar, the stress is on the first and the fourth quarter. Note, this music example is a combination of the patterns used for Stage 1 and Stage 2 of the exercise.

Stand in place and count aloud all the quarters, from one to six; mark the stressed quarters by clapping your hands. Practice this task several times until the mistakes eliminated. Now, walk forward/backward, moving continuously for odd bars and with halted steps for the even bars.

Repeat exercise several times, moving forward or backward or mixing both modes. Pay attention to the transition from stillness to motion and back to stillness; constantly monitor your posture and gait.

Stage 4
Music – see Appendix 8.

Listen to this music and try to detect all the nuances expressed in it. Now, listen again to the first and the second bar only. Notice that in the first bar, the stress is in the first, third, and fifth quarters, but in the second bar, a soft sound is only in the first quarter.

Begin with your right foot and walk forward continuously in halves. Your fourth step would coincide with the first quarter of the second bar or with that peculiar signal. Take this fourth step and begin to turn gradually about-face over your right shoulder. Finish the turn at the end of the second bar facing upstage. In other words, to complete the turning, you have five quarters of music. While turning, keep both feet on the ground to help you maintain the balance. Also, as you make the about-turn, gradually shift the weight of your body from the left foot to the right.

Repeat this exercise four times or until all the movements and transitions are smooth, and the balance is perfect all along. Monitor your gait and posture constantly. Repeat the exercise but in reverse, i.e., begin it with your left foot and, accordingly, invert the rest of the moves.

Now, begin with the right foot and repeat it one more time. Execute the about-turn this time in the following manner. First, move your eyes, then continue turning with your head, then your shoulders, followed by your upper body, pelvis, and finish by rotating your legs and feet. You may justify such physical behavior by the action, "I want to see the source of that particular sound without attracting much attention." Please distribute all various movements evenly through the five quarters of the music.

Methodological guidelines: Since this exercise contains given circumstances and particular actions, the instructor should carefully watch the reaction of the performers to the signal and get rid of any attempt to overreact. As permission to "perform" finally allowed, some students would probably act scared or surprised, et cetera. If anything like this happens, one should explain that so far, there were no specific suggestions to act in any particular way.

However, suggest the accompanist present different interpretations or dynamics with every new repetition. In this case, encourage the students to react according to the message given by the music.

Please, pay attention to the way we suggested the physical action in the description above. We determined it, as "I want to see the source of the peculiar sound without attracting much attention." It seems it would be enough to ask the students to perform this about-turn "cautiously." Many would not see much difference between the two, except that the latter is much shorter. However, the truth is, the former motivates a very particular physical activity, whereas the latter recommends an action "in general." That is a straightforward example of how the Method of Physical Actions by K. Stanislavsky truly works.

Nevertheless, the action suggested in the previous exercise should not be in the least degree considered the only correct one established for this situation. The same pattern, used in a different play, in other circumstances, with diverse music, et cetera, would call for a particular interpretation of physical action. Besides being precise, this description must provoke the actor's imagination and the emotion sought for this specific moment of the performance.

Stage 5
Music is the same, as in Stage 4. Note: For this stage of the exercise, the accompanist should play the entire piece without accentuating the fourth quarter in the third bar and playing it instead, just like a stressed quarter.

Formation – a crowd.

Listen to the music assigned for your next exercise. Notice that the stressed quarters in the first bar are the first, third, and fifth. Stressed in the second bar is only the fifth quarter; in the third and the fourth bar stressed are the first and the fourth quarter.

Beginning position is regular stance, your hands on hips.
Begin with your right foot, and repeat all the movements precisely as you did in Stage 4 of the exercise for the first two bars of music. Then, for the third measure (immediately after the turn,) begin kneeling and touch the floor with your left knee on the 3rd quarter; for the rest of the bar, stay on your knee motionless. Now, for the 1st quarter of the next (last) bar, begin gradually rising and finish it, pulling your left foot to the right at the end of the music. Maintain the balance through the entire exercise and watch your posture and gait.
Repeat exercise several times.
Now, repeat the entire exercise in reverse, i.e., begin walking with your left foot, then make the about-turn over your left shoulder, and kneel on your right knee.

Methodological guidelines: At this stage of training, the instructor should inform students that exercise "Hamlet" involves the etiquette of the sixteenth century. For instance, kneeling was customary for men and women in the Sixteenth and Seventeenth centuries while praying, giving an oath, accepting the knighthood, et cetera. As these occasions were formal and solemn, it would be embarrassing for a person to perform it awkwardly. However, as kneeling is uncommon for modern human beings, the actor must practice it to acquire a skill. The students should learn how to spread the body weight between the knee and the foot evenly to maintain the balance when performing this ritual.

Stage 6
Music – the accompanist plays the full version of the music sample (Appendix 8) with all the nuances written in it; make the stress in the third bar sound threatening.

Listen to music and recognize all the nuances.

Begin with your right foot and take four continuous steps forward; then make a smooth turn and kneel as you did before in the previous exercise. Now, with the stress in the third bar, make a sudden about-turn over your left shoulder and shift the weight of your body from left knee to the right knee. Stay in this position motionless for the rest of this bar. Finally, gradually get up for the next six quarters and pull your feet together at the end.

The sudden turn about-face in the third bar is the only novel element for you in this stage of the exercise. Believe the new signal as a startling noise behind your back, which calls for an immediate investigation.

Practice the exercise several times and then repeat it several times, beginning with the left foot and reversing all other motions.

Methodological guidelines: Before moving to the final stage of this complex exercise, make sure the students perform all the techniques precisely as prescribed in the previous stages of the exercise. Apply your judgment to determine when the group is ready for the final stage of this exercise. Consider the fact that it is going to be a skit and one of the major exercises of the Essential Stage Movement. As such, include it in the Test Lesson at the end of the program.

Stage 7 (final)
Music is the same, as in Stage 6.

From now on, let us call this exercise "Hamlet." Listen to the narrative: Hamlet, Prince of Denmark, received a rumor that the Ghost of his dead father appears every night on the walls of the Elsinore castle. Hamlet came here in the middle of the night to see it firsthand. The night is moonless, windy, and cold. He moves slowly on the top of the wall. Suddenly, he hears a light but bizarre noise behind his back. The Prince turns around and sees an unusual light illuminating the Ghost of his father, Claudius. He kneels and stretches his arms toward the Ghost as if inviting him to come closer. Just then, a loud and threatening noise (as if a heavy sword fell on the cobblestones of the castle) makes Hamlet turn around. Impulsively, he grabs his dagger with his right hand and even half-draws it. Only after Hamlet assured in the absence of immediate danger, he slowly gets up and conceals his weapon.

The narrative you just heard gives you some given circumstances and suggests additional physical actions. First, perform the exercise paying attention to the new movements, such as stretching your arms toward the Ghost, grabbing the handle of the dagger, and sending the blade down the holder. Fit all elements of the story into the rhythm of the music and match musical nuances.

Repeat the exercise several times to achieve the flawless performance of all the techniques, including gait, posture, balance, and rhythmicity.

Now, we are moving into the final performance of this exercise/étude. Think of the given circumstances: the place, the time of the day, the state of nature around you, the image of the Ghost, et cetera. Out of all images that come to your mind, choose those that are the brightest.

Now, analyze the actions that you must perform. The first action is, "I want to make sure that the rumor is true." There are two events (Stanislavsky's term) in this skit. The first event is a strange sound behind Hamlet's back. The reaction to this sound or your next action could be "I want to explore," or "to scrutinize what caused this sound without being exposed." The second event is a sound threatening noise. Your next action here might be "I want to confront a possible attack," or "I want to defend myself." After Hamlet sees that nothing had happened, his next and final action in the skit could be "I want to expose the evidence."

Perform "Hamlet," considering all the circumstances and actions discussed above. You should add personal visualizations and circumstances to what has already suggested converting this exercise into a truthful and exciting sketch. The individual elements, based on your experience and knowledge, would be able to enhance your imagination and color your physical actions uniquely and emotionally.

Methodological guidelines: This exercise/étude is one of the essential exercises of our method. In addition to the apparent useful training of several faculties, such as Rhythmicity, Balance, and Coordination, it also develops certain habits, such as Concentration, Precision of Physical Act, Tempo-Rhythm of Physical Act, as well as Correct Posture and Correct Gait. Combined in this exercise are the unique movement pattern, or choreography, and essential elements of acting, such as given circumstances, actions, and events. As our method based on the Stanislavsky's System of acting, the student of the Essential Stage Movement program must have some understanding, and possibly skills, in the execution of the System's techniques. At this phase of movement training, the truthfulness of physical actions must become the most desirable quality.

Any tendency to overact, to "show off," must be criticized politely by the instructor. If overlooked, such superficial behavior might be interpreted by a student as a personal success and perhaps erase all the teacher's efforts in acting class. However, the lack or sometimes-complete absence of expression might be an indication of disbelief in the given circumstances. It might be a sign of a student who did not bother to create the images in his/her mind to act on them.

Do not expect the student to play a character in this particular exercise, but only to consider the given circumstances and actions.

Repeat the exercise several times in a series of lessons.

To train the Awareness and Concentration further, during one of the repetitions of this exercise, the accompanist might surprise the students, by substituting the threatening signal in the third measure with a modest unstressed sound. Most likely, the students would perform the sudden turn anyway, as it already became a routine.

Use this as an excuse to explain that something like this could happen on stage in live production intentionally or unintentionally. The actor must react only to an event that is happening on stage, to something, the audience is also seeing or hearing. An actor's reaction to an event that did not occur is capable of ruining the scene and sometimes the entire production.

In the future repetitions perform the exercise with and without the emphasis. When there is no event, the students should continue the favored action of that moment, which in our skit is to "make the Ghost to approach." They have to wait until the end of the bar, and then get up on the fourth measure as usual.

Repeat the final stage of the exercise in two or three consecutive classes and then abandon before it becomes trivial. However, from time to time, return to the exercise later in the program. With every repetition, accompanist should vary shades of stresses and the mood of the whole piece, thus challenging the students to respond to all those changes.

Be sure to include this exercise in the test class at the end of the program. According to Stanislavsky's System, the actor should change the visualizations slightly, and given circumstances to make every new performance of the same skit refreshing and exciting. Also, remind the students now and then that this exercise included in the stage movement program mainly to improve correct posture and gait. It would be inappropriate for the student to consider possibly using the technique in a particular production.

At this point, one should expect the movement patterns executed automatically to make room in the minds of students for more essential and more delicate matters. However, in a class situation, they should always try to control the movements incorporated in the skit and flawlessly shift their attention from one to another. They must understand that even most substantial feelings on stage look pale without appropriate and precise gestures.

A convincing performance of the final stage of "Hamlet" exercise, in a sense, would indicate that the group is on the right track. Moreover, it would mean they are ready to undertake other, more complicated tasks if it happens around the middle of the program.

CHAPTER SEVEN

AWARENESS AND MOTOR COORDINATION

The exercises presented in this chapter explicitly designed to develop Awareness and Motor Coordination. It is a widespread belief that most people who reached adulthood have these qualities already developed adequately, so they do not have to worry about it much. It might be right for people's everyday activities and for occupations that do not require much of these qualities. However, most often, the ordinary level of coordination is not sufficient for those who choose acting as a profession. Moving about the stage (TV or Movie set) is not the same as moving in a real-life environment. To make a stage presentation look like reality, the actor must develop Awareness and Motor Coordination to a much higher level.

Any theater or movie director or any choreographer would tell you countless stories about how often they had to simplify planned for production tasks merely because a professional actor could not execute them properly. Naturally, this substantially reduces the quality of the scene or movement sequence. For a strange reason, it became common for dramatic actors. Also, in the movie production, for any slightly intricate movement pattern, a stuntman is hired. Why is it different from, let say, dance production? Try to explain to a ballet choreographer that this group of dancers cannot perform a "Grand Fouetté Relivé." His answer would be straightforward: "Sorry, I won't be able to choreograph "Corsair Ballet" with this group."

The fact is, without highly developed Awareness and Motor Coordination actor is quite helpless and is not ready to meet the demands of the profession. It is true that many nonperformance professions also demand strong coordination skills. For instance, an experienced corporate secretary finds no difficulty typing on a keyboard while talking on the phone at the same time. A woman-seamstress working in a factory has no problem executing very complicated maneuvers on a sewing machine while listening to the instructions of her manager, etc.

Moreover, almost everyone who drives a car can carry on a conversation with a passenger at the same time. Some drivers even dare to speak on a cell phone while driving. Does this mean that all these people have their movement coordination developed sufficiently enough? It does not! One can successfully establish an isolated skill or even a combination of movement patterns through constant repetition; even so, some need more repetitions than the others do.

The acting profession requires a more refined level of these qualities, which would enable the actor to be believable in any form of any character, any trade, or any historical period. In other words, a performing artist, if the part so required, must look like a skillful typist, or a clever seamstress, an accomplished boxer, or a professional of any kind. More importantly, the actor must achieve all these skills and learn the basic movement patterns in a limited time, determined by the rehearsal duration. In many instances, this period is much shorter than an average individual would need to develop a similar skill in real life.

However, the most critical aspect of this is that life on stage is secondary. The actor, who performs a complex combination of moves and speech, or even movements and singing, does it while transforming into another person, which we call the character. The transformation alone takes a lot of awareness and concentration. The conclusion is -- an actor needs to drill the Awareness and Motor Coordination expressly and develop it to the highest possible degree.

It is for the exercises of this chapter more than for other parts of training, the critical methodological principles of our method, the performance of exercises from a verbal description, is fundamentally applied. According to this principle, the drill goes as follows. One begins performing the exercise only after the task is evident in one's mind. Visualization works well when the actor manages to perform the movements in his mind simultaneously with the instructor's description of them. In the beginning, many students having problems with this technique, as the vast majority has a secure habit of learning movement patterns from the demonstration. Moreover, some students have difficulty understanding why they have to do it now in any different way. Few even get upset with this proposition because it feels illogical for them. Their experience tells them that to learn a pattern from the demonstration is more straightforward and faster. In other words, the conventional sense or rationality hints at what is best for them.

Nevertheless, the goal of a verbal explanation of a task is not to achieve the results fast. It is to obtain a sophisticated skill -- to create an image in mind first, and then accomplish it with the body. The students must also understand that movements copied from the demonstration will most likely be short of individuality. Although, it might take longer to learn a movement pattern in this manner at the beginning, obtaining a valuable skill, makes this technique more critical perhaps than a brief inconvenience.

Exercise 88 ARMS COORDINATION #1
Music is improvisation 4/4-time, slow chords.
Formation – a crowd.

Methodological guidelines: At the early stage of training, the instructor should introduce a formation that we determined as "The Crowd." In theater to create an illusion of a multitude of people or a crowd with a limited number of actors, we routinely spread them evenly across the stage, to create an illusion of a crowd. For many exercises in the Essential Stage Movement, this formation turned out to be the best. It keeps the students in an assembly and, at the same time, provides them with enough space to perform physical exercises without interfering with each other.

The best and quickest way to create a "crowd" is to ask each student to find a place in the classroom where he/she can freely extend both arms without touching other students. Let them find a spot from which one can see the instructor well. Last but not least, the condition for this formation is still to look like a group or a crowd. Spreading around the room too much would break the illusion. Philosophically speaking, a "crowd" is also a group of people united by a common characteristic, or a cooperative idea. This definition is akin to the goal of our training.

Stage 1

The beginning position is heels together, toes slightly apart, hands along the body, i.e., regular stance. Be prepared to listen, understand, and memorize the following exercise from a verbal description. Try to picture yourself executing the movements while you listen to the descriptions.

You are going to perform four movements with your right arm. The first movement – extend it forward with the palm facing down; the second movement – gather fingers in a fist, the third movement – open your fist; the fourth movement – bring your straight arm down to the beginning position. Take one quarter of music for each motion. Perform this sequence four times. Note, you have to perform the exercise from the first attempt. Try to memorize the pattern to be able to repeat it without prompting.

Now, you are going to perform four different movements with your left arm. The first movement is extending your arm to the side with fingers gathered in a fist; the second – open your fist; the third movement – collect fingers in a fist; the fourth movement – bring your straight arm down and open hand simultaneously. Repeat this sequence four times and take one quarter of the music for each motion.

Now, try to perform the movements of your right and left arm together at the same time. Move both arms in quarters and repeat the exercise four times.

Methodological guidelines: The instructor should discourage the attempts to perform the movements while they described. This action, in many cases, is involuntary as the students wish to succeed. However, convince the group that it is more beneficial to learn to visualize the movements first.

If the students are not able to perform the exercise with both arms from the first attempt, go back to perform it separately with one arm, then another, and only then try to put together all the motions again. Repeat each exercise four times. Another technique to accommodate the students is to slow down the tempo of the music. Move to the next stage of the exercise only after every student in the group performed the combination correctly.

The instructor should see that the students maintain the "crowd" formation during the exercise. Besides, the instructor needs to find a spot in the classroom, from which he/she can see practically every student in the class and be able to notice the errors timely.

Another technique to help the students master the combination faster is to switch the position. For instance, suggest everyone turning right-face or about-face, and then repeat the exercise four times in the new attitude. Changing the circumstances suddenly creates a new challenge and, in turn, enhances the concentration. This technique would also discourage some students from trying to mimic the classmates' movements, as the additional task would further confuse such students.

Stage 2

In your mind, reverse the movements of Stage 1 of the exercise so that your right arm would adopt the motions of your left arm and vice versa.

Now, perform the exercise with the right arm only and repeat it four times.

Perform the exercise with your left arm and repeat it four times.

Now, perform the reversed version of the exercise with both arms at the same time and repeat it four times.

Stage 3

Now, when you accomplish the two variations of the same pattern (Stage 1 and Stage 2), do the following -- begin with the initial version of the exercise and perform it with both arms once; then, continue the exercise and perform the reverse version of the exercise once. Keep alternating the two versions and repeat the sequence four times in a row. Practice it several times in a single lesson.

Methodological guidelines: As usual, repeat each version of the exercise until everyone does it satisfactory, and only after this, move to the next stage. Try to complete all three phases of this exercise within one lesson. If it takes longer than 7– 8 minutes, finish working on it in the following lesson.

Exercise 89 ARMS COORDINATION #2
Music is the same, as in the previous exercise.
Formation – a crowd.

This exercise is similar to the previous; the difference is in the pattern of movements.

Movements for right arm: the first movement is bring the extended arm forward, second – put it sideways, third – again forward, and the fourth – bring it down. As you did before, first try to imagine yourself doing these movements while the instructor describes them; after that, perform it with music; take one quarter of the musical accompaniment for each motion.

Now, here are the movements for your left arm: first movement – sideways, second – forward, third – sideways, and fourth – down. Repeat it four times with your left arm only.

Put together the movements of both arms and repeat the exercise four times.

Reverse the movements of your arms in your mind, one at a time. Now, try to perform the new, reverse version of the exercise right away with both arms, i.e., without first practicing with each arm separately.

Now, perform the exercise and alternate the two variations as you did in Stage 3 of the previous exercise. Begin with the initial version and repeat the sequence four times.

Methodological guidelines: If sensing confusion, return to a previous stage, practice with one arm at a time, and put both arms together again. The instructor should explain to the students why they repeat a new combination four times. The first repetition is producing a rough draft. On the second repetition, they should make corrections; on the third, they should practice already assembled pattern, and only on the fourth repetition, they finally perform the exercise freely.

Exercise 90 ARMS COORDINATION AND WALKING
Music is improvisation 4/4-time.

Repeat the initial version of the previous exercise with both arms standing in the spot.

Now, begin with your right foot, walk forward in quarters, and perform the exercise with both arms at the same time. Try to control both, correct walking (gait and posture) and the movements of your arms. Go over the exercise four times, then stop, turn about-face, and repeat it four more times walking upstage.

Now, repeat the arms' sequence four times walking forward, and then continue moving the arms and walk backward for another four bars of music.

And now, repeat this combination of walking and arms' movements and walk forward for the duration of six bars of music instead of four. Try to use precisely the same space as you did when walking forward for four bars. That means you have to consider the area available for moving forward. Notice, you still must walk continuously with even steps during this exercise, and indeed, preserve all the qualities of your posture and gait. It will be an error if you walk forward for four bars and the rest of the exercise walk on the spot.

Now, repeat the sequence eight times, walk forward and keep walking even if your steps would have to be smaller.

Note: This and other exercises of the present chapter, along with Coordination, Rhythmicity, and Awareness, develop such habits as Awareness of Space and Proper Gait.

Exercise 91 COORDINATION #3
Music is the same, as in previous exercises.

The concept of this exercise and the order of developing it is the same as in two previous exercises.

The movements for the right arm are -- first movement – forward, second movement – arm straight up, third movement – sideways, fourth movement – down. Repeat this pattern with the right arm four times.

The movements for left arm: first movement – sideways, second – forward, third – extend your arm up, fourth movement – down. Repeat these also four times.

Now, combine the movements of both arm and repeat the sequence four times.

Walk forward/backward and perform the combination with both arms at the same time. Attention, make sure from this point on, you move your arms assertively while walking continuously. Always monitor your gait.

Walk forward and repeat the exercise six times; finish it at the same spot as when you performed only four sequences.

Repeat the exercise one more time, walk forward for eight bars of the music, and finish it at the same spot.

Now, walk forward, move your arms, and for every fourth quarter, clap your hands in front of your chest, instead of bringing them down. After you clap your hands, continue the exercise as usual.

Methodological guidelines: In exercises of this kind, there is often a tendency to transform a crowd formation into a line or several lines in the process. It happens when students in the rear of the crowd, unintentionally move to the forefront. It is natural, as the tasks given to students overwhelm their minds, and maintaining the crowd formation becomes insignificant for them. Explain this at the end of the exercise and request to eliminate this common mistake as soon as possible. However, the instructor needs to gradually add new tasks, only after the students absorb the previous ones.

Exercise 92 COORDINATION #4
Music is improvisation 4/4-time.

The order and the way of mastering the exercise are the same as in previous Motor Coordination exercises.

Perform the following four movements with your right arm. The first movement – extend arm forward, the second movement – bend the elbow and put your arm across the chest (see Figure 19), the third movement – bring the arm to the side, the fourth movement – extend your arm down. Repeat it four times.

Perform the following four movements with the left arms: first movement – straight arm sideways, second movement – down, third movement – forward, fourth movement – down. Repeat it four times.

Perform the exercise with both arms simultaneously and repeat it four times.

Now, put your hands on your hips and keep them there during the next exercise.

Figure 19

Begin with the right foot and walk forward in quarters in the following pattern: three steps forward and a step backward. Repeat this walking pattern minimum four times.

Now, put together the walking pattern and the exercise with both arms; begin with the right foot and repeat the sequence four times.

Methodological guidelines: Sometimes, students tend to peep at classmates trying to copy the movements when a new pattern offered for performance. The instructor should advise against this, as it slows down developing Coordination. Remind your pupils -- it is not the result we are after; most important is the process.

It would take a different amount of repetitions for various groups to achieve satisfactory results. However, one should not rush with the results taking as much time as needed to make sure students perform the final stage of each exercise correctly.

Exercise 93 COORDINATION #5
Music is improvisation ¾-time, moderate tempo.

The beginning position is the regular stance, your hands on hips. Start with your right foot and walk two steps forward, then a step backward. Repeat the pattern eight times. Alternate your feet and never pull your feet together.
Here are new movements for your arms. Bring your right arm forward for the first quarter of the bar; bring your left arm sideways for the second quarter (do not move your right arm); put both arms down for the third quarter. Coordinate these movements first in your mind, and then perform it four times in a row standing in the spot.

Now, put together the walking pattern and the arms' combination. Begin with your right foot and walk forward continuously. Repeat this exercise four or eight times.

Notice, the rhythm of this exercise is different from all previous coordination exercises. When moving in the ¾-time, make sure you alternate your feet and walk continuously while moving your arms energetically.

Exercise 94 COORDINATION #6
Music is improvisation 5/4, moderate tempo.

The beginning position is a regular stance, your hands on hips.

Start with your right foot and take three steps forward, then a step sideways, then a step backward. Repeat the exercise four times.

Remember, the odd number of steps in this pattern makes you begin every new sequence with a different foot.

Now, stand in place and perform the following five movements with your right arm: forward, across the chest, a pause, sideways, and down. Repeat this pattern four times.

Now perform the following five movements with your left arm: sideways, straight up, forward, sideways, and down. Repeat this pattern four times as well.

Stand in place and practice the exercise, moving both arms at the same time.

Now, put together the walking pattern and the arms' combination. Go over the sequence four times, then stop, turn about-face, and repeat it four more times.

Exercise 95 COORDINATION #7
Music is improvisation 4/4-time, moderate tempo.

Visualize now the following new pattern—your right arm: forward, across the chest, sideways, and down. Your left arm: sideways, extend up, forward, and down.

Perform all the stages of the previous exercises in the same order -- first, with right arm only, then with the left arm, then with both arms together standing in place.

Walk forward, then backward, and move both arms at the same time. Repeat the pattern four times in each direction.

Now, walk forward in half-notes continuously and move your arms in quarters as you did before. Notice, you would have to perform two movements with your arms for each step. Walk continuously but move your arms assertively.

Next, change your walking pattern: for the first bar stroll in quarters, for the second, walk in halves, then again in quarters, and back in halves. Try to combine this new walking pattern with the movements of your arms still performed in quarter-notes.

Methodological guidelines: Use coordination exercises to drill each new pattern with all the variety of complications and unexpected tasks such as change the tempo, the mode of walking, in the middle of the exercise make the group cease walking, but continue moving arms, etc.

Exercise 96 COORDINATION #8
Music is improvisation 4/4-time.

The technique and the order of learning are the same as in the previous exercises.

Right arm: sideways, place the hand on the back of your neck, bring straight up, down.

Left arm: forward, sideways, across the chest, down.

Perform the exercise four times with right arm only, then four times with left arm only, and then with both arms together. Repeat it four times standing in place.

Reverse the movements in your mind's eye and then perform the exercise with both arms standing in place.

Perform the exercise standing in place and alternate the initial pattern with the reverse pattern; repeat the exercise four times.

Now, walk forward in quarters and move your arms, alternating the two variations.
Walk backward and alternate the two variations of the same arms' pattern.

Now, begin the exercise by walking forward and changing the direction according to the instructor's command.

Exercise 97 COORDINATION #9
Music is the same as in previous exercises.

Right arm: forward, sideways, across the chest, down. Perform it in quarters and repeat four times.

Left arm: same movements as for the right arm; perform these movements in half-notes.

Repeat the exercise four times with the right arm only, then perform four times with left arm only, and then perform the exercise with both arms at the same time. Notice, the entire sequence will take two bars of music in contrast to one bar in previous exercises, i.e., for each movement of your left arm, there will be two movements of your right arm. Repeat the sequence four times.

Now, combine the movements of both arms with walking forward in quarters.

Walk forward in halves and perform the combination with both arms.

Walk forward alternating the two walking patterns – in the first bar walk on quarters, in the next, in halves, and so forth; maintain the arms' pattern established for this exercise.

Reverse the movements of your arms and go over all the stages you went through when developing the initial exercise.

* * *

All exercises presented in this chapter have one common goal: to train Coordination and Awareness. For best results, the instructor should apply the following essential Methodological technique to all of them – after an exercise performed satisfactorily, there is no need to repeat it. Understand, an extra repetition or two will not hurt, but the time it takes one can use for another, more challenging exercise.

The exercises of this chapter, mechanical as they might appear, serve as the preliminary ones for more complex exercises, as presented in the following chapters. The latter designed to develop Awareness and Coordination as well but include some artistic elements.

The variety of movement patterns presented in this chapter might look abundant. However, both the modern science of Psychophysiology and our practical experience proves that various patterns mastered by an individual have a direct impact on how fast one learns a new pattern and how long it will remain in memory.

Among other essential qualities, the exercises of the current chapter would actively develop such a habit as Awareness of Space.

Konstantin Stanislavsky continually advised actors to learn how to "position the body in the stage space." The reality of this is that just understanding the problem would not change much in solving it. In the exercises of this chapter and other exercises of this textbook, one should always remind the students to maintain the initial shape of "crowd" formation as well as other formations used, such as a line, file, circle, or semi-circle. Another way to drill Awareness of Space is having the students fit a different number of equal steps within the same space without changing the features of a pattern.

Originate a separate segment of the lesson for the exercises of this chapter. This segment should not last more than seven to ten minutes per class due to the intense concentration and multifaceted awareness that the exercises demand from the student.

CHAPTER EIGHT

DEVELOPMENT OF SPEECH-MOTOR COORDINATION

Let us agree to the actor's activities on stage as correlation and interaction of motion and speech, conditioned by circumstances of the play. In other words, the actor in a performance situation is committed to executing invented actions and words in limited spaces and fixed tempos. These conditions tend to overwhelm the actor's mind so much that it prevents him from devoting himself to "honesty of passions and truthfulness of feelings" (K. Stanislavsky.)[1]

Therefore, the actor needs to make certain motions work semi-automatically in the shortest possible time. The actor must perform the character "movements of every day" on stage naturally as if they are his, actor's habits. Among other things included are the gait, the gestures, and the poses of the reality of a particular play. The "reality" for an actor is the circumstances of the drama, the time in human history, the age of the character, the character's social status, and many other conditions.

The exercises described in this chapter would further help the future actor to free the body of the muscle tensions that subconsciously arise every time a new or unfamiliar physical pattern introduced. Accomplish this using the advanced and creative technique. In the Speech-Motor Coordination chapter of Essential Stage Movement, you will find simple rhymes and poems included in the exercises. The idea to engage the student in reciting a meaningful text or singing a song while performing various movement patterns stems from the scientifically proven principle that a muscle tension creates obstacles to the speaking, not to mention the singing.

The undertaking of reciting a precise text logically on stage, especially of reciting poetry, permeates the actor's mind so much that the only way to perform any relatively intricate movement pattern at the same time is to perform it semi-automatically. Moreover, if this movement pattern alien to the actor, the physical performance would appear weak, sometimes even strange. In many cases, there will be no movement at all. For instance, observing an opera singer, one can notice that in the essential part of a solo in opera, the artist stops moving.

However, if these imposed on the actor movements are reduced to semi-automatism or, in other words, if they become habitual, it would free the mind for the logical and artistic delivery of a text or a song. In a situation of stage movement class, the instructor would notice that a high level of coordination and concentration habit achieved. That would be when a combination of speech and movement comes out comfortable.

In our daily lives, we often see people executing various kinds of physical work while simultaneously talking about things that have absolutely nothing to do with their physical activity. For example, it is natural for a person to sing a popular tune while cleaning the room. It is natural for a person to stroll next to a friend and tell him the content of a movie he saw the day before. It is easy for a mother to commission her son the chores he must do while making breakfast. In reality, the disconnection between a physical act and a verbal expression is typical and comes naturally.

This model gave us an idea to use the abstract movements combined with logically constructed texts to train Speech-Motor Coordination – one of the most valuable skills the actor needs to develop in a stage movement class. Introduce the exercises of this chapter around the middle of the program and practice in every lesson afterward.

Exercise 98 MOTOR COORDINATION AND RECITATION OF
            NUMBERS
Music is improvisation 4/4-time.
The formation is a crowd.

Stand in place, perform the following four movements with your right arm, and repeat the pattern four times: extend it forward, bend across the chest, extend it to the side, and put it down.

Now perform the following movements with your left arm: out to the side, forward, out to the side, down. Repeat it four times.

Put together the movements of both arms and perform the exercise four times.

Now, standing in place, move both arms together and simultaneously recite odd numbers beginning from "one." Pronounce one number for each quarter; inhale between bars.

Now, begin with your right foot, walk forward in quarters, recite odd numbers, and move both arms, all at the same time. Repeat the pattern four times.

Now, repeat the exercise one more time; walk this time forward for only two bars of music and then walk backward for another two bars.

Repeat the exercise and walk forward continuously in half-notes; move your arms assertively in quarters and recite odd numbers simultaneously.

Methodological guidelines: As soon as the exercise becomes a routine and noticeably loses its appeal, change the task, or add a new complication. For instance, recite even numbers, etc.

A helpful technique to change the circumstances and to drill the speech-motor coordination with this kind of exercise is to ask the group to repeat the task facing the upstage wall, facing another wall in the room, or moving forward but upstage instead of downstage, etc.

Exercise 99 MOTOR COORDINATION, RECITE MULTIPLICATION
          TABLES
Music and technique are the same as in the previous exercise.

Right arm: out to the side; put the hand on the back of your neck, forward, down.

Left arm: bend across the chest, forward, out to the side, down.

Follow the same order of execution as in previous exercises and perform the task with the right arm only, then with left, then with both arms. Now, put your hands on hips and recite Multiplication

Tables for "two" in time with the music standing in the spot; pronounce the words as follows:

1st quarter	2nd quarter	3rd quarter	4th quarter
Two	*times one*	*is two*	(pause take a breath)
Two	*times two*	*is four*	(pause, take a breath),
and so on.			

Now, perform the movements with both arms and recite the Multiplication Tables for "two" simultaneously. Make sure you pronounce the text clearly and loud. However, make sure you do not outvoice your classmates, but the instructor can still hear your voice. Repeat the exercise four times standing in the spot.

Begin with your right foot and walk forward in quarters; move both arms in the established pattern and recite Multiplication Tables for "two."

Repeat the exercise, this time move forward in half notes.

Repeat the exercise and walk forward in quarters, and then walk backward in halves.

Methodological guidelines: Pay attention to the way the students pronounce the text. Repeat this exercise in several consecutive lessons. However, in the following lessons suggest reciting Multiplication Tables for "three," then for "four," etc. to refresh the task. Before doing that, advice students to change the way the words consisting of two or three syllables pronounced, for instance:

1st quarter	2nd quarter	3rd quarter	4th quarter	
Three times	*eight is*	*twenty-*	*four*	or
Four times	*nine is*	*thirty-*	*six,*	etc.

In these situations, the students must inhale between the bars.

Methodological guidelines: After performing several variations of this exercise in some lessons, we suggest that the instructor would offer a game where he would tease the group by expressing doubts about the results of the multiplications. Do it in the process of the exercise with words like "That's impossible!" or "Are you sure?" or "I don't believe it!" etc.

That would instigate the students to "argue" with or try to "convince" the instructor. In other words, it would make them react in reply to the instructor's actions. However, students cannot stop reciting. With this technique's help, the instructor would be able to test the quality of students' performance of movement patterns and the text. However, the instructor himself must act candidly expressing his/her doubts. A false intonation or lack of sincerity might prompt the students to overreact and might destroy the honest interaction.

Exercise 100 MOTOR COORDINATION, RECITATION OF POETRY
(Version I)
Music is improvisation 4/4-time.

Stage 1

Right arm: forward, across the chest, out to the side, and down. Repeat it four times in quarters.

Left arm: same pattern as for the right arm, perform it in half-notes and repeat four times. Remember, move the left arm in the first and the third quarter of a bar.

Now, combine the movements of both arms and repeat the pattern, which is two bars length, four times.

Begin with your right foot and walk forward in quarter notes; perform the exercise with both hands. Repeat the pattern four times; it will take eight bars.

Now go over the exercise four times and walk backward.

Methodological guidelines: If the students have a problem performing the combination from the first attempt, try the following technique: make them count aloud the quarter notes from one to eight and move right arm only. Then, make them count quarter-notes again and move left arm only. Then ask them to combine the movements of both arms, still counting the quarters. Work on this exercise for five to seven minutes in a single lesson and repeat it over in the next class before moving to Stage 2.

Stage 2

Repeat the combined pattern of Stage 1 four times.

Now, put your hands on hips and walk forward, then backward in half-notes.

Begin with your right foot and walk forward in halves; this time, combine walking pattern with arms' movements. Repeat it several times, first walking forward, and then backward.

Now, walk forward in quarters for one bar, then walk in halves for the next bar; perform the movements with your arms at the same time. Continue the exercise alternating the walking patterns.

Now, walk forward in quarters, move both arms, and recite Multiplication Tables for "two" (or "three," or "four.")

Stage 3

Music is improvisation 4/4, chords.

Repeat Stage 2 of the exercise four times.

Now, read and memorize the nursery rhyme "Little Miss Muffet." Standing in place recite the rhyme in time with the music; distribute the lines of the poem in quarters, but make a pause for the fourth quarter in the second and the fourth line. Utilize the gaps to take a breath.

> *Little Miss Muffet sat on her tuffet,*
> *Eating her curds and whey; (pause)*
> *Along came a spider, who sat down beside her,*
> *And frightened Miss Muffet away. (pause)*

Pronounce each word clearly and correctly. Recite the rhyme several times and try to pronounce all the words jointly, like a narration.

Now, combine the movements of your arms and the recitation of the rhyme, standing in place. Repeat the arms sequence two times (four quarters) to match the length of the verse.

Stage 4

Perform Stage 3 of the exercise.

Begin with your right foot and walk forward in quarters; move your arms, and recite the rhyme at the same time.

Repeat the entire exercise, but this time walk in half-notes.

Now, repeat the exercise and walk one bar in quarters and the next bar in half-notes.

Repeat the exercise and rotate walking in quarters with walking in halves; for two bars, walk forward and for the rest of the exercise walk backward.

Methodological guidelines: Practice the last stage of this exercise in several consecutive lessons with all possible combinations of tempos, rhythms, and modes of walking. The instructor should continuously challenge the students to achieve satisfactory results in all the elements of this complex exercise. The recitation of the rhyme must be logical and continuous; see that the lines pronounced clearly and rhythmically and the Gait is correct too.

Every so often, delegate the drill to the accompanist, who would vary the tempo at his will. That would let the instructor pointing out any errors in the performance, without interrupting the exercise.

When this exercise reaches the level of effortless and semi-automatic performance, the instructor should introduce the following new task.

Explain that to effectively communicate an image expressed in words to a listener, a performer must have this image in mind. That is precisely how it happens in reality. When someone tells about what happened to him two hours ago or yesterday, one most likely has this story in his mind in the form of images. The listener would be genuinely interested to hear the story when the storyteller sincerely sees the pictures with his inner vision. Probably, that is why people with weak imaginations are boring storytellers.

Why should it be different for a stage presentation? The difference, though, is that the story the actor delivers did not happen to him before, or he did not witness this event. The essence of telling a fictitious story is in creating visualizations in the mind of the narrator in advance.

So, think about the story of "Little Miss Muffet" and create a series of bright images in your mind that would illustrate this tale in the best possible way.

One way to begin this work is to ask yourself a series of questions. Who is Little Miss Muffet? How is she dressed? How does her tuffet look? How is she eating her food? How big is the spider? Suggest that the students create a string of pictures in their minds about everything this story tells us. Besides, the more details one can visualize, the more interesting the story would sound.

Give the students several minutes to do this work and then suggest performing the exercise walking forward in quarter-notes, moving both arms, reciting the rhyme, and visualizing all the images that they just created.

K. Stanislavsky once wrote, "Out of all these moments inside us there generates a continuous and perpetual chain of inner and outer moments of visualizations, sort of reel of film." 1

This kind of work requires time and patience from the instructor and the students. We recommend choosing a student whose performance of the rhyme was exceptional and, to encourage the group, have him/her demonstrate the exercise in front of the group.

Consider the absence of any character playing at this stage of the exercise, as there were no given circumstances yet.

Stage 5 (final)

Perform the final combination of the previous exercise once.

Now, let us assume that "Little Miss Muffet" is a short play. It has all the elements of a play: lines, story, and chain of events, climax, and the conclusion. There are two characters in this play, Miss Muffet, and Spider and conflict between these two characters. Think of what had happened. Little Miss Muffet had been eating her breakfast without bothering anyone. However, Spider had come in and scared her away. What was the reason for Spider to do that? He could have many different reasons. Maybe he just wanted to make friends, or perhaps he planned to frighten Miss Muffet, or he was hungry and came in hoping to have some of her food, etc. Why did Miss Muffet have to leave? Was Spider huge or small? Was he threatening, or was he ugly? You must choose the circumstances and actions.

All these and maybe more questions need to be answered before continuing with this play. Take the abstract movements established so far as choreography and the lines that you recite as the narration of your play.

Now, perform all the elements plus the given circumstances and the actions chosen for your characters. Based on these circumstances and actions, act accordingly. Perform the exercise several times, trying to improve your visualizations, and specify your actions.

Now, imagine a group of kindergarten kids sitting in front of you on the floor. Perform the play for them.

Methodological guidelines: The final stage of the "Little Miss Muffet" exercise contains all the elements for acting. The instructor should see that the presentation would appear significant, believable, and sincere. Allow some of the motions to change slightly to accommodate a student's visions and thoughts. It is normal and acceptable. We should always welcome the unique interpretation of the story. Nevertheless, breaking the movement pattern, or moving out of rhythm or tempo, would be a mistake that requires immediate correction.

If you decide to repeat the final version of exercise two or more times in a single lesson, we recommend changing some visualization, or some circumstances slightly to refresh the outcome.

Every so often, the instructor would have to offer a set of given circumstances and actions for everyone to consider, in case some students could not create compelling visions, circumstances, and actions on their own. However, in the following repetitions, the instructor should insist on the individual approach.

Occasionally, radically change the circumstances of the play. Suggest them thinking of it as a satire, or a tragedy, or a musical, etc. However, one must be cautious with such modifications, as they would demand a significant alteration of the visualizations, given circumstances, and the actions. Otherwise, the students would easily fall into a cliché.

Include the final version of the exercise in the Test Lesson with some new circumstances.

Exercise 101 MOTOR COORDINATION, RECITATION OF POETRY
                (Version II)
Music is improvisation 4/4, moderate tempo.

Stage 1

This exercise is similar to the previous one. Therefore, the order of learning, techniques, and methodology is the same.

Right arm: forward, down, out to the side, down.

Beginning position for left arm – straight forward, and the pattern is down, out to the side, up, forward.

Perform the four movements with the right arm and then with the left arm, and then with both arms at the same time.

Put your hands on hips and walk forward in the following pattern – make a step forward with the right foot on the first quarter, pull your left foot next to the right for the second quarter; then, make a step forward with your left foot, pull your right foot next to your left. Repeat this pattern four times.

Now, combine the movements of your arms with the walking pattern. Go over the combination four times, then stop, make an about-turn, and repeat it four more times.

Stage 2

Music is the same, as in the previous stage of this exercise.

Read first, and then recite nursery rhyme "Humpty-Dumpty."

> *Humpty-Dumpty sat on a wall;*
> *Humpty-Dumpty had a great fall.*
> *All the king's horses and all the king's men*
> *Couldn't put Humpty together again!*

Recite this rhyme several times with music until you memorize it; distribute each line to fit 4/4-time musical accompaniment.

Now, perform the movements with both arms and recite the rhyme while standing in place.

Stage 3

Begin with your right foot, walk forward using the pattern learned in Stage 1 of the exercise; move your arms, and recite the rhyme at the same time. Perform the sequence four times to match the terms of the verse. Make sure you recite all the lines audibly.

Repeat the exercise, but move backward.

Stage 4 (final)

Use the same technique you did for the *Exercise 100* to create visualizations for this story. Your images can be conventional, or unconventional, but they must be bright and colorful with as many details as the format of the poem permits you to create.

Perform Stage 3 of the exercise and include in it the visualizations created by you.

Repeat the exercise and slightly change your images; keep doing it in subsequent repetitions, until you find the visualizations that best represent your idea of the poem and the ones that excite you the most. After you succeed, try to stick to these visualizations in the future repetitions. You can add more details every time you repeat the exercise to make it even more exciting for you to perform.

Now, explore the text and create given circumstances and actions. After you do this work, repeat the exercise and include all the elements already established in previous repetitions.

Perform the final stage of the exercise with the following objective: along with your classmates, you are protesting against child neglect. Use rhyme and movements choreographed, especially for this event. Imagine walking along the street, perhaps in front of public office or a courthouse protesting against regulations that facilitated such neglect to occur.

Methodological guidelines: We recommend completing the entire exercise within three lessons working ten to twelve minutes in each lesson. Go over this exercise occasionally in the following lessons but use different circumstances and actions.

Exercise 102 "THE BRICKS"

Note: Exercises with imaginary objects are a significant part of acting education in the Stanislavsky System of Actor training. We included this concept in our program intentionally because of our method of stage movement is based upon and supportive of the Stanislavsky System. However, this exercise is somewhat different from all the other exercises in this chapter. To benefit from it, the students must be familiar with the concept and the goal of exercises with imaginary objects.

Music is improvisation 4/4, slow chords.

Stage 1

Imagine that a simple construction "brick" set on the "table" to the right of you within your reach. The size of the "brick" is about 8 X 4 X 2 inches.

Grasp the imaginary brick with your right hand from above and arrange your palm and fingers in such a way that it would look a

Figure 20a

lot like you holding a real brick (see Figure 20a). In this sort of exercise, you must believe in your action and actually "see" (imagine) the object with your inner vision. So, visualize the size of the brick, its rough surface, its color, and the shape before you grab it.

Now, carefully lift the "brick" off the "table" and observe for a while. Attention, make sure you do not show the action "I observe," but instead genuinely observe it with the help of your imagination. Notice that it has cavities, spots of different colors on it, all kinds of imperfections, etc. Turn it upside down in your hand to observe the other side of the "brick"; weigh up in your palm to determine its weight; turn it upside down again and put the "brick" back on the "table." Make sure you place the "brick" carefully for not to damage the "table" or your fingers. When the "brick" is finally on the table, *relax your hand and take it* away from the object. Now, repeat the same manipulations with the "brick" only with your left hand. Pick it from the "table" located to the left of your body. Try to vary the actions

Figure 20b

you did before with your right hand; change the order of actions, or create new adjustments.

Now, perform the following four physical actions, one for each quarter of music:

Figure 20c

1. First quarter – grab the brick from above with your right hand.

2. Second quarter – bring the brick in front of your chest and immediately grasp it from above with your left hand (see Figure 20b).

3. Third quarter – first, release your right hand and then turn the brick in your left hand upside down; execute these two actions simultaneously to fit the music (see Figure 20c).

4. Fourth quarter – hand over the brick to the left to imaginary partner; preserve the position of your hand (see Figure 20d).

Figure 20d

Attention, try not to "crack" the brick in half in action #3. Quickly take your right hand off the brick first, and only then turn the brick upside down in your left hand.

Repeat this exercise four times with the music and try to accomplish the continuity of physical actions. Remember, you must take every next brick with your right hand on the downbeat of each bar.

Repeat the exercise; this time, follow each brick with your eyes up until you pass it to your "partner" on the left. Make sure you shift your eyes back to the "table" to "see" the next brick a bit before you pick it up.

Practice in passing bricks in a faster tempo. See that you perform all the accepted movements even when you have less time to do it.

Repeat all the stages of this exercise in reverse: pick up bricks with your left hand and pass them to the right.

Methodological guidelines: The instructor should explain why the exercises with imaginary objects introduced to acting training in general and to stage movement program, in particular. One of the reasons is that the task of handling imaginary objects demands undivided attention from a performer. Taken entirely by the inspiring mission, the student, for the time being, ceases thinking about the fact that other people are watching his actions. It would help the performer to concentrate on the task and bring the "self" to a sound state of mind.

After repeating the exercise with the same object many times, the student begins to do it semi-automatically. The mind liberated from the intense work begins to invent actions "in general," to fill up the gap. It is a proper time for the stage movement instructor to change the task or the object, or to make the task even more complicated.

The exercises with imaginary objects develop imagination and the attention to the detail; they help a beginner to believe in imaginary things as if they are real. This skill would help them later to believe in given circumstances, in fictitious situations, and perhaps in that a partner on stage is not just a fellow actor, but also a character, created by this actor.

Stage 2
The formation is a semi-circle; students are two to three feet apart from each other.

Now you will transfer a single brick from hand to hand along the semi-circle. Use the movements you have learned in Stage 1 and do it in time with the music.

The first student on the right side of the semi-circle begins the exercise by picking up a brick from the imaginary table on the right. Perform four movements and pass the brick to the person on your left. The next student picks up the brick straight from the partner's hand, passes it further, and so forth. The last student in the semi-circle places the brick on the "table" to the left of his/her body. Attention, on the down bit of every bar, one must hold the brick in the left hand until a partner takes it away. If you relax your left hand before this moment, your "brick" will "fall." Notice, the brick must change hands always in the first quarter of a bar, or on the downbeat.

Repeat the exercise several times; switch places to have a different person on the right side of the formation.

Methodological guidelines: The common mistakes in this exercise are -- student "drops" the brick before someone picks it up; the student takes the brick not from a partner's hand, but next to it. This exercise is one of the few in the entire Essential Stage Movement program, where the classmates have the opportunity to observe each other. We recommend having the students point to the errors at the end of the exercise. That would drill observation skills and raise the responsibility of the individual performer.

Maintaining the rhythm is crucial. The best way to do it is to switch the attention from the movements to the music. The timely reminders of the instructor would help the performers to do it right.

Stage 3

Repeat the exercise, and this time pass not one, but five or six bricks one after another. Notice, this would create a substantial challenge because, in the first quarter of each bar, you would have to pick up a new brick with your right hand while giving away the brick, which is still in your left hand. In other words, you would have to perform two different actions simultaneously. It means that to execute both actions correctly, you must spread your attention. After you pass the last brick, relax, and watch your classmates perform the exercise. The last person in the semi-circle should store the bricks on the imaginary table on the left.

Repeat the exercise and pass the bricks in the same way but from left to right of the semi-circle.

Now, assign each brick you are passing, a particular number from "one" and up, and as you pass bricks, announce them in the following manner:

1st quarter	2nd quarter	3rd quarter	4th quarter
"First"	*brick*	*take a*	*brick,*
"Second"	*brick*	*take a*	*brick,*
"Third"	*brick*	*take a*	*brick,* etc.

Notice, there are four syllables (words), one for each physical action that you perform with the brick: pick up the brick, transfer it to another hand, turn the brick upside down, and pass the brick.

Now, pass five or six bricks one after another; everyone announces the brick's number when picking it up (on the downbeat). Continue the exercise until the last brick set on the table at the end of the formation.

Repeat the exercise, and this time, the first student on the right of the semi-circle will decide how many bricks he/she would pass. State each number loud and clear; however, the last brick should be announced as "Last brick, take the brick," so every participant would know when it is coming.

Methodological guidelines: Repeat the "The Bricks" exercise in several consecutive classes with students switching positions in the formation. Make sure the students pronounce words clearly and loud enough for the next partner to hear, but not too loud to outvoice the classmates. The goal of the exercise is to control the speech/voice, tempo-rhythm, and the movement pattern simultaneously by switching attention from one object to another.

By introducing this exercise, you will find it to be an excellent source to train speech-motor coordination.

Stage 4 (final)
Music is improvisation 4/4-time.
The formation is a semi-circle.

Imagine that the bricks you are about to pass painted in different colors: red, blue, white, green, and yellow. Repeat Stage 3 of the exercise but announce the bricks by their color instead; while brick is in your hands, try to visualize its color. Similarly spread the text as you did with numbers:

1st quarter	2nd quarter	3rd quarter	4th quarter
Red	*brick*	*take the*	*brick*
White	*brick*	*take the*	*brick*, etc.

Everyone, who is going to be the first in the formation, would improvise both the colors and order the bricks passed. The rest of the students must follow the game set by the leader.

Now, repeat the exercise and add the following given circumstances: the time is the Eighteenth Century; the place is

England, the event – an annual ball in King's Palace. The guests at this fantasy ball are the Bricks of different colors. You are a Stewart, which announces the arrival of each distinguished guest. The Palace is massive and many stewards are announcing the guests one after another, as guests move along.

Methodological guidelines: The changes and new complications in this exercise are introduced for several particular reasons: to train the precision of the physical act, the rhythm, and the adjustment of the voice in a crowd. It would be a mistake to instruct the students to announce the guests louder. Let the actors consider the circumstances by themselves.

Repeat this exercise in several consecutive lessons and practice it for five to seven minutes in each. Move to the next stage of the exercise only after the previous one performed flawlessly. To rejuvenate the appeal to this exercise, offer it for performance unexpectedly in one of the lessons later in the program. This time, give the bricks the names of classmates. Also, every so often, offer the students to perform the exercise in reverse.

In the skit with Stewards, the instructor should see that the students avoid acting as characters and follow the given circumstances instead.

Note: This exercise actively trains *Speech and Movement Coordination* as well as *Concentration, Rhythmicity, Awareness of Space, Precision of physical action,* and *Tempo-rhythm of the physical act.* Repeat the Final Stage of the exercise occasionally in the following lessons; include it in the Test class with a fresh set of complications.

Exercise 103 "FOLLOW THE LEADER"

Music is improvisation 4/4-time.
The formation is a crowd.

Stage 1

Standing in place, recite "Little Miss Muffet" in time with the music (see Stage 3, Exercise 100).

Appoint one of the students the Leader. Imagine that every player in the crowd attached to the Leader by an imaginary pole. The Leader will move forward, backward, and occasionally stop. The group would have to recite the rhyme in time with music and follow the Leader at the same time. Notice, everyone would have to maintain the initial distance between you and the leader while moving in a direction the Leader "pulls," or "drives" you. The Leader does not have to recite the rhyme, as his/her task is to change the directions. We suggest the Leader stand still for a while before initiating any movement. Besides, the Leader may improvise not just the direction (backward/forward) but the amplitudes of steps as well.

Stage 2

Now the Leader will move not only forward and backward, but also sideways, and even walk along the arc. Recite the rhyme in time with music and follow the Leader. Repeat the exercise with another player as the Leader.

In addition to previous complications, the next leader will also vary the tempo of execution by changing the speed of the steps. Both the students and the accompanist should follow the Leader.

Note: The goal of this exercise is to develop the ability to recite a logical text while reacting to spontaneous changes in tempo-rhythm and modes of movements. Make sure you maintain a clear and reasonable performance of the rhyme no matter the changes of circumstances.

Stage 3

The next Leader will break the rhythm intentionally, i.e., make all kinds of unexpected moves, such as squats, jumps, dance moves, etc. Nevertheless, the group must continue reciting the rhyme in the tempo-rhythm suggested by the music. In other words, the accompanist in this exercise would maintain the tempo-rhythm of the music.

Recite the rhyme in time with music and follow the Leader. Do not forget the imaginary poll you are attached to the Leader with, but the additional movements suggested by the Leader perform as a mirror reflection. Recite the text in an audible articulate voice despite the extreme positions.

Methodological guidelines: Have every student try the role of Leader at least once over several successive lessons. Every new leader should create engaging new combinations of movements. To avoid monotony, repeat this exercise no more than three times in a single class. Welcome a spirit of competition between leaders should.

Stage 4 (final)
Formation and music are the same, as in previous stages of the exercise.

Standing in place, recite "Little Miss Muffet" with all the visualizations, given circumstances, and actions that you established in the Final stage of Exercise 100.
Now, follow the Leader and try to preserve all the elements that you just displayed.

Note: Repeat the final stage of the exercise occasionally in the future in selected lessons. Include a version of this exercise in a Test class as well.

Exercise 104 "THE WEST WAS GETTING OUT OF GOLD"

Stage 1
Music is improvisation 4/4, plain chords.

Perform the following four movements with your right arm in quarter-notes -- forward, in front of your chest, out to the side, down. Repeat the exercise four times.

Perform the following three movements with your left arm: forward, out to the side, down. Repeat these three movements continuously (without interruption) for three bars of music.

Now, move both arms at the same time, each arm in its unique pattern. Notice, unlike previous motor coordination exercises, you have four movements for your right arm and only three movements for your left. As a result, your arms' juxtaposition would continually change during twelve quarters (or three bars of music). It is only for the twelfth quarter when both arms would go down along your sides. On the twelfth quarter, your right arm would complete only three full sequences, while your left arm would complete four sequences.

Perform the exercise with both arms for three bars and finish it by slapping your thighs with both hands. That would indicate the end of the sequence. Make an about-face turn and do this exercise again standing in place.

Methodological guidelines: In case the students would still make mistakes or be confused after several attempts, go back to executing the exercise with each arm independently and then combining the movements of both arms again. Try to perform the exercise at a slow tempo. Gradually increase the speed with every next repetition.

Stage 2
Music – "The West was Getting out of Gold" without effects (see Appendix 9).

Listen to the entire piece of music once and notice that it consists of twelve bars in 4/4-time or 48 quarters.

Now, stand in place and perform the exercise with both arms for the duration of the musical piece. It means you would have to repeat the entire sequence three times.

Now, begin with your right foot and walk forward in quarter-notes;
perform the pattern with both arms at the same time. Repeat the
twelve-bar sequence only once; make sure you end it with both your
arms down.

Stop, and then repeat the same walking backward.

Now, repeat the exercise and walk forward for three bars of
music, then continue and walk backward for another three bars of
music.

To develop this exercise further, you would have to learn the
poem "Looking for a Sunset Bird in Winter" by Robert Frost.

Recite the poem without the music and maintain the rhythm
as follows:

1st quarter	**2nd quarter**	**3rd quarter**	**4th quarter**
The West	*was getting*	*out of*	*gold,*
The breath	*of air*	*had died*	*of cold,*
When shoeing	*home*	*across*	*the white,*
I thought	*I saw*	*a bird*	*alight.*

* * *

In summer	*(pause)*	*when I passed*	*the place*
I had	*to stop*	*and lift*	*my face;*
A bird	*(pause)*	*with an angelic*	*gift*
Was singing	*in it*	*sweet*	*and swift.*

* * *

No bird	*was singing*	*in it*	*now.*
A single	*leaf*	*was on*	*the bough,*
And that	*was all*	*there was*	*to see*
In going	*twice*	*around*	*the tree.*

Notice the pause in the second quarter in the first and the
third line of the second verse.

Now, recite the poem in time with music and incorporate these pauses; try to achieve a rhythmical and audible pronunciation of the lines.

Methodological guidelines: We recommend displaying a poster with the poem so that the students could learn the lines from it; another way is to distribute a Xerox copy to everyone.
The instructor should work with the group on the articulation of the poem and, among other things, explain that the two pauses in the second verse need to be fashioned to sound logical. It is most likely that at the beginning, the students would stress each word to match it with a quarter-note. One should explain that such recitation makes it almost impossible to understand the meaning of lines, so the words in lines must be delivered jointly and logically.

However, make sure the poem recited rhythmically but without stressing every word. It is also a common blunder to pass the first word of the poem, which is "the." It happens unintentionally because the next word "west" corresponds to the downbeat. Make sure "the West" pronounced clear but not over-amplified.

Stag*e* 3
The formation is a crowd.

The beginning position is a regular stance, your hands on hips. Recite the first verse of the poem standing in place; begin with your right foot and walk forward in quarter-notes, while reciting the second verse; walk backward and recite the third verse. Stop at the end of the poem and pull your feet together on the last beat. Walk continuously and remember to continuously monitor all the elements of this exercise: the correct gait, the rhythmical recitation of the poem, the continuity, the logic of the text, etc. From now on, consider this arrangement as the basic pattern for this exercise.

For drilling, repeat the exercise and walk forward and backward in whole-notes instead of quarter-notes.

Methodological guidelines: Perform this stage of the exercise in several consecutive lessons and do not move any further until this arrangement mastered and performed with confidence.

Stage 4
Music is the same, as in the previous Stage.

Methodological guidelines: The work towards the artistic interpretation of the poem begins at this stage of the exercise with the emphasis on logic, consistency, visualizations, objectives, and actions.

The instructor should explain that this poem consists of three parts, each of them represented by one verse. Read the poem for the students and point out that each section has a different state of mind. We offer a very general interpretation of the piece. The first verse expresses hope, the second is a flashback that conveys joy, and the last part is a cheerless manifestation of disappointment. To reveal the true meaning of this poem, the students should attempt to bring up these three different emotions – the hope, the joy, and the disappointment through the recitation of the poem. According to Stanislavsky, any attempt to play a feeling directly would unavoidably result in overacting. Therefore, we must find a way to create the sensation of these emotions, employing different means. First, we should discover appropriate images and given circumstances that would help the players to create these sensations.

From the poem, we already know that the first part occurs during the sunset; it is freezing, the field covered with deep snow, so it is challenging to walk on it. Also, we can suggest that the narrator already exhausted by a long walk and monotonous landscape. This place is familiar to the narrator; it is where he would usually stop and relax in the shadow of the tree; this is where he would listen to a beautiful song of the Sunset bird. The players should create individual images in their minds, which they would later visualize when reciting the poem.

The second part gives enough facts to create colorful images in mind familiar to one, something one can believe in without difficulty.

This place looks much different in the summertime. Everything is sweet to one's heart – the tree covered with green leaves, the breezy shadow, the gentle sun, and the singing bird.

The third part's circumstances are similar to that of the first part only with more details: monotonous white snow everywhere, brutally cold weather, lonely bare tree, and no place, where an exhausted body can find rest.

After all given circumstances are thoroughly selected and defined, the players must create their personal, unique visualizations of the situation based on these circumstances. Encourage the players to bring their recollections of places they visited and use images from movies and TV shows. They must use their imagination and create a chain of images, "a reel of the film" that they would turn on every time they begin reciting the poem.

Now, standing in place, recite the poem in time with the music; roll the "reel of the film" in your mind as you recite. Perhaps, you would have to repeat the exercise several times to make it work. It is not an easy task and demands a lot of practice. If it is novel for you, give it careful consideration.

Now, recite the poem, move both arms, and follow the choreography established in Stage 3 of the exercise, i.e., perform first verse standing in place, second – moving forward, and third verse – moving backward; walk on quarters.

Methodological guidelines: To prevent mechanical repetitions, perform this stage of the exercise no more than two or three times in a single lesson.

Stage 5 (final)
Music is a full version of Appendix 9 with all the nuances.

Listen to the complete version of the music and notice all the nuances presented in it. To further develop this exercise into an étude, we have to establish one crucial aspect of the presentation. It is the purpose we recite this poem to the audience. Using the Stanislavsky System's terminology, we must identify the *objective*.

Analyzing this and some other works of great American poet Robert Frost, we may presume that his poem "Looking for a Sunset Bird in Winter" has a symbolic meaning, conveyed in the poem through impersonation of the winter and the summer. There is a contraposition between these two seasons in the poem. One is desirable, favored, and the other is unwanted, dismissed. One is about a life full of joy and warmth; the other is about bereavement packed with cold and emptiness. This attitude suggests identifying the objective, as "I wish that summer was always."

Declare this objective with the help of words and pauses given by the poet. Have it in every image created by you. Include it in every choreographed movement. The music is there to help you to accomplish your objective.

Perform the entire exercise conforming to the music. Remember, the first four bars stay in place; the second four bars walk forward, and the last four bars walk backward. By this time, make sure the conditional movements of your arms are performed semi-automatically to allow you to concentrate on the meaning of the poem and to make your objective apparent through visualizations, words, intonation, and movements.

Methodological guidelines: Understandably, different students in the group will present the final stage of this exercise slightly dissimilar. That is how it should be. Nevertheless, the students must comply with the essential elements such as tempo-rhythm of the étude, given circumstances, and the objective. It would create an ensemble performance with every member of the ensemble having his or her visions and adaptations.

The final stage of this exercise should demonstrate your students' ability to transform a literary work combined with movement patterns into a creative stage presentation. For practicing purposes, we included the conditional movements in the exercise intentionally. The idea of such training is that if a student can perform a logical text along with these kinds of movements, it would be easier for him/her to incorporate logical and natural movements of every day later in professional life.

The instructor should see that the pronunciation of the text is audible and consistent with the objective. Minimal knowledge of the Speech for the Actor would come handy for the instructor. With all the exciting visualizations and circumstances, the impression from the étude would remain marginal if the text delivered in a weak voice, and the lines make no sense. Make sure also that the movements are expressive of the meaning and the objective of the piece. The students must consider the movements as not an obstacle, but something they should integrate into the presentation.

Repeat the final stage of the exercise no more than two or three times in a single lesson. Include the exercise occasionally in selected future lessons and certainly make it a part of the Test Lesson.

CHAPTER NINE

DEVELOPMENT OF SINGING-MOTOR COORDINATION

Exercise 105 "MARY HAD A LITTLE LAMB"

Stage 1
Music is improvisation 2/4-time consisting of eighth notes, clear and slow.
The formation is a crowd.

The beginning position – feet in 3rd dancing position[1] – right foot in front, and your hands on hips (see Figure 21.)

Figure 21

Take a small step forward with your right foot, and then pull the left foot to the right to a 3rd dancing position. Repeat this pattern four times.

Switch the position of your feet to a 3rd position with your left foot in front; repeat the same four steps forward with the left foot in front.

Now, begin with the right foot and repeat the sequence (four steps) four times alternating feet.

Now listen to music and note that it has four eight notes in each bar, with a stress on the first and the third note. There are two up-beats (1st and 3rd beats) and two down-beats (2nd and 4th beats) in each bar. Begin with your right foot and perform the steps in time with this music; match your step forward with the stressed beat, and pull your feet together to 3rd position on the upbeat. Repeat the exercise for the duration of four bars of music. Now, repeat the same with your left foot in front; maintain the 3rd position every time you pull feet together.

Repeat the exercise and make four steps forward (one sequence) with the right foot; continue and make four steps forward with your left foot. Repeat this pattern and swap feet for the duration of eight bars of music; do not pause when switching feet.

Methodological guidelines: To avoid confusion, suggest counting aloud the up- and down-beats in the following manner: "one and, two and, one and, two and." Pronouncing "one" on the down-beat, recite "and" on the upbeat.

Now, repeat the exercise without the music; make four steps forward with your right foot and place the left foot behind in the 3rd dancing position only after the first three steps. After the fourth step, though, stomp your left foot behind the right instead; spring it up immediately after the stomp. This way, you would finish the pattern with your left foot off the floor. It would make it more convenient for you to continue the exercise forward with your left foot. Repeat the exercise now with your left foot in front.

Now, begin with your right foot in 3rd position and perform the sequence four times alternating feet. Remember to stomp your foot only after each fourth step. Perform this version of the exercise several times in a single lesson.

Let us now modify the first three steps in the pattern. Every time you pull the back foot to the front foot on the up-beat, make a semi-squat, or as they say in ballet, a *"demi plié."* Make this movement soft and smooth. So, after the 1st, 2nd, and 3rd steps pull feet together with a semi-squat. However, after the 4th step, stomp your foot behind and bounce it up as you did before. Repeat this version of the exercise several times until performed with ease.

Put your hands on hips, right foot in front in 3rd position; move forward in time with music, swap feet after every four steps. Repeat the pattern four times.

Finally, add one small feature to make the exercise inclusive. When moving forward with the right foot, turn your right shoulder halfway forward, when traveling with the left foot, twist your left shoulder halfway forward. To accommodate this, move your torso slightly and keep staring ahead. Perform this as a kind of dance moves and repeat it several times in a single lesson.

Stage 2
Music and Formation are the same as in Stage 1.

Stand in place, hands on your hips, count aloud in time with music in the following manner: "one and, two and, three and, four and," with the numbers matching the down-beats.

Now, count out again and perform the following movements with your arms: on count "one" open right arm forward/sideways with palm up; on count "two" open your left arm the same way. Now, cross both hands on your chest on count "three"; finally, clap your hands in front of your chest and immediately put hands back on your hips on count "four." Make sure you perform every movement on the downbeat; only the very last movement – bringing your hands to hips – must match the upbeat. Stand in place and repeat this combination four times.

Now, combine these movements of your arms with the steps that you learned in Stage 1. Repeat the sequence four times moving forward and remember to twist your shoulder (matching the leading foot) slightly forward. Try to remove any unnecessary tension in your body to make the movements appear effortless and graceful.

Methodological guidelines: As the complexity of the exercise increases, we recommend slowing down the tempo of musical accompaniment for some time. Increase the speed again, as the performance appears more confident. If combining the arms and feet movements presents a problem, repeat the arms' movements separately, and then put them with steps together again. See that the students keep turning the torso slightly forward along with the leading foot; that gives the exercise a dance-like quality.

Stage 3
Music – "Mary had a little lamb" (see Appendix 3)

Listen to the music that is probably familiar to you. Nevertheless, it is good to know that the music is by Wolfgang Amadeus Mozart. One Lowell Mason set a well-known nursery rhyme, "Mary had a little lamb" to this melody in 1830. Read and memorize this rhyme.

Mary had a little lamb,
Little lamb, little lamb,
Mary had a little lamb,
Whose fleece was white as snow.
And everywhere that Mary went,
Mary went, Mary went,
And everywhere that Mary went,
The lamb was sure to go.

Now, sing the song along with the music. Repeat it several times and make sure you follow the right key and the tempo. See also that you pronounce all the words in this song correctly.

Stage 4
Music is the same as in the previous exercise.
The formation is a crowd.

The beginning position – 3rd dancing position, right foot in front; right shoulder turned slightly forward; hands on hips; stare ahead.

Begin with your right foot, move forward alternating feet after every four steps; sing the first verse of the song. Repeat the movement pattern four times and stop, feet together, your right foot behind in a 3rd position.

Turn around and repeat the exercise, moving upstage; sing the second verse of the song.

Now, do it without music in your tempo; begin with your left foot and execute only four dancing steps forward (one sequence). After the last step, <u>stomp</u> your right foot behind as usual and simultaneously make an about-turn over your right shoulder. After it bounces, your right foot would be off the floor, so continue moving in the opposite direction, starting with it. However, to make this turn smooth, you would have to prepare your body for it in advance. The trick is, when making the last step, place your left foot down, and turn it a bit inside. It would help you to complete the turn. Practice this rotation several times without music.

Now, perform four sequences of the exercise beginning with your right foot as usual; at the end, make this turn about-face over your right shoulder that you practiced before. Then continue the exercise with your right foot moving upstage. After four sequences completed, make another about-turn over the right shoulder and stop with your feet in 3rd dancing position, right foot in front.

Methodological guidelines: The rotation might confuse students at the beginning, as this motion is quite uncommon. Make sure every student performs the turn correctly, before including it into the composite exercise.

A common mistake is stomping and springing the right foot at the end of the exercise after the second about-turn. The exercise ends with setting the foot down in the 3rd position. This mistake is natural because springing foot after the stomp could already become a habit. The instructor should point out n the fact that this is the last motion that indicates the end, the finale.

To emphasize the end of a gesture (motion) is an essential habit for the actor, the lecturer, or the orator. It is a way to make the audiences tell one bit of business from another. In everyday reality, people do not think much about it, even though they occasionally use this technique spontaneously to make a point. So, this exercise gives an excellent chance to begin training the habit.

The duration of a pause at the end of the exercise depends on the tempo-rhythm of preceding action. Eventually, the students will understand it, but for the time being, the instructor should help them to maintain a pause, just the right amount of time. One can do it by a simple command, "Stay!" followed by a call, "Relax."

In dance programs, the participants acquire this habit early in the process, and this is another reason why actors must have a dance class.

Stage 5
Music and Formation are the same as in the previous exercise.

Repeat Stage 4 of the exercise; sing the first verse when you move downstage, perform the turn at the end; then sing the second verse when you travel up the stage. Make another turn at the end and stop; do not move for several seconds, indicating the end of the exercise. Make your turns smooth, so they do not affect the singing.

Now, listen to the music standing in place, and clap your hands on the first downbeat of every bar; repeat the exercise for the duration of eight bars of music.

And now, combine the steps, song, and the clapping of hands in one complex exercise; begin with the right foot and move downstage; make the turn at the end and continue the exercise moving upstage; make another turn and stop.

Stand in place, clap your hands on the second downbeat of each bar, and practice it for eight bars of music. Now, perform the entire exercise and clap for the second downbeat.

Now, combine the two previous hands' patterns with the primary exercise in the following manner: clap your hands on the first downbeat and repeat it for the duration of one sequence (eight bars); for the next sequence, clap your hands on the second downbeat. As usual, move downstage for the first verse, and upstage for the second verse; make an about-turn over your right shoulder at the end of the first verse and the end of the exercise.

Practice the exercise several times in a single lesson or until performed flawlessly.

Stage 6
Music and Formation are the same as in the previous exercise.

The beginning position is feet in the 3rd dancing position, your hands on hips.

Stand in place and repeat the movements for your arms from Stage 2 of the exercise – open right arm; then open left arm; cross arms on your chest; clap hands on the last downbeat of the sequence and quickly put your hands on hips for the final eighth note of the sequence. Repeat the exercise for the duration of sixteen bars of music.

Combine the hands' pattern with singing and perform two verses standing in place.

Then perform the exercise as follows: move downstage, then upstage, sing the song, and move your arms in the above-established pattern. Try to control all the tasks by quickly switching your attention from one to another.

Methodological guidelines: Practice this version of the exercise in several consecutive lessons until performed flawlessly and effortlessly. To prepare for the final stage, make sure all the elements mastered and delivered by everyone semi-automatically.

Stage 7 (final)

Here are some given circumstances and actions for this stage of the exercise.

A drunken cowboy is heading home from a local bar. The night is dark while the cowboy decides on the closest path – across the field. He's got "one too many" and being in a jolly good mood he is singing and dancing. Halfway home, he realizes that he left his brand new Stetson hat in the bar. He turns around and swings back to the bar. He finally reaches the bar only to see the bar closed.

Perform the skit utilizing all the steps that you learned previously plus the movements of arms and the song from the final version of the exercise "Mary had a little lamb." Stay with the music and the rhythm, although the given circumstances and the actions may suggest you to improvise some of the elements occasionally.

Repeat the exercise one more time and update some circumstances, perhaps even create a different ending.

Methodological guidelines: As with other exercises involving acting techniques, the instructor should be particular in the selection of the circumstances and other elements to avoid overacting and buffoonery in this skit. However, this skit would noticeably demonstrate the ability of the students to coordinate their movements and singing in extreme circumstances of the skit.

If the company is not prepared to create additional circumstances for the skit on the request, the instructor may want to suggest some for the skit's ending. The cowboy trips over a stone and falls, or the cowboy opens the bar door and falls over the threshold, or the cowboy stops and freezes eyeing a sheriff, etc.

As this is one of the fundamental exercises of the Essential Stage Movement program, consider including its final stage in the Test Class, perhaps with a new set of circumstances.

The objective of introducing different actions and complications into the exercise is to develop *Singing-Motor Coordination, Rhythmicity, and Awareness*. Do not allow the students to neglect the choreography and the rhythmical performance getting carried away with acting; as this is a stage movement class, pay special attention to the task's physical performance.

Exercise 106 CANON ONE, "Frère Jacques"[2]

Stage 1
Music is improvisation 4/4-time in the following pattern:

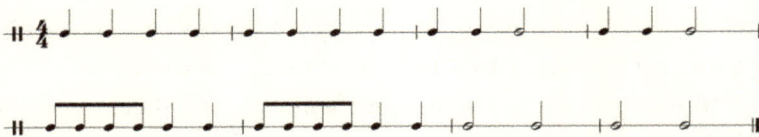

The beginning position is the regular stance.

Listen to this rhythmical pattern several times and notice that the piece consists of eight bars and that the rhythm changes every two bars. In the first two bars, there are only quarter-notes; in the next two bars, there are two quarters and one half-note in each; in the next two bars, there are four eighth-notes and two quarter-notes in each bar, and in the last two bars, there are half-notes only.

Listen to music again and try to identify all the diversity of the piece.

Now, the accompanist would play one bar of music at a time; repeat the pattern of each bar by clapping your hands, as you did, let say in Exercise 65 (see Chapter 5).

Let us now divide the exercise into four parts with two identical bars of music in each. Let us call them Part 1, Part 2, Part 3, and Part 4.

Stand in place and clap your hands in time with music, imitating the rhythmical pattern of each part and the nuances of the entire piece.

Form a crowd.

Put your hands on hips, and prepare to learn new steps. Take a step by planting your heel on the ground first, and then step on the entire foot, thus making two distinguished motions. The first motion would fall on the first beat, the second motion on the second beat. Let us call these steps, "heel-foot steps." Begin with your right foot and perform four such steps forward, two for each bar of music. That would complete Part 1 of the exercise. Repeat the exercise several times.

Let us slightly change the steps of this part of the exercise. Every time you step on the whole foot, gently bend the knee and, at the same time, lift the other foot behind slightly off the floor. Perform Part 1 of the exercise with these modifications; practice these steps with music for the duration of eight or sixteen bars or until you do it with grace and ease.

Now, listen to the rhythmical pattern of Part 2 and clap your hands accentuating the notes. Notice, there are two quarters and one half-note in each bar. Begin with your right foot and walk forward, imitating this rhythm with regular steps. Repeat this pattern four times in a row.

Now, combine Part 1 and Part 2 of the exercise and perform it continuously four times with music.

Listen now to musical pattern Part 3 of the exercise and imitate the sounds by clapping your hands. Note that this part consists of two bars, and there are four eighth-notes and two quarter-notes in each.

Now, begin with your right foot and imitate this rhythmical pattern by running forward in passing steps for the eighth-notes and taking regular steps for the quarter-notes. Repeat Part 3 four times.

Now, combine the three parts of the exercise, one following another, and repeat it two times.

Part 4 of the exercise also consists of two bars, two half-notes each or four half-note altogether. Begin with your right foot and imitate the beats with regular steps; however, on the last beat, pull your left foot next to the right to finish the exercise.

After practicing all four parts separately, put them together, and perform one after another in time with the music continuously. After you finish the exercise, stop, make an about-turn, and repeat it, moving upstage.

Stage 2
The formation is a crowd.

For drilling purposes, repeat the exercise this time without the musical accompaniment. Try to make your music with your steps imitating the rhythmical pattern. Nevertheless, maintain a common tempo-rhythm with the rest of the group.

Now, the accompanist will play bare quarters instead of the patterns. However, perform all four parts of the exercise, as usual, imitating the rhythmical patterns.

Let us make a small adjustment to Part 4. From this point on, perform the first two steps forward, next, take a step with your right foot in front and across your left foot, and for the fourth quarter, get up on your toes, make an about-turn and lower your heels on the floor. Notice, you must execute all three movements for one beat of the music! Besides, do not forget to perform the rotation over your left shoulder. Practice this new development without music several times and try to execute the turn smoothly and gracefully.

Now perform the entire exercise four times with the music, including last change; start every sequence with the right foot and maintain the balance.

Now, perform the exercise twice: first time moving downstage, making the about-turn. Then continue moving upstage; make another turn and stop; stay still for a while to indicate the end of the exercise.

Repeat the entire exercise, and this time, make sure you finish it precisely at the same spot where you began.

Now perform the entire exercise in reverse, i.e., begin the exercise with your left foot, move downstage, turn over your right shoulder, move upstage, and then make the about-turn again over the right shoulder and stop.

Stage 3
The formation is a crowd.
Music – "Frère Jacques" (see Appendix 10).

Listen to the music. It might sound familiar, as it is a universally familiar French nursery rhyme.

Perform the pattern that you accomplished in Stage 2 with this new musical complement moving downstage, and then upstage. Make turns and stop at the end.
Learn the lyrics for this rhyme. As this is a French song, so you have to sing it properly in French.

> *Frère Jacques, Frère Jacques,*
> *Dormez-vous? Dormez-vous?*
> *Sonnez les matines! Sonnez les matines!*
> *Ding, dang, dong. Ding, dang, dong.*

Stand in place and sing the song along with the music; repeat the verse twice.

Now, begin with your right foot and perform the entire exercise that you did previously; move downstage and then upstage and make the turns, sing "Frère Jacques" twice.

For the next performance of the exercise, the accompanist would play only plain quarter-chords; execute the steps and the song with this music.

Stage 4 (final)
Music is the same as in the previous stage.
The formation is a line, in order of height.

Perform the exercise "Frère Jacques" in the line formation. It is essential to maintain a straight line through the entire exercise, so when at the end, everyone turns about-face, there still must be a straight line.

Now, begin from the first person in line and count off from one to four.

In the following exercise, those with the number "one" will begin the exercise first. After number "one" players finish Part 1 of the exercise and begin Part 2, players number "two" join in the exercise by performing it from the top, i.e., starting with Part 1, and so forth. In other words, every two bars of music next number should begin the exercise. Notice, each "number" must enter the exercise from Part 1 and perform it in the order, established previously, i.e., every "number" would have to complete the sequence twice – downstage with the about-turn at the end, and then upstage with the about-turn and stop.

Before joining in the exercise and after finishing it, stay still until it is your turn; at the end, have everyone in one straight line.

Perform the exercise *by numbers* with the rhyme music but do not sing yet. Instead, concentrate on joining in the exercise on time. Also, while moving in groups, the members of the same numerical group must maintain a line between them.

Now, perform the entire exercise by numbers and sing the rhyme at the same time; begin singing altogether and continue repeating the verse until group "four" finishes the exercise. Sing whether or not you physically doing the exercise. Repeat this exercise several times, switching numbers with every new repetition. Now, perform the exercise by numbers and sing the rhyme by the numbers as well, i.e., begin singing the song from the top as you start moving. The different parts of the song would sound at the same time. That is precisely why this exercise called "Canon." However, to accommodate this, everyone should adjust the voice level so that one can hear you, and yet, one could hear the rest of the group singing. If you hear only yourself, it indicates that you are too loud. Repeat the exercise several times in a single lesson switching the numbers.

Methodological guidelines: Develop this exercise gradually to reach its final stage over several lessons. Keep practicing it in every class beginning from the second half of the semester until the end of it. Each stage of the exercise would probably take two to three lessons to master. However, repeat a previous level of the exercise in the next class before a new modification introduced. Practice this exercise no more than 10 to 12 minutes in a single lesson. Offer the complex tasks, such as the ones presented in exercise Canon I or similar exercises, to a group able to manage them.

Here are some particular guidelines for the accompanist. For the final stage of the exercise, the accompanist should repeatedly play the song until group "four" finished the exercise. When the company sings in *canon*, make the accompaniment harmonic chords only. Also, we recommend introducing one harmonic chord as a sign to begin the exercise. The accompanist may use a short Introduction (perhaps four bars) that would serve as a command to start the exercise as well as set the tempo.

For drilling purposes, change the tempo each time the exercise repeated. Towards the end of the semester, the speed could vary slightly in the progression of the performance. However, carefully measure the degree of such changes according to the abilities of a particular group of students.

In mastering of the first stages of exercise, make sure the students pull both feet together and then continue moving with the right foot every time they make an about-turn.

To switch the roles (numbers) while standing in line, the instructor should ask the student at the beginning of the line to move to the end of it, and make the company count off from one to four again. Make sure every student has a chance to perform all different numbers.

After the exercise performed flawlessly and with ease, we recommend letting the students present the final version of the exercise without the music, or *"a cappella."* However, save this variation for the Test Class.

Exercise 107 CANON II, "Battle Hymn of the Republic"
Music is improvisation 4/4-time or March in the following pattern:

The formation is a crowd.

Stage 1

Listen to this rhythmical pattern several times. Notice that the first and the third bars are identical and consist of four quarters; the second bar has a quarter-note with a dot, one eight-note, a quarter-note, and one quarter-pause; the fourth bar consists of four eighth-notes and two quarter-notes. Let us conditionally divide this piece into four parts, each part one bar long.

Stand in place and clap your hands in time with music, marking every sound of the pattern.

Now, let us establish particular movements for each part of the exercise.

For Part 1, begin with your right foot, walk forward, and take four regular steps in quarters. Do not pull feet together at the end. Just remember it.

Execute Part 2 of this exercise as follows: take a step forward with your right foot on the quarter with a dot (remember, it lasts a quarter plus ½ of a quarter). Then, on the eighth note, jump sideways to the left, arrive on your left foot, and quickly plant your right foot next to the left on a quarter-note; hold a quarter-pause to complete this bar. If the description is too cumbersome to comprehend, just imitate the rhythm of music with the steps described above.

Practice this part of the exercise several times and start it with your right foot each time.

Now, perform Part 1 and Part 2 one following another. Repeat it four times successively.

Part 3 consists of four quarters; walk in the spot marking each of them. However, unlike Part 1, instead of planting your feet for each beat, mark each beat by yanking your knees up. Begin with your right knee up and walk on the spot alternating feet. If you execute this task correctly, after four such steps, your left foot will stop off the floor.

Repeat this part of the exercise four times. Make sure you begin with lifting your right knee and finish with your left knee up in the air.

Now, put together the first three parts of the exercise and repeat it several times in a single lesson. Make the transition from one part to another smooth and natural.

Listen to the rhythmical pattern of Part 4. Then clap your hands, imitating the pattern.

Perform this pattern with your feet, by making light steps on the spot and alternating feet.

Now, begin with your left foot and run forward on your toes for the eighth-notes; then make one more step forward for a quarter-note, and finally jump forward and land on both feet for the last quarter of the bar. Repeat this exercise four times without music; begin with your left foot each time.

Now, put together all four parts of the exercise and try to make all the transitions effortless. Repeat the entire exercise several times or until all the tasks and transitions executed sufficiently.

Methodological guidelines: Try to accomplish this stage of exercise within one lesson. The students might have trouble with Part 3, as lifting knees on the downbeat in walking is quite unusual. It would prevent some students from performing the task correctly right away. However, after several repetitions, this action would become natural.

Stage 2
Music and Formation are the same as in the previous stage.

Let us make two small adjustments to this exercise.

The first adjustment: in Part 3, walk backward instead of walking on the spot. Still, yank the knees up for each beat. Lift the right knee as usual, and execute the steps moving backward. Attention, shift first, the weight of your body slightly back to move timely backward. Practice this part of the exercise several times without music.

Now, repeat the entire exercise; incorporate the changes made in Part 3.

Notice an additional complication this change creates in the transition from Part 3 to Part 4 -- in Part 3, you move backward, and in Part 4, you must run forward. Repeat the exercise. Try to find adjustment by shifting the weight of your body a bit in advance to prepare it for moving in the opposite direction.

The second adjustment – in Part 4 jumping forward and landing on both feet on the last beat, perform an about-turn over the left shoulder at the same time. To execute the turn successfully and land in a balanced position, prepare your body for this by adequately positioning your left foot just before jumping. Place your left foot with your toe turned out (to the left), so the turn already begins with this step. Repeat this part of the exercise several times to find necessary adjustments.

Repeat the entire exercise incorporating the adjustment you made in Part 4.

Now execute the exercise twice – first time downstage with the turn at the end, second time upstage; make another about-turn and stop; stay still to indicate the end of your performance.

Methodological guidelines: Try to accomplish this stage of the exercise within a single lesson; this would not be difficult if, by the time the exercise introduced into the program, your students prepared for these sorts of things. However, if you need two lessons to develop Stage 2, repeat the last variation once or twice in the next class, and then continue working on it.

Stage 3
Music is the same as in the previous stage.
The formation is a line.

Perform the exercise as before, but this time in the line formation. Perform it twice: first moving downstage and then moving upstage; maintain a straight line through the entire exercise.

Now be prepared, the accompanist would interrupt the music at his will any time during the performance; however, carry on and maintain the tempo initiated by the music.

Methodological guidelines: Include this stage of the exercise for drill purposes, and repeat several times changing the tempos. The instructor should watch for a common mistake in Part 4 – the students often tend to increase the speed while running forward in eighth notes. If this occurs, stop the exercise, point out on this error, and, if necessary, make the students repeat the rhythmical pattern of Part 4 by clapping their hands first, then stomping their feet, and then running forward with the jump/turn at the end.

The instructor should persistently remind them to maintain the line through the entire exercise. Make them accept that it is a part of the exercise, a specific choreography. Sometimes it helps to bring as an example of the Rockettes from Radio City Music Hall, whose synchronized movements alone create an emotional reaction in the audience. It pays to work continuously on the sustaining a pause at the end of each exercise, and on the notion to finish it in the same spot, it started. The latter would drill the *Sense of Space*.

Stage 4
Music – "Battle Hymn of the Republic" (see Appendix 11)
The formation is a line.

Listen to the chorus part of the song "Battle Hymn of the Republic." It is good to know that Julia
Ward Howe wrote the lyrics for this famous song of American Civil War period, and set it to already-existing music by William Steffe.
Read and memorize the chorus part of the song:

> *Glory, glory, hallelujah!*
> *Glory, glory, hallelujah!*
> *Glory, glory, hallelujah!*
> *His truth is marching on.*
> *Glory, glory, hallelujah!*
> *Glory, glory, hallelujah!*
> *Glory, glory, hallelujah!*
> *Since God is marching on.*

Stand in place and sing the chorus twice.
Now, repeat Stage 4 of the exercise along with this new music but do not sing yet. Make sure your movements match precisely this musical piece. Notice that the rhythm of the song does not exactly repeat the rhythmical pattern that you perform with your feet. That

would be an additional challenge for you. Practice the exercise several times and try to achieve flawless performance.

Now, combine the movement pattern with the singing in one complex exercise; make sure the movements that you perform (especially running and jumping) do not affect your singing. Articulate every word in the song.

Stage 5
Music is improvisation 4/4-time with each first quarter of a measure stressed.

Assemble a line; count off from "one" to "four" beginning from the right end of the line. Participants with the number "one" will start the exercise first. Each number-group must perform the task twice: once moving downstage with the turn at the end, and then once upstage with a final turn. Make sure you return to the initial spot and stay still until group "four" finishes the exercise. Every next group begins the exercise with a delay of precisely one bar.
Perform the exercise in time with music by order of numbers. The music will last until group "four" finishes the sequence. Practice the exercise several times in a single lesson, switching the roles (numbers).

Methodological guidelines: A complex task of a Canon II exercise sometimes creates confusion. It is common to observe some students looking around and trying to copy their partners during the performance. Notice such attempts early in the process and explain that copying can only further confuse a player. One must concentrate on the task and try to correct possible mistakes in the next repetition. For training purposes, suggest performing Canon II exercises with no music at all, so that the sound of steps would imitate the rhythm.

Now, perform the exercise by numbers, and sing the song at the same time. Sing the first and the second verse altogether. Notice, group "four" will finish the exercise and return to the initial line with several bars left before the song is over. Therefore, everyone should continue singing standing in place until the end of the second verse. Repeat the exercise several times in a single lesson, switching roles (numbers.)

Now do the following: perform the exercise in the same order as the last version; when all players of group "four" are back in line and for the final four bars of the music, perform the sequence one more time altogether moving downstage as a straight line. At the end of this last sequence, do not make the turn; jump forward instead and land on both feet, concluding the exercise in a straight line. Notice, there is one bar of music left after company "four" returns to the line; all of you would have to sing this bar standing in a spot so that you continue forward with the last two lines.

Now, perform the exercise by numbers; each numbered group should begin moving and singing the song independently; sing only when you perform your sequences and stop singing when you return to the line. Then continue the exercise altogether (singing and moving) and perform one sequence forward. Perform the last jump forward and stop indicating the end of the exercise. When singing different parts of the song, as in Canon I exercise, try to control your voice so you can hear everybody, and everyone can hear you.

Methodological guidelines: As different modifications are involved in performing various roles (numbers,) every participant must experience each of these roles.

The task to finish the exercise with the jump forward would surely present a challenge, as by now, turning about-face already became habitual. This variation was included in the process intentionally because breaking a routine at will is one of the qualities the actor must own. Repeat the exercise and eliminate this error if it occurs.

Stage 6
Music – "Battle Hymn of the Republic," play solemnly (Appendix 11). The formation is a line.

Imagine that you are a service member of US Marines and ready to stride on Veterans Day parade in Washington. You and your fellow Marines had been practicing the steps and the song for some time in preparation for this special occasion. There are crowds of people along your path in the stands, eager to see you marching. Imagine also that you carry a rifle in your hand, dressed in ceremonial Marine uniform complete with white gloves.

Perform the entire exercise for the duration of one verse, and on the last beat jump, then make the turn, stop and freeze as if you are "standing guard" from this point on.

Begin the skit after a two-bar introduction. Repeat the sequence two times (downstage and then upstage) along with singing. Make sure you maintain a straight line at all times.

Methodological guidelines: Repeat this version of the exercise in several consecutive lessons changing the tempo and some details of given circumstances. Make sure students reflect on the changes in the performance of the task. Drop this version after several repetitions and move to the next one.

Stage 7 (final)

Music – "Oh, Susanna" (see Appendix 2)

Note: Develop this variation of Canon II in a similar order you did in the previous version.

Music for this exercise is traditional, lyrics by Stephen Foster.

> *I came from Alabama*
> *With my banjo on my knee,*
> *I'm going to Louisiana*
> *My true love for to see;*
>
> *O, Susanna,*
> *O, don't you cry for me,*
> *I've come from Alabama*
> *With my banjo on my knee.*

This song is a lot different from "Battle Hymn" in the style, mood, and content. Also, the tempo is faster, which would create additional challenges.

Listen to music, learn the lyrics, and then perform the movement pattern of Canon II exercise first with music only, and finally singing the song and moving simultaneously.

Practice the exercise in different variations similar to those with the music of "Battle Hymn."

Now, perform this variation with all established elements but in the style of a Country Dance. You can improvise the movements of your arms and other parts of your body, but perform the steps as established initially.

Caution, this song has a "pick-up" preceding the first downbeat. This pick-up is only two sixteen-notes. Make sure you begin your first step on the downbeat of the song.

Methodological guidelines: For training purposes, combine Canon II with the music of different styles, for instance, a Tango "Hernando's Hideaway" from the musical "The Pajama Game" by Richard Adler and Jerry Ross. You can suggest performing this pattern with the song "It's a Small World" By Sherman Brothers, etc. The instructor should create new complications and the given circumstances to drill the essential skill called *Singing-Motion Coordination.*

Choose the amount of material, and the assimilation pace always depending on progress. Every group of students is different. This textbook offers enough exercises to fill up the program, even for most advanced students.

Include one of the variations of the Canon II exercise with a surprise task in the Final Lesson.

Exercise 108 "OLD MACDONALD HAD A FARM"

Stage 1
The formation is a crowd.

Music is improvisation 4/4-time in the following pattern:

Listen to this rhythmical pattern several times and notice that the sequence consists of two bars of music. In the first bar, there is a quarter-note followed by two eighth-notes, and another quarter-note followed by another two eighth-notes. The second bar is different. There is a quarter-note followed by two eighth-notes, and then a quarter-note with a dot and an eighth-note. Listen to the pattern again and imitate the rhythm by clapping hands.

Now, execute the rhythm by tapping your feet on the spot. Alternate your feet as usual.

Now, begin with your right foot and perform the pattern along with music by walking forward; repeat it two times in a row. Make sure you hold the quarter with a dot in the second bar long enough to make your last step for the eighth-note. Note, as the number of steps in this pattern is odd, you will begin the second sequence with your left foot. Practice the exercise several times until it presents no problems.

Now, begin with your right foot and perform the sequence twice, walking backward.

Stage 2

Music is improvisation 4/4-time, first in plain quarter-chords, later jazzy style.

Begin with your right foot and perform the exercise moving forward. Repeat the sequence two times then stop and do the exercise two times, moving backward.

Perform the exercise two times forward and then two times backward without a pause.

Repeat the exercise, but this time, the accompanist would play only quarter-notes.

Perform the exercise one more time. The music will be a syncopated jazz improvisation in 4/4-time; you still must perform the initial rhythmical pattern.

Methodological guidelines: For drill-purpose frequently change the tempo and the style of music and finally allow the speed to fluctuate during the performance of the exercise.

Stage 3
Music is the same, as in Stage 1 of this exercise.

Stand in place and count quarters while the accompanist plays the rhythmical pattern. Remember, there are eight quarters in two bars of music, so you have to count aloud from one to eight.

Now, begin with your right foot and walk forward in the pattern established previously. Count quarters from one to eight aloud at the same time. With "five," execute the last forward step and perform the rest of the pattern moving backward. Execute this new variation for the duration of one sequence and stop.

Repeat this exercise and begin the pattern with your left foot. As previously, make your last step forward on count "five," and perform the rest of the pattern moving backward.

Perform the sequence moving forward and repeat it four times; from this point on, walk in the new manner only, which is again -- for the first five counts (not steps) move forward and for the rest of the sequence move backward. Do not forget to alternate feet at all times, so every sequence you would begin with another foot. Repeat the exercise without counting the quarters.

Now, reverse the exercise. Face upstage, begin with your right foot and move backward until count "five" and then continue and perform the rest of the sequence moving forward. Repeat the exercise four times in a single lesson.

Stage 4
Music – "Old Macdonald Had a Farm" (see Appendix 12)

The formation is a crowd.

Listen to the music several times. Now, begin with your right foot and perform the last version of Stage 3 four times moving forward, then backward with the music.

Repeat the exercise and walk backward first, and then forward.

Learn the lyrics of this traditional children's song:

> *Old Macdonald had a farm, E-I-E-I-O*
> *And on his farm, he had a cow, E-I-E-I-O*
> *With a "moo-moo" here and a "moo-moo" there*
> *Here a "moo" there a "moo,"*
> *Everywhere a "moo-moo."*
> *Old Macdonald had a farm, E-I-E-I-O.*
> *Old Macdonald had a farm, E-I-E-I-O*
> *And on his farm, he had a pig, E-I-E-I-O*
> *With an "oink-oink" here and an "oink-oink" there*
> *Here an "oink" there an "oink,"*
> *Everywhere an "oink-oink."*
> *Old Macdonald had a farm, E-I-E-I-O.*

Stand in place and sing the song along with the music.

Now, perform the exercise moving forward first, then backward, and sing the song simultaneously. Repeat the exercise for the duration of one verse and stop pulling feet together with the last beat of the music.

Repeat the exercise and move backward first, then forward. Make sure you finish the task with your feet together. Stay motionless for a few moments.

With every repetition, vary the lyrics by introducing a new animal in the text (chick, duck, horse, etc.)

Methodological guidelines: At a certain point in the training, surprise the students by changing the direction of moving in the course of the exercise. That would help to drill the *Awareness* and *Attention*. Also, for training purposes, suggest a particular animal just before the moment comes to mention it in the song.

Stage 5 (Final)

Stand in place, sing the song; when you mention the farm, make a gesture with your right hand towards the "farm" on your right. When you introduce an animal, make a gesture with your left hand towards the corral on your left. Singing the line "with a moo-moo here" gesture first with the right hand and then with the left hand to indicate that the animals are scattered all over the farm. Indicate the line "everywhere a moo-moo" with broad movements of both arms. Repeat the exercise for the duration of two verses to memorize the order of the motions.

Here are some given circumstances for your consideration. Imagine that you are a tour-guide showing the site where famous Old McDonald once had a farm to a group of tourists. The farmhouse is stage right, and the corral is stage left. Your action as a tour-guide could be "to amaze" your tourists.

Perform the exercise moving forward, and then backward, sing the song and act according to the given circumstances and the action established previously. Try to justify the sudden change in the direction of moving with the help of your imagination.

Repeat the exercise in reverse, and move backward first, and then forward.

Methodological guidelines: Practice the final stage of the exercise in several consecutive classes. Introduce a new task or a unique circumstance with every repetition. Create new or different circumstances and actions for this short sketch. For instance, a real estate broker is trying to sell the farm to a family, etc. If you happen to have guests in your classroom, ask the students to sell the farm to these real people, instead of imaginary buyers.

Exercise 109 "DO-RE-MI"

Stage 1
Music is improvisation 2/4-time, clear chords, moderate tempo, stress the first beat in each bar.
The formation is a crowd.

The exercise consists of four_parts; each part takes four bars of the music.

The beginning position is squatting down, feet and knees together, palms placed on the floor.

Part 1, on the first bar stand up feet together; for the remaining three bars, walk forward beginning with your right foot in quarter-notes and take six steps. Pull your feet together with the last step. Count quarters aloud from "one" to "eight" and perform it once without the music.

Count quarters, do the exercise in time with the music, and memorize the pattern.

Part 2 and Part 3 are identical. Begin with your right foot and make a small step sideways to the right, then pull your left foot next to the right; now repeat the same steps to the left. Execute all these steps in half-notes.

Repeat this pattern four times for the duration of the next eight bars of music (four bars – Part 2 and four bars – Part 3). Perform the exercise first without music, but counting quarter, and then repeat it one more time with the music.

Now, perform Part 1, 2, and 3 in succession. Stop, turn about-face, and repeat the combination.

Part 4 is also four bars long. Begin with your right foot, walk forward in quarter-notes and make two steps forward, then one step in front and across the left foot, and then one step backward with your left foot and finally, pull your right foot next to the left. Notice, all together that would make five steps. Now swiftly squat down, put your knees together, and put the palms on the floor. In other words, get back to the beginning position for the sixth quarter. Stay in this position for the remaining two quarters. Perform this pattern first without music, count quarters aloud instead, and then repeat Part 4 along with the music and try to memorize the pattern.

Now, assemble the entire exercise – repeat the four parts in succession and try to make all the transitions smooth. Remember, each art takes four bars of 2/4-time music or eight quarters. Practice the exercise several times and try to coordinate your movements with those of the company.

Methodological guidelines: Offer this exercise in the last quarter of the semester, as it requires a high level of motor coordination. We recommend going over each part separately before trying to put them together. An excellent technique to employ is to make students count quarters aloud along with the movements. Drop the counting after everyone in the group distributes the choreography correctly. Avoid a demonstration, even if you have to repeat the explanation several times.

Try to get this stage of exercise accomplished in one lesson. Offer this stage of the exercise in the next class, before moving any further with it.

Stage 2
Music and Formation are the same as in Stage 1.

The beginning position is squatting down, palms on the floor.

Go over Stage 1 of the exercise. Remember, you must stand up for the first bar, and then walk forward with your right foot. Now repeat the exercise two times in a row. It means that after you finish the first sequence and squat down, wait for the end of music (skip two quarters), and then repeat the sequence.

Now, there are small adjustments to the pattern you have to make. In Part 1, after you stand up, put your hands on hips; hold them there up until you squat down.

In Part 2 and 3, while making sideways step to the right, turn your right shoulder slightly forward and with a step to the left, turn left shoulder; keep looking forward. Also, bounce slightly with each step.

In Part 4, as before, squat down and place your palms on the floor; lift your head and stare forward.

Perform the exercise two times in a row, trying to adopt all the adjustments described above. Pay special attention to the transition from Part 1 to Part 2, because in Part 1 you move in quarters, whereas in Part 3 in halves.

Stage 3
Music is a song "Do-Re-Mi" from "The Sound of Music" by Rodgers and Hammerstein (see Appendix 13)
The formation is a crowd.

Read and memorize this chorus from the song "Do-Re-Mi."

> *Doe- a deer, a female deer*
> *Ray- a drop of golden sun*
> *Me – a name I call myself*
> *Far- a long, long way to run*
> *Sew- a needle pulling thread*
> *La- a note to follow so*
> *Tea I drink with jam and bread*
> *That will bring us back to do*

Listen to music and notice that the entire piece is thirty-two bars long.

Stand in place and sing the song.

Now, squat down in the beginning position of the exercise and sing the first four lines of the chorus in this position. Starting from the fifth line, *"Sew, a needle pulling thread,"* begin the movement sequence that you learned in previous stages and perform the entire sequence while singing the rest of the song.

Repeat the exercise several times in a single lesson or until all the movements and the transitions executed flawlessly. See that the movement part of the exercise does not affect your singing.

Stage 4 (Final)
Music is the same as in the previous stage.
Formation – a line.

Lineup and count off from right to left in notes on the music scale, i.e., Do, Re, Mi, Fa, Sol, La, Ti. It would break up the company into seven smaller groups – each called after a note in a music scale (group "do," group "re" etc.) Every such group should prepare to sing only the line that represents this group in the song. For instance, a group named "Do" will sing the line *"Doe, a deer, a female deer,"* a group called "Re" will sing the line *"Ray, a drop of golden sun,"* and so forth. The entire company will also sing the last line, *"That will bring us back to Doe."*

Members of each group must begin moving and singing at the same time. Remain in squat position until it is your turn to join in the exercise. Also, every group must perform Part 1, and the entire company performs Part 4 of the exercise altogether by singing the last line, *"That will bring us back to do."* The difference is that each group, after it executes Part 1, will perform sideways steps for as long as it takes until the last line of the song. For instance, the group "Do" would perform Part 1 and then repeat sideways steps six times in a row, group "Re" would have to repeat the pattern five times, and so forth. Incidentally, the group "Si" has no time to do the sideways steps at all. So, after performing Part 1, it would go directly to Part 4 to finish the exercise with all other players.

Repeat the exercise several times to master all the tasks; switch roles after every repetition.

Now, standing in the spot, sing the song in turns as you did in the previous exercise. This time, while one of the groups sings its solo, the rest of the company will sing only a particular note and sustain it for the duration of the line. For example, sing "Do-o-o-o-o," "Re-e-e-e-e," and so forth. Make sure the choir's vocals sound as a background. Perform the exercise with this new adjustment several times; switch roles after each repetition.

Repeat the exercise one more time, and in the last two bars of the song, squat down sequentially like a wave one group at a time. Group "Do" would go down first, followed by the group "Re," and so forth. Remember, you have only three quarters to finish "the wave." Spread the wave evenly.

Perform the exercise several times in several consecutive lessons, switching roles after each repetition.

Methodological guidelines: To switch roles, have a person on the right of the line move all away to the end of the line, then count off again in order of notes.

This exercise is quite complicated and could be a piece of choreography for a musical.

Plan the program so that there will be enough time to bring the final stage of this exercise to a satisfying level. If a new complication creates confusion, you did not practice the previous version long enough. In a case like this, it would be smart to go back to the previous exercise and make sure the players do it flawlessly.

We suggest rehearsing the song standing in place and trying to achieve a precise and harmonious sound, and only then to combine the singing with the movement pattern.

Repeat the exercise in several consecutive lessons and then begin including some given circumstances in it. For example, this is an audition for Broadway production of the musical "The Sound of Music." Everyone has a chance to present only a small portion of the song to attract the casting director's attention. Challenge the students to include their visualizations connected with the line and other circumstances.

Divide the company into groups of seven and have each group perform the exercise separately with the rest of the company watching them. To create additional complications, switch the roles with every new repetition.

Include one of the versions of this exercise in the Test Lesson.

Exercise 110 "MY FAIR LADY"
Music is improvisation 4/4-time in the following pattern:

The formation is a crowd.

Stage 1

Listen to the music and understand that the sequence consists of four bars of music and that the first three bars are identical – one-half-notes followed by two quarter-notes. Only the last bar is different – two half-notes.

Begin with your right foot and walk forward continuously imitating the rhythmical pattern; on the last half-note, make a step, pull your feet together and stop. Repeat the sequence by walking backward; at the end, pull your feet together.

Now, turn left face and imitate the rhythmical pattern moving sideways. Begin with your right foot and make a sideways step; subsequently, move downstage by crossing left foot behind the right; alternate your feet. With the last half-note step, pull your right foot together with the left.

Perform the exercise moving sideways to the left. Accordingly, begin with your left foot and cross the right foot behind the left. Pull your feet together at the end. Remember, when you move sideways to the right, your right foot is always in front of the left and vice versa. Stand in place and count aloud half-notes from "one" to "eight" along with the music.

Now, begin with your right foot, state half-notes, and perform the pattern sideways. This time take the last step to the right on "five," and then perform the rest of the sequence moving sideways to the left; pull your feet together at the end as usual. Repeat the exercise several times or until the new variation comprehended.

Repeat this exercise in reverse – begin moving sideways with your left foot until "five," and then move sideways to the right for the rest of the sequence. Repeat the exercise several times and make sure you position your feet correctly – when moving to the right, cross the left foot behind, when moving to the left, cross your right foot behind left.

And now, repeat the exercise twice: first time begin moving sideways to the right then to the left; when you finish the sequence and pull your feet together, continue the exercise and move sideways to the left then to the right. Repeat this exercise several times in a single lesson and make all the transitions look natural and smooth.

Stage 2
Music is the same, as in the previous stage.

Begin the exercise with your right foot and move forward. Perform the entire sequence once forward. In the end, pull your feet together and make a left-face turn at the same time. Continue and perform the next sequence sideways to the right, and then, without a pause, perform it again to the left; at the end, turn "right face" (facing forward) and simultaneously pull your feet together. Continue starting with the right foot and perform one sequence backward. Pull your feet together with the last step and stop. That is going to be your basic pattern for the next stages of the exercise. Note, you change direction on count "five" only when you walk sideways.

Repeat the entire exercise one more time and try to memorize the choreography.

Listen to the song "Wouldn't it be Loverly" by Frederic Loewe and lyrics by Alan Jay Lerner, from the musical "My Fair Lady" (see Appendix 14.)

> *All I want is a room somewhere,*
> *Far away from the cold night air*
> *With one enormous chair*
> *Oh wouldn't it be loverly?*

Lots of choc'late for me to eat,
Lots of coal makin' lots of heat,
Warm face, warm hands, warm feet
Oh wouldn't it be loverly?
Oh, so loverly sittin' abso-bloomin'lutely still!
I would never budge 'till spring crept over my windowsill.
Someone's head restin' on my knee;
Warm and tender as he (she) can be,
Who takes good care of me
Oh wouldn't it be loverly?
Loverly, Loverly
Loverly, Loverly…

Listen to the song several times and try to memorize the tune and the lyrics.

Sing the first two verses of the song standing in place.

Now, perform the movement pattern learned previously, and sing the first two verses of the song simultaneously. Remember, to perform one sequence moving only forward, then perform next sequence moving sideways to the right/left; now one more sequence move sideways to the left/right. Then move only backward for the last sequence. Do not forget to pull your feet together at the end of every sequence. Repeat the exercise several times in a single lesson and match the steps with the song. Try to achieve the flawless performance of all the elements in the exercise.

Stage 3
Music is the same as in the previous stage.
The formation is the pairs in line with other couples.

The beginning position is standing next to your partner hand in hand (females on the right side of males).

Without singing the song yet, perform the combination of four sequences from Stage 2. Male partners begin with the left foot, females – with the right. Perform the first sequence moving forward downstage, at the end turn facing each other, and pull your feet together. Then, both partners begin with the right foot move sideways to the right/left, thus fulfilling the second sequence. Notice, by doing that, you would separate with your partner. Continue, and together move sideways to the left/right; at the end of this sequence, players get together again and turn facing downstage. Continue, and perform the last sequence holding hands and moving only backward.

Repeat this combination several times until fully mastered.

Music – "Wouldn't it be Loverly," verses 3 and 4.

We continue developing the choreography for this musical skit.

Female partners will perform one sequence forward only and stop with their feet together. After that, male partners will complete the sequence forward once and join in next to a female partner.

Next, both partners perform one sequence moving forward and holding hands; at the end, stop and turn facing each other. Perform this part once and stop.

Put together new elements. Perform the pattern with the music of the third and the fourth verse of the song. Repeat this combination several times to memorize the choreography.

Now, try to put together the entire exercise with music but without singing yet. Repeat the exercise several times or until you feel comfortable and ready to combine the choreography with singing.

Stage 4
Music is the same as in Stage 2.
The formation is the couples standing in line.

Perform Stage 3 of the exercise once without singing, and then include the song in your performance. Attention, both partners sing the first two verses together, beginning from *"Oh so loverly..."* female partners sing solo as they move forward alone; next line, *"I would never..."* male partners sing solo while catching up with the female. The last verse both partners sing together moving forward and performing one sequence; sing the rest of the lines altogether standing in place and facing each other.

Practice the entire exercise several times in a single lesson or until you feel comfortable with all the elements and all transitions.

Repeat the exercise one more time, and this time, after the last verse is over, the male partners sing "loverly" and offer both hands to the female. Then female partners sing "loverly" in reply and put their hands into the hands of males. Holding hands sing "loverly" together last two times, looking into each other's eyes.

Stage 5 (Final)
Music and Formation are the same as in the previous stage.

Imagine the following given circumstances: you are on a date in a city park. The day is warm and sunny. You and your partner stroll along the alleyway are enjoying the good weather and each other's company. In addition to these primary circumstances, create other unique ones and actions that would justify the physical behavior in this exercise. You may also create some specific movements and transitions. For instance, when you are separating for a little while, perhaps you do it to observe an object (a plant, a small animal, a bird, etc.). Perhaps you want to be alone with your thoughts for a while. But soon, you are together again, making plans for your future or declaring your devotion to each other. Take a few minutes, discuss it with your partner before the beginning of the exercise, and make sure you both agree on a particular set of circumstances and the actions. Make sure you use specific circumstances and not general concepts, which might bring you to the overacting or force you to portray emotions. When choosing your actions, avoid verbs expressing feelings, like, "I am confused." Instead, choose an action, "I am guessing whether she/he loves me."

The challenge in the final stage of the exercise is to perform all the actions you choose and consider all the circumstances at the same time as you sing the song. The content of the song should not necessarily coincide with your actions. Besides, the movements that you do are not exactly what you would like to do in these circumstances. However, you must take into account that this is not a scene from the popular musical, but an exercise intended to develop your *Voice and Motion Coordination*. Along with the outer manifestations, there must be an inner dialogue between two people who are perhaps in love with each other. Be truthful in your actions.

Perform the exercise several times with the same set of actions and circumstances and try to find modest adjustments to be sincere.

Methodological guidelines: The work on the Final Stage of the exercise should begin with a repetition of the previous stage. It would be beneficial to ask one or several pairs immediately after the performance about the circumstances they created. Take this advantage to make sure that the circumstances are particular, unlike "I saw something on the ground and decided to get closer." There should be no general visualizations. The students must understand that it is impossible to imagine "something"; one can only imagine a particular object or a subject. As to the actions, the students must understand that to say "I just walk away from my date" does not help to be truthful in a presentation. The actor must know precisely why he or she is making a particular movement and justify this movement by the given circumstances of the skit.

In case a pair is not able to find all the elements for this étude by themselves, help them to make adjustments to the given circumstances and actions. Make sure all the details are logical, consistent, and clear for both partners. In case the students are not able to come up with a complete set of circumstances, offer your assistance.

Repeat this stage of the exercise no more than two or three times in a single lesson, and switch partners occasionally.

Keep the exercise in the "repertoire" and repeat it once or twice in the selected following lessons. Make the exercise a part of the Final Class with some unexpected new circumstances and actions offered for every pair. For instance, an old couple married for fifty years on their golden anniversary declares respect for each other, and the joy they shared. It happens in the presence of their numerous children and grandchildren, etc. Create a different set of circumstances if you wish, but make sure it is logical and related to the lyrics, the music, and the choreography.

CHAPTER TEN

SPECIAL EXERCISES IN BALANCE

Many exercises described in this textbook some way or another help to develop one of the essential faculties - the *Balance* or Equilibrium. This ability happens to be an integral element of various *Habits* and *Skills*. Even simple motions like slow-paced walk, or body rotation would look awkward without proficient balance. Moreover, when it comes to specific stunts in acrobatics, stage falls, and stage combat, well-developed *Balance* becomes a necessity. The importance of this particular ability is so great that we felt it necessary to present a group of unique exercises in *Balance*. We recommend using the exercises of this chapter in a separate part of a lesson and have the intensity of them gradually increased. However, special exercises in *Balance* should take no more than three to eight minutes in a single lesson.

The process of cultivating the body regarding the balance is a two-way avenue: while acquiring certain habits and skills, one improves equilibrium involuntarily; on the other hand, by expressly developing the balance, one increases the quality of Habits and Skills.

To be able to improve the balance consciously, one should become familiar with the mechanics of it. The delicate organs which control our balance are located in the innermost part of the ear or the *inner ear*. The skull bones correctly protect these organs. They collectively call the vestibular (or balance) organ, and it is about the size of a quarter. This inner ear consists of a maze of tubes filled with fluid to different levels and positioned at different angles. The three hollow tubes are directly related to balance. Floating on the liquid are very tiny particles of *calcium*. The tube itself contains millions of microscopic hairs that stick out and are in contact with the liquid and calcium.

When the head tilts front, back, or sideways, the calcium granules push against the hairs and bend them in a different direction. It sends off rapid messages to the brain, which immediately sends out instructions to the muscles to adjust the body's position.

There are several gymnastic apparatuses specially designed to exercise the balance. Among them, a device called Swedish Bench invented in the Nineteenth Century and transformed into a Balance Beam later. Swedish Bench used to be a standard accessory of every gymnasium and exercise room, including those intended for future actors training. Unfortunately, you cannot find them anymore in theater departments and schools.

The exercises in balance often called the exercises "on reduced support." The following is a collection of exercises specially selected and developed for the Essential Stage Movement program. These exercises intended to be performed on the floor. An effective amalgamation of physical and artistic elements makes these exercises most appropriate for a stage movement program. We recommend executing a diverse group of these exercises in as many lessons as possible for five to eight minutes in a single lesson.

Exercise 111 "THE GOALKEEPER"
Music is improvisation 4/4-time, every 1st quarter stressed.
The formation for this exercise is a crowd.

The beginning position is standing feet apart, hands free.

Imagine that you are a goalkeeper practicing on a soccer field. The players pitch balls into your box, and you are trying to catch, or at least to repel the attack. Trying to score, the players send shots in different places and various levels, so with every new pitch, you would end in a different position. Most likely, you would not be able to catch all the balls. You would redirect some of them, miss others, and let some pass. After each action, you ought to lend necessarily on one foot and freeze.

Jump to the right for the first quarter of music and try to catch the ball. Land on your right foot, freeze and stay in this position for the rest of the bar (for three quarters.) Next, repeat the same action in the opposite direction.

Repeat the exercise for the duration of eight or sixteen bars of the music.

Methodological guidelines: Ensure that the students remain motionless during the pause and encourage them to take extreme poses. The justification for such behavior could be that a local newspaper photographer is on the field, taking the pictures to publish.

Note: Along with *Balance,* this exercise also develops *Strength, Amplitude of movement,* and *Velocity.*

Exercise 112 THE HERON
Music is improvisation ¾-time, slow waltz.
Formation -- a crowd.

Figure 22

The beginning position – stand on your half-bend right leg, use hands to place your left foot on the top of your right thigh, spinal column straight, and hands free (see Figure 22).

Perform exercise "The Fish" (see Exercise 154) staying in this position; do it with both hands for the duration of sixteen bars of the music. Then stop, reverse the position of your legs and perform "The Fish" for another sixteen bars.

Methodological guidelines: In the following lessons, make the students switch the position of legs without stopping and losing the tempo-rhythm.

Offer this exercise around the time when exercises for *Expressive Hand* already introduced. This way, you can combine "The Heron" with basic hand exercises and later move to the more complicated ones described in Chapter 12. Also, combine it with simple exercises in movement coordination from Chapter 7. The instructor should continuously remind the students to relax the muscles not involved in maintaining the balance.

Exercise 113 "THE BARRIER GATE"
Music is improvisation 4/4-time, legato, and adagio.
Formation -- a crowd.

First version

Figure 23a

The beginning position is standing feet together, arms extended upward, palms facing each other (see Figure 23a).

Imagine yourself being a garage Barrier. One of your legs would function as an "operator/stand," while another leg, together with your upper body and arms, would function as an "arm" of the barrier. Staying on your right foot only, gradually tilt the "arm" of the gate to a horizontal position by the end of the bar (see Figure 23b). Take four quarters for this action. For the second part of the exercise, gradually return to the beginning position. Now, repeat the exercise standing on the left foot. Make sure your arms, upper body, and one of the legs form a straight line. The supporting leg must also be straight. Repeat the exercise four times on each foot.

Figure 23b

Second version

The Beginning position for this version of the exercise is different: stand on your right foot and bring your left leg, the torso, and the arms in the horizontal position, i.e., your gate is "closed." Alternate your feet after each sequence. Now, the first half of the routine would be opening the gate, the second --closing it.

Perform the exercise "Barrier Gate" this time as a sketch. Here are the given circumstances: you are working as a barrier gate at a public garage. Besides, you happened to be a car connoisseur who likes fancy cars and detests the ordinary ones. Perform the mastered pattern and improvise the kinds of vehicles that are passing by when you open the "gate." You must visualize every passing car: model, color, condition, etc. You are free to turn your head in any direction if you have to. Also, depending on your preferences, you can vary the speed the "gate" opens or closes. However, open and close it within one bar of the music.

Repeat the exercise four times on each foot.

Methodological guidelines: we suggest introducing the second version of the exercise later into the semester after the concept of given circumstances already presented. The instructor should eliminate any attempt to "play" a character. Instead, have the students concentrate on the given circumstances. They might be different with every repetition of the exercise. For instance, the Barrier Gate is a nitpicker who works on a highway as a tollgate. Some of the passing cars are clean, and the others are dirty.

However, no matter what kind of given circumstances, this exercise is in the program mainly to develop the *Balance*.

Figure 24

Exercise 114 "THE JUMPING JACK"
Music is improvisation 4/4-time with stress in the third quarter.
Formation -- a circle.

First version

The beginning position is standing on your right foot, with the knee of your left leg pulled by your hands to the chest (see Figure 24).
For the first and second quarters, let your body gradually tilt forward so that you start losing the balance. With the third (stressed) quarter of a bar, jump forward on your right foot and quickly restore the balance. Stand still for the rest of the bar. Continue

moving in a circle and repeat the sequence eight times. Stop, switch feet positions, and repeat the exercise eight times on your left foot.

Second version

Repeat the exercise "The Jumping Jack" but move backward instead. For that, you would have to tilt your body back, lose the balance, jump on the third, and restore the balance in the fourth quarter. Repeat the exercise eight times standing on your right foot, then switch feet positions and repeat it eight more times.

Third version

Combine the first and the second versions, and switch feet after every four bars of music.

Fourth version

Perform the First version and jump forward with a turn about face (180°) and over your left shoulder at the same time. Repeat the exercise eight times on your right foot, then stop, switch the feet positions, and repeat it eight times.

Fifth version

Perform the First version and jump forward, but this time make a 360° turn over your left shoulder, land facing the same direction that you started the exercise. Repeat the exercise eight times on your right foot, then stop, switch feet positions, and repeat it eight more times on your left foot.

Sixth version

Perform the Forth version of the exercise. After you turn and land, continue and perform the Second version. Keep moving in the circle. Repeat the exercise eight times.

Methodological guidelines: Watch that the exercise performed strictly in time with the music. It would help to drill the *Tempo-rhythm of Physical Act* and *Rhythmicity* along with the *Balance*. If you wish to make this exercise even more challenging, suggest that students recite a logical text while performing the jumps and turns.

Exercise 115 "THE TIGHTROPE"
Music is improvisation ¾-time, tempo moderato.
Formation -- a crowd.

The beginning position is standing, both feet in a straight line -- right foot in front of the left, the toe touching heel, hands extended out to the sides, look forward -- a typical position of a tightrope walker.

Move forward in time with the music in the following pattern: slide your right foot forward as far as you can for two bars of music, then, for another two bars, slide left foot forward to the beginning position. Make sure your feet are always in a straight line. Do not look down! Keep your body erect and look forward. Repeat the pattern three times, and then for the next four bars of music, turn gradually about-face over your left shoulder. Make this turn on the heels of your feet.

Now, repeat the exercise with your left foot in front. In the end, turn over your right shoulder, and stop. Maintain the balance during the entire exercise.

Methodological guidelines: After practicing this exercise in several consecutive lessons, suggest that each student holds an imaginary "pole" for balance. Hands should support the "pole" with palms turned upward. The pattern remains the same – three sequences forward, then the about-turn.

The students often begin "playing" a tightrope walker mimicking the sudden loss of balance, etc. Prevent this, as it takes the attention away from actually maintaining the balance. Repeat the exercise four times in a single lesson.

Exercise 116 KNEE TO FOREHEAD
Music is improvisation 4/4-time, slow chords.

Formation -- a crowd.

The beginning position is the regular stance.

With both hands grab and lift your left knee, simultaneously tilt your head forward until you touch your knee with your forehead. Take four quarters of music for this. For the next four quarters, gradually return the leg to the beginning position. Repeat the exercise and lift your right knee. Keep breathing rhythmically through the routine. Continue alternating your legs and repeat the exercise eight times.

Methodological guidelines: Repeat this exercise in several consecutive lessons and then offer the students to recite multiplication tables for "two" while performing the actions.

Exercise 117 *"THE* CORK OPENER"
Music is improvisation ¾-time, moderate tempo.
Formation --a circle or a crowd.

Figure 25

The beginning position is standing on the right foot with the left leg across your right, in front of it, the toe touching the floor, body weight is on your right leg, hands on the back of your head, elbows to the sides, and the chin slightly up (see Figure 25).

Before the music begins, get up on your toes and, on the first four bars, gradually turn over the left shoulder for a complete 360°. Sink all the way slowly down at the same time. You must perform these two different movements simultaneously to imitate the motion of a cork opener. Do not move your feet and support your body on your toes only. For the next four bars, gradually rotate in the opposite direction, lifting your body at the same time to the beginning position. Keep your upper body upright at all times. Inhale while going down and exhale on your way up.

Perform the exercise four times, then stop, switch your legs position, and repeat it four more times in reverse.

Note: This is an excellent exercise to develop your *Balance*; it also drills *Stamina* and *Muscle Strength*.

Exercise 118 STRETCHING ARM AND LEG
Music is improvisation 4/4-time, slow tempo.
Formation -- a crowd.

The beginning position is standing on your knees, the palms of your hands on the floor, so your body looks like a bench; drop your spinal column slightly down; raise your head and stare forward (see Figure 5, Page 84).

First Version
Gradually extend your right arm forward and simultaneously stretch your left leg backward. Take four quarters of music for that. For the next four quarters, slowly return to the beginning position. Continue the exercise in reverse and this time stretch your left arm and right leg. Make sure you maintain the balance at all times and keep your head up, staring forward.
Repeat the exercise four times, switching knee positions.

Second version
Perform this exercise and gradually stretch your right arm and right leg simultaneously, and then continue and stretch your left arm and left leg. Repeat the exercise eight times, alternating the right and left sides. Maintain your torso in a horizontal position at all times. Breathe rhythmically and continually.

Methodological guidelines: To drill the *Balance* further with this exercise, increase the speed of the performance. For instance, perform one sequence in two beats instead of four.

Note: This exercise develops *Balance, Strength, Flexibility,* and *Stamina.*

Exercise 119 SIT NEXT TO KNEES
Music is improvisation 4/4-time, moderate tempo.
Formation -- a crowd.

Figure 26a

The beginning position is standing on your knees, placed shoulder-width, feet stretched, upper body upright (do not sit on your heels), arms free, chin slightly up (see Figure 26a).

Gradually sit all away down on the floor to the right (see Figure 26b), and keep the position of your knees. To preserve the balance, extend your arms in the opposite direction. Take four quarters of music to complete this portion of the exercise. Then gradually lift your body off the floor to the beginning position. "Gradually" is the keyword in this exercise. Repeat the pattern and sit down to the left. Repeat the entire exercise four to six times.

Figure 26b

Methodological guidelines: It is common for some students to fall on a side when trying to sit down. Our experience demonstrates that after several repetitions in consecutive lessons, the students eventually would find adjustments to perform it correctly. The main thing is to discover how to keep the balance in these unusual positions of the body. Another error is a player jerking his body to get off the floor. Though it is natural for humans to find the most comfortable way in physical actions instinctively, poised movement in this exercise is crucial.

After the primary form of this exercise mastered, have the students perform it in a more rapid tempo. When the sufficient level achieved by the entire group, introduce a complication -- have the students put the hands on the back of the neck and to keep them there. That would make the exercise even more efficient.

Further complications might include a simultaneous recital of a sensible text.

Note: This is an excellent exercise to develop *Flexibility, Strength,* and *Balance.*

Figure 27a

Exercise 120 STEP OVER CHAIR
Music is improvisation 4/4-time, moderate tempo.
Formation -- a crowd.

The beginning position is the regular stance. Stand on the side of the chair with your left flank towards the seat (see Figure 27a).

Figure 27b

Continuously step over the seat of the chair with your left foot without touching it (see Figure 27b). Take four quarters of music to do this. For the next four quarters, gradually bring your right foot over the chair and place it next to the left. Continue the exercise and step over the seat of the chair with your right foot first, and then with your left back to the beginning position. Maintain the balance at all times. Repeat the entire exercise four times.

Methodological guidance: You can make the exercise even more complicated by introducing some given circumstances. For instance, hold an imaginary bowl full of hot soup in your hands while stepping over the chair, etc.

Offer the exercises in *Balance* in a separate segment of a lesson and perform them one following another. Combine two or three exercises in a single lesson and alternate the patterns and tempos. However, if a lesson contains other activities that partially drill *Balance*, exclude the special *Balance* segment.

Exercise 121 SEMI-SQUATS ON ONE FOOT
Music is improvisation ¾-time, moderate tempo.

Formation -- a crowd.

The beginning position is -- stand feet together, hands extended out to the sides.

Figure 28a

Figure 28b

First variation

Gradually, half-bend your right leg and, simultaneously, slide stretched left foot forward (see Figure 28a). Take the first two bars of music for that. For the next two bars, gradually lift the left leg (toe still pointed) to a horizontal position (see Figure 28b). Maintain the supporting leg half-bended. For the next two bars, lower your foot on the floor, and finally, stand up and pull your feet together for the last two bars. Now, repeat the exercise in reverse, switching the legs. Alternate feet and repeat the exercise four to six times.

Note: For better balance, turn the supporting foot a bit out.

Second variation

Repeat the exercise, but this time, when lifting your leg, move it sideways instead of forward. Still, keep your upper body upright, and the working leg stretched. Repeat the exercise in several consecutive lessons.

Third variation

Slide and then lift your extended left leg backward, then return to the beginning position. Continue and switch legs.

Now, repeat the exercise and perform all three versions – once forward, once sideways, and one time backward. Execute this with the left leg first, and then with the right.

Note, the exercises described in this chapter specifically designed to improve the *Balance*, and we recommend including several of them in each lesson as a separate segment. However, they also can be a part of a warm-up group of exercises.

Balance is an essential quality for the actor. Drill it regularly and continuously using various exercises of this program. Even after the student concludes basic training, *Balance* must be one of the qualities to perfect perpetually in Dance class, in Combat class and any other physical exercise class.

CHAPTER ELEVEN

EXERCISES IN ACROBATICS

Exercises in acrobatics are included in the Essential Stage Movement program to improve critical faculties and habits such as Balance, Coordination, Velocity, Muscle control, and Suppleness yet further. However, the most important role of acrobatic exercises in our program is to develop *Courage* and *Decisiveness*. These qualities are of great importance to the actor. Nevertheless, many acting and stage movement programs consistently ignore such due to underestimation and the shortage of suitable exercises. Acrobatics perhaps is the only effective tool to develop Courage and Decisiveness in a class setting.

We would like to emphasize that the objective of the following group of exercises is not to master specific acrobatic skills. Frankly, the majority of actors would never have to perform a forward roll or a cartwheel in their entire professional life. However, the faculties and habits improved and newly acquired by way of acrobatic exercises would come useful and would stay with the actor for a long time. Besides, in case a student would have an opportunity to engage in other forms of movement training later, such as Stage Combat or Stage Fencing, the skills acquired in Acrobatics would turn out to be most beneficial.

Nevertheless, such faculties as *Courage and Decisiveness* might become very functional on a variety of professional life levels. It is too apparent that hesitation and indecisiveness are not very good friends of an actor. Incidentally, these are not desirable in acrobatics as well. Once an acrobat initiates a move to perform a stunt, changing the mind in progress can be painful. Acrobat understands this very soon in the process. In his book "Actor's Prepares," K. Stanislavsky said, "Acrobatics is wanted by the actor more for internal, then external application; it is wanted for most intense moments of emotional passion, and for creative inspiration. I need acrobatics to produce decisiveness in you."[1]

In our profession, *Courage* might be a desirable habit for the actor to make a decision on or off stage. For instance, a resolve to take on a challenging role or a decision to choose an action that looks too extreme requires courage from a person. Decisiveness, being a psycho-physical quality in itself, is beneficial for any activity, though developed with the help of the physical exercises.

Most of the exercises in this chapter are widely known and familiar to many students. Some of them might have never tried them before, but most likely, they had a chance to see them more than once performed by other people. That alone perhaps excludes the necessity of demonstration. The instructor must explain the techniques and the common mistakes ahead of execution in detail to eliminate any possible harm or injuries. However, if a student has any physical deficiency, either from birth or due to previous injury or surgery, he/she has to consult a physician and notify the instructor about it before committing to these activities.

Have the students perform all exercises in this chapter on a gym mat. Besides the sense of security, it gives the student real protection from any harm, in case he or she makes a mistake.

We also believe it to be essential for the future actor to perform some of these exercises in combination with music and speech. Moreover, the program would require some techniques performed in different rhythms, tempos, and within limited spaces. We recommend later in the process to offer performing some exercises on the floor. It would develop *Courage and Decisiveness* further. However, do it with all the precautions, and only after you are confident in the already acquired skills. Practicing acrobatic stunts on the bare floor might be a good idea also in anticipation of performing these techniques on stage, where, as a rule, there is no padding.

Exercises presented in this chapter in actuality are elementary. Our experience shows that intricate acrobatic techniques are not practical in a stage movement program. It takes a long time to learn them, and most likely, the players would never have a chance to use them on stage. It is factual that basic techniques serve our purpose just as good as the spectacular stunts.

The truth is, when developing *Courage and Decisiveness*, an acrobatic stunt loses its drilling quality soon after the student realizes there is no danger or pain. At this point, transform the stunt into something more challenging, more complicated. Another method is to combine this stunt with other elements, such as reciting a logical text or even singing. It would compel the student to distribute the attention, thus help to develop automatism of the physical action.

Another reason why we recommend the exercises of this chapter is -- they serve as preparatory exercises for *Stage Falls, Stage Lifts,* and *Hand-to-Hand Combat.*

We recommend introducing acrobatics in the second half of the semester and coordinate several exercises in a separate episode of the lesson.

Methodological guidelines: We highly advise engaging in acrobatic exercises only after a warm-up. If acrobatics were just a part of regular stage movement class, the warm-up completed at the beginning of the lesson would be adequate.

For the acrobatics segment of the lesson, set the gym mats in such a fashion, that they constitute a truck where a number of students standing in line and facing this truck could practice simultaneously. If the group is too large, break it into two or three smaller groups so that each student can comfortably fit on this line of mats. Make sure your mats are six feet by three feet in size minimum and at least two inches thick.

Exercise 122 ROCK ON YOUR BACK
Music is improvisation ¾-time, slow tempo.
Formation -- a line in front of mats

The beginning position is -- lye on your back on the mat, legs straight, and arms along your body resting on the mat.

Figure 29

Stage 1

Bend your knees, then grasp them with both hands and gently pull up to your chest. At the same time, simultaneously lift your head and bring your chin up to the chest. Tuck your body together tightly, so only a portion of small of your back touches the mat (see Figure 29). Take two bars of music for that.

For the next two bars, bring your knees and your body back to the beginning position. Repeat exercise four times, trying to gather your body as tight as possible.

*

Next, repeat the exercise, but tuck in swiftly, on the downbeat of the first bar, then keep this position for the second bar's duration, and then open up rapidly on the downbeat of the third bar relax for the fourth bar of music. Repeat exercise at least four times.

Stage 2

The beginning position is lying on your back with your legs and head tucked to the chest.

Gently rock your body back and forth several times. When moving backward, ensure touching the mat with the back of your neck; when rocking forward, touch the mat with your heels. Then open up, lie on your back, and relax. Repeat this exercise several times without music.

*

Music is the same, as in the previous stage.

Now, get in the same folded position and rock in time with the music. Rock forward and then backward on the downbeat of each bar of music. Make sure your swinging movements are increasingly stronger. Then, force your body on the third bar hard enough to finish in the squat position. If you succeed, stand up on your feet in the fourth bar.

Lie down and try it again. After two or three attempts, you should be able to conclude the exercise by standing up in the fourth bar of music. Notice, you have to gain enough force to get up on your feet. We call this force a momentum. We will use this term more than once because the momentum plays a critical role in acrobatics and other extraordinary movements.

Stage 3

The beginning position is stand with your back to the mat, feet slightly apart.

Begin the exercise by gradually bending your knees and sitting down on the mat. Then lie down on your back and tuck in legs and head. Allow your body to roll back, so the back of your neck touches the mat. Take four bars of music for that. Do not help yourself in any of these movements with your hands. Use the momentum you gain in the first part and propel your body forward for the next four bars. Stand up on your feet and finish the exercise. Repeat the entire sequence four times.

Find the exact amount of momentum that would help you get up on your feet, but make sure it will not cause you to lose the balance or even fall forward.

Note: This exercise works best when you keep your body tucked, so it resembles a ball.

Methodological guidelines: Include this exercise in several consecutive lessons until all the students execute it with ease and maintain a sound balance. That was a preparatory exercise for the *Forward roll.*

Figure 30b

Exercise 123 ROLL ONTO RIGHT KNEE

Formation -- a line in front of mats

Figure 30a

The beginning position is lie on your back, bend your right leg and place the knee on the mat and the foot under the knee of your straight left leg. Hands resting on the mat along your body (see Figure 30a).

Figure 30c

Preserving the position of your legs, lift both of them gradually up and continue moving legs until they are above your chest. This action would force your buttocks to lift off the mat (see Figure 30b). Now, still maintaining the position of your legs drive them vigorously forward and down. Use the *momentum* and roll your body up off the mat. Find yourself standing on your right knee with your left foot set firmly on the floor. Make sure your left leg bent (see Figure 30c). Take your time to examine your new position. It must be a balanced and comfortable pose with your weight spread evenly between your right knee and left foot. If you keep your legs in the initial position, the shin of your right leg will end up at the right angle to your left foot. Keep upper body upright, and hands free next to your body. Correct the errors, then stand up and relax. Repeat the exercise several times and make sure your final position is as described above.

Note: A common mistake is to point your right knee up instead of sideways in the process. That would make you finish the roll with your shin parallel to the left foot. This pose is unstable and awkward. Remember, in the final pose, your right knee must rest on the mat and open to the side.

*

Music is improvisation ¾-time with a stress on the 1st beat of the third bar.

The beginning position is the final position of the previous exercise -- stand on your right knee extended to the side, and the left foot (see Figure 30c).

Perform the exercise as follows: softly lie down on your back and bring your legs above your body in the same position as in the previous exercise. Complete the action for the first two bars of the music. Remember to keep your right foot under your straight left leg. Then, on the downbeat of the next bar, drive your legs forward/down and finish the sequence in the beginning position. Relax for the last bar of music. Perform the exercise four times in a row.

Practice the exercise in several consecutive lessons and change the tempo slightly with each repetition.

*

Now, begin this exercise from standing position. Gently squat down, lie on your back, and lift your legs for two bars of music. For the next two bars, force your legs forward/down and use the *momentum to* stand all away up on your feet over your right knee. To perform this action effectively, give your body a bit stronger *momentum.*

Repeat this final stage of the exercise in several consecutive lessons until you perform it with ease and strictly in sync with the music.

Exercise 124 SHOULDER STAND
Formation -- a line in front of mats.

Figure 31

The beginning position is lying down on your back, arms alongside your body, palms resting on the mat.

Lift your straight legs gradually and continue moving them until you touch the floor behind your head with the toes. Now, keeping your elbows on the mat, bend your arms, and place the palms under your lower back. Gradually and slowly extend your legs up to a vertical position with toes pointed. Align your legs with the body (see Figure 31). Stay in the Shoulder Stand position for four to five seconds, then bend your right leg and position the knee jut to the side and the foot under your straight left leg. It must be the same position that you used in Exercise 123. Now, quickly remove your hands. Your body and legs, obeying the gravity, would begin to fall forward. Use *momentum* to get up on your feet over the right knee precisely as in the final version of the previous exercise. Perform the exercise several times in a row.

Repeat the exercise in several consecutive lessons without music, working at your own pace.

Music is improvisation 4/4-time, slow chords.
The beginning position is the same as above.

Now, perform Shoulder Stand with the music and distribute the actions as follows: lift your legs and get right into Shoulder Stand for two quarters of music. Stay in this position for the next two quarters. Then, for the next two quarters bend your right leg, place it under left leg, and roll forward on your right knee and left foot (do not stand up!) Finally, for the last two quarters lie down on your back, stretch both legs and relax in the beginning position. Repeat the exercise four times in a row then practice it in several following lessons.

Methodological guidelines: By the time you offer this exercise to the students, make sure you are confident in the group's readiness for this kind of act. Some students might have difficulties keeping their bodies and legs aligned in the Shoulder Stand. The reason could be fear, lack of coordination, or strength deficiency. Encourage the students to overcome the fear as there is no danger involved in this particular exercise, mainly when performed on the mat.

In some cases, the instructor should physically assist a student by helping to lift legs to a proper position until they aligned with the body. As to other shortcomings, they should not be the case if all the previous exercises of our program managed properly from the beginning. The instructor should be persistent with the acrobatic exercises from the start, making sure that every student completes any stunt in the end.

Exercise 125 "THE BRIDGE" (Backbend)
Music is improvisation ¾-time.
Formation -- a line in front of mats.

The beginning position is lying down on your back. Place your feet apart as close as possible to your buttocks, lift your arms, and place palms of your hands on the mat on each side of your head (see Figure 32a).

Figure 32a

Gradually lift your body, arching it as you do, and continue until your legs and arms are straight; simultaneously tilt your head backward until you see the ground (see Figure 32b). Stay in this position for three to four seconds, and then gradually lie down and return to the beginning position. Relax your muscles for several seconds and repeat the exercise.

Now repeat this exercise four times successively with the music. Take two bars to arch up, for the next two bars stay in the position, then, for the next two bars, lie down, and relax for the last two bars. Do not hold your breath -- inhale for two bars and exhale for another two bars of music.

Figure 32b

Repeat this exercise in the following lessons in different combinations with other acrobatic techniques.

Exercise 126 THE FROG
Some call this exercise "squat hand balance."

The beginning position is: squat down and put your palms on the mat in front of you about a foot apart, so the arms half-bent. Mount your right leg and then left leg on the top of your bent arms just above the elbows but keep the toes on the ground yet. Make sure your head tilted back in this strange pose. Establish the balance, then push off slightly with your toes and try to lift them off the ground. You would find yourself balancing the entire body on your hands only. Stay in this position for several seconds, then land back on your toes, take the legs off your arms and stand up.

Repeat the exercise several times and each time try to stay in this position a bit longer.

*

Now, repeat the exercise, and when you get in the balancing position, try to rock gently forward and backward. Notice, maintaining the balance on your hands is similar to balancing your body standing on your feet. For example, when you feel like you lose balance and begin to lean forward, you will press on toes. In the "frog" position if you lose balance and start leaning forward, press on your fingers. When tilting off balance backward, strain the heels of your hands.

*

Get into the "frog" position and gently rotate your body first to the right, then to the left. Try to lift and lower your head and observe how it affects your balance. Get back on your feet and relax.

*

Now, get into the "frog" position and walk forward; begin with your right hand, take a small step, and then continue with the left hand. Make several steps and get up on your feet.

*

Now, try to jump forward with both hands while in the "frog" position. For that, you would have to lean slightly forward until you begin slipping off balance, and then make a jump forward and regain the balance.

Now, while in the "frog" position, try to rock gently in all directions, then walk forward and then jump.

Repeat this exercise in several consecutive lessons in different variations and combinations.

Note: This exercise prepares you for some acrobatic techniques described in this chapter. Besides, it is an excellent exercise in *Balance* by itself.

Exercise 127 FORWARD ROLL

Stage 1

The beginning position: squat down and put your palms on the edge of the mat, fingers together, and pointed forward. Position your bent knees between your arms, tilt your head down, and press

Figure 33a

 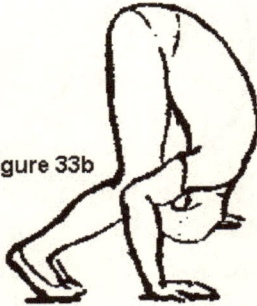 

Figure 33b

Figure 33c

your chin against the chest, curve your back (see Figure 33a). Now, slightly bend your elbows and drive the tucked body to turn over your head. For that, you would have to push off your feet (see Figure 33b). Doing this, you would provide your body with *momentum* to perform the roll forward. However, be careful, you must touch the mat first with the back of your neck and the shoulder blades (see Figure 33c). Your tucked-in-tightly body and momentum would make you roll over your curved back (see Figure 33d, e.) Another adjustment in this stunt is to grab your shins immediately after your hands are off the ground. If the momentum were strong enough, you would find yourself on your feet (see Figure 33f).

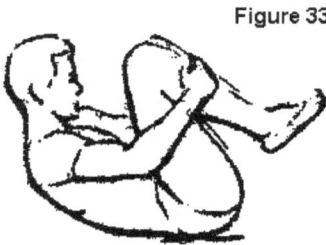

Figure 33d

The most important thing to understand about this (and other acrobatic stunts) action is -- do not change your mind once you launched it! The next important thing to remember is to keep your body tucked up to the end when you find yourself on your feet in a squat

Figure 33e

Figure 33f

position. Once you are there, gain the balance and stand up. If the momentum was weak, or you opened up early, you would finish the forward roll sitting on the mat. Do not worry about it, and correct this error in the next repetition.

Repeat the exercise several times without the music at your own pace. Adjust the momentum that sets your body in motion to roll. Little by little, you will find the ultimate position and the right momentum to perform the Forward Roll properly. Remember, you must land on the mat with the back of your neck first. Never fall on your head! To adhere to this rule, you must keep your chin touching your chest.

You can help yourself maintain the body in a tucked position by grasping your knees with your arms as soon as your arms are free. Maintain your own pace and repeat the exercise several times or until you succeed with this new stunt.

Methodological guidelines: A common mistake in executing the forward roll is to land first on the crown of the head. It is not just wrong but also dangerous. You should continuously remind to those making this error to press the chin to the chest. Occasionally, the instructor should get down on his knee, gently press the student's head down to the chest, and remove it just before the back of the student's neck touches the ground. Ensure everyone keeps the body tacked in the process of the stunt, and relax the muscles only when the momentum expires.

Have the players repeat this stage of exercise several times in a single lesson and practice it in the following lessons until everyone feels completely comfortable performing this stunt.

Stage 2
Music is improvisation ¾-time, slow waltz.
Formation – a line.

The beginning position is standing in front of the mat, feet together.

Begin the forward roll from standing up position. Try to perform the following actions as one continuous action: squat down, put your palms down knees between arms, and execute the forward roll as in Stage 1. Begin accumulating the momentum from the first movement. Remember, you have to finish forward roll and stand on your feet, body upright. Repeat the exercise four times or until it performed flawlessly.

*

Now, execute two consecutive forward rolls with music. Perform your first roll, stand up on your feet for two bars of music, and then make an about-turn over your right shoulder on the third bar. Pause and prepare for your next roll for the fourth bar of music. Then repeat the stunt once more and stop.

Practice this exercise in the following lessons until you feel comfortable with it.

Note: From this point on, when practicing the forward roll, always perform it from standing up position.

Stage 3 (Final)
Music is the same as above.
Formation – a line.

Perform three forward rolls from standing up position in the same manner as in the previous stage of the exercise and take four bars of the music for each roll and the turn.

*

Repeat the exercise and take only two bars of the music for the roll and the turn. Notice, the pace of your rolls will double. Repeat the exercise several times in a single lesson.

Methodological guidelines: While performing two or three rolls, some students might feel slightly dizzy. Usually, students communicate it one way or another. The instructor should reassure them that it is reasonable, so they would stop worrying about it. The body reacts this way because it is an unusual activity. This ailment would fade away after practicing it in several consecutive classes.

However, the ultimate goal is to perform the forward roll quickly. That would reduce pressure on the parts of the body that are in contact with the ground. The pressure is much stronger when the roll performed slowly. The requirement to complete the forward roll in sync with music helps to develop *Decisiveness* further. The student, carried away with the task, has little time for hesitation or assessment of a possible risk. Nevertheless, to avoid potential harm and even injuries, the instructor should make sure the previous stages of the exercise grasped and performed safely before moving to the next stage.

Exercise 128 ROLL FORWARD, STAND UP OVER KNEE

Formation – a line in front of mats

Repeat the final stage of the previous exercise several times. Now, independently repeat the final stage of Exercise 123, and then merge these two exercises in one combination. From standing up position roll forward, finish the roll standing on your right knee. Remember to put your legs in the proper position while rolling to finish the roll on your right knee. Repeat the exercise several times at your own pace to get accustomed to the combination.

*

Next, repeat the exercise and apply a stronger momentum this time, enabling you to get up on your feet over the right knee. Notice, finishing a forward roll using this technique is more convenient than getting up on both feet.

*

Music is improvisation ¾-time, moderate tempo.

Now perform three consecutive forward rolls over your right knee. After each roll, turn about the right shoulder and then complete your next roll. After the last roll, make another turn and stop. Take two bars of music for a roll and another two bars for the turn.

Repeat the exercise, trying to finish every roll with your feet on the edge of the mat.

Exercise 129 THREE CONSECUTIVE FORWARD ROLLS

Set three mats in a path.
Formation – a lineup at the beginning of the path.
Music is Appendix 29, slow and clear.

The first player in the lineup would perform three consecutive forward rolls in the same direction and stand up after each roll. Take two bars of music to execute the roll and the stand-up. After the last roll, the player should stand up, step aside from the mat and move to the end of the lineup.

Attention, every next student will begin the combination only after the previous one completed all three rolls. Continue practicing until everyone performs the exercise.

*

Now, repeat this exercise, and instead of standing up after each roll, perform all three forward rolls continuously. It is more convenient to finish each roll on both feet in a squat position. Use the momentum from the prior roll to execute the next one. Get up on your feet and step out after concluding the last roll. Perform all your movements in time with the music and take only one bar of music for each roll. On the fourth bar, get up and step aside. Match the overturn (the most energetic movement) precisely with the downbeat of the bar. The next student should begin this combination only after the previous one finished all three rolls.

Methodological guidelines: To make this exercise extra stimulating and also to add the excitement, have every next student begin the exercise after only two rolls executed by the previous. Later, make every next student begin the exercise after the previous student performed only one roll. In this scenario, everyone depends on partners to perform this chain of rolls smoothly and safely. However, the instructor should oversee the process and stop the exercise immediately if any unsafe situation occurs.

Note: In addition to *Awareness of Space, Awareness of Time, Balance,* and *Coordination,* this exercise develops a very important for actor quality, the interdependence of partners on stage.

Exercise 130 FORWARD ROLL IN SLOW MOTION
The music -- improvisation ¾-time, slow waltz.

Perform a forward roll and take two bars of music to roll and get on your knee. Then take another two bars to stand up and make an about-turn. Caution, you would have to do all the movements a bit slower to unite them with the music. That is quite tricky to accomplish as the gravity forces you to finish the roll sooner than you want to. To adjust the speed of your motions, one should restrain certain groups of muscles. Practice the slow-motion roll in several following lessons and try to achieve continuous and smooth transitions. You would find that performing forward roll in slow motion is just as challenging as the fast execution.

Methodological guidelines: Explain that in everyday life, people rarely change tempos and rhythms of physical behavior drastically. Everyone owns his or her tempo-rhythm. However, the reality of stage demands a much larger variety, perhaps because the time in performance is often compressed, requiring frequent adjustments to new tempo rhythm. The actor's body should react to such changes instantaneously. We believe that the introduction of unusual (and at times inconvenient) tempos and rhythms into the exercises helps to develop a well-rounded actor.

Exercise 131 THREE FORWARD ROLLS, CHANGE DIRECTION

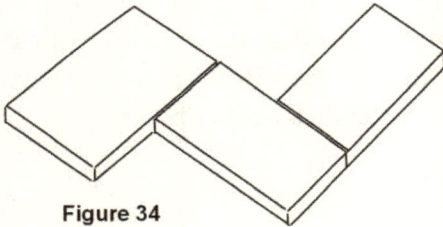

Figure 34

Set three mats in a zigzag figure at the right angle to each other (see Figure 34).

Formation – a lineup at the beginning of the path.
Music is a slow waltz.

Perform three forward rolls on the zigzag-shaped chain of mats. Execute one forward roll and stand up over the right knee, turn right face, and execute the second roll in the same manner. Then turn left face and perform your last roll. Stand up and move to the end of the lineup. Take two bars of music for the roll and the turn. The next person in lineup begins the exercise only after the previous one finished all three rolls.

*

Now, repeat the exercise in a chain, so everyone joins in after only one forward roll performed by a previous player. Attention, strict compliance with the rhythm of the music would prevent you from a collision with partners.

Note: This exercise would train *Awareness of Space,* among other abilities. It is beneficial to perform it in a swift tempo to make the drill noteworthy.

Exercise 132 FORWARD ROLL, SHOULDER STAND

Formation – a line in front of the path of mats.
The beginning position is standing facing the mat.

As the title states, this exercise is a combination of two stunts. Perform a forward roll getting up over the right knee, then squat down, sit on the mat, and lie down on your back. Execute the last three motions continuously in one extended movement. Now, using the momentum from the previous action, lift your legs and get into a shoulder stand position. Stay in this pose for a little while, then bend your right leg, drive your legs forward, and stand up over your right knee to conclude this combination. All the elements are familiar to you by now, so put them together in the order described above.

*

Music is improvisation ¾-time.

Now, perform this combination in sync with the music in the following order:
Roll forward and stand up – 2 bars, lie down and get into shoulder stand position – 2 bars, pause in shoulder stand position – 2 bars, bend the knee and stand up – 2 bars.

Repeat the exercise twice in a row – after the first sequence, make an about-turn, and repeat it in the opposite direction.

Exercise 133 "FROG," FORWARD ROLL

This exercise is yet another combination of two stunts. First, get in a "frog" position (see Exercise 126). Rock gently forward/backward, then tilt your chin to the chest and purposely lose the balance; roll it over your head and perform the forward roll. Use the momentum and stand up over your right knee.

Repeat the exercise several times in a single lesson, and practice it in the following lessons.

Exercise 134 BACKWARD ROLL

Methodological guidelines: Offer the backward roll only towards the end of the semester and after the forward roll performed flawlessly and in different combinations by everyone in the group. The main concept of this stunt is similar to that of a forward roll. One must execute it swiftly to avoid pressure on parts of the body that touch the ground. Make sure the players keep their bodies compacted while rolling.

Preliminary Exercise

The beginning position is - squat down with your back to the mat, tuck your body in tightly - press knees to the chest, place the chin on your chest, clasp knees with your arms (See Figure 33f).

Now, maintaining this position let your body fall backward, so you land on your buttocks first. Use the momentum and roll on your back then on the shoulder blades. Remain folded and rock forward and backward several times, increasing the momentum with each movement. After two or three such swings, push forward a bit harder and finish the exercise on your feet in a squat position.

*

Now, repeat the exercise and let yourself rock backward only once, and on your swing forward, make an effort and get to the beginning position. Repeat exercise several times, and each time retreat to the squat position. Retain the balance each time you finish the routine.

Main Exercise

The secret of a successful backward roll is in the momentum, which you must give to your body; the more robust the momentum, the lesser the pressure on your back and neck. A strong momentum provides you with faster speed and reduces the time your body interacts with the ground.

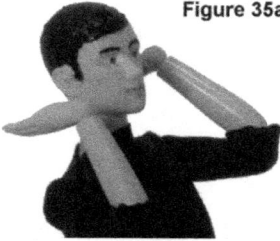

Figure 35a

Here is an additional technique to ease this pressure: the moment your back contacts the mat, take your hands off the legs, and place the palms on the ground next to your head (see Figure 35a and b). The moment you feel the pressure on your palms, push off with your hands to take the weight off your neck. However, keep your legs tucked. With a sound momentum and the support of your hands, you would overturn your body to find yourself standing on your feet in a squat position. Remember, press your chin to the chest, and do not turn your head left or right. If you follow all the rules described in this paragraph, your neck and the head would hardly touch the ground.

Figure 35b

Use the preliminary exercise to rock on your spine forward and backward, increasing the momentum with each sway. Do it two or three times and then suddenly force your body back, quickly place your palms on the mat next to the head, and overturn to complete the backward roll. Repeat the exercise several times and adjust the force to regain the balance at the end.

*

The beginning position is squat down with your back to the mat, put your palms on the floor, lean on your hands. Perform the backward roll from this position by driving your body backward on the mat. Remember, you must first touch the mat with your buttocks and then tuck in. To avoid "killing" the momentum, try to land your buttocks as close as possible to the heels of your feet. Repeat this exercise several times until you succeed and then continue practicing it in the following lessons.

*

Perform the backward roll from standing position. Begin it by vigorously squatting down and use this action to gain momentum. Continue the roll in the same way that you know from the previous stage and stand up at the end of the roll. Notice, if you execute all the adjustments correctly, this stunt lasts all but a few seconds.

Repeat the exercise several times in a single lesson, and continue practicing until it turns light and natural for you. Only after that, incorporate the backward roll in combinations with other acrobatic stunts and techniques.

Exercise 135 TWO BACKWARD ROLLS
Music is improvisation ¾-time, tempo moderato.

The beginning position is regular stand with back to the mat.
Perform a backward roll from standing position and get up on your feet, turn about-face over the right shoulder. Perform the second backward roll, stand up, make another turn about the right shoulder, and stop. Take two bars of music for a roll and two bars for a turn. Repeat exercise two or three times.

*

Practice the next exercise on the path of mats.
Perform two consecutive backward rolls. After the first roll, stand up and then perform the second roll in the same direction. Try to maintain the tempo-rhythm. Repeat the exercise two or three times.

Exercise 136 THREE BACKWARD ROLLS
Music – see Appendix 30.
Formation – a line.

The beginning position is stand with your back to the mat.

Repeat the previous exercise and perform three backward rolls on one mat. Make a turn over the right shoulder after each roll. Accomplish continuous and smooth transitions between the rolls.

Notice, the music is 4/4-time, thus perform a backward roll and the turn within one bar of the music. Take the interval at the end of the bar (duration of one eighth) to prepare for the next roll.

Repeat the exercise one more time, but this time make the about-turn over *the left* shoulder after each roll.

Perform this exercise several times in the following lessons, along with other combinations that include a backward roll.

Exercise 137 ROLL FORWARD, ROLL BACKWARD, ROLL
            FORWARD
Music is improvisation ¾-time, tempo moderate.

The beginning position is stand facing the mat.

Perform this exercise on a single mat. Roll forward and stand up over your right knee. From this position, roll backward and stand up. Then roll forward again and get up over the right knee. Execute this simple combination and take two bars of the music to perform a roll, and two bars to stand up and prepare for the next roll.

*

Next, perform the exercise and take only one bar of music for a roll and one to stand up.

Repeat both versions of this exercise several times in a single lesson, as well as in the following lessons.

Exercise 138 ROLL BACKWARD, ROLL FORWARD, ROLL
            BACKWARD

The beginning position is stand with your back to the mat.

Perform the rolls in the order described in the title. Begin each roll from standing up position. Repeat the exercise several times in a single lesson to achieve continuity and grace in your performance.

Next, repeat the exercise and increase the momentum. Use extra force to jump up at the end of each roll. Land on your feet and then perform the next roll. Repeat exercise several times in a single lesson.

To make sure you can control the momentum, perform the sequence twice -- in the first repetition jump up after each roll, and in the second, do not jump at all.

Exercise 139 ROLL BACKWARD, ROLL FORWARD, SHOULDER
       STAND
Music is improvisation 4/4-time, plain chords.

Begin from standing up position, perform a backward roll, and stand up, spread the movements for the whole bar of music. Roll forward and stand up for the second bar. Roll on your back and get into Shoulder Stand for the next bar of music. Bend the right knee and stand up over your knee for the last bar of the music. Notice, at this point in acrobatics training, it is essential that you perform all the composition elements in sync with the music. Consider this as a particular choreography.

Repeat the exercise three or four times in each of the several consecutive lessons.

Methodological guidelines: In this combination and the similar ones, the instructor should offer to execute the same exercise simultaneously by several students and demand synchronization.

Exercise 140 ROLL FORWARD, LIE DOWN ON BACK, STAND UP

The beginning position is squat down in front of the mat.
Perform a forward roll, but instead of rolling all away and finishing it on your feet, open up your body just as soon as you touch

the ground with your shoulder blades. This maneuver would "kill" the momentum. Then, before your legs unfold on the mat, quickly bend your right leg and place the right foot under the left leg (the same position you take when performing a forward roll over your knee). The final pose is lying on the mat with both legs on the ground. Now lift your legs off the floor (maintaining the position) then thrust your legs forward/down to get up on your feet over your right knee. Repeat this combination several times without music, at your own pace.

*

Music is improvisation ¾-time.

Repeat the exercise with the music. Take two bars to roll forward and unfold your legs on the mat, take another two bars to relax in this position, and then take two more bars of the music to lift your legs, and, finally, for two bars, get up on your feet. Practice the exercise several times in a single lesson.

*

Repeat the exercise twice -- after the first repetition, make an about-turn over your right shoulder and perform the task second time.

Methodological guidelines: Advise your students to be alert when unfolding their bodies because the left leg, driven by the momentum, might strike the ground with undesirable strength and even hurt the heel. Ask them to lower the leg intentionally instead of letting it fall.

By this time in the program, one should expect the students to acquire the habit of keeping their bodies tucked-in when performing a forward roll. However, this particular exercise demands just the opposite – the opening of the body in the process of the stunt. It might present some problems in the beginning. Our experience in working with this exercise shows that the students tend to keep the body folded a bit longer than needed for this particular task. As a result, the shoulders would move up off the ground. Prompt the students to relax the upper body immediately after the shoulder blades touch the ground. Nevertheless, be patient, as it would take some time to do it right.

Exercise 141 ROLL FORWARD, FINISH ON BACK, "BRIDGE," STAND UP

Perform a forward roll and finish on your back as in the previous exercise. Put your hands and feet in the position for a backbend. Perform the backbend and stay in the place for 2–3 seconds, then lie down on your back and bend the right leg in preparation for getting up. Lift your legs and then drive them forward to stand up over the right knee. Repeat the exercise several times without music to set the order of the techniques in your memory.

*

Music is improvisation ¾-time.

Repeat the exercise with the music. Take two bars to roll forward and lie on your back. Relax on the ground for the next two bars, and then take two bars to prepare your hands and feet for the backbend. Next, take two bars to lift your body into a backbend position, and maintain this position for the next two bars. Then, for two bars, lie down on your back and bend the right leg at the same time. For the next two bars, lift your legs and stand up on your feet for the last two bars. Notice, the entire combination would take sixteen bars of music. Make sure you match all the motions with the music precisely as described above. Repeat exercise two or three times in a single lesson.

*

Now, perform the same combination of acts and transitions in the same order as before, and pack it all into eight bars of music. Make sure all the actions are yet graceful and smooth.

Methodological guidelines: Explain that the combinations of acrobatic stunts offered in this chapter represent the training of a paramount quality called *the Economy of Movement*. To perform a stunt safely and gracefully, the player must get rid of non-essential moves. Incidentally, it is also the goal of an actor in a production.

Also, it is essential to find a way to perform any movement or any technique with minimal effort. That would save the player a lot of energy so much needed for long hours of rehearsals, exhaustive performances, or tedious work on the set of a film or TV production. Moreover, the *laconic* movements are typically most expressive movements. The physical behavior becomes artistic when it is void of unnecessary movement. Only purposeful actions on stage are inspiring.

This notion, however, applies to all physical actions on stage, and not only to acrobatic exercises. It is imperative to concentrate the students' attention on this aspect of physical performance from the early stages of the Essential Stage Movement program. That would give enough time to develop an adequate habit of removing all non-essential movements from a purposeful physical activity.

Exercise 142 ROLL FORWARD, ROLL BACKWARD

The following is a combination of two stunts already known to you. However, one element included in the exercise is new. It is a backward roll from the standing-on-right-knee position. Practice the following combination first without music.

The beginning position is stand facing the mat.
Perform a forward roll and finish it standing on your right knee. Now, from this position, perform a backward roll. For that, you would have to accumulate momentum with fewer possibilities at hand. So, lean your upper body slightly forward and curve your back, and then drive upper body back to attain enough force for your backward roll. Repeat the combination several times and discover the necessary adjustments.

*

Music is improvisation ¾-time.

Repeat the combination and take two bars of music for your forward roll, and another two bars for the backward roll. Repeat the combination several times in a single lesson and practice it in the following lessons.

Exercise 143 FORWARD ROLL OVER ONE HAND

The beginning position is stand in front and two feet away of the mat, place your feet shoulder-width.

Figure 36

Make a decisive step forward with the right foot, bend over, and place the palm of your right hand on the mat directly in front of your body with the hand turned inward. Using the momentum from this action, perform a forward roll, as usual (see Figure 36). The apparent difference is that you would have to support your body with one hand instead of both. Note, while performing the forward roll, keep your left arm out to the side. It would be a miscalculation to put it behind your back because then your tumbling body would press on it. Finish the roll with your right knee touching the ground, stop, and stand up. Repeat exercise several times.

*

Music is improvisation ¾-time.
The beginning position is the same.

Perform three forward rolls on one mat using the right hand only. After each roll, get up over your right knee and turn about over the right shoulder, then take two steps backward. Perform each roll for two bars of music, and take another two bars to get up, turn and step back. The entire combination would take twelve bars of music.

*

Repeat the exercise, and this time take only six bars of music to perform the entire combination. It means you would have to move twice faster. However, preserve all the elements of the stunt.

*

Perform the same combination and roll over your left hand. Remember, you must step forward with your left foot and position the palm directly in front of your body with your hand turned in.

Practice this exercise in several consecutive lessons, alternating hands.

Exercise 144 SIDEWAYS ROLL

The beginning position – squat down with your right flank toward the mat, arch your back, and clasp the legs with your hands, press your chin to the chest.

Drive the tucked body onto the mat with enough force to overturn and finish the sideways roll on your feet, and in the squat position. To get enough momentum, shift the weight of your body on the left foot just before the drive. Repeat the exercise several times and strive to finish it on both feet, and not on the shins of your legs.

*

Perform the stunt in reverse -- begin it with your left flank toward the mat, roll, and finish it in a squat position standing on both feet. Repeat the exercise several times in a single lesson.

*

Music is improvisation ¾-time.
Arrange mats in a path.

Perform four consecutive sideways rolls in time with the music. Take one bar of music for each roll and stand up only after you finish all four rolls. Perform the exercise once over your right shoulder, then stop, turn around, and do it again.

Methodological guidelines: As in previous exercises, the students need to find the intensity of momentum to perform the sideways roll properly and to finish it on both feet. It is easier to finish it on the shins, which many students would tend to do. Point out to this error and insist on the correct execution of this stunt.

Another common mistake to avoid when executing several rolls in a row is the tendency to roll away from the path of mats. That would indicate the inability to control the actions. Encourage the students to make an effort and keep moving in one straight line.

Exercise 145 DIVING ROLL

Note: we do not recommend attempting the diving roll before both forward and backward roll mastered and performed in all various combinations. We suggest mounting two mats (one on the top of another) when attempting the diving roll. Only after the technique is perceived and performed safely can the students return to practice this stunt on a single layer mat.

Stage 1

Place one mat on top of another. Put an obstacle such as a backpack or a medium-sized stuffed animal on the edge of the mat.

Figure 37
Figure 37
Figure 37

The beginning position is standing in front of the mat.

Your task is to jump over the obstacle by pushing off with both feet (see Figure 37). Land on the palms of your hands and use the momentum accumulated by the jump to roll over your head the same way you do when performing a forward roll. After you touch the

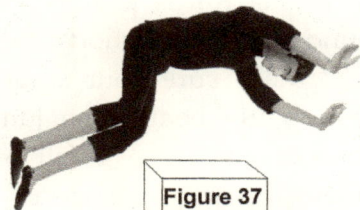

ground, roll over you curved back. Finish the roll and get up over the right knee.

Attention, do not lock your elbows! Instead, have your elbows slightly bent. These tactics would help you to soften the landing on the back of your neck. Remember to quickly tuck your body in, as you do when performing a regular forward roll.

The skill acquired in the execution of the forward roll would help you with this stunt, as the difference between the two is the way you provide your body with a momentum. In a forward roll, it is vigorous bending over, in a diving roll - jumping. Repeat the exercise several times in a single lesson and continue practicing it in the following lessons.

Methodological guidelines: Consider this stunt as a substantial step in developing *Courage and Decisiveness*. It will take several repetitions to get the proper results. Yet, expect all kinds of excuses in the beginning. Most of them would arise simply to cover fear. Be persistent and encourage the students to complete the task. However, make sure every player in your group by this time is proficient in a regular forward roll. Some students would try to perform the diving roll by quickly bending over and placing hands on the mat instead of jumping over the obstacle. Make it clear that the correct performance of a diving roll is to have both -- the feet and the hands, off the ground for at least a short time.

Make sure your students understand why they must keep arms slightly bent when jumping over the obstacle. Locking the elbows might cause a fall on the back, which is an undesirable incident. Having experienced this can discourage the student from further attempts.

The *obstacle* used in this exercise is a simple psychological trick to help the student overcome fear. Position it low enough so no players can brush it. Remove the ploy only after everyone performs the roll successfully once or twice.

To drill the *Courage and Decisiveness* further, use a simple rod or a thin pole and hold it in front of a student to jump over it.

However, consider the individual abilities of each student and change the height accordingly. In other words, combine a challenge with common sense. Raise the bar slightly for those who successfully conquered a lower height. Expect some students even asking to raise the bar trying to contest each other and their fears. Repeat this exercise several times in a single lesson.

Stage 3

Begin the exercise five to six steps away from the mats. Run forward a few steps, jump, land on both feet in front of the mat, and then push off with both feet to execute the diving roll. All the above actions are to gain momentum for the forward roll. Notice, this momentum would come considerably stronger. Adjust the force by increasing the length of your dive. Mark the spot where you begin the jump and, with every repetition, land a bit further away. That would make you fly up in the air a bit longer, also reduce the momentum.

Practice the Diving Roll in several consecutive classes or until you achieve a perfect performance.

Methodological guidelines: The transition from executing a diving roll from standing position to the "run-and-jump" technique is a significant step forward in developing *Courage and Decisiveness*, as the increase in the force is substantial. If the students are not ready for this, keep practicing diving roll in different combinations. Be careful, too strong of momentum sometimes could cause an uncontrollable jerk of the player's head. Advise the students and suggest pressing the chin to the chest purposely during the roll.

Diving roll is beneficial in the stage movement program not only because it improves *Decisiveness and Courage* but also because this stunt would come handy in *Stage Falls* and *Hand-to-Hand Combat*. Therefore, students need to master it. However, there is a certain risk involved in the process. Remind always the basic rules -- to land first on the back of the neck and the shoulder blades, to alleviate the fall by bending arms, and to arch the back the moment the shoulder blades touch the ground. Practice the stunt on a pile of mats until you are sure the technique mastered. Only after that, offer to perform the stunt on a single mat.

When using a rod for an obstacle, be reasonable, and avoid pressing the students. In the process of a diving roll, you may lower the rod to accommodate the execution. Moreover, always remember -- you are not preparing them for athletic competition.

Exercise 146 DIVING ROLL, FORWARD ROLL

Set three mats in a path.
Formation – a lineup.

The beginning position is normal posture. The first person in the lineup positioned eight to ten feet away from the mat.

Exercise one student at a time; run forward and perform a diving roll over the rod held by the instructor (or one of the students). Employ the momentum gained from the diving roll, perform a regular forward roll. Get up on your feet over the right knee and incur the balance. Finish the diving roll on both feet and the regular roll by standing over the right knee. Step to the side to make space for the next student.

Methodological guidelines: Adjust the height of the bar for each student according to the capability and lower it in the process of the stunt in case a student obviously failing the height. Repeat the exercise with musical accompaniment and have the students match their movements with the rhythm of the music.

After the skill is secure, we suggest performing this exercise in a chain, i.e., one student following another immediately, but maintaining a safe distance. The accompanist should play a cheerful musical piece as a background for this performance, a kind of a circus "*Charee-Varie.*"[2]

The attempt to perform it in improvisation style and unified tempo-rhythm would create in your students an ambiance of joy and a feeling of an event.

Exercise 147 DIVING ROLL, FORWARD ROLL, SHOULDER STAND

Formation – a line.

Practice this combination of stunts on a single mat.

Integrate your skills acquired in this chapter and perform the combination in the order described in the title.

After the diving roll, turn about over the right shoulder, after the forward roll stand up over the right knee, and then lie down on your back, use the momentum and raise your legs for the Shoulder Stand. Pause, then bend your right leg with the knee out to the side, drive your legs forward and stand up over the knee. Perform this combination without music, but try to establish your tempo-rhythm and maintain it throughout the combination.

Repeat the combination several times and vary your tempo-rhythm with every repetition. Once a tempo-rhythm established, maintain it until the end of the combination.

Remember, your attempts to perform a series of stunts or a combination of techniques without music are most beneficial for you because creating your tempo-rhythm would help you gradually develop a critical skill – the *Tempo-Rhythm of Physical Act*.

Exercise 148 "CARTWHEEL"

Formation – a line, each player faces individual mat.

The beginning position – stand with your right (or left, depending on preference) shoulder toward the mat with arms up and apart.

Lift your right (or left) leg off

Figure 38

the ground and tilt your upper body slightly backward. It serves as a preparatory movement to attain momentum for your *Cartwheel*. Think of your arms and legs as spokes of a wheel (see Figure 38).

Now, energetically bend at the waist sideways and down and drive your body in the direction of the mat. As you begin the rotation, place right (or left) foot on the ground first, then the palm of your hand, and then, as you shift the weight of your body further, place on the ground the palm of another hand, and finally your left (or right) foot. Notice, your arms and legs touch the ground alternately. In process, keep your legs and arms locked and your body aligned at all times during this stunt. That would prevent you from collapsing in case the momentum was not strong enough. Finish the stunt in the beginning position.

Repeat the exercise several times until confident. Keep practicing the Cartwheel in the following lessons until you perform it effortlessly. Increase/decrease the momentum to find the right force to make your body turn over supporting arms and legs.

Methodological guidelines: Initial attempts to perform the Cartwheel usually end up with the student bending at hips and landing on both feet. It is all right since a student learns that this stunt is quite safe, and it is hardly possible to hurt yourself by doing it. Explain that as long as one maintains arms and legs locked, there is little chance for one to fall.

However, to complete the Cartwheel, a player must integrate three things: first, to arrange all the "spokes" of the wheel in one line, second, to tilt the head back and third, to maintain the body along with legs and arms in one flat surface (plane).

Again, as it is with most acrobatic techniques, one must provide the body with enough momentum to complete the stunt. A weak momentum would cause the body to halt in the middle of the rotation. It might even collapse if the hands are bent. Also, bending at hips would hinder the momentum and prevent the legs from landing in the straight line.

Some students would probably perform *Cartwheel* properly from the start, as many learn this stunt as children from adults or friends. You would have to coach those who never tried it before. Only after everyone in class performs this stunt safely, offer to execute it with another leading foot. It would present an additional challenge and further train *Courage and Decisiveness* in students.

Use both versions later in the program in combination with other techniques to drill these skills.

Figure 39

Exercise 149 "HANDSTAND"

Stage 1

Note: Moving forward by *skipping* is a natural motion, usually acquired by humans in early childhood. This mode of moving is familiar to you from Chapter 4 (Opening and Concluding Exercises) of this program. You should remember that *skipping* helps to jump. It is because this action assists in gaining momentum.

Now you can use this technique in acrobatics as a distinctive supply of momentum for many stunts. That was one of the reasons we introduced skipping early in the program.

Run forward several steps, then push off with left foot and jump. Repeat this several times, and when you are up in the air, lift your right knee and bring both arms up above your head. Now, repeat the preliminary exercise, then lend on your left foot first, and then immediately on your right foot, and stop. Realize that you just performed a single skip. Notice also, swinging your arms up helps you to jump higher, thus to gain stronger momentum. Repeat the exercise several times at your own pace.

Stage 2
Set the mats on the floor next to a wall.

The beginning position – stand on the mat facing the wall, at a distance of two to three steps away.

Lift your right leg, then make a forceful step forward, bend over, and immediately place palms on the mat about one foot away from the wall. Use the momentum gained by this motion to kick your legs up. Your feet would touch the wall, with your body curved. This pose is the *Handstand* (See Figure 39). The wall prevents you from falling. However, keep your arms locked. Repeat the exercise several times and find the appropriate force. A weak momentum would prevent you from contacting the wall. If momentum were too strong, your feet would thump the wall. Remember, you must keep your arms locked through the entire stunt. Besides, tilt your head back so you can see the ground.

Repeat the stunt several times in a single lesson and keep practicing it in the following lessons.

Stage 3
Arrange mats on the floor next to a wall.

The beginning position is a regular stance, five to six steps away from the wall.

Perform the *Handstand* and incorporate the *Skipping* technique that you learned in Stage 1 of this exercise.

Run several steps forward, then skip, bend over and place hands on the mat. The momentum would bring your legs up to a *Handstand*. Stay in the position for a few seconds and keep your body arched and head tilted back. Then push slightly off the wall and get your feet down on the mat.

Repeat the exercise several times and attempt to find the right force of the momentum and balance of your *Handstand*.

Methodological guidelines: We find it beneficial to combine the skipping technique with the handstand. Incorporate this skill later in many different stunts and exercises.

Exercise 150 "CARTWHEEL" WITH SKIP

Set a path out of mats placed next to each other.

The beginning position -- stand five to seven steps away from the mat.

In this exercise, combine the cartwheel and a skip. Run forward several steps, and then perform a skip turning your right flank to the mat at the same time. Use the momentum, execute a cartwheel. Keep in mind that the skip would provide you with strong momentum and be prepared to break it in the process to obtain the balance. Notice, it is easier to perform a cartwheel using a skip. Repeat the exercise several times in a single lesson and keep practicing it in the following lessons.

*

Now, using the "run and skip" technique, perform two consecutive cartwheels. Try to perform these two wheels continuously, without a pause. One can achieve this by providing the body with enough momentum.

Methodological guidelines: Use the *Cartwheel* to continually develop *Courage and Decisiveness* by combining several cartwheels, right and left hand cartwheels, and including the stunt in different combinations with other stunts. For many students, it would be challenging for others -- something to defeat. However, do not move to more complex exercises until the previous version performed with confidence and ease by every player.

Exercise 151 CARTWHEEL, FORWARD ROLL
Music is improvisation ¾-time, moderate tempo.
Formation – a line.

Set two or three mats in a path.

The first person in the lineup is standing by the beginning of the path. Perform a cartwheel from standing position, then pull your feet together and turn at the same time in the direction of travel. Continue the combination and execute a forward roll from standing position. Take two bars of music for the cartwheel and another two bars for the roll. Stand up and move to the side, clearing the way for the next person. As the music continues, the next player begins the exercise on the following bar so there would be no pose in the performance.

*

Now, perform the exercise in the same tempo-rhythm but switch your forward roll to a diving roll. Remember, you must execute the diving roll from both feet. Repeat this version several times in a single lesson.

*

Repeat the exercise and have the players follow one another after only two bars of the music, i.e., the next person joins in after the previous completed the cartwheel and starts to roll. Notice, to avoid a collision, each player must strictly keep the tempo-rhythm.

Exercise 152 "HEADSTAND"

Figure 40

Formation – a line in front of mats.
 The beginning position -- squat down facing the mat, palms on the mat shoulder width, fingers pointed forward.

Place your forehead on the mat directly in front of your hands to create a triangle. Lift your buttocks, and position it on the top of this triangle. Stay in the position for several seconds and then return to the beginning position. Repeat the exercise several times and maintain the triangle between your hands and head. Also, make sure you are comfortable in this position.

*

Repeat the exercise, and when you obtain the balance, try to get your toes gently off the ground. Stand up after you succeed. Execute the exercise several times, and with every repetition, try to stay with your feet off the ground a bit longer. Notice, only your hands and the head support your body. Make sure your head touching the mat with the forehead and not with its crown. Also, maintain an equilateral triangle between your hands and head.

*

Repeat the exercise, get your toes off the ground, maintain the balance, and gently bend your knees. When you realize that your entire body is up over the triangle, gradually extend your legs up and get into *the Headstand* position (see Figure 40). Stay in the position several seconds, then bend your legs, lower them to the floor, and stand up. Repeat the exercise several times and practice it in the future to acquire a steady skill.

Methodological guidelines: The key to this stunt is in maintaining the triangle for proper support and balancing the body on the top of it. Make sure the players find how to distribute the body weight evenly between these three points of support. It is an excellent exercise to develop both *Balance* and *Courage*. As soon as the stunt mastered, include it in various combinations of acrobatic stunts and continue drilling a wide array of habits and skills.

Introduce acrobatic stunts one by one into the program, and then make it a segment of every lesson from the middle of the semester and up. This part should take no more than ten to twelve minutes of a single lesson. Remember that the major goal of this training is not a perfect technique. A good mixture of acrobatics and music, acrobatics, and a sense of space, acrobatics and speech, etc. is the way to drill the essential habits and skills. However, the safety of the students must be your major concern.

As soon as a stunt performed accurately, shift the objective to other elements such as artistic techniques. Incorporate them into the exercise or a combination of exercises. Always remember that this training in acrobatics is for actors and not for athletics competition.

However, an entirely and harmoniously executed stunt in production can often become emotionally impressive. In our trade (and in our method, in particular), we use movements willfully to convey a thought and make every effort to avoid using a movement for the sake of demonstration.

Therefore, a simple task of performing a forward roll in time with the music or in any particular style becomes much more valuable for our profession than an athletic performance of it.

However, there is a risk in taking on the acrobatics in stage movement class. Students unprepared psychologically and physically for this kind of training might experience some pain and even injury when challenged with acrobatic stunts. It might discourage a young person to the extent that he/she would never try it again.

The instructor should be very cautious when introducing the acrobatic stunts. It is essential to determine the time to begin the introduction and the doses of elements introduced. Always work with each student individually. One should take the recommendations of this text very seriously and consistently follow all the methodological guidelines to present every exercise accurately and timely.

CHAPTER TWELVE

SPECIAL DEVELOPMENT OF EXPRESSIVE HAND

The development of expressive hands deserves a special place in actor training since the hands play a significant role in communication between people. The essence of human nature, occupation, and profession exposed better through the appearance and movements of hands, then through any other part of the human body. Just like a change in the intonation of speech, the slightest gesture change might alter the nature or content of the action. Look at modern sign language to assume the vividness of gesture.

We can declare with confidence that next to human speech, the gesture has the most vibrant diversity in the history of humanity.

Unfortunately, the importance of hands in communication on stage is much too often underestimated by the actors. A great Jewish-Russian actor Solomon Mikhoels wrote, "Gesture for me is the expression of thought ... The thought is accustomed to going through my fingers. The gesture must act out instead of serving merely as an interpretation of a spoken word."[1]

Sadly enough, "mere interpretation of a spoken word" is what one can observe much too often in theater, particularly in the musical theater. Young actors and even hapless stage directors, who do not know any better, tend to substitute visualizations and thoughts with explanatory gestures. They wholeheartedly believe that this is the theatrical way to deliver the message to the audience.

However, theatrical scholars widely agreed that a gesture helps a great deal of a character's creation. Some even compare the actor's hand with the actor's soul. Nevertheless, there is little concern with the development of the expressive hand in theater education. Moreover, no one had approached this aspect with the Stanislavsky System of actor training in mind. However, the great Stanislavsky maintains that body movements and gestures must express not just the logic of the character, but also all the complexity of the character's feelings and emotions.

Some of the books written in the Nineteenth - beginning of the Twentieth century on this subject, trying to help the actor, had offered ready-to-use sets of gestures. According to these authors, one gesture would express despair, another – a plea, yet another – obedience. Their books filled up with dozens of illustrations of various emotions, so all an aspiring actor had to do, was to practice these gestures in front of the mirror, memorize them, and then use them in a suitable situation on stage. Humorous as it sounds nowadays, the demonstration of a pose or a gesture is still a common practice in theaters and theater schools around the world.

We strongly believe that the tutoring of specific expressive gestures is an unreasonable practice. A genuine expressive gesture must come naturally as a continuation of thought. One can achieve this with hard work in class as a particular part of the development of a well-rounded actor. Gesture ought to emerge naturally in the process of the actor's creative work. However, one must pave the way for the arrival of living gestures that express the individuality of a character and inner image. The actor's gesture becomes expressive only when hands are subservient to the thoughts. One can only achieve such harmonization by reaching a high level of skill. To obtain such skill, one should devote oneself to a systematic and continuing training.

Concentrate the process around one primary goal: to develop the ability to express a precise and exciting action with hands. When gestures on stage are void of logic and lacking in emotionality, they represent nothing and thus are useless, if not damaging.

Exercises in dance and stage fencing are excellent to develop the large movements of arms. They train the flexibility and mobility of shoulders, elbows, and, to some degree, of wrist joints.

However, the exclusive capability of human hands and fingers can reveal the most delicate thoughts and actions. Without adequately flexible and obedient hands, the actor of the Stanislavsky trend would be unable to employ the so-called *Subtext*. This concept is habitually contradictory to the words pronounced, and expressed on stage with gestures. Friedrich Nietzsche once wrote, "Fanatics are picturesque, mankind would rather see gestures than listen to reason."

Considering the importance of training the expressive hand, we dedicated to dedicate an individual chapter in the Essential Stage Movement to attend to this need. However, various exercises in other sections of this book include specific movements for hands. For instance, Chapter 5, Improvement of Rhythmicity, has a group of exercises based on *Conducting*. One of these exercises' objectives is to make the actor's hands act purposefully and willfully to express logic and emotions residing in music.

There are many exercises for hands used by various teachers of specific disciplines to develop flexibility and mobility of joints. The problem is -- most of them are mechanical motions not connected with physical actions. For example, there is a popular notion that juggling might help develop an expressive hand. We would agree that juggling helps to improve quick reaction but not necessarily the expressive hand.

We believe that relying on the occasional training of hands with the help of random exercises would not produce significant results. Only an organized and comprehensive training that employs specially designed exercises can and will stimulate the development of the expressive hand.

The collection of exercises we are offering in this chapter starts with *Simple Motor exercises*. The training continues using *Imaginative exercises* that already incorporate simple physical acts. We conclude it with special *Exercises/Études*, in which a physical action is the main component.

Simple Motor Exercises

Exercises included in this chapter develop flexibility and mobility of wrists and fingers. We pay special attention to the advancement of the left hand. In daily life, the right hand does most of the work, including gestures. It is okay with most people, and they do not even think of that as an inconvenience. However, from the perspective of our profession, we cannot overlook the fact that actors regularly have to use their left hand for the jobs typically executed by the right hand.

Our experience demonstrates that regarding the flexibility of hands, one can achieve significant results with the help of just a few selected exercises. However, one has to do them as often as possible, not only in the stage movement class but also in morning exercises and a warm-up of any kind.

Exercise 153 THE TARDY HAND

Music – slow waltz (see Appendix 15).
Formation – a crowd.

The beginning position is the regular stance.

Gradually lift the right arm to the side and begin the act with your elbow. Then have your forearm and hand follow the elbow. When the upper arm reaches a horizontal position, continue moving only the forearm with hand following it until your hand is in line with the forearm and the upper arm. Take four bars of music to complete all the motions (see Figure 41 a, b, and c.)

Figure 41a

Figure 41b

Figure 41c

For the next four bars of music, gradually let your elbow down with forearm and hand following it. Continue and lower your forearm. Finally, lower your hand and bring your arm to the beginning position. Repeat the exercise with another arm, and then repeat it four to eight times with each arm separately. Make sure all transitions are smooth and continuous.

Notice, your hand finished the motion last, or in other words, it was tardy. That justifies the title of the exercise.

*

Next, perform the exercise and move both arms simultaneously up and down in time with the music. Switch your attention from one arm to another to control the accuracy of movements. Practice this exercise in several consecutive lessons.

*

Repeat the exercise, but move both arms in front of your body. Practice it four to eight times in a single lesson.

*

Now repeat the exercise and move your right arm to the side and left arm in front of your body. Perform this version of the exercise four times, then reverse and repeat four more times in a single lesson.

*

The beginning position – regular stance, left arm extended to the side.

Begin the exercise "The Tardy Hand" with both arms; lift your right arm to the side and simultaneously let your left arm down. Repeat the exercise four times in a single lesson and practice in the following lessons.

Methodological guidelines: After practicing *The Tardy Hand* in numerous lessons, we recommend experimenting with the tempo, making it faster or slower, and reminding the students to maintain fluency in the motions of arms and hands.

Exercise 154 THE FISH
Music – see Appendix 16.

Formation – a crowd.

The beginning position is standing feet together, arms extended forward and slightly bent, palms turned inward facing each other, fingers together (see Figure 42).

Imagine that your forearms are fishes and hands are their tails.

Gradually move your forearms horizontally backward pass the sides of your body, and simultaneously sway your hands (not the forearms!) right-and-left imitating the fishtail movements. In addition to swaying, make your fingers smoothly bend at every single joint. For three bars of music, move your "fishes" backward as far as you can, and on the fourth bar, swiftly return hands to the beginning position. While moving your forearms backward, try to execute as many swaying motions with your hands and fingers as you possibly can. Repeat the exercise four times.

Notice, if you perform the exercise correctly, it would quickly tire out your hands. It is the effect we are after. So, please do not overdo it, instead, repeat the exercise only four times in a single lesson and keep working on hands' flexibility.

Figure 42

Methodological guidelines: A common mistake is to leave the fingers immobile while swinging the hand. It would be a waste of time. Make sure the students bend fingers at every joint. It helps to perform this exercise with one hand at a time, so the students can concentrate on one hand and find the necessary adjustments. Point out that the left hand is not as compliant as the right and encourage the students to exercise their left hand heartily.

Exercise 155 THE CLAWS
Music – see Appendix 17.
Formation – a crowd.

The beginning position – regular stance, arms bent in front of the body, palms facing down, and fingers widespread.

Bend your fingers sharply one phalange at a time, beginning with the 3rd row of the phalanges (or the tips of fingers). For the first three eight bits of music, bend your fingers and close your fist sharply for the fourth eight-note. The second half of the exercise is - open your fist and then open one phalange at a time in reverse order. It would take another four eighth-notes. The motions described above should be sharp as well. Notice, the entire sequence takes one bar of music. Think of your fingers being the claws of a predatory bird. In the first half, the bird sinks its claws into prey, and then lets the victim go in the second part of the exercise.

Repeat the exercise eight to twelve times in a single lesson, and practice it in the following lessons.

Exercise 156 THE SNAKE
Music – see Appendix 18.
Formation – a crowd.

The beginning position – stand feet together, arm out to the side, palm facing down; fingers together, the tip of thumb touch the tip of the index finger to resemble the head of a snake (see Figure 42b.)

Figure 42b

Keeping the upper arm in a horizontal position, begin gradually rotating your hand at the wrist until the palm faces up. Continue the movement by rotating the forearm at the elbow joint. Continue till bringing your hand down to the armpit. Take two bars of the music for that. Continue moving your hand, passing it under the armpit and extend the arm out to the side with palms facing up. In the last moment (last quarter of the music), return your hand to the beginning position. i.e., palm down. Take another two bars of the music to perform this second half of the exercise.

During the entire exercise, make sure your body is relaxed. Imagine that your arm is a snake, and the rest of your body is a trunk of a tree. Repeat the exercise with another arm, and then perform it with both arms simultaneously.

Repeat the exercise four to six times in a single lesson and keep practicing it in numerous following lessons.

Exercise 157 RIGHT ANGLE
Music is improvisation 4/4-time, slow chords.
Formation – a crowd.

The beginning position is regular stance. Press the palms against each other in front of the chest, so your forearms and hands create a right angle (see Figure 43a).

Gradually draw your hands away from each other as far as you can while maintaining the right angle and keeping forearms parallel to the ground. Take four quarters of the music to move your arms apart, and then another four quarters to draw palms together back to the beginning position.

Figure 43a

Perform the exercise four times, then drop your hands and gently shake the wrists to relax your muscles from the stress. After that, repeat the exercise four more times.

Figure 44a

Practice this exercise in each of the following lessons.

Exercise 158 THE GEARS
Version 1

Music – see Appendix 19.
Formation – a crowd.

The beginning position is -- stand with your feet shoulder-width. Extend your arms forward, the palms of your hands facing outward. Now cross the right hand over the left and press the palms against each other. That is the (see Figure 44a).

Imagine that there is an axis running through the center of your hands.  Keep the hands pressed and gradually turn them around this imaginary axle (See Figure 44b). Continue the rotation and make a 360° revolution (see Figure 44c). Notice, your hands would come to the same position as the beginning one only now the left hand is over the right. To accommodate the rotation, you would have to bend your arms slightly in the process. Take two bars of music to perform this part of the exercise.

Figure 44b

Now, rotate your hands around the axle in reverse, and bring them back to the beginning position. Repeat the entire sequence four times.

*

The beginning position for the next stage of this exercise is as follows: hands in the same position as before, but turn your upper body and arms to the extreme left.

Rotate hands in the same manner as before and simultaneously move arms along with your torso to the extreme right. Take four bars of music for the sequence. Then take another four bars and rotating hands in reverse, bringing them to the beginning position.

Figure 44c

Methodological guidelines: Because positions and actions in this exercise are stylized (not the movements of every day), we recommend demonstrating them at least once to the students. After the basic concept is understood, suggest keeping elbows straight while rotating the "gears." It might take some time and many repetitions until this task achieved, but better flexibility would come as a reward. Repeat different versions of the exercise in numerous lessons. Later in the process, make the students perform the two parts in just four bars of music.

Version 2
Music and Formation are the same as in the previous version of the exercise.

The beginning position is the same as before, but arms stretched up above the head and eyes fixed on hands.

Begin rotating the "gears" and, simultaneously, bend the upper body along with arms forward to a horizontal position. Take four bars of music for this portion of the exercise. Now, rotate hands in reverse and return to the beginning position. Repeat the exercise four or eight times in a single lesson.

Repeat the exercise and take two bars of music to bend forward, and another two bars to return to the beginning position.

Version 3
Music and Formation are the same as before.

This stage of the exercise is a mixture of Versions 1 and 2.

The beginning position – stand feet apart, upper body and arms turned to the left, palms pressed.

For two bars, rotate hands and move your arms to the extreme right.

For another two bars, rotate hands in reverse and bring your arms up above your head.

For two more bars, rotate hands and bend forward at the same time.

For yet another two bars, rotate hands, unbend, and bring your arms to the beginning position.

Repeat this version of the exercise several times in a single lesson and practice it in as many upcoming lessons as possible.

Exercise 159 THE FAN
Music – see Appendix 20.
Formation – a crowd.

The beginning position – stand feet apart, arms extended forward, palms facing down.

Version 1
Moving only fingers, fold them gradually as a hand fan -- move your little fingers out first, and then cover them with ring fingers, then with middle fingers, then with index fingers, and finally, cover up the index fingers with thumbs. Keep the palms fixed. Take one bar of the music for this portion of the sequence.

For the next bar, move your fingers in reverse order: first thumbs, then cover them with index fingers, followed by the middle fingers, then ring, and, finally, little fingers cover the ring fingers.

It is essential to stretch all fingers during the entire sequence vigorously.

Repeat exercise eight or sixteen times in a single lesson.

Version 2
Perform the exercise and, at the same time, gradually move your arms apart out to the sides for the first half, then bring them back for the second half of the sequence.

Repeat exercise four to six times in each following lesson.

Methodological guidelines: If the students have difficulties in performing *The Fan* exercise with both hands simultaneously, have them learn the technique with one hand, then with another, and only after that, make them perform the task with both hands.

Exercise 160 "WAVE MAKER"

Music is a slow waltz (see Appendix 21).

Formation – a crowd.

Version 1

The beginning position – stand feet apart, arms bent, hands in front of your chest, palms facing forward (see Figure 45a).

Imagine yourself being immersed in water (pool, lake, or ocean) up to the chest.

Push the "water" forward with your palms bending forward, trying to push it as far as you can to produce a wave (see

Figure 45a

Figure 45b). Then relax your arms and hands and return your body to the beginning position. Take two bars of music to push a wave, and another two bars to recover. Spread your fingers wide when pushing the water, and relax the fingers when

Figure 45b

pulling hands back. Repeat exercise four times in a row.

Perform exercises four to six times and keep practicing it in several following lessons.

Version 2

The beginning position is the same as in Version 1, but have your bent arms and palms turned outwards.

Perform the same exercise sideways. Sway your body first to the right and make a wave with your right hand, then to the left with your left hand. Continue the exercise and alternate hands. Repeat it four to eight times.

Version 3

The beginning position is the same as in Version 1, palms in front of the chest.

Repeat the same exercise, this time pushing "water" downward with both hands. Bend over to extend your movements, maintain the same tempo-rhythm.

Version 4

The beginning position – squat down knees apart, elbows bent, hands on the sides of your head, palms facing up.

Imagine yourself completely immersed in water. Perform the movements with both hands pushing the "water" up and straighten up your knees simultaneously to extend the motions all away. Then return to the beginning position. Repeat the exercise four times.

Version 5

Combine all four previous versions of the exercise and perform them in succession four times each: move forward, then sideways, then down, and then up. Get in a squat position just before you begin Version 4.

Methodological guidelines: Offer different versions of the exercise to practice in numerous lessons. Make sure the "pushing away" movements are energetic and robust, and returning to the beginning position is soft and relaxed. Encourage the students to create the impression of resisting water pressure. Initiate a different mood by changing the tempo and the music while training the flexibility of hands.

Exercise 161 THE KITTEN
Music – see Appendix 22. Perform it light and playful.
Formation – a crowd.

The beginning position – stand feet together, arms half-bent, hands in front of the chest, palms facing forward, fingers spread and relaxed.

Stage 1

Gently, but swiftly tap the pads of your index fingers against pads of thumbs three times following the rhythm of the music. Continue the exercise and tap your middle fingers against the thumbs, then the ring fingers, and then little fingers. Bounce your fingers back after each touch. Perform the actions in quarters so it would take four bars to complete the sequence. Make your movements light and graceful. Repeat the exercise four to six times before moving to the next stage.

Stage 2

With a quick motion, bend and unbend all your fingers at the knuckles for each quarter of music and repeat this motion for the duration of four bars (or twelve times). Your movements should resemble those of the claws of a kitten playing with a toy.

Repeat the exercise several times before moving to the next stage.

Stage 3

Make a fist and immediately open your hand three times, once for each quarter of the music. Repeat this motion for three consecutive bars of music and then, on the downbeat of the fourth bar, close your fist one more time and hold it until the end of the bar. This final movement should resemble the claws snatching the toy.

Repeat this part of the exercise several times before moving to the next stage of the exercise.

Stage 4

This stage of the exercise is a combination of the previous three stages.

Repeat Stage 1 for the first four bars of the music, then continue with Stage 2 and repeat it for only two bars. Then go on with Stage 3 and perform for one bar only (three motions) plus one last action on the downbeat of the last bar. Perform the exercise several times. After each repetition, stop and relax your hands.

*

Now, assume the following given circumstances: in the first part of the exercise, the kitten plays with a mouse, in the second part your kitten becomes angry and roughs the mouse up, and in the third part the kitten finally strikes the mouse and catches it with the last snatch.

Repeat the exercise in several following lessons as a part of the *Special Development of the Expressive Hand* section.

Methodological guidelines: While playing the music, your accompanist should go along with the given circumstances to help the players create a skit.

Exercise 162 THE BOWL
Music is improvisation 4/4-time, slow tempo.
Formation – a crowd.

The beginning position – stand feet apart, right arm bent at the side of your body, an imaginary "bowl" resting in hand (see Figure 46a).

Figure 46a

Figure 46b

Figure 46c

Imagine yourself holding a bowl in your hand filled up with water to the brim.

Begin the exercise and turn your hand gradually inward under your armpit, then continue the rotation (see Figure 46b and 46c) and lift your hand, and bring the bowl up above your head. Remember, the bowl filled with water, and you do not want to spill it. So, twist your upper body to accommodate this maneuver. Continue and transfer the bowl over the head until you bring it to the right of and slightly above your head (see Figure 46d).

Do not take your eyes off the bowl at all times. Move your hand continuously. Take two bars of music to complete this part of the exercise.

Figure 46d

Now, perform "The Bowl" exercise in reverse and, going through all the stages, finish it in the beginning position. Take another two bars of music for this half of the exercise. Repeat the sequence four times.

Perform the entire sequence now with your left arm and repeat it four times.

Repeat the exercise several times, alternating arms.

Next, perform the exercise with both hands simultaneously. Coordinate the movements of both hands with the adjustments of your body to balance two "bowls." You would have to switch your attention frequently from one element to another. Notice, to accommodate this quite complicated combination of movements, bend forward when moving hand under your armpit; when transferring them over your head, bend backward.

Repeat this exercise four to six times in each following lesson.

Imaginative Exercises

After basic techniques learned and fulfilled, the exercises of this group become simple études. They would own sensible content and, while carrying no specific action, actively engage students' imagination. The image-bearing title and a thoroughly selected music would assist in transforming them into a little presentation. Our experience shows that even a simple movement performed in a particular tempo-rhythm creates a specific association in the mind of a player and motivates him/her to perform the exercise with a purpose. As a result, it impresses as having dramatic content.

Imaginative exercises provoke the student's mind to engage in an action. The next step in transforming the exercise into étude is to justify the choreographed movements with the help of imagination. Finally, encourage the players to create their own given circumstances. That would motivate them to act individually and not generally. According to the Stanislavsky System of actor training, only through these stages can one adorn the actions with genuine emotions in harmony with the movements and music.

Exercise 163 PAINTING THE FENCE

Preliminary exercise

Stand in front of an imaginary fence and imagine that your right hand is a paintbrush, and your fingers represent a bristle dipped in paint. Carefully place "the bristle" on the fence above your head and begin "painting" it moving the "paintbrush" gradually down. Bend over to reach the bottom of the fence. Now run the "paintbrush" slowly up, back to the beginning position. Notice, when you change the direction and begin moving your paintbrush up, it is the back of your hand that will stroke the wall. That is how the real brush would do.

So, watch your movements closely when the brush changes directions. Make sure the hairs of bristle transfer gradually into a new

position. Make sure your "paintbrush" touches the surface at all times
to cover the fence with paint evenly. Repeat the exercise several times
at your own pace and make your movements purposeful and smart.

Repeat the exercise several times with your left hand.

Stage 1
Music is improvisation 4/4-time, slow and continuous.
Formation – a crowd.

The beginning position
– stand feet apart, right palm
rests on the "fence," slightly
above the head.

Gradually move your
right hand down to one bar of
the music; take another bar and
move your hand up. Imitate the
movements of a painter and, at
the same time, control the
position of your "paintbrush."
Repeat the exercise four times.
Stop, and then repeat it four
more times with your left
hand.

Figure 47a

Figure 47b

Now, perform this exercise with both hands and try to control
the movements of your hands and your body (see Figure 47a and b).
Repeat the exercise several times in a single lesson.

Stage 2
Imagine that the fence is so high that you would have to get
up on your toes to reach the top edge. Also, you have to "paint" this
fence with both hands all away to the ground. Take one bar of music
to move "paintbrushes" down and another bar to move them up; find

all necessary adjustments to cover the surface evenly from top to bottom. Control your balance in the process.

Repeat the exercise several times in a single lesson.

Stage 3
Music is the same, as in the previous exercise.

The beginning position is standing feet shoulder-width; bend sideways and extend arms to the extreme right; palms are resting on the "fence."

Paint by moving your hands horizontally. Begin to move hands to the left and gradually straighten your body until you bring the "brushes" to the center in front of you. Then make a transition and move them to the right, back to the beginning position. Take two bars of music for the entire cycle. Remember to turn your hands smoothly when changing the direction of strokes. Repeat the exercise four times.

Now begin with your hands on the extreme left of your body and repeat the exercise four more times. Find the adjustments to produce smooth and graceful movements.

Stage 4 (Final)
Music is the same, as in the previous exercise.

This exercise is a combination of Stage 2 and Stage 3.

"Paint" the fence down/up twice, then paint it twice from right to the center, then twice from left to the center, and then again, down/up twice. Take four bars of music for each of these parts of the exercise and perform it for the sixteen bars. Make sure you switch from one part of the next in an orderly and graceful manner. Maintain the tempo-rhythm through the entire exercise.

Practice this exercise four to six times in the following lessons.

Methodological guidelines: This complex exercise would train *Expressive Hand,* along with *Coordination, Sense of Space,*

Rhythmicity, and other essential qualities. Plan to have all the stages of the exercise accomplished in a single lesson and then repeat the final stage of the exercise in the following lessons along with other exercises for hands.

To make this exercise even more beneficial, try to combine it with a song. For instance, make your students sing, or hum, or even whistle *a cappella* a tune "Oh, what a beautiful morning" from musical "Oklahoma," by Richard Rodgers and Oscar Hammerstein with the final stage of the exercise.

Exercise 164 RINSING A CLOTH
Music is a slow waltz.
Formation – a crowd.

The beginning position – stand feet apart shoulder width.

Stage 1

Imagine yourself standing in front of a bathtub filled with water. Imagine also that you hold a handkerchief by the corner with two fingers of your right hand. "Dip" the scarf into the tub at the extreme right.

Stand in place and gradually pull the handkerchief to the extreme left side of the tub. Take two bars of music for this. Now, drag the scarf to the far right, back to the beginning position.

Repeat the exercise four times and observe your imaginary handkerchief moving in the water. Keep it "submerged" in the water, and see how the scarf folds and unfolds when changing directions.

Repeat this exercise four times with your left hand; see that your hand is moving along a horizontal line.

Stage 2

Imagine now that your hand is the handkerchief that you rinse in the bathtub. Perform the exercise with the right hand and make your hand imitate the movements of a scarf, especially in switching directions. Repeat the exercise four times, stop, and perform it with your left hand.

*

The beginning position – stand feet apart; both hands to the right of your body dipped in "water," left palm facing up, right palm facing down. Move both hands to the left, then to the right, and switch the position at the turn.

Imagine now that your hands represent a beach towel that you are rinsing in the tub. Use the technique that you just learned and drag hands from extreme right to the extreme left, then reverse the positions of palms and drag the "towel" in the opposite direction. Take two bars of music to perform half of the sequence. Make sure you keep your hands just below the surface at all times.

Repeat this exercise in numerous lessons in different variations.

Methodological guidelines: A common mistake is involuntarily lifting hands out of the "water." It removes the tension from the wrists, making the exercise unproductive. Make sure the students find the right adjustments for their bodies' position, the ones that would serve the purpose in the best and natural way. Practice the exercise in several following lessons and change the tempo-rhythm with every repetition, i.e., make the students perform it once for the duration of eight bars of music, and another time for two bars of music. Watch how the tempo-rhythm changes the ambiance of this simple physical action. In one case, it would look perhaps as if the job was done meticulously, in another case, as if the person is in a hurry to finish the job.

Next step -- suggest creating simple given circumstances that would justify doing the job slow or fast.

Make the students execute the exercise in the following consecutive lessons until the end of the program.

Exercise 165 THE PRAYER

Stage 1
Music is improvisation 6/8-time, plain chords, slow.
Formation – a crowd.

The beginning position – stand feet together, arms bent, hands touching each other along the sides, so the palms are in front of the face; fingers together. The position should resemble an action "reading a book" (see Figure 48a).

The exercise consists of six consecutive motions, and each one performed for one quarter of the music. As the motions are quite uncommon, we explain them below one by one.

1st motion: begin rotating your hands inward but keep them connected; continue the rotation and stretch your arms with palms facing outward and hands at a right angle to your

Figure 48a

forearms and touching each other along thumbs (see Figure 48b). Execute this motion without the music gradually and slow to grasp the technique, and then repeat it several times at your own pace.

Now repeat the action as one swift and energetic movement. Perform it several times to get comfortable with this unusual movement, and then pause in the final position to prepare for the next motion.

Figure 48b

2nd motion: begin from the final position of the 1st motion. Bend your arms slightly and then stretch them downward; simultaneously, turn hands inward palms facing down, so

Figure 48c

the tips of your middle fingers touch. End this motion with hands at a right angle to your forearms (see Figure 48c). Practice this motion several times, first gradually, and then swiftly and energetically. Stop hands in the final position and prepare for the next move.

3rd motion: begin from the final position of 2nd motion. Elevate your hands slightly up and swiftly turn them palms up, and immediately extend your arms down with hands at a right angle to forearms. Note, the tips of middle fingers still touch each other (see Figure 48d). Repeat the motion several times and stop in the final position.

Figure 48d

4th motion: bend your elbows slightly, twist your hands again, palms down and stretch your arms down. Position hands at a right angle to forearms (see Figure 48c). This position is the same as the final position of 2nd motion. Practice this motion several times and stop in the final position.

5th motion: lift your hands in front of your body up to the face level, then separate your arms and bring them the shortest way to the sides of your head. This motion should resemble the opening of a flower. The final position is -- arms bent at a right angle, hands turned outward at a right angle to forearms, palms facing up (see Figure 48e). Execute this motion slow to grasp the technique, then repeat it energetically several times and stop in the final position.

Figure 48e

Figure 48f

6th motion: From the previous motion's final position, bring both hands back to the beginning position. First, connect your fingers above the head (see Figure 48f), then lower your arms, so the palms turned toward your face, and hands touching each other (see Figure 48b). Perform this motion also several times in a slow tempo, and then repeat several times swiftly and energetically.

Note, you must perform each motion energetically because there is only one beat of the music allocated for it.

*

Perform all six motions one by one and strive to do it continuously and in harmony with the music. Repeat the exercise four times in a row in a single lesson.

Methodological guidelines: This exercise choreographed with stylized motions. However, one can describe them as they consist of simple movements. Moreover, it is what we are precisely attempting to do in this program. The instructor should avoid demonstrating the entire exercise. Nevertheless, you may demonstrate some positions briefly just to save time. Graphics included in this textbook are there for your convenience, and you may display them to the students as well. That would be better than a demonstration by the instructor.

See that the transitions from one position to the next are smooth and swift, and the movements performed in accord with the music. Practice each position separately and then put them together without the music. Then, finally, make them perform the exercise several times in time with the music.

To drill the expressive hand properly, make sure that the students stretch their arms completely where it is required and maintain the right angle in every position, except the first and the sixth.

Repeat this stage of the exercise in several following lessons and require a continuous and precise performance.

Stage 2
Music is the same as in the previous exercise.

The beginning position – stand feet together, your hands on hips.

Begin with your right foot, walk forward, taking steps on the 1st and the 4th quarters of each bar. Travel in a halted manner, i.e., stop after each step and pause until the next step. Maintain the balance during the pause and relax your muscles. Make eight such steps and stop.

Now, walk eight steps backward in the same manner. Move on the first and the fourth beat of each bar; maintain correct *Posture and Gait.*

Stage 3
Music – see Appendix 23.

The beginning position is the same as in Stage 1.

This stage of the exercise is a combination of the previous two stages. Listen to the music composed for this exercise and notice that it is in ¾-time, i.e., there are three quarters in each bar.

Begin with your right foot, walk forward, take a step for each bar's downbeat, and move your arms in quarters. As "The Prayer" routine consists of six motions, it takes two music bars to perform them. Yet, you will make only two steps. Also, move your arms continuously even though your walk is halted. Repeat the sequence four or six times walking forward.

Now repeat the exercise and walk backward in the same manner.

Figure 48g

Practice the exercise in several following classes standing in place, walking forward, and backward.

Stage 4
Music is the same, as in the previous stage.

As the motions for your arms remain mostly unchanged,

you are now going to learn four new patterns for your legs and the body.

The beginning position – stand feet together, your hands on hips.

Part I. Make a step forward with your right foot on the bar's downbeat and begin to kneel. Continue and kneel on your left knee with the third quarter of the bar (see Figure 48g). Next, put your right knee down on the next bar's downbeat and continue sinking until you sit on your heels at the end of the second bar. Repeat this new choreography several times and mark that it takes two bars of music.

Part II. The beginning position for this Part is the final position of *Part I,* i.e., sitting on your heels, only your hands free. From this position, bend over (see Figure 48h) until you touch the ground with your forehead and then return to the beginning position. Take one bar of music (or three quarters) to bend and another three quarters to unbend. Repeat this Part several times.

Figure 48h

Part III. This Part is precisely the same as Part II and takes two bars of music.

Part IV. Begin from sitting on heels position gradually lift your body off the heels, then place the right foot on the ground with the third quarter of the bar. Then, continue rising and put the left foot on the ground for the next bar's downbeat. Stand up on both feet by the end of the bar.

Repeat this Part several times, and try to deliver a smooth and continuous performance.

*

Now, perform all four parts of the exercise one following another. Notice, each Part takes two bars of the music or eight bars for the entire exercise. In short, you must kneel and sit on your heels, bend over and unbend (twice), and then get up on your feet. Maintain the balance throughout the entire exercise.

Repeat the combination several times in a single lesson and attempt to sustain continuity and precision of choreographed movements.

Stage 5

Music and Formation are the same, as in the previous stage.

Combine the four parts of the exercise that you learned in Stage 4 with the arms and hands movements learned in Stage 1. One small adjustment, though, is that you would have to stretch your arms along the sides of your body instead of in front of it when performing bending forward and unbending.

Practice the combination in several following lessons.

Stage 6

Music and Formation are the same, as in the previous stage.

Perform the exercise "The Prayer" in the following order: for the first four bars of music, move your arms, standing in place. For the next eight bars, continue moving your arms and walk forward, taking steps on each bar's downbeat. For the next two bars of music, kneel and sit on your heels; then for the next four bars bend and unbend twice, and then get up on your feet for the next two bars. Finally, for the last eight bars of the musical piece, move your arms and walk backward, making steps down each bar's downbeat. Pull your feet together with the last step and stop having your hands in front of your face.

Practice the entire combination several times in a single lesson and repeat it in various following lessons to improve your technical performance.

Stage 7 (Final)
Music is the same as above, with all the nuances included.
Formation – a crowd.

Perform the entire combination and consider the following given circumstances: you belong to an ancient cult whose way of praying is similar to what you learned in previous stages of this exercise. The prayer takes place first on the porch and later inside of an ancient temple. When entering the temple, you see a sacred hearth. Your faith strictly forbids interrupting the prayer while in the temple. You approach the fire, kneel and pray, stand up and pray, and finally, leave the temple moving backward because the faith also forbids turning your back to the hearth.

Before you begin performing this étude, you may create additional circumstances for yourself, such as "who you are," "why did you come here?" and "what exactly are you praying for?" Repeat the exercise several times in a single lesson and with every repetition slightly change or add more given circumstances.

Methodological guidelines: Save the full version of the musical piece for the Final Stage of the exercise to provide a fresh impression to the performers. Before the Final Stage performed, have the students listen to music once to grasp all the nuances, stresses, and dynamics. This ploy might inspire them for a more artistic performance.

Nevertheless, make sure all the movements in the exercise polished and precise before offering any given circumstances. It would be beneficial to have a guest(s) to watch the final stage of this exercise and other imaginative exercises. That would make the students feel compelled for the technique and the inner visions they carry on in the performance.

The typical error is when students being carried away with the given circumstances cease to control the movements. Have them repeat the exercise many times, so the choreography performed semi-automatically. Request that students concentrate on the objective of the prayer, which could be "to save someone's life," or "to divert a catastrophe," etc.

Include this exercise in the Test Class at the end of the semester.

Exercises/Études

Exercises of this group are similar to sketches, customarily offered in acting classes to students of the Stanislavsky oriented program. The presence of *physical actions*, the *given circumstances*, and the *objectives is w*hat makes them related. However, we prefer to call them exercises and recommend performing them repeatedly and frequently in stage movement training. The primary goal of these exercises is to develop the *Expressive Hand*, whereas, in a similar situation in acting class, the goal could be different – to achieve a logical action, to obtain a proper reaction, to get an honest emotion, etc.

Moreover, we believe that allowing the performance of dramatic skits in a stage movement class is an unnecessary and potentially harmful duplication of acting teacher's job. We strongly believe that the student must acquire essential skills in movement, singing, and voice in corresponding classes to use these skills to his/her advantage in acting class. As the acting profession is a very delicate one, it is easy to confuse a trusting pupil. Also, not every stage movement instructor can claim a broad familiarity with the acting profession's sensibilities, in our case, with the Stanislavsky System of actor training.

Every exercise in the following collection possesses the beginning, middle, and end. Also, in some of these exercises, the student would be dealing with "imaginary objects."

We suggest performing exercises of this group purposefully and successively, as they are chains of actions. The requirement is to comprehend these actions first, independently create in one's mind second, and then execute physically. This way, the results would be individual and unique and would vary with every student in a group.

Exercises/Études in this chapter of the Essential Stage Movement training include providing the student with a good notion of a human hand's abundant resources. However, the instructor should be patient and continue improving abilities consistently and purposely. The students must commit themselves to a complete truthfulness of the actions. They must demonstrate a total concentration and display their creativity. Merely mechanical repetition of the exercises perhaps would improve one's flexibility, but it would not develop the *Expressive Hand*.

Exercise 166 THE MOSQUITO
Music – see Appendix 24.
Formation – a crowd.

Catch a buzzing "mosquito" in front of you with your right hand and bring your fist to your face. Begin with your index finger, carefully finger by finger open your fist. Realize that you missed the mosquito. Repeat the exercise with your left hand.

Now, repeat the exercise with the music in 4/4-time specially composed for this étude. Catch the mosquito in the 1st quarter, then for the 2nd and 3rd quarter open your fingers one by one, and then in the 4th quarter, look for another mosquito. The technique is quite simple, but you must plainly distinguish the following actions – "I look for a mosquito," "I see a mosquito," "I catch the mosquito," and "I want to make sure I've got it." Go over the exercise several times with your right hand, stop, and repeat it four times with your left hand.

Next, repeat the exercise four times with the right hand, then continue without pausing, and repeat it with your left.

Repeat the exercise with both hands simultaneously. Open your fists close to your eyes so you can check both hands together.

Now, imagine yourself in the middle of a rain forest, and the nasty mosquitoes are everywhere. You are trying to catch them with both hands anywhere you can reach. Open your hands to check the results. Repeat the exercise for the duration of twelve bars of music.

Now, include your classmates or potential observers in the act. Try the following actions: "I want to demonstrate my successful catch" or "I want to demonstrate my dexterity" or "I want to prove that this place infested with mosquitoes," etc. Repeat the different variations of this exercise once or twice in the following lessons.

Methodological guidelines: Explain to the students that this exercise is designed to develop the *Expressive Hand*. With this goal in mind, one should be very particular about the movements, the tempo-rhythm, and the coordination. When changing given circumstances, the instructor should expect a change or reactions from the students and point out the lack of such, when appropriate. It often comes because of intense concentration on the technique. Explain that the students must believe in given circumstances and sincerely carry out the actions established for this étude.

Exercise 167 THE COIL
Music – see Appendix 25.
Formation – a crowd.

The following exercise is contrary to the previous one by the manner of motion. In "The Mosquito" exercise, the stress had been on clasping the hand. In this exercise, the stress is on the opening your hand.

Imagine that you have a small coil on the palm of your hand. Squeeze it gently with your fingers overcoming the resistance. Note, the more you squeeze a coil, the stronger the resistance. Then, when you press it almost to the limit, your fingers suddenly give up and the coil "springs up" out of your hand. Follow the coil's trajectory, catch it, and open up your palm with the coil resting on it. Repeat the exercise several times with your right hand and then repeat it several times with the left hand without music at your own pace.

Listen to the music and notice that it is in 4/4-time. Perform the exercise with one hand and then with another in time with the music. Work in the following way -- gradually squeeze the coil for the first bar, the coil would spring away on the downbeat of the second bar, catch it in the last quarter of this bar.

Now repeat the exercise with both hands simultaneously and notice that catching two coils simultaneously in different spots is quite challenging.

Repeat the exercise four or eight times in a single lesson next after "The Mosquito" exercise.

Methodological guidelines: After the technique was comprehended, we suggest working with two coils simultaneously but on different levels improvising the locations with every repetition. One may suggest some given circumstances. For instance, "you are demonstrating a new toy/game to customers in a department store" or "you are testing new equipment for a technical laboratory," etc. Practice the exercise with one hand, then another, and then both hands together.

Exercise 168 THE SPIDER
Music is improvisation ¾-time with a stress on the 1st beat of every next bar.
Formation – a crowd.

The beginning position – stand feet together, right arm bent, one hand in front and on the side of the chest, palm facing forward; index finger pointed up, the other fingers are half-bent and relaxed.

Imagine that your right hand is a giant spider that froze on his cobweb waiting for prey. The index finger represents the spider's head; your other fingers are his legs.

Imitate a spider climbing up the cobwebs with the help of "spider's legs." Move your hand up, gradually for the first bar of music, keep your index finger straight at all times. Cease moving your hand and fingers suddenly on the downbeat of the second bar. Pause for the rest of this bar. Continue in the same pattern and move your hand to the extreme left, but keep the "spider" head up. Next, move your hand down, and then move it to the right, back to the beginning position. Notice, as a result, your "spider" would travel along a square.

Repeat exercise several times. Make sure you move your fingers as quickly as you can, while your hand travels gradually from one frozen position to another.

Perform the exercise four times with your left hand.

Practice the exercise four or eight times in every following lesson.

Methodological guidelines: See that your players actively use the thumb along with other fingers. Point out that all fingers (except index) must move equally fast.

Some given circumstances would make this exercise exciting and purposeful. For instance, spider inspects the cobweb checking it out for prey or spider stops to listen for any possible vibrations of the cobwebs. It is after the evaluation that the spider decides to move to a new location, etc.

Practice the exercise and one day, suggest improvising the direction the "spider" moves, including moving diagonally, or even along a curve.

Figure 49a

Exercise 169 "COME IN - GO AWAY"
Music – see Appendix 26.

The beginning position – stand feet together, arms bent, elbows at your sides, hands *relaxed,* so they dangle, thumbs touching abdomen (see Figure 49a).

Figure 49b

Lift your hands slightly up, and without changing your upper arms position, turn your hands, so palms look up and let them hang down relaxed (see Figure 49b). Now move hands in reverse and return them to the beginning position. Repeat the exercise several times and relax hands completely after each turn.

*

Now perform the exercise with the music and turn your palms up or down for the downbeat of the bar. Along with the movements, try to produce what we call the *"internal monologue."* With the first movement say wordlessly, "Please, come in," then with the second movement, wordlessly say, "Go away." Make an effort to restrain yourself from including your facial expression and any other body movements. Instead, try to express the meaning with your hands only. Note, it is quite natural to add the facial expression, body movements, and even the voice in the act. Still, the limitations are intentional in our case to make you express the propositions solely with your hands.

Repeat the exercise four or eight times in a single lesson.

*

Now let us change the statements you are expressing with your hands. Perform the first movement as if you are saying, «Give me that!" and "I do not want it," with the second movement. Make sure you perform the exercise in sync with the music.

Methodological guidelines: This exercise illustrates the fact that gestures alone can express different actions. To express a particular action with the same gesture, one must change tempo-rhythm, the shade of motion, force, etc. According to Stanislavsky, the actor must avoid using prearranged gestures to express specific physical actions. Instead, one should make one's hands accommodating and capable of expressing numerous details and shades, which would appear involuntary following the actor's thoughts and desires.

Vary the "internal monologue" from one repetition to another. Try this one, "My hands are clean" with the first movement, and "Sorry I was wrong" with the second, or create new ones.

Exercise 170 A BIT OF FLUFF
Music – see Appendix 27, slow waltz.
Formation – a crowd.

Basic Exercise

The beginning position – stand feet apart, right arm bent, hand relaxed in front of the body.

Imagine yourself resting in a park on a lovely sunny day. There is almost no wind, so bits of poplar fluff are slowly falling around you. Single out one bit of fluff and watch it moving in the air; carefully take it with the tips of your fingers. Play with the fluff, moving your hand softly up and down several times, and observe it following the movements of your hand. Finally, let it fly up and follow its descend with your eyes.

Now let us coordinate these basic movements with the music. Listen to music and notice its peculiarities. Now, start observing the fluff and choose a bit you are going to play with shortly before the music begins. The "pick-up" part of the musical piece will alert you to start the motion so that you take the fluff with your two fingers on the bar's downbeat. Play with it for the duration of the first and second bars. Lift your hand for downbeat, and then lower it by the end of the bar. On the downbeat of the third bar, lift your hand again and let the fluff go. Watch it flying in the air for the rest of this bar and the entire fourth bar. Repeat this sequence four times or for the duration of sixteen bars of music.

*

Listen to the entire musical number again and notice that it ends with a strong chord.

Now perform the exercise and repeat it four times; make sure the movements of your hand gentle because you are "handling" a very light and delicate object. Remember, before you take a bit you must choose it out of myriads of bits around you. Try to single out bits in different places – above your head, to the right, below your waist, etc. At the end of the fourth repetition on the stressed chord, abruptly grab the fluff with your fist and finish the exercise. However, you would have to justify such unexpected motion. One of the reasons to squash the fluff could be, "I am bored to play with this bit of fluff!"

Repeat the exercise four times with your left hand. Improvise the spot around you where you choose a fluff.

Methodological guidelines: See that all the physical actions in the exercise, such as "choose the fluff," "catch the fluff," "play with the fluff," or "let the fluff go," performed realistically. Try to eliminate any attempt to demonstrate the action instead of executing it.
Exercises with imaginary objects do not suggest that the student should hallucinate or pretend to see the object. However, using the power of imagination, one can visualize any desired object in detail to handle it properly according to its shape, weight, utilization, and substance.

It is important to guard continually that the actions are truthful and believable. Students not familiar with the principles of the Stanislavsky System often tend to admire themselves performing exercises of this kind, try to imitate elegance, gracefulness, or even worse – fake joy or tenderness "in general," i.e., to express the emotion itself. That is hugely damaging to the profession as it cultivates falsehood and exhibits clichés. Failing to stops such a performance could make the student think it is okay and continue doing it in the future.

Having some experience in basic acting techniques would be vastly beneficial for an instructor before offering this and similar exercises, described in the Essential Stage Movement program.

Offer the following variations of the exercise "A Bit of Fluff" only after the basic exercise mastered.

Version 1

Consider the following given circumstances: a wicked witch has frozen your body, leaving alive only your right hand and eyes. Perform the entire exercise using only the hand and eyes. Make sure you maintain the rhythm, and your movements coincide with stressed notes in music.

Methodological guidelines: Stillness is an abnormal state of our body unless we are sleeping. Most movement programs constantly remind us that the actor's body must be free and that the actor must always use his entire body. However, *stillness* is not a rarity on stage and actually could become a potent means of expression when suggested by the logic of given circumstances of the play. We believe that *stillness* is a skill that must sit in every movement program on a par with other essential skills.

Version 2
The wicked witch now froze your entire body and left alive only your head and your left hand. It gives you a chance to turn your neck freely and follow the fluff's flight with your eyes as well.
Repeat the exercise with these new circumstances.

Version 3
The wicked witch froze only your legs and hips and left animated the rest of the body. Perform the exercise with one hand, then with another, and then with both hands simultaneously.

Version 4
The witch has freed your body and the legs but glued your feet to the floor. Nevertheless, try to pick up your fluff in the most uncomfortable places around you without moving your feet. Repeat the exercise with one hand, then with another, and then with both hands.
Note, through the previous versions of the basic exercise, and you were engaging gradually different parts of the body in action. Version 4, among other things, further develops your *Balance*.

Version 5

Perform the initial version of the exercise with the new given circumstances: a gentle breeze in the park blows away the fluff. To catch a bit of fluff, you would have to follow it everywhere it flies – you may walk, or run, or even jump to accomplish your objective. You are free to move in any direction, and pick up the fluff with right or left hand anywhere in the room.

Methodological guidelines: The players of the final version most likely would move around the room chaotically. Stop the exercise and explain that possible collisions with each other and with the walls or furniture are highly undesirable. Along with others, this would become an additional circumstance for the performers to consider. The actor needs to be able to navigate dexterously within a confined space.

We recommend performing the last version of the exercise for the duration of two consecutive repetitions of the musical piece and designate the final chord only at the end of the second round. See that the players manage to stop the motion effectively at a moment when they catch the fluff. That would indicate a reasonable control of the momentum.

"A Bit of Fluff" is a good exercise to train, among other abilities, the *Sense of Space*, a habit often neglected by many stage movement programs.

Exercise 171 THE GOBLET
Music – see Appendix 28; perform it slowly.
Formation – a crowd.

The beginning position – stand feet together, arms crossed on chest, head tilted down (see Figure 50a).

This exercise consists of eight parts. Perform each part for one bar of the music. Note, the music is in 4/4-time. This exercise features an imaginary

Figure 50a

goblet.

Part 1. Lunge forward with your right foot and lean forward gradually stretching your right arm; reach for the imaginary goblet, which rests on the ground (see Figure 50b).

Figure 50b

Part 2. Pick up the goblet with your opened hand, so that the stem of it is between your middle and ring finger. Lift the goblet off the ground and stretch your arm as if offering it to someone; simultaneously tilt your head down (see Figure 50c).

Part 3. Gradually move back to an upright position: first, shift the weight of your body from right foot to the left; then pull the right foot next to the left. At the same time, bring your hand with the goblet to the right side of your body on the waist level (see Figure 50d).

Figure 50c

Figure 50d

Part 4. Gradually twist your hand inward under your armpit; continue rotating your hand and lift it simultaneously. Then continue the rotation and pass your hand with the goblet over your head (see Figure 50e, f, and g); and then complete the rotation and .bring the goblet to the right, slightly above your head. This action is similar to the one described in Exercise 162, "The Bowl" of this chapter.

Figure 50e

Figure 50f

Figure 50g

Part 5. Hold your hand with the goblet in the position and cross your right foot in front of the left on the first quarter of the bar, then get up on your toes and make a full-circle rotation over your left shoulder. Get down on your hills at the end of the bar.

Part 6. Lunge forward with the right foot and stretch your hand with the goblet forward as far as you can.

Part 7. Gradually lower your right hand and put the goblet on the ground.

Part 8. Push your right foot off the ground, lift yourself and bring right foot next to the left in the first quarter of the bar; for the rest of the bar, gradually cross your hands on the chest and tilt your head down.

*

As this exercise is intricate and each part of it later will acquire a special meaning and action, practice each part separately without the music until you find adjustments and positions to maintain the balance, which would play an essential role in this exercise.

*

Now perform each part separately but with the music and repeat it several times; stop after each repetition. Make sure you begin each part on the downbeat of a bar and end in the last quarter.

*

Now, put all the parts together and perform the entire exercise with the music; try to achieve continuity and smooth conversion from one part to the next.

Repeat the exercise several times in a single lesson and practice it in the following three or four lessons before moving to the next stage.

*

Perform this exercise and take into account the following given circumstances: the event is taking place at the court of a medieval tyrant. You are a slave whose job is to serve wine to the master. This ritual consists of specially choreographed movements, which no one can alter or break. Any mistake is punishable by death. However, you are a party to a conspiracy to destroy the tyrant, and during this ritual, you must find a suitable moment to drop a poison secretly into the goblet filled with wine.

Let us agree that the slave's objective in this étude is "I want to destroy the tyrant." However, you must consider several psycho-physical actions to accomplish this objective. First, "I want to arouse the tyrant's desire for wine." Perform this action in the 1st and 2nd part of the exercise. Second, "I want to tease the tyrant to make him eager." Apply this action to part 3. Next, "I want to diver tyrant's attention" to be able to drop poison in the goblet. Perform this action in part 4 of the exercise and find the right moment to place the poison in the goblet. The next action is, "I want to buy time," so the poison would dissolve, which you will accomplish in part 5 of the exercise.

After you served the drink in Part 6 and realized that your offer turned down, your next action is, "I want to hide my true feelings and retire in submission." Perform this action in the last two parts of the exercise.

Perform the exercise with these given circumstances, the objective, and actions and never forget to perform all the motions gracefully as wine-server job demands. And make sure (God forbid!) not to spill the wine.

Practice exercise in several lessons and perform each action separately, and then all together.

*

Repeat the entire exercise, and begin it this time with your left foot first; accordingly, perform all the movements in reverse.

*

Now repeat the exercise twice, first time with the right foot and second time with the left foot. You can justify the repetition by the desperate attempt of the slave to accomplish the goal.

Methodological guidelines: Consider the fact that players would need some time to digest the variety of actions suggested for this exercise. We recommend giving students some time to practice individually without the music to put all the tasks together before demonstrating the entire exercise as a group.

The fact that this exercise combines a variety of amplitudes and tempo-rhythms of movements with various actions makes it exceptionally useful. It would require a reasonably high level of many faculties and habits, such as *Flexibility, Mobility of joints, Tempo-Rhythm, Awareness of Space, Balance,* and others to be mastered by this time in the program. Provided all the exercises described in the Essential Stage Movement comprehended on time, this would not be a problem.

Nevertheless, do not forget, this is still an exercise to develop the *Expressive Hand,* so pay maximum attention to the precision and expressivity of hand movements.

This exercise must become a part of the Final Lesson at the end of the semester. Prepare new circumstances and actions as a surprise for this particular event.

CHAPTER THIRTEEN

STAGE FALL TECHNIQUES

Stage Fall Techniques are special skills in performing deliberate and calculated falls on the ground. Both the contemporary and historical plays are full of different situations requiring the actor to perform a fall. The circumstances that might result in a fall are numerous. Some of them are -- a character falls shot or wounded; a character tumbles from elevation; a character stumbles over an object or subject. Any such stunt in the production always associated with risk.

In modern movie productions, dangerous stunts usually performed by stuntmen and stuntwomen, the professionals specially trained in all kinds of aerial tricks. In theater and TV shows, most of the time, there is no option to use doubles, so the actor should be prepared to perform simple stunts.

There are always two essential aspects of performing a stage fall – it must be safe, and it should be convincing. Safety has the priority because it concerns the actor's health and subsequently, his entire career. My mentor, Professor Ivan Koch, used to joke, "A good actor is a live actor."

The variety of situations that would call for a stage fall is so great that it would be practically impossible to learn all the potential techniques. However, our experience shows that it is unnecessary. The actor can repeatedly use the same set of techniques by merely changing the power, the angle of view or the style to suit a particular situation, a period in human history and specifics of the character.

One way or the other, many experts in stage movement agree that a stage stunt consists of only 20% technique and 80% acting. We strongly believe that the actor is capable of mastering the basic principles of stage falls within a reasonable time. Along with several particular techniques, one can use these skills for the rest of one's career. Without a doubt, *Stage Falls*, being unique skills, should be practiced from time to time to remain an actor's secure assets.

Another condition for its successful application is definitely to be in good physical shape.

In the Essential Stage Movement program, we distinguish two different types of stage falls. One is when a character collapses because of losing control over muscles, for instance, when one passes out. In these cases, the muscles alleviate gradually. Another is when a character falls in a fight, a violent intervention or stumbling, etc. In this instance, the muscles purposely stressed, as the character would instinctively try to maintain the balance.

It turns to be more challenging to imitate the first type of falls then the second in which the actor can use all kinds of deliberate safety techniques such as body turns, extended limbs, or dodging. In stunts of this type, the actor does not have to conceal from the audience the muscle strain and the auxiliary motions. Such physical behavior is natural for a human when resisting the fall.

It is more complicated to act "unconscious" or "dead," and the actor forced to use special techniques to make the landing safe. Besides, the player has to hide these techniques from the audience at the same time.

When performing stunts, the body's most vulnerable parts are the head, the sacrum, the knees, and the elbows. A common rule in the premeditated fall is to land on fleshy, soft spots of the body, such as the calf, thigh, and upper arm. Make sure any stage fall technique mastered first on a gym mat and only then practiced on a bare floor. However, even meticulous training in the stage movement class should not restrict the actor from an individual search of adjustments and perhaps new techniques when a real situation in production occurs.

Consider the techniques recommended in this chapter, just an essential matter. One may expand the skill in the future depending on the capacities of a group and other circumstances. The techniques offered in this chapter would help the future actor to choose the most economical, precise, and safe motions for a real situation on stage.

Besides accomplishing a useful mission of obtaining special skills, exercising *stage falls* would further develop such essential qualities as *Muscle control, Precision of the physical Act, Sense of Space,* and *Courage, and Decisiveness.*

Use these skills effectively later in different combinations with hand-to-hand combat techniques, and it is then when they would utilize the best.

Introduce exercises of this chapter into the program soon after the drill in Acrobatics started. It would be beneficial to include exercises in Stage Falls in the Acrobatics block of the lesson, thus saving valuable time on the setting up of the mats.

Exercise 172 FALL TO THE SIDE
Formation is a line in front of the path of mats.

The beginning position – squat down in the middle of the mat, palms are resting on the mat.
Perform this exercise first at a reasonable pace so you would weigh up the positions of different parts of your body, and understand the stages of relaxing certain groups of your muscles. Execute one at a time the following four stages of the exercise and make short pauses in between.

Preliminary exercise
1. Tilt your head and curve the torso to the left, then lose the balance and let your body drop on the side of your right calf. With your right hand, prevent your body from falling completely.
2. Now place your right thigh down on the mat, still supporting your body with your hand, and preventing it from collapsing.
3. Let your body fall now on your upper arm and the shoulder by

Figure 51

taking your right hand away; quickly move the elbow to your abdomen. Still, keep your head tilted to the left (see Figure 51).
4. Gently place your head on the ground and relax all your muscles.

Repeat this succession of movements several times and thoroughly avoid touching the ground with your knee or elbow. With every repetition, try to make pauses between the stages of the exercise a bit shorter. The goal is to perform all four stages as one continuous motion.

Repeat all stages of the *preliminary exercise* with pauses but fall on your left side instead, and then perform it continuously.

Practice both variations in the following lessons until you do it efficiently and with grace.

Methodological guidelines: In this exercise, the fall occurs from a minimum height. We recommend beginning the drill with this exercise to prevent fear and prepare the player for more complex stunts in the future. Successful performance of a simple exercise would help the student gain confidence in unusual stunts.

Exercise 173 FALL WITH A TWIST

The beginning position – squat down in front of and facing the mat; feet together, knees wide apart, hands holding the knee; arms curved; tilt your head forward and to the left.

Twist your left shoulder together with the torso slightly forward, lose the balance, and let your body fall. Land in succession on your left calf, then thigh, and then on upper arm and shoulder; if you keep your muscles strained, your body will rock. Use this as a momentum to rock back and return to the beginning position. In case you fail to return from the first time, rock back and forth several times and gain enough momentum to finish the exercise on your feet.

Repeat the exercise several times until you feel comfortable with the fall. Remember, as in the previous exercise, avoid touching the ground with your knee or elbow.

*

Squat down in the beginning position; extend your left arm up with palm turned outward. As in the previous exercise, twist your body left side forward. Begin falling on your calf, then thigh, and then continue falling on your side and slap the mat with your left palm. Only after that, lower your head on your shoulder. Note, reaching the ground with your palm as far as possible, would help you to complete the fall safely. Besides, the sound produced by the slap would serve as a good sound effect for this fall.

Methodological guidelines: The beginning position for this exercise is quite unusual. Make sure the players execute it precisely. It might even be necessary to demonstrate the position once. Having left arm extended is very important. It serves as a double-protection from possible injury of the head. It also protects the elbow from striking the ground. The rule of reaching far forward and slapping the mat with the palm is a trick to make your students keep the arm straight. Otherwise, obeying the instinct of self-protection, some would most certainly bend the arm. Command the students in the first several repetitions to extend the arm before falling. Later, they would do it at the last moment, or even in the process of the fall.

After the technique mastered, make them perform the fall on the right flank and to slap the mat with the right palm.

Repeat both versions several times in a single lesson, and then practice the stunt in the following lessons until it performed with ease.

Exercise 174 STRIKE YOUR CHEST, TWIST BODY, FALL

Formation is a line in front of the truck of mats; the distance between students four to five feet.

Preliminary Exercise

The beginning position -- stand feet together facing the mat about its left corner.

There are four parts in this stunt that you have to learn one by one and put them together afterward.

1. Lunge forward, placing your right foot on the mat and strike your "opponent" with the fist of your right hand; extend the left arm backward for balance (see Figure 52a).

Figure 52a

2. Without changing the position of your legs, gently strike the left side of your chest with the palm of the right hand imitating a reply from the "opponent; simultaneously, toss your left arm up, palm turned outward (See Figure 52b).

3. Gradually begin rotating your body together with the head to the left; keep turning until you can see the ground behind you. Attention, do not move your feet; perform rotation on the balls of your feet instead (see Figure 52c, d).

Figure 52b

Figure 52c

4. After you see the ground, lose the balance, and begin falling. However, do not fall at this time, but restore the balance making a step with left foot instead.

Repeat the exercise several times. Make sure the lunge forward is substantial. That would bring your body closer to the ground. Remember, the lunge position requires your front leg to be bent and back leg straight. Also, before you

Figure 52d

begin the fall, you must twist your body far enough to be able to see the floor.

Main exercise

The beginning position is the same, as above.

Perform all the movements successively, then lose the balance and fall on the mat (see Figure 52e). As in the previous exercises, land successively on the side of your calf and then on your thigh. Then slap the mat with your left palm and finally put your head on the shoulder. Only after this, relax all your muscles. Note, obeying the momentum, your right leg should fly over left and land in front of your body. That would indicate that you performed the fall correctly.

Figure 52e

Repeat the exercise several times in a single lesson and keep practicing it in the future until performed fearlessly and smoothly.

*

Music is improvisation 4/4-time, stress on the 1st and 3rd beat of the first bar.

Perform this fall in time with the music as follows: for the downbeat of the bar strike, the "opponent." Get "hit" in reply on the third beat. Take the next bar to twist your body and fall on the ground; slap the mat with the palm of your left hand precisely in the last quarter.

Methodological guidelines: The beginning position requires the student to stand close to the mat's left corner. It has a practical reason because the fall would take most of the space of a single mat. Neglecting this rule might result in hand and even knee hitting the floor.

Although this exercise sounds and looks risky, it is quite safe for a performer. The students must understand that being close to the ground in the lunge position makes the fall even safer. A precondition for this fall is to make sure one catches the sight of the ground before falling. There is no secret in it – if one can see the ground, one is in the correct position to perform the last stage of the fall. After everyone in the class successfully completed this fall many times, suggest trying it on a bare floor. The floor, however, should be carpeted or wooden. Attention! Never make your students fall on concrete or a tile floor!

This spectacular stunt could fit a situation stage when a character hit by a sword or by a bullet.

Exercise 175 "SUICIDE" (Fall Forward Arching)
Formation – a line along the path of gym mats, the distance between students 2 to 3 feet.

Preliminary exercise

Figure 53a

Figure 53b

The beginning position is standing in front of the mat, feet apart.

Learn the techniques one action at a time and then put them together to create the final version of the exercise.

1. Grab the handle of a "dagger" with your right hand on the left of your waist (see Figure 52a).
2. Draw the "dagger" out and lift it above your head (see Figure 53b).
3. Grab the handle with your other hand also (see Figure 53c).

Figure 53c

4. "Stub" yourself in the stomach with the "dagger," then bend over, bend your knees, and lift your heels off the ground -- all at the same time (see Figure 53d).

5. Pull the "dagger" out with both hands and raise it above your head. At the same time, straighten up and get on your toes.

6. Gradually turn left face without moving your feet then arch your body in the opposite direction from the mat, i.e., to the left (see Figure 53e).

Figure 53d

7. Lose the balance and begin falling sideways. Stop short from falling by making a step sideways and obtain the balance.

Repeat these actions several times in order they presented, pausing after each one; check every single motion for precision and balance.

Main exercise
The beginning position is the same, as in the preliminary exercise.

Repeat the seven actions of the preliminary exercise continuously and fall on the right side of your body. Keep your body arched while falling and follow the same order as in previous exercises -- the side of your calf, the thigh, the torso, and finally, place your arms on the ground. Note, your head protected as it would arrive at your arm. In the end, relax all your muscles. Your body's final position must be lying on your right side, with both hands extended and still holding

Figure 53e

the "dagger." Have your right leg bent and its foot placed under the left leg (see Figure 53f).

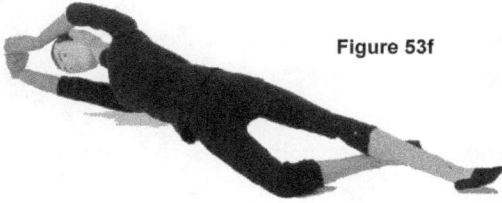

Figure 53f

Notice, the fall is safe as long as you touch the ground with the "fleshy" spots of your body. Avoid hitting the ground with your knee or elbow. Lastly, secure your fall with an extended hand. We took care of everything already. Just relax the parts of your body in succession just as soon as they touch the ground.

Perform the exercise several times in a single lesson; keep working on this stunt in the following lessons.

Methodological guidelines: A common mistake in the execution of this stunt is bending the right knee while falling. It happens out of fear to get hurt, and it could be harmful even executed on a mat. Make a point that both legs must be straight and the entire body curved. This stunt is safe precisely due to the arched body.

It is essential to remind the students to ease both legs' muscle tension at the end of the fall. With this not being taken care of, the legs will leap up in the air, producing a comical effect, which conflicts with the content of the exercise. Let your students find their own adjustments and various details to make the fall appear realistic and spectacular.

After the technique practiced in several consecutive classes and accomplished by the students, begin including simple actions in the exercise to turn it into a skit. To justify the movements in part four, for example, let them know that muscles of a person experiencing a sharp pain weaken suddenly and involuntarily. This fact represented in the exercise by bending knees and bending over. In Part 5, the action is "I want to live!" The player finds the strength to pull the blade out and get up on toes. In Part 6, the action could be, "I want to call for help!" In Part 7, the player faints and then falls unconscious.

From our experience, we know that this stunt always received with enthusiasm and with readiness to "act it out" by the players. The instructor should encourage any expression of interest in performing it. However, alert the students to remain truthful about the circumstances and to avoid overacting in such a dramatic situation like this.

When the skit performed satisfactorily, ask the pianist to improvise a simple musical accompaniment that would help the performers to feel the tension of this action.

Repeat the exercise several times in a single lesson and practice it in the following lessons.

Include this skit in the Final lesson at the end of the program.

Exercise 176 FALL FORWARD ARCHING, TURNING FACE DOWN

Note, offer the following exercise after the exercise "Suicide," because it utilizes the same techniques.

The beginning position – stand facing the mat, feet together, arms along the body.

Imitate a strike of a sword or a knife, a gunshot to your back. React by getting up on your toes and swinging both hands up. Then gradually turn over your left shoulder, as if trying to see your attacker, simultaneously arch your body similarly to what you did in exercise "Suicide," and fall on your right side, lifting your hands. Swiftly turn on your abdomen and relax when your entire body is on the ground.

Repeat the exercise several times in a single lesson.

Perform the exercise with the instructor or the accompanist imitating the strike unexpectedly, as a surprise; react to the sound immediately.

Methodological guidelines: This stunt supposed to make the impression that the actor falls forward on his face. The effect depends on how fast the player can turn face down at the end of the stunt.

Exercise 177 FALL ON THE BACK

Formation – a line along the path of the gym mats, the distance between participants 2 to 3 feet.

The beginning position is stand with your back to the mat one full step away from it, feet apart (see Figure 54a).

Preliminary exercise

Figure 54b

Figure 54a

Figure 54c

Figure 54d

Make a decisive step back with your right foot (turned outward) and stomp the floor next to the mat. Lift your left leg for balance; simultaneously, slap the back of your right hand against the palm of your left in front of your face and immediately swing hands up and apart (see Figure 54b and c.) Note, make sure your foot lands parallel to the edge of the mat. Also, slap hands at the same moment as the stomp. Both these sounds would imitate a punch to your face.

Next, turn right face (the position of the supporting foot would assist you in this) and arch your body to the opposite side from the mat. Now lose the balance and begin falling, but make a step and gain the balance instead (see Figure 54d).

Repeat the exercise several times and try to coordinate all the movements described above in logical order to create the impression that "punch in the face" happened suddenly.

*

Repeat the exercise but with your left foot stomping the ground. Accordingly, reverse all the motions and begin falling on your left side, but discontinue the fall and gain the balance.

Methodological guidelines: From the experience of several generations of pedagogues and choreographers, we know that the actors must perform most stunts, including falls and combat techniques, somewhat slower than similar acts in real life. That is because a real fight happens so fast that the witnesses sometimes have a problem understanding the outcome. It is not suitable for the stage. Performing the stunt slower would give the audience a chance to understand the incident and to appreciate the technique. The falls and punches performed too fast are confusing for the audience as they often come as a surprise. It is especially true for stage performances, where the attention of the spectators spread. It is much easier to concentrate the attention of the spectators in a movie or TV production, where the camera picks up the most critical moments.

Advise the students to take a little time between arching the body and falling. It would make the action look similar to a "slow-motion" effect.

Main exercise

Perform the preliminary exercise, and then fall on your right side, landing successively on your calf, then thigh, then right flank, and finally, place your arms on the mat. Remember, keeping your arms extended would protect your head from incidentally hitting the ground. Swiftly turn on your back after you complete the fall.

Practice exercise four to six times.

Methodological guidelines: This stunt must create the effect of falling on the back. The instructor should warn the students that falling directly on the back, even successfully, is a dangerous stunt and needs much longer training in Acrobatics and motor coordination. However, the fall described above, when performed correctly, gives just about the same impression. The quick spin on the back at the end would do the trick.

Constantly remind the students always to arch the body before the fall. Falling with the straight body and tense muscles can cause injury and generate unwanted fear of performing similar stunts in the future.

Exercise 178 FALL FORWARD OVER YOUR HEAD

Formation is a line along the path of mats.

The beginning position – stand feet together facing the mat, a step away from it.

Make a step forward and begin executing a slow forward roll; use one hand for support. Then, instead of finishing the roll and getting up to your feet, remain on your back and unfold the legs with right leg bent under your straight left leg. In other words, finish the exercise lying on your back. Now lift both legs and stand up over the right knee (see Exercise 140, Chapter 11). Repeat the exercise several times and make sure your head and shoulders remain on the ground while your legs unfold on the mat.

*

Begin the exercise five to six steps away from the mat. Run several steps, skip, and begin the exercise as a roll forward. Open up the moment you touch the ground with the back of your neck and finish the stunt lying on your back. From now on, let us name it "fall forward over your head." Attention, since you are going to gain a substantial momentum due to running and skipping, be prepared to experience a slide down the mat after the fall. It is normal, and the stunt would create an impression of a person who tripped or shot while running.

Repeat exercise three or four times in a single lesson and keep practicing it in the following classes until the stunt becomes a reliable skill.

Methodological guidelines: By this time, the basic pattern is familiar to the students from Acrobatics. At this point in the program, the instructor should present this stunt as a "Fall Forward over Head" and try to include it in combination with some other stunts and perhaps to introduce some given circumstances.

The common mistake students make in this stunt is letting left foot fly uncontrollably. Point this out and always remind the students to hold the left leg from hitting the ground. Offer this exercise only after the students proficient in all variations of the forward roll.

Exercise 179 JUMP DOWN FROM ELEVATION

Jumping or falling from elevation *is* a stunt used quite often on contemporary stages. In film production, stuntmen hired to perform an act like this use all kinds of safety devices. In the theater, the actor himself is the stuntman without any devices. Therefore, his stunt must be a hundred percent safe and spectacular at the same time. A fake or a clumsy stunt might spoil the meaning of the scene, or even of the entire play. An intense dramatic situation can turn pathetic, etc. That is why it is so important for the actor to become proficient in these techniques.

Preliminary exercise

The beginning position – stand on mat feet together.

Jump up as high as you can, land on the tips of your toes, then bend your knees and soften the landing by placing the palms of your hands on the ground. Stop for a second, then fall on the right flank using the skill that you acquired in Exercise 172 of this chapter, i.e., land successively on your calf, thigh, the upper arm, and shoulder.

Relax your muscles at the end of the fall. Repeat the exercise several times.

Main exercise

Assemble a sturdy table and a mat at the base of it in the middle of the room. Use a platform or a big cube no higher than three feet to serve the purpose. Put a chair next to this elevation for climbing upon it.

Formation – a column.

The beginning position – stand on the edge of the platform feet together.

Drop down and land on the mat, touching it first with the tips of your toes, then soften the landing with your hands. Make sure the arms slightly bent! Then fall on your side as in the preliminary exercise. Attention, keep your head slightly tilted back to avoid collision with your knees at landing.

Repeat exercise several times, falling on your right side, then fall and land on left flank. Try to achieve a smooth and swift fall; perform the entire fall as one continuous motion, so make no pause after you touch the ground with the toes.

*

Now repeat the exercise and begin it standing on the very edge of the platform with your heels; let yourself fall by leaning forward until you lose the balance, then sliding down. It would create an impression of falling into the "ravine." Fall on the mat using the technique attained previously.

Methodological guidelines: Expect some students to be terrified even to try this stunt. By this point in the program, the students must obtain trust in the instructor. If so, you would be able to convince a group that the stunt is safe. A hesitant student must be encouraged to perform the stunt here and now. Do not accept any excuses and promises to practice "at home" or "later." For the sake of the student, use the authority to overcome a fear like this and insist on the immediate performance of the stunt. If necessary, explain the exercise again specifically for this student, perhaps with more details. That would save the instructor a lot of time in the future in similar situations. In the end, a successful (maybe not perfect at first) performance would raise your authority and advance the courage level in students.

Increase the height of the elevation gradually up to five or six feet when every student in the group performs the stunt with ease. We do not recommend offering the students to fall from elevations higher than six feet. A height like this becomes potentially dangerous, and theaters should prohibit actors to perform stunts like this as well — this program designed to train actors and not stuntmen.

Exercise 180 *FALL OVER OBSTACLE*

The stunt you are about to learn extensively used on stage in situations when a character must fall tripping over different kinds of furniture such as sofa, table or desk, etc.

Mount a sturdy table (2.5 to 3.5 feet wide) in the center of the classroom and put a mat at its base.

Preliminary exercise

Lie on the top of a narrow table on your back. Extend both your arms and legs up and slightly apart. Place a mat to the right of the table on the floor. Now, maintain the position of your arms and legs, tilt your entire body to the right, and let yourself drop down to the mat over the edge of the table. Land first on your feet, then on your hands, and then continue the rotation and fall on your side. Make sure you do not lend on your knees or elbows.

Execute exercise several times to make sure all the movements performed properly, and your landing is safe.

*

Next, stand two feet away from the table, so the mat is on the opposite side, left flank towards the table.

Tilt to the right and lift your left leg and left arm up to gain the momentum. Then, make a sharp step toward the table and drive your body on top of it. Lay first your left arm and shoulder, and then roll over your flat back. Extend your legs and arms up and finish the fall, as in the previous exercise. Obey the momentum, and drop over the edge on the other side of the table. Land safely on the mat using the technique you learned in the previous exercise.

Repeat the stunt several times and try to find the best spot to put your left arm on the table, so that after you roll over the back, your right flank would align with the edge of the table. In other words, adjust your technique to the particular table (or piece of furniture).

*

Now repeat the exercise and try to roll over the table without even placing the arm first. Place your left flank on the top of the table instead. Notice, this adjustment would create a stronger momentum.

Repeat the exercise several times then practice it in numerous consecutive lessons.

Main exercise

The beginning position is stand six to eight feet away from the table.

Run forward several steps, skip and roll over the table, and fall safely on the other side as before. Be aware, the momentum in this exercise might be more significant. Therefore, be ready to make a roll sideways after the fall to offset the momentum. Try to finish the roll laying on your back by using one of the techniques learned in Acrobatics.

*

Repeat the exercise and try to finish it in standing up position. To accomplish that, you would have to make a roll sideways after the fall and get up on your feet.

Repeat the exercise several times.

Now, try to perform the stunt in reverse – place your right flank on the table first. Go through all the stages of the initial version of the exercise.

Methodological guidelines: Offer to perform this stunt on a bare floor, but only after being entirely confident in the adequate performance of every student.

To further train this skill, substitute the object used as an obstacle after several lessons with another one, different in size and shape. Work with each student individually and help to find just the right force of the momentum for a particular apparatus used for this stunt. The goal is to adjust to a new obstacle quickly.

Exercise 181 FALL OVER OBSTACLE AFTER PUNCH

This exercise is a combination of the previous exercise and "punch in the face" from Exercise 177 of this chapter.

The beginning position is standing feet apart six to eight feet away from and with your back to the table.

Imagine getting "punched" in the face, stomp back with your right foot and slap your hands against each other in front of your face precisely as you did in Exercise 177. Lose the balance, and begin falling back as if trying to regain your balance. Nearing the table, turn your right flank toward it, lie on the top of the table with your right side, then use momentum, roll it over it, and fall on the other side of the table on the ground.

Repeat the exercise several times and then perform this combination in reverse, i.e., turn your left flank toward the table; correspondingly lie on the table on your left side and so forth.

Practice both versions of the exercise in numerous lessons to make the skill safe and spectacular.

* * *

The exercises and stunts offered in this chapter of the Essential Stage Movement further develop such essential qualities as *Flexibility and mobility of Joints, Strength, Courage and Decisiveness, Sense of Space,* and others.

These stunts would be very useful in a Stage Combat class and, combined with fight techniques, would help to choreograph a stage fight.

Another application of stage fall techniques is that in ever-changing situations of live production in case of an unexpected incident or accident on stage, the actor's body is prepared and would react instantly to find a solution and even transform it to the advantage of the character.

CHAPTER FOURTEEN

LIFT AND CARRY TECHNIQUES

Lifting a partner or carrying a partner is a theater reality starting from ancient times to modern days. Many plays have various situations in which one character has to lift and carry another, or two or several actors have to carry a player. It is essential to perform such a physical act dexterously whether a circumstance is dramatic, tragic, or comedic. A failed attempt might damage the fragile sense of stage truth and break the trust between the actors and the audience, which is not easy to establish in the first place. A clumsy lifting might ruin a scene and even the entire play. Imagine a dramatic situation in production when an actor awkwardly trips and drops his partner, a "mortally wounded" character. It might raise laughter in the audience instead of compassion.

There are specific techniques that the actors should know to avoid situations like this. Moreover, the actor proficient in these skills would perform *lifts* or *carries* with a minimal physical effort and would be able to make them spectacular if the play calls for it.

By the time the following stunts offered to the group, the students should have *the strength* and *flexibility of joints* developed to a reasonable degree with the help of various exercises described in this textbook.

The techniques depicted in this chapter are, actually particular skills. At the same time, they are excellent physical exercises, which would further develop *strength, coordination,* and *tempo-rhythm of physical action*. Most importantly, these exercises improve physical interaction between the partners. There are not many easy exercises around to develop a unified tempo-rhythm of physical communication through the sensation of muscles. In this sense, the *lift and carry* exercises are unique and are of great value as they drill the ability to combine and to coordinate the physical efforts of the partners.

Notice, when practicing "one carrying one" technique, the instructor should be careful to pair off students according to their weight. We do not recommend letting anyone lifting or carrying a partner whose weight is considerably larger. It is especially unsafe for women. Professional actors must follow this rule as well, because of the evident danger to actors' health.

We recommend starting the introduction of *Lift and Carry* in the second semester of the stage movement training or at least after basic acrobatic techniques comprehended.

Exercise 182 SEVEN CARRY ONE

The beginning position – seven students assigned to play the carriers line up in order of height and then, beginning from the tallest in line, count off from "one" to "seven." A student who plays "casualty" lies on the floor with hands crossed on the chest; muscles tighten. The "carriers" positioned four steps away from "casualty." Carrier #1 – opposite the head, carriers #2, 4, and 6 to the right, #3, 5, and 7 to the left of "casualty."

Music is a funeral march, slow and solemn, or improvisation 4/4-time in the same style.

Carriers: Begin with the right foot and make four steps toward «casualty»; move continuously in quarters; pull your feet together with the last step. Kneel on your right knee and tuck your hands under the body of "casualty" in the following order. Carrier 1 – under the head, carriers #2 and 3 – under the shoulder blades, carriers #4 and 5 – one hand under lower back, another hand under the thigh, carriers #6 and 7 – under the calves. Perform the above actions for the next four quarters of music (one bar).

For the third bar of music, working strictly in sync with each other, gradually lift the "casualty" on the level of your chest. Then take another four quarters of the music and rise to your feet, and, simultaneously, turn slowly in the direction of "casualty's" feet. Now lift the body slightly and tuck your shoulder under it by the end of the bar. Attention, support the body with both hands.

Carefully synchronize your movements with those of your partners to assist *"casualty"* to remain motionless at all times. Notice, because of the difference in the height of carriers, the head and shoulders of the *"casualty"* should appear slightly higher than the feet. Consider this a proper position for a corpse.

*

Now perform all movements in reverse -- take four quarters of music to turn and face the *"casualty;"* kneel on your right knee and lower the *"casualty"* on the ground for another bar of music; stand up gradually for the next four quarters. Then begin with your right foot and make four steps backward in quarters; pull your feet together at the end.

Repeat the exercise with another group of carriers.

*

Perform a new version of the exercise as follows: leave the first part unchanged, then, after *carriers* line up facing forward, continue and extend your arms gradually; lift "casualty" and support it with straight arms. Take four quarters of music for this. Notice, this maneuver should preserve the tilted position of the body.

Begin with the right foot and walk forward in quarters. Make twelve steps for the next three bars of the music; with the last step, pull your feet together, and stop.

And now, perform this version in reverse, i.e., lower *"casualty"* on your shoulder, turn facing it, kneel and lay it on the ground; get up on your feet and walk backward; stop in the beginning position feet together. Notice, the entire exercise should take twelve bars of the music.

Repeat the exercise once with a set of participants in a single lesson and practice it in the following lessons switching the roles with every repetition.

Methodological guidelines: The instructor should watch that all the motions performed in accord with music and synchronized between the *carriers* so that the "casualty" would remain undisturbed. The student who plays the "casualty" role must tighten his/her muscles to help the *carriers* work with the body. Besides, weak or relaxed muscles would result in parts of the body sagging. Synchronism of all movements is utterly necessary not just to create a stage effect, but for the safety reasons as well. In any event, the instructor should be near the performers in case of an emergency.

Also, advise the players to walk carefully with small steps while supporting the «casualty» in their extended arms, considering a rather short distance between the *carriers*.

This exercise does not require exceptional strength in students, so everyone in the group should try it. Practice it in several consecutive lessons and make sure that everyone has a chance to try different roles, playing the "casualty" on one occasion and supporting different parts of the body as a "carrier" in another.

After all techniques of the exercise performed adequately, introduce some given circumstances to turn this exercise into a simple sketch. For example, Hamlet's friends carry his dead body away in a ritual of that historical period in Denmark.

Exercise 183 FIVE CARRY ONE

Music is the same as in the previous exercise.

This exercise is similar to the previous one. Use the same order of actions and the same rhythmical pattern as in exercise "Seven Carry One."
The beginning position is stand four steps away from the *Casualty*.

The tallest Carrier (Carrier #1) opposite the head, Carriers #2, and 4 – to the right of the Casualty, Carrier #3, and 5 – to the left.

Take four steps in quarters and approach the *Casualty*. Kneel on the right knee and tuck your hands under the *Casualty* in the following order. Carrier #1 – under the head, Carrier #2 under the shoulder blade, Carrier #3 – under lower back, Carrier #4 – under the thigh, and Carrier #5 – under the calves.

The order of movements and the tempo-rhythm is similar to the exercise "Seven Carry One," except for one adjustment. Form a file under the Casualty while lifting it and support the body with your straight arms. Walk forward with small steps and maintain the distance to avoid stepping on each other heels. Do not look down.

Repeat the exercise several times in a single lesson and have everyone try it in turns.

Methodological guidelines: This variation is certainly more spectacular than the previous though it demands additional physical effort from the carriers. Consider this stunt as dangerous for the balance in a situation like this is unstable.

Assign a tall but lightweight student to play the Casualty. Practice the exercise several times in a few consecutive lessons, then leave it out, and then offer it again later as a surprise to check how the students memorized the pattern and the adjustments.

Exercise 184 FOUR CARRY ONE

Formation – four *carriers* stand four steps away from the *Casualty*, Carrier #1 and Carrier #3 on the left, and Carriers #2 and Carrier #4 on the right side of the *Casualty*.

Music is the same as in the previous exercises.

The technique and the rhythmical pattern are the same as in two previous exercises. Support the body as follows. Carrier #1 supports the head and shoulders, Carrier #2 the lower back, Carrier #3 holds the thighs, and Carrier #4 supports the shins.

Methodological guidelines: Assign a lightweight student to act as *Casualty* and physically fit students for the roles of *carriers*, as this exercise is a physically challenging one.
Make as many students perform the exercise, as you consider fit to carry the weight load. The instructor must be near the performers in case of an emergency.

Exercise 185 THREE CARRY ONE

This exercise is similar to the previous; however, it is even more challenging physically.

Formation – Carrier #1 and #3 are on the right side of the *Casualty*, and Carrier #2 is on the left side.
Support the body as follows: Carrier #1 lifts the shoulders, Carrier #2 lifts the lower back, and Carrier #3 the shins.

Methodological guidelines: If all the previous exercises performed successfully, this particular exercise should not cause any problem. Make sure that the most robust student supports the shoulders. However, this exercise might be challenging for a student playing the *Casualty*. He/she would have to strain the muscles through the lifting and carrying and be responsible for maintaining the balance. Notice, Carrier #1 supports the shoulders, so the *Casualty* must relax neck muscles and let the head tilt back. Let as many students as possible try different roles and various positions in the stunt.

Exercise 186 *ONE* CARRY ONE ON SHOULDER

Divide the company into two equal parts.
Formation – two lines are facing each other, about 4 to 5 feet apart; in one line all are *carriers*, in another – *casualties*.

Preliminary Exercise 1
Part 1
Casualty: raise your hands. Carrier: approach the Casualty, bend your knees slightly, and lean forward. Position your right (or left) shoulder under your partner's stomach around the thigh joint.

Part 2

Casualty: bend over at your thigh joint and lay your body on your Carrier's shoulder; let your arms dangle.

Part 3

Carrier: clasp your partner's legs with your arm and move closer to position yourself under your partner. Then gradually unbend your body and knees and lift the partner on your shoulder (see Figure 55). Casualty: relax all your muscles.

Figure 55

Part 4

Carrier: hold the Casualty for a few seconds, then slowly bend your knees, lean forward, and carefully return your partner on his/her feet. Now, switch roles and repeat the exercise.

Preliminary Exercise 2

Formation – two lines facing each other.

The beginning position: Carrier – regular stance; Casualty – lie down on your back, legs together, feet toward Carrier, arms crossed on chest.

Part 1

Carrier: bend over, take *Casualty's* left leg, bending it, and place his left foot close to buttocks. Then position your right foot turned inward against your partner left foot; lean forward, reach for your partner's wrists; grab the wrists from above. Casualty: play lifeless; relax your muscles, and do not resist any actions of your partner.

Part 2

Carrier: lean back, pull your partner by the wrists up and towards you with a quick and robust movement; lift your partner until he/she is up all away and hold partner in this position.

Casualty: invisibly help the *Carrier* to lift you by bending your upper body forward and straightening your left knee; however, coordinate your movements with those of your partner to create an illusion that your body is lifeless.

Part 3

Carrier: let go of your partner's hands, swiftly bend over, and place your right shoulder under your partner's stomach around the thigh joint. Casualty: As soon as the Carrier leaves your hands, drop them down, and "collapse "on your partner's shoulder.

Part 4

Carrier: lift the *Casualty*; hold it for a few seconds, then put carefully down.

Repeat the exercise several times, then switch roles and repeat several more times.

Main exercise

Arrange two gym mats each at the opposite walls of the classroom. The beginning position -- the *Casualty* lies on the mat, arms crossed on the chest.

Carrier: Approach the Casualty and repeat all the actions of Preliminary Exercise 2. Lift the Casualty on your right shoulder and carry him/her over to the classroom's opposite wall. Stop at the mat with your right shoulder toward it. Then slightly bend your knees and sharply spring them up to toss the Casualty on the mat.

Casualty: Land first on your feet and perform a fall using the technique from Exercise 179, "Jump Down from Elevation."

Methodological guidelines: Practice these techniques until every student finds adjustments in playing both roles. See that students who play *Casualty* are fully relaxed while being carried.
Pair up students according to their weight and height at the beginning, but after the technique is accomplished, let them choose the partners for themselves.
Explain that a carrier must walk smoothly and avoid twisting and bouncing to prevent any pain that it may cause to a partner.

Switch roles after each performance, switch partners after two or three performances of the exercise and finally transform this exercise into a skit.

Exercise 187 TWO CARRY ONE

Divide the company into groups of three.

The beginning position – Carrier #1 and Casualty stand with their backs to each other, Carrier #2 stands to the left of the Casualty with the right arm around the Casualty's waist.

Part 1

Carrier #1: Press your back against the Casualty back then push your arms through and under your partner's arms behind your back; bend your knees and slightly lean forward so the body of the Casualty would rest upon your back; now receive the Casualty on your back and unbend your legs.

Casualty: Let your body rest upon the back of Carrier #1; still stand on the ground with both feet.

Carrier #2: Help the Casualty to lean softly upon the back of Carrier #1.

Part 2

Carrier #2: Move to face the Casualty; bend over and grasp his/her legs under knees with both hands; lift the legs and hold them on both sides of your waist.

Casualty: Relax and obey the actions of your partners.

Part 3

Carriers #1 and #2: Begin with your right foot and walk forward. Make eight steps, then stop and let the Casualty down in reverse order -- put down first the feet, and help the player get off the back of Carrier #1.

Repeat the exercise several times to achieve a smooth performance. Change partners and roles and repeat the exercise several more times.

Now lift the Casualty from the ground as in Exercise 186 of this chapter, and then continue with the current technique of "Two Carry One."

Methodological guidelines: Turn the last combination into an étude with a set of uncomplicated given circumstances and later even demonstrated in the Final Lesson.

Exercise 188 FOUR-HAND SEAT CARRY

Formation – each group of three finds a spot in the classroom to practice.

The beginning position – two carriers facing each other; Casualty is between them at the right angle to carriers.

Carriers: assemble your hands in a "seat" – both carriers grasp your left wrist from above with the right hand, and then clasp the other Carrier's wrist from above with your left hand. That would form a "seat."

Now, both carriers tilt your head back and lower the "seat" to allow the Casualty to sit on it.

Casualty: put your arms over carriers' shoulders and gently sit down on the "seat."

Carriers: lift the Casualty, half-turn forward, and walk a few steps. Stop, lower the "seat" and let the Casualty stand up; return to the beginning position.

Repeat the exercise several times in a single lesson switching roles after each repetition.

Methodological guidelines: Let the students know that this technique is suitable when two people have to carry a wounded but conscious person.

Exercise 189 ONE-MAN CARRY ON SHOULDERS

Formation – two lines 4 to 5 feet apart, players are facing each other.

The beginning position: Carrier – regular stance, Casualty – right shoulder to the Carrier, right arm extended upward.

Carrier: approach the Casualty and clasp his extended hand by the wrist with your right hand; bend forward so you can enfold his right leg with your left arm. Now, position your shoulders under Casualty's waistline. Gradually and carefully, overturn your partner's body and take it on both your shoulders. Unbend and lift the body. Hold the Casualty for several seconds, and then move in reverse order, carefully putting the body back to the beginning position.

Casualty: keep your body sturdy to assist the Carrier in performing the lift.

*

Now repeat the lift and this time transport the Casualty across the room. Stop and lightly let Casualty down on the gym mat, so his/her legs touch the ground. Next, Casualty performs the fall using one of the techniques learned previously.

Repeat the exercise several times, switching the partners and roles with every repetition.

Methodological guidelines: Make sure no one carries a partner whose weight is substantially higher than that of the Carrier. Suggest a different ending for the exercise -- instead of tossing the Casualty down carefully lower your partner on the ground.

Exercise 190 ARMS CARRY

Preliminary exercise
Formation – two concentric circles, everyone is facing the center; each student in the outer circle is immediately behind his partner in the inner circle.

The beginning position – students in the outer circle: stand feet-apart shoulder width, grasp the waist of your partner in front of you so that your thumbs rest on the partner's back; students in the inner circle: regular stance.
Students in the inner circle – bend your knees slightly, then jump up; land on your feet.
Students in the outer circle assist him/her in jumping up, and making a soft landing by supporting partner with hands holding the waist.
Repeat the exercise several times, then switch partners and repeat it with a new partner.

Methodological guidelines: One way to switch partners in a formation like this is to make the students of the outer circle move clockwise to the next partner in the inner circle.
The Preliminary exercise is supposed to train the coordination of movements between the partners. See that the students jump straight up, keeping their backs straight and land noiselessly. The switching of partners drills the ability to adjust quickly to a new tempo-rhythm. At a certain point in the exercise, the instructor should switch the roles of the students. Make the students of the inner circle trade places with the students of the outer circle.
Practice the Preliminary exercise several times and then move to the Main exercise.

Main exercise
Formation – the same as in Preliminary exercise.

The beginning position – Carrier in the outer circle is facing the center, and the Casualty is standing with the right shoulder to the Carrier.

Music is improvisation 4/4-time in minor, solemn.

Part 1
Carrier: clasp the wrist of your partner's right hand with your right hand and put his/her arm over your shoulders. Embrace the waist with your left arm, then bend forward, and embrace your partner's right leg under the knee with your right hand. Now slightly bend your knees and pick up the Casualty, coordinating your motion with that of your partner. Catch his/her other leg and straighten up your legs holding Casualty up in your arms (see Figure 56.)
Casualty: invisibly help the Carrier to lift you by coordinating the jump on your left leg with the lift furnished by your partner. Then bring this leg up into your partner's arm. Then let your head drop back or put your head on the Carrier's shoulder for the final pose.

Repeat the exercise several times with one partner, then switch partners and continue practicing striving for perfect timing.
Now perform the exercise in time with the music. For the first bar of music prepare for the lift; on the downbeat of the second bar lift the Casualty and hold it until the end of this bar; for the third bar of music gently lower the Casualty to his/her feet; for the fourth bar move to the next partner.

Have outer circle switch partners by moving clockwise to the next person in the inner circle and repeating the exercise with each new partner until you return to your initial partner.

Methodological guidelines: At the early stage of learning this technique, the instructor should note that it would be much easier to hold and to carry the body by bringing the «casualty» up to the chest and tilting the upper body slightly back. This way, the Carrier would support the «casualty» by his/her entire body rather than have a partner hanging on the Carrier's arms. The Carrier would be able to hold the Casualty longer and perhaps even speak or sing with the «casualty» in his/her arms. Also, the student who plays the Casualty must hold on to the Carrier's shoulders with the right arm once in the final position.

To test this technique's accuracy, the instructor should command "Carriers hands down!" when the performers are in the final position. If the Casualty manages to remain in the position and doesn't slip down, the exercise performed correctly.

When the basic technique is comprehended, adjust the exercise and make the carriers walk around the circle several steps with their partners in arms; then, stop, put the partners down, and then move to the next partner. Arrange this version of the exercise in time with the music.

Part 2

The beginning position – Carrier holds Casualty in arms; pairs evenly spread around the circle.

Carrier: begin with the right foot and walk forward four steps around the circle. Make your last step with the left foot and stop. Gradually kneel on your right knee, still holding the «casualty» in your arms.

Casualty: slide down and sit on the Carrier's left knee; then, as soon as your feet touch the ground, gradually stretch your legs; tilt your head back and slightly arch your body up.

Now, with the right hand, Carrier takes his partner's right hand and brings it to his/her chest; then, using the right hand lifts the Casualty's head and tilts it forward. That would serve as a sign for the partner to relax all his/her muscles.

Casualty: relax your muscles and gradually slip down on the ground.

Now Carrier: help «casualty» to lie down on the ground supporting your partner's back.

Notice, the Casualty does most of the job in this part of the exercise, while the Carrier just mimes the actions. When the Casualty is on the ground, the Carrier stands up and steps back.

Repeat the exercise several times in a single lesson, switching roles and partners.

Methodological guidelines: Practice the exercise in several consecutive lessons and then combine the first and the second parts. While the techniques gradually learned, practice it six to eight times in a single lesson, but after mastering, several repetitions per lesson would be enough. Otherwise, the exercise becomes tedious. To make the performance more dramatic, include music in it.

Part 3
Formation – pairs next to each other in a circle.

The beginning position – Casualty is lying on the floor, head toward the center of the circle, legs straight, hands folded on the chest. Carrier stands facing "casualty" at the partner's feet.

Carrier: turn your left foot outward and press it against your partner's feet; then, lunge forward with your right foot and bend over the "casualty." Grasp your partner's wrists from above, and then gradually pull the "casualty" by the arms into the sitting position.

Casualty: imperceptibly help the Carrier to bring you up in the sitting position, and then relax the muscles of your back and neck so that your head drops forward.

Now Carrier lets the "casualty" slightly back as preparatory aim motion, and then with a sharp movement pulls his arms up and over.

Casualty: while being lifted slide forward with your straight right leg and bend the knee of your left leg, then push off the ground with your left foot to help the Carrier lifting you up.

Carrier, having his partner standing with the right flank toward him, lets Casualty's hands go, and when the body begins sinking, he swiftly kneels on his right knee and positions his bent left knee under the body. At the same time, Carrier grips his partner's waist with his left arm.

Casualty: while sinking, drop your right arm over your partner's shoulders.

Carrier: once you have the "casualty" in a position familiar to you from Part 1 of this exercise, take your partner up in your arms and carry him/her over, making several steps; stop and put the «casualty» down on the ground.

Methodological guidelines: After all three parts of the exercise comprehended, combine them all, and practice it in the following lessons. Make the students perform the combination with different partners until the end of the semester.

By introducing a set of given circumstances, transform this combination into a skit that for individual performance. After observing individual performances, the instructor might point out that the same technique executed by different performers acquired unique details and even elements of emotion.

It is recommended to combine exercises of this chapter along with Acrobatics in a separate block of a lesson. However, as the learning progresses and the students become skilled at more techniques in Lift and Carry, use these exercises in a separate block of a lesson and practice them for seven to ten minutes in a single lesson.

PART III

THE METHODOLOGY

CHAPTER FIFTEEN

THE METHODOLOGY OF THE SUBJECT

The methodology of theater pedagogy is the analysis of the principles and procedures of inquiry in the subject of teaching theater arts. The methodology is the most critical part of any learning process. When it is accurate and based on scientific facts, the methodology provides the resolution of a subject's set tasks in the shortest viable time. It determines the selection of educational material and suggests the timely interpenetration of related disciplines.

In Stage Movement, a set of exercises alone, even carefully selected, would not guarantee successful training. Conversely, a theory indicating the importance and benefits of exercising won't do the job either. Even a combination of the previous two components would not prepare the actor's body for creative work on the physical expressiveness of the character. Only a scientific, based on numerous experiments methodology would help organize the learning process in a way that the theory and the practical material channeled in the right direction.

The Methodology of Stage Movement, along with educational problems common for many other subjects, undoubtedly has its specific tasks. These unique requirements, as well as the need to achieve maximum results in the shortest time, led to the creation of original teaching principles and exclusive methodological techniques procured out of the pedagogical experiences of many teachers.

Throughout the years, the author of this text had studied the actor's physical training's many different approaches. The major problem with the majority of the systems and techniques is, in fact, the lack of methodology. If we agree that the establishment of compelling connections with adjacent disciplines is an essential part of any methodology, there is an apparent disconnect between teaching movement disciplines (Stage Movement, Dance, Mime, etc.) and teaching acting in the North American Theater Education. In many of the established programs, only a particular style of movement taught under the pretense of movement training. The lack of serious research in this area of pedagogy and the absence of criticism created a very colorful picture in the physical education of future actors.

A recently published book, "Movement Training for the Modern Actor" by Mark Evans[1] inspires hope that significant research in this field of education would finally occupy the minds of talented and objective critics. That would be a tremendous support for thousands of movement tutors destined to speculate on how to teach their students better and faster.

We want to assure our consumers that the Methodology presented in this textbook persuasively rests on modern notions of Psycho-physiology and the experiences of many leading experts in the field.

An educational program in Acting that claims to be comprehensive must be a fine blend of different disciplines offered in appropriate proportions within the appropriate time. Unfortunately, there are still scores of programs that provide Stage Combat to students who have yet to learn a proper walk. A respectable Acting program must be thoroughly designed and continuously supervised by an experienced Acting teacher. This person should be aware of the outcome of each special class, be it Stage Movement, Speech, Dance, or Acting. Secretive sorcery behind closed doors is a negative phenomenon in our very public profession. One must open every class to colleagues' observation and discussion of the methods and techniques used in it. Only insecure and unprofessional instructors are uncomfortable with guests. Moreover, in our trend, the opportunity to perform even a simple exercise in the presence of someone else besides the teacher must be saluted as it cultivates the most essential quality of the actor – the ability to create publicly.

Any learning process without methodological justification is similar to sailing without navigation device – accidentally, you might reach your destination, but most likely, you will lose your way in the ocean. In education, one cannot rely on experience or intuition only, even if this experience is extensive, and the intuition has helped once or twice. However, a combination of solid training, intensive research, and the comprehensive expertise of many pedagogues can guarantee success in such a complicated field, as the teaching of others.

That is why we pay special attention to the Methodology of teaching Stage Movement in the present textbook. Below, we will discuss in detail the problems of systematic physical training of the actor.

K. Stanislavsky pointed out the importance of special physical training adaptation to the education of actors and theater directors.

Such a consideration of a program can be achieved only through a particular methodology, a refined set of specific teaching principles and techniques to be used calculatingly in the classroom. The principles and techniques expounded in this chapter emerged as a result of summarizing the experience of many teachers in Russia, the US, and elsewhere. Ivan Koch, Head of Stage Movement Department, professor of the Leningrad Institute of Theatre, Music, and Cinematography, has formulated most of them. However, many of the objects are published for the first time. They are the result of the subject's extensive teaching, specifically to the students in North America.

Major Methodological Principles

Five fundamental principles define our Methodology:

I. The performance of exercises from a verbal description of the instructor.
II. The alternation of contrasting elements within a lesson and an exercise.
III. The assortment of tasks in a lesson and an exercise.
IV. The gradual transition from simple tasks to complex ones.
V. The performance of exercises must be purposeful, efficient, and precise.

Let us contemplate each of these principles individually.

The performance of exercises from a verbal description of the instructor

It is still a common practice in teaching Stage Movement to demonstrate exercises to students physically. The teachers routinely combine demonstration with a description in such a way that the display of an exercise comes first and then comes the technique's explanation.

Modern Physiology distinguishes the First- and the Second-Signal Systems. The First-Signal System is present in virtually all animals and humans, and the Second is predominantly characteristic of humans. A movement demonstrated to a human activates his First-Signal System. The depiction of a movement gives rise to corresponding nerve stimulation, and an unconditional reflex of imitation snaps into action. This process does not involve the Second-Signal System, which enables humans to form an abstract image.

A demonstration of a movement pattern gives the viewer only a rough idea. Therefore, the teacher should not require the execution of the pattern after a display, as the student does not have a detailed impression of it yet. Only after adequate verbal explanation of the exercise, the student develops a full and accurate idea of what to perform. Word as a stimulus activates the Second-Signal System and enables the trainee to form an image that is closer to the desired result than the one demonstrated by the teacher. Based on this image, the student would be able to reproduce the required motor pattern more efficiently.

Trying to reproduce a pattern from the demonstration, the student would merely imitate the technique without involving his Second-Signal System. Indeed, the student would try to do his best, but such a performance would lack personality. However, imperfect as it is, this way of learning a physical pattern is effective in dance, illusion mime, stage fencing, and period movement. In a word, in all stylized forms of movement, a known method or demonstration followed by a verbal explanation is mostly productive.

Nevertheless, for most areas of the Essential Stage Movement, this mixed-method is inappropriate. Imitating a movement pattern does not contribute much to establishing the right skill because the psycho-physical capacities of the student cannot be fully engaged this way.

We strongly encourage utilizing the method of verbal explanation without any demonstration when presenting natural, organic movements of the everyday. Scientific research and experience have recognized that performing exercises by verbal description only makes the student create the pattern faster and sustain it longer.

Furthermore, this is precisely how a proper physical action, according to K. Stanislavsky, is found. It is not from the demonstration of the director, but the selected exact words, expressing the essence of action that inspiring the actor to act. However, at the beginning of the learning process, this method might come across as one, which is too complicated and time-consuming. It should not discourage the instructor. Soon enough, after the student understands the advantages of it, the method of verbal explanation of a task would work invariably.

Building a motion based on verbal instruction is productive also because the aspiration to begin the execution comes up immediately after the student fully comprehends the task. That is equally true for a simple motor exercise, an ordinary stage action, or a dramatic skit. The teacher should utilize this principle, as it gradually develops the need to assess the assignment carefully and to monitor actions.

To further understand the advantages of this method being applied to the actor's profession, let us examine the shortcomings of the demonstration technique where the instructor displays the exercise first and then invites pupils to repeat it. By doing this, the teacher attempts to show a model piece of work so that students would get an idea of how a perfect performance looks. As a result, the students try to duplicate it as best as they can, imitating against their will the manner of the performance as well. That does not allow the student to express his/her individuality in the assignment and constrains his initiative. Besides, what if the teacher himself is not skillful enough or already lost his former agility? The most important for us is what the demonstration method does not do: it does not develop logical thinking and creative imagination.

Another deficiency is that all students begin to look like their teacher, and therefore, to look alike. Demonstration deprives them of the ability to act independently. Many still think that it is faster to acquire a technique this way, but in reality, it hinders the process. Besides, certain types of skills picked up by demonstration, rarely become an active item in the repertoire of expressive means of the artist. The associative links just do not form when a pattern learned from the demonstration, and the actor rarely uses it in a similar situation on stage. Conversely, a pattern created by the actor by his imagination, becomes his skill and stays for life. This movement pattern, related to a particular situation, spontaneously manifests in physical action on stage when given circumstances similar to those created by this skill.

We suggest the following instructions when using the method of verbal description: first – the teacher outlines the task and confronts students with an accurate, realistic problem. Do this even if it will only lead to the creation of simplistic motion. Next – after the students understand the task, they should begin in their minds selecting appropriate means for its execution. Third, the students perform the task as best as possible, and the teacher observes the group. Fourth – the errors should be fixed verbally, but not by demonstration. One should expect errors in the initial performance and correct only those that change the exercise's logic. Additionally, do not correct the various small deviations from the ideal that appears to be the individual means of expression.

As you can see now, The First Methodological Principle helps to train the Higher Nervous Activity, thus accomplishing the primary task of stage movement education. The fact of similarity between the process of visualization before execution and the creation of physical action in mind before materialization makes our principle entirely justified.

To sum up the previous, there must be two conditions for the student to begin a physical action: he/she must have a clear idea of what to do, and he/she must have a desire to do it. The former should come from a refined description of the exercise, and the latter would arrive if the task is challenging enough. That is why it is vital to select the exercises for the program with full responsibility. These exercises should have a quality to them that would allow the student to comprehend the totality of circumstances and would stimulate him/her to start the physical act.

It is likely that at first, some students would resist the verbal explanation method. Usually, they are the students who had some experience in dance training or a High School Drama program. It is understandable because the previous experience of the majority of young people has made it habitual to learn physical behavior from the demonstration. Since childhood, humans learn by mimicking parents, siblings, and friends. Later, in school, this way of learning a movement pattern is almost universal. It happens because it is the fastest way to learn a motion. The result of imitating may be imprecise, but an attentive individual would correct it later by observing other people perform the same pattern or by listening to critical comments of a teacher or a friend.

Many students who enroll in a theater program already have experience in performing on stage from participating in a drama program in their school or community organizations. These students already have a corrupt habit of recreating movement sequences from the demonstration, as most mentors who introduce them to stage performance do not have time to teach acting correctly. In many cases, the drama teachers and directors-volunteers do not know better. Therefore, they do their best – they demonstrate all the moves and even the emotions they feel. By the time a young person enrolls in a theatrical school, he or she already "know" how to act.

The instructor should explain why the verbal method is better than the demonstration and see that all students would comply. It must become apparent to the students that they have to create an image of the motions described by the instructor in their mind, as if they imitate these motions mentally, "in their heads." Soon, this would become a useful new habit, and the students will be able to imagine themselves doing these movements. The proven fact is that a movement pattern created this way is more accurate and lives much longer than the one learned from a demonstration.

Nevertheless, for some time, the instructor would notice some students still try "unwillingly" to do the movements, while they described. It is quite logical - a stable habit is often hard to break. The instructor should remind the student politely that this is not right. In reality, with some students, it would take a while to acquire a new habit of learning a movement pattern from the description.

The alternation of contrasting elements within a lesson and an exercise

By the alternation of contrasting elements, we mean a logical rotation of exercises with different tasks, patterns, qualities, and characteristics to them. A single exercise should consist of contrasting elements, as well. This methodological principle challenges the student to make instant transitions from one environment to another. For example, one part of the exercise requires a slow and smooth motion, and a next a quick and abrupt one, or a part of the exercise is fast and quiet, and another dense and halted, etc. These attributes are more achievable in imaginative exercises, in sketches and improvisations than in motor type physical routines.

Regarding the entire lesson, this principle translates into the selection of exercises and topics that would be contrastive to one another. For instance, a single lesson might consist of an exercise to improve Posture and Gait, few exercises for the improvement of expressive hand, a practice in a particular Period Style, and a fighting technique in Hand-to-Hand combat. The idea is to make the student frequently switch from one kind of movement to another, from one tempo-rhythm to another or from exercising one group of muscles to applying another, etc. This principle of diversity and contrast creates a continuous confrontation, eliminates monotony from the lesson, and reduces fatigue. It also helps the student to develop the ability to switch from one tempo-rhythm of physical action to another quickly. To set up the lesson of this kind, draw the exercises from different sections of the program.

The principle of alternation of contrastive elements in stage movement class imitates the very essence of the dramatic play with its constant collisions of interests of characters, which manifested through conflicting actions. These events and actions sometimes gradually but often rapidly change the relationships between the characters in the play. These changes, in turn, give rise to a gradual or abrupt modification of tempo-rhythms of physical action. Thereby, to accommodate all these transitions, the actor must be able to switch from one kind to action to the other, from one emotion to another (often at odds with the previous) virtually instantly.

However, this is easier to proclaim than to do, and most aspiring actors are not born with this specific quality. On the contrary, a human being tends to exist in a certain tempo rhythm, and his self often aggressively resists to any changes. Acting is perhaps one of few known occupations requiring the professional to appreciate an abrupt shift in tempo-rhythm. This quality is especially essential for a performer in modern plays. An actor might play several characters within one scene or have to act in real-time, followed by a flashback scene that calls for a sudden change of place, time, and circumstances.

See that this skill is a subject of a continuous drill. One way to do it is to diversify every lesson with the exercises of different tempos and rhythms, of different amplitudes of movement, and with various expenditures of energy. Proper rotation of exercises in a single lesson subliminally develops a quality that enables the actor to move from one type of action to another and from one tempo-rhythm to the other gracefully and naturally.

Undoubtedly, the same ability actor would obtain working intensively and continuously in a series of different productions for some years. Nevertheless, we want our students to begin their careers already equipped with specific abilities. That makes our second primary methodological principle appear very significant for the learning process.

There is another essential aspect of this principle that we merely mentioned before. The scientists have proved that a lengthy repetition of the same subject or pattern tires not only muscles but also the nervous system. Incidentally, the majority of exercises presented in this textbook do actively influence the emotions of the students. So, a numerous and monotonous repetition of the same exercise (or similar exercises) causes the student to lose interest in it, and then inevitably brings about emotional fatigue.

The continuous research of the efficiency of different teaching methods in various branches of knowledge suggests that the student learns the material much better and faster when the lessons are lively and exciting. In contrast, boring lessons, and the tasks performed under the pressure of the teacher have an opposite outcome on learning. As our experience demonstrates, the exercises' alternation with a different effect on the body and the mind within a single lesson enables the instructor to make the process diverse and exciting. As a result, students perform with absolute dedication throughout the lesson. In our case, such a technique has a positive influence not only on the nervous system but also on the student's physique. Therefore, a lesson built on the principle of alternation of contrastive elements is more productive than one consisting of similar type exercises.

It applies not only to the diversity of exercises within a single lesson but to variety within an exercise. It works by presenting the same action in small, medium, and large amplitudes combined with a corresponding change of tempo. For example, such an approach would help the actor to acquire an assortment of movements of various periods in human history that are quite different from modern everyday activities. The utilization of all kinds of accessories in plays, such as fans, walking sticks, lorgnettes, hats, etc. might become an excellent means of expressiveness in character. However, to make it look natural, the actor should practice these patterns in a variety of amplitudes and with different tempos. Otherwise, the actor would just hold these accessories on stage and feel uncomfortable doing it.

Executing exercises with periodically changing tempos, amplitudes, and styles would gradually develop a necessary skill, so the instructor should always consider it when picking exercises for a particular lesson. It means that if the tempo of one exercise is slow, the next routine should be fast; if one consists of small-amplitude motions, include large amplitudes in the following; if previous uses minor muscular tension, next should suggest substantial tension. In a single lesson, many different types of movements should be at hand, such as rounded, soft, and continuous, as well as sharp, intense, and halted. It would actively train the ability to switch from one type of movement to another by will, either instantly or gradually.

The students usually have no problem changing tempos or amplitudes in the exercises of the simple motor type. All the instructor has to do is to spell out a concrete task. However, exercises that contain some semantics require particular skills and experience from the instructor regarding appropriate changes in the tempo-rhythms of performance, as it is always important to preserve the logic of action. One should be careful when imposing a tempo-rhythm in skits because the given circumstances and psycho-physical actions *are* the factors that naturally determine a particular tempo-rhythm of physical behavior in an individual sketch. Our textbook offers the teacher an assortment of movement sketches that vary in content and differ by subject, given circumstances, and, as a result, by the tempo rhythm.

The assortment of tasks in a lesson and exercise

This principle means that in selecting exercises for Stage Movement course the preference should be given to the exercises that develop not just a single ability, but a complex of faculties, habits, and skills. For example, in bodybuilding, most of the exercises designed to develop one particular quality, often only individual muscle. Stage movement should be different from other movement disciplines and employ exercises that have more than one task. However, at the beginning of training, the exercises could be simple and instantly recognizable to avoid information overload. Nevertheless, as soon as the students understand and accept the "rules of the game," the instructor should introduce the exercises that develop a range of qualities.

The straightforward exercises described in Chapter Four of the text should be included mostly in the Preliminary part of the lesson. Most of them intended to warm up the muscles, to stretch the ligaments, and to prepare the body for the forthcoming series of more complex exercises. Some of the exercises of this type summoned to develop certain groups of muscles, others to improve correct breathing, still, others to regulate the cardiovascular system. However, even these exercises upon closer examination reveal the complexity of tasks. For instance, exercise "The Spring" actively develops flexibility and mobility of joints, strength, rhythmicity, and correct breathing.

Most importantly, however, is the complexity of tasks in a lesson. A standard lesson in Essential Stage Movement includes exercises derived from five to eight different themes. Within a single lesson, the students offered exercises in Gymnastics, in Motor Coordination, in Posture and Gait improvement, in developing Expressive Hand, in Balance, and Acrobatics. A lesson saturated with a variety of tasks compels the student body and mind to the simultaneous development of a range of psycho-physical capabilities.

It is what makes our method unique and different from many other known methods and techniques. The principle of an assortment of tasks is precisely what K. Stanislavsky had in mind in his search for the actor's proper physical training. The variety of topics in each session makes this training comprehensive. It does not mean that dance, stage fencing, or Mime does not contribute to the actor's physical preparedness. On the contrary, each of these disciplines improves the actor's plastic apparatus in its unique way. However, in the Essential Stage Movement, the same problem is resolved based on natural or organic movements of the everyday. We consider this as a significant benefit for the dramatic actor. Applying the principle of an assortment of tasks, we successfully achieve a comprehensive training of plasticity in the natural movements.

The assortment principle in a stage movement course would realize by gradually reducing the number of exercises containing one or two tasks, giving way to more complex exercises as the training progresses. The more tasks exercise presents, the more nerve/muscle stimulation it creates. By practicing exercises of this kind, an individual progressively develops the ability to learn new patterns in a shorter period. It helps to train multifaceted attention and motor memory, but most importantly, the principle of an assortment of tasks significantly accelerates the process of "training and drilling" itself.

The gradual transition from simple exercises to complex ones

This important methodological principle of our method has a notion that each new exercise or a variation of them should present a challenge, so the student would have to make an effort to perform it. Every new practice must be scrutinized to verify the motions and to represent the teacher's task correctly. We highly recommend that once the technique learned and the errors corrected by the instructor, repeat it until executed semi-automatically. That would improve such qualities as attention and coordination. From this point on, use a primary exercise reached a semi-automatic level to develop more complex qualities and skills. One can achieve this by adding details to the basic pattern or by adding new parts or by combining techniques learned before with this basic exercise. This way, the student challenged every time a new element added. However, this new task is easy to conquer with a relatively moderate effort. This process should continue until the exercise reaches its final stage.

Repeat the exercise thereafter in the following lessons as training material. Nevertheless, introduce some new circumstances, such as a change of tempo, music, partners, etc. Therefore, the impressive performance of an exercise in the classroom is not a goal, but a pretext for more complex and challenging training, in which the exercise's intricacy would gradually increase. If a physical exercise becomes a routine, it converts into dull skeletal muscle gymnastics, which is insignificant for the actor's training.

Using this primary methodological principle, the instructor can achieve maximum levels of concentration and attention of the student. Besides, it actively trains motion memory, quick reaction, instantaneous adaptation to changing conditions, and raises enthusiasm about unexpected new tasks, all of which are essential qualities for a future actor.

The practical application of this principle begins from an initial lesson in which the instructor originates the exercise's approximate technique. At first, the tasks themselves must be simple enough, even primitive, because the instructor is not going to demonstrate them, but just explain to the students what to do. Of course, some difficulty must be present yet in these tasks. These first exercises should not be too demanding on the part of psycho-physical quality. Otherwise, it would overwhelm the beginners and might even create a psychological blockade in some of them.

However, the instructor must be sensitive and observant to understand when an exercise does not present a challenge. In this case, he/she should make the tasks more difficult immediately or in the following lessons. The main goal is to keep the group in a state of constant psycho-physical mobilization. One can achieve this by merely changing the tempo or the amplitudes of motions. If the teacher manages to maintain such a condition throughout the lesson and through the entire program, the students would gradually build up a solid concentration skill and endurance of the nervous system, which is crucial for young actors.

Let us discuss now a common problem that, one way or another, is present in the learning process everywhere. The problem is that there is always a significant difference in the level of previous training and preparedness between students in a particular group. This heterogeneity stems from the reality of students of different backgrounds, various education qualities, different age groups, and students trained in different methods (or no methods at all) assembled in one group.

An experienced pedagogue should choose exercises of such complexity that would be somewhat difficult for some students and yet doable for others, who would have to make a more considerable effort. One should remember that the exercises that are too easy never captivate students; engaging in such activities is boring, and the subject's interest diminishes rapidly. As a result, the quality of training drastically reduced. On the other hand, introduced to exercises that are too difficult, students lose faith in their abilities and often get discouraged. It would inevitably lead to a reduction in interest in the class.

Sometimes the instructor should temporarily abandon this principle "from simple to complex" and offer an exercise that is simpler than previous or perhaps a simpler variation of it. Such a reverse act would be acceptable only when a teacher by mistake offered a new task, complex to the degree that students were unable to execute it. By doing this, the instructor should consciously admit a pedagogical error made. Generally speaking, the instructor should always try increasing the number of exercises that would be grasped by students within the time allotted. Only through a diverse selection of tasks included in the training, a teacher can obtain a real skill or a firm habit. Any such skill or habit would become the actor's source of expressive means. When the student manages to perform an exercise semi-automatically, his mind acquires the opportunity to invite yet another task and visualization. One can only achieve that with hard work, or as Stanislavsky put it, with "training and drill."

The training outcomes depend on the instructor's ability to plan the material for the term in such a way that the student would master the maximum possible number of skills. This planning should consider the time allocated the degree of preparedness of the group, and the general psycho-physical load suitable for the group. Build your plan with the following notion: one must install various skills into the student and not just acquaint him/her with them. Merely information or knowledge about the necessary skills, though broadens the horizon, does not enable the student to use these skills in their future stage practice. Therefore, movement training must be both versatile and profound.

The primary principle "from simple to complex" in our method also makes us shift from training a body that bears purely technical nature to the full psycho-physical action on stage, formed by the will of the individual performer.

The performance of exercises must be purposeful, efficient, and precise

The actual training of Faculties, Habits, and Skills in Essential Stage Movement begins from the moment the student can execute an exercise purposefully, efficiently, and precisely, in other words, when the external form of an exercise grasped. By this time, have all technical errors corrected and unnecessary motions eliminated. In the following work on the task, the performance should gradually become purposeful and efficient in each part and totality.

To adhere to this primary methodological principle, the instructor should seek in his students a desire to execute an exercise correctly, even when the activity is the simplest. That would demonstrate that students have already acquired the need to perform the task set by the instructor thoroughly. The instructor needs to detect this moment to maintain the taste for proper execution in his students.

The nature of human motion based on the quality of the motor analyzer. Similarly, the psycho-physical abilities, which provide physical actions of the actor in the role, depend on the quality of motor analyzers of the individual performer. The improvement of these analyzers is the responsibility of an instructor, regardless of the movement subject he or she teaches. This process is not a simple one and takes a rather long time to accomplish. However, the motor analyzers are adequately tuned and tuned in the first stage of training with the help of simple motor exercises. They begin to serve the student on a higher level, which is closer to the creative process. The skills obtained by such training would continue to assist the student in a study with an acting instructor, and later in the professional work on the role.

A useful device to develop motor analyzers even further is a group of exercises with imaginary objects. They create an additional obstacle for the mind in the area of management of skeletal muscles because of the student's awareness in such activities occupied by the extreme illusory situation. However, in programs where acting taught by the Stanislavsky method, the exercises with imaginary objects are already part of the curriculum. In this case, we do not recommend duplicating this training in the movement class. Otherwise, such exercises might be included later in the stage movement program as a segment of regular lessons, but on a higher level – as skits with given circumstances.

Our experience shows that the transition from simple motor exercise to a skit must be gradual. Through the introduction of intermediate exercises, the instructor should delicately encourage the students to use their imagination in creating some given circumstances. If the instructor is skillful in this kind of work, the students begin to apply their given circumstances during execution, and soon a formal movement pattern miraculously and often involuntarily turns into a meaningful behavior. The subsequent process of transforming such exercises into the skits becomes much more manageable. At the final stage of the program, certain appropriate exercises with given circumstances proposed by the instructor would make the students perform specific physical actions.

The experience of many generations of pedagogues has shown that the most helpful exercises for this kind of training are those that can develop the abilities gradually from the simple motor pattern up to the level of meaningful behavior. Naturally, the task of the Introductory exercises and Gymnastic exercises presented in this text is simply to train muscles, cardiovascular and respiratory apparatuses. It does not make sense transforming them into expressive physical behavior. They will always remain just this, motor exercises. However, even these exercises could be exciting and "artistic," as we demonstrated in Chapter Four and Chapter Ten. In short, with the help of simple motor exercises, we train the reaction through fluctuations of tempo-rhythm in combination with variations in the range of movements.

However, the Essential Stage Movement's main subject matter is not gymnastics, but rather unique exercises. One should keep in mind that in activities with a semantic task, motions might slightly fluctuate due to the play of student's imagination. The instructor should accept such movements as a natural manifestation of creativity. As for the exercises/études (or skits), the training of adaptive reactions is possible only through changes in given circumstances. It is the circumstances that define and organize the essence of physical behavior and its tempo rhythm.

A crucial element in stage movement pedagogy is the method of evaluation of muscle tension. In an "old school," this method reduced to a subjective impression of the instructor who would provide a student with advice based on observation only.

It turns out to be quite simple to determine the failure of muscle tension: if the effort is insufficient, the student will not accomplish the exercise. To detect the overstress of muscles is more difficult because, in this case, the student, as a rule, will complete the task. In the practical part of our book, some exercises would help to determine muscle overstress. Most of them are in the Chapter "Special exercises in balance," where activities on reduced support combined with the recitation of logical text or singing, would noticeably demonstrate the student's ability to control muscle tension. The trick is, it is impossible to speak, much less to sing when the muscles clamped.

Another group of exercises, which would demonstrate the correct muscle tension, is acrobatics. In it, any muscle imbalance leads to failure. However, since an acrobatic stunt lasts all but several seconds, the student must learn to control the muscle tension before practicing it.

The instructor should continuously point out any excessive muscle tension but demand the precision of the pattern's execution. That would ensure the transformation of external control into self-control. These corrections would mobilize the consciousness, which in turn would manage the function of skeletal muscles in the right way.

The instructor must monitor each performance of an exercise in the program on account of the accuracy of muscle stress, as it affects the *harmonious activity of the movements*. That is the primary goal of the entire methodology of the Essential Stage Movement.

Methodological Techniques

Major methodological principles described above will work when applied to the program through the entire period of training. However, the following *Methodological Techniques* work best when employed selectively; they belong to particular exercises and specific situations. However, some of the techniques are relevant to most of the training. We will identify these general methodological techniques below.

We suggested conducting the lessons in the Essential Stage Movement no more than two or three times a week, depending on the intensity of the program. Each lesson should last a minimum of one hour and fifteen minutes and a maximum of one and a half hours. Different timetables might create problems. For instance, administering classes less than twice a week would result in students forgetting the material from one lesson to another. On the other hand, more than three lessons per week might tire students, thus reducing the discipline's interest. Besides, the experience shows that humans systems need time to "digest" a new material. The length of a lesson suggested above gives the instructor enough time to include 5 to 8 different themes in one lesson. Besides, it is not too long to wear out the students.

Ensure that all lessons are connected methodically so that every next lesson is a continuation of the previous.

It would be a fundamental miscalculation to believe that the movement pattern learned by the student in the Essential Stage Movement program is the end objective. One should remember that the actor's physical behavior on stage is the external expression of feelings and thoughts of the character created by him/her. In athletics, the movement in itself is mostly the result desired. The same thing is in Dance, Stage Fencing, etc. A dancer would spend hours and days working on the *Fouetté en Tournant* for the sake of... *Fouetté en Tournant.*

An instructor, who does not understand the difference between athletic training and that of the actor or between dance training and stage movement, would never be beneficial to our profession, even though some of the exercises and patterns they use are similar in comparable disciplines.

Let us take, for instance, a Forward Roll. In athletics, a coach would be very particular about how fast the athlete performs a forward roll, or how high he or she should jump to execute it. In stage movement class, a basic form of this stunt is sufficient, as we use Forward Roll in the program for many different reasons. One is to develop an essential habit called *Courage and Decisiveness*, and another is to train *Awareness of Space* – the ability to distribute the movements within a given space. Thirdly, we use this stunt to drill the transitions from one tempo-rhythm to another. Finally, one can use this technique as a preliminary exercise for Stage Falls. Incidentally, they rarely use it in theater productions as a stunt by itself.

In selecting the techniques and exercises for the program, we should always remember that learning a skill that has nothing (or very little) to do with acting on stage, TV or Movie, is a waste of precious training time. For instant, juggling looks like a good exercise, theatrical too. However, why spending time on the development of this skill if most would never have a chance to use it on stage? However, the actor should have his psycho-physical abilities developed to the degree, which would allow him to learn a simple juggling routine in a brief period in case the role would require it.

Another general methodological technique is the use of one exercise for numerous different reasons. However, in doing this, the instructor should follow the right order of the tasks represented in the exercise. For example, a simple exercise like Running is used in the

Essential Stage Movement mainly as a tool to train cardiovascular and respiratory apparatuses. Nevertheless, before suggesting to the students to control their breathing while running, we should first teach the exercise's correct technique. Later in the program, use this same exercise to drill a Sense of Rhythm, Sense of Space, Endurance, etc. Before using an exercise for a particular reason, one has to make sure all the previous tasks performed satisfactorily.

The Essential Stage Movement is not a finished edifice or an outright method. Developed by many pedagogues during a substantial period, it is still in the process of widening. Methodological principles and techniques, application of exercises, exercises themselves all are subject to modification and changes. With new developments in theater arts, one should revise the method and bring it in conformity with the demands. ESM is a mobile system that attempts to assemble different topics into a comprehensive training of the actor's psycho-physical apparatus.

Methodological techniques described below are specific ways of using one or several exercises most productively. These techniques are comprehensive and plenty to choose from to employ them in teaching many themes and a majority of exercises described in this text. The instructor is free to use any of the techniques when it feels necessary. It is difficult to predict when and which technique would be more effective in a lesson. Use a particular methodological technique only when there is a specific need for it. The employment of these techniques also depends on the composition of the group, and abilities of individual students – their interests, the degree of talent, technical level, the state of health, and physical preparedness.

One can better understand how the Methodology of Essential Stage Movement works only when teaching it with the simultaneous exploration of the major principles and techniques. It might be a good idea to familiarize yourself with the video version of the Essential Stage Movement course by taking it from the beginning to the end to feel its impact on you practically.

The level of mastery of this method by an instructor depends on many qualities of the individual, such as knowledge of theater arts, acting and movement skills, experience, teaching abilities and incentive, etc. Only when a teacher mastered the basic methodological principles and standard techniques, is capable to timely and adequately apply them, and can manipulate the exercises offered in this text, could this individual considered for representing the subject.

To learn the methodological techniques and to memorize the exercises would present no problem for individuals with decent memory and sheer persistence. However, this knowledge would not be adequate for conducting the classes in Stage Movement masterfully and confidently. Only after a sufficient period of pedagogical practice would the instructor manage to develop his/her style of teaching. Only then he or she would be ready for the professional work.

This text offers an accumulated experience of many distinguished pedagogues. The knowledge obtained from this source combined with live examples from the Video Instructor course would give a contender enough material to try to conduct his/her class. To get a feel of the subject, one should be able to experiment with the exercises described here freely and to apply the different methodological principles and techniques, as well as to create new ones. It will take the time to become a real pro, but this is the way to go. However, we must warn from oversaturation of lessons with a variety of methodological techniques described above. These should be used carefully and only with specific exercises.

Accompany the exercises by live music

This procedure is something quite unusual for stage movement training in North America but is common in Russia and some European countries. Somehow, no one is surprised that dance classes always accompanied by live music. Sadly, for the last thirty years or so, live music gradually disappeared from dance classes because it substituted with a cheaper source – boom box. This seemingly harmless replacement had been, in fact, a significant setback in dance aesthetics. Recorded music, though convenient to use, makes the dance *exercic* mechanical and robotic. The recorded music piece always sounds the same, and the performer of the exercise after several repetitions knows ahead of time what to expect. As a result, this kind of musical accompaniment provides merely the rhythm. Thus, the dynamics and nuances became not relevant, and hip-hop music now can compete with the classical as a source of dance accompaniment.

This is precisely why we insist on having live music (piano) to accompany movement classes. The advantages of having live music for training psycho-physical abilities are too obvious. Live music is random in the sense of tempo; one can change both the rhythm and the tempo at any time by choice, and live music performed by a professional accompanist has an emotional quality to it. Using live music in class helps to infuse an artistic taste in students and to comprehend esthetics. A contemporary generation has little chance to listen to classical or folk music. They surrounded day and night by pop or hip-hop sounds that hardly can assist future actors in developing a sense of beauty, or imagination.

Live music in the Essential Stage Movement has yet another task. A good portion of exercises in the program designed with a piece of particular music in mind to accompany them. As the exercise developing, this music would sound in many different variations. The instructor would change the tempo-rhythm of the music, the intensity of different parts, the meaning of it, etc. The students would be required to reflect these nuances and changes in their movements.

For instance, one of the exercises that drill Rhythmicity called "Echo" can be performed only with a live accompanist, as it is the accompanist who leads the group in this exercise by perpetually presenting a new musical pattern, one bar of music at a time.

Students who never before had a chance to exercise with live music soon find it very amusing and work with great interest. One way or another, there is no better way to train the sense of tempo and rhythm than using live music in class. It is common for the theater pedagogues to think that musical literacy belongs to future musical theater actors only. Does this mean that the dramatic actor would never be working with music? Nowadays, students who understand the importance of musical education for the actor seek such an opportunity on the side.

Being quite uncommon, the proposition to have an accompanist for movement classes might raise no enthusiasm with the administration of many schools in North America. However, if one is serious about providing the authentic movement training, one has to convince the administrator and to insist on having it.

Demonstrate "how not to" instead of "how to"

When more than one student makes an error in a newly introduced exercise and a simple statement can easily correct it, it is an excellent occasion to demonstrate ... the error! That's right, intentionally show them not the proper execution, but exaggerated wrong one. This demonstration "how not to" attracts the immediate attention of the group. However, using this technique, the instructor should carefully avoid pointing personally at the student(s) who made a mistake. Those responsible would instantly understand this by themselves. If one does such a demonstration with a fair share of humor and performs it artistically, it would perhaps raise laughter. It is a good sign, as it would encourage floppers to correct the error in the next repetition.

Follow the demonstration of "how not to" by perhaps a more detailed description of the task with another repletion followed. If this would not solve the problem, the instructor should try again and explain how to correct the error verbally using different words.

It is a very effective methodological technique, but it should not often be used to avoid turning the lesson into a comical spectacle or some kind of entertainment. That can take away the students' attention from the learning process and drastically change the rhythm of the lesson.

Maintaining tempo-rhythm of the lesson

Every lesson definitely should have its tempo-rhythm just as every theatrical production should. The instructor has to put together each lesson like a small production with its own, if you wish, dramaturgy. It should have the beginning, the development, the climax, and the resolution. The beginning, for example, is the Preliminary exercises, the resolution – Concluding exercises, and the instructor's farewell words.

Should the instructor manage to create each lesson in such a way, the entire training process would become extremely close to what the students trained for – the sense of integrity of the stage presentation. It would establish the responsibility to execute every task with a maximum effort. It would also raise the emotional set of mind in students, and as a result, after the lesson, it would create a genuine sense of accomplishment. Sometimes, in our practice, when the students are overwhelmed with this kind of sensation, they applaud the teacher at the end, which is traditionally done only in dance classes.

However, it takes time and effort to reach a level when the instructor would be able to build a lesson in such a fashion. The "secret" is in blending themes (or different groups of exercises,) tempos, and amplitudes in such a way that a tempo-rhythm of the lesson produces a sensation of an invention rather than hard work. A novice instructor should thoroughly plan each lesson and analyze each exercise – its place in the lesson, its length, musical accompaniment, etc. This should become natural after teaching the Essential Stage Movement to several different groups of students over a period.

Correcting errors made by a student in exercise

After each performance of the exercise, the instructor should make a short comment so that the students would know whether the performance was successful or not. It is sometimes necessary to stop the exercise as soon as it began when it is evident that the majority of students misunderstood the task. Letting them finish it would just take away valuable time for no good reason. In cases like this, the instructor should quickly understand why most of the group failed to perform the task. Sometimes it is a distraction that prevented students from listening, or perhaps the description of the exercise has not been explicitly conveyed. Eliminate the obstacles or rephrase the task before repeating the exercise.

If incidents described above happen at the beginning of the program, do not get alarmed, as it takes time for the group to adjust to a new subject, teacher, or method. However, if things like this continue to occur, it could be an indication that the students do not take this class seriously. One should change this attitude drastically, and perhaps an additional explanation of the program's objectives would help fix this.

When one or several students make a mistake, the instructor should point it out to them, explaining what was wrong without scolding or degrading them. However, if a student makes the same mistakes repeatedly, talk to him/her after the class and try to understand the reason. It happens much too often that young people overestimate their inclination and, as a result, find themselves in the wrong profession. The honest thing for a mentor is, to tell the truth, and to prevent the young person from wasting time. For sure, this youngster will find another profession in which he or she will be more successful.

Correction of common errors by displaying a poor performance

Another technique to let the students understand a common mistake is to ask a student whose performance was the least suitable to demonstrate the exercise in front of the group. The instructor's proposition should sound simple, leisurely, and without any hint of deception to avoid alarming the student. After the incorrect performance, the instructor should ask the class to comment on this performance. When the students would point on mistakes that they notice, the instructor should explain what caused the errors and how to correct them.

This technique would often help to alert a careless student, as it would raise his self-esteem. However, the instructor should never overdo it to make it look offensive but instead, turn it into a joke.

Presence of outside observers in class

It is beneficial to invite outside observers to class once and again. They can be students from other groups, teachers who teach other disciplines to this group, instructor's friends or students' friends and family members visiting campus, etc. The presence of the "audience" would mobilize the students and give them a sense of performance.

The so-called "stage fright" is an unpleasant fact in our business, and it is no secret that many young people often have it. This methodological technique would help such students to get rid of this sensation gradually. The fact that the entire group performs the same exercise makes it safe; it should not instigate the overacting or "showing off." At the same time, it would give the students a bit more satisfaction from their work done, especially if they would sense a positive reaction from the observers. However, the students should not be distracted by the presence of observers and execute the tasks with usual enthusiasm instead.

When having guests in the class, the instructor should not ignore them but give those not familiar with the training a brief explanation of what is going on and what the exercises' objectives are. From the students' point of view, having unexpected guests in class is like considering a new set of given circumstances. The performers have to accept it as such instead of pretending as if nothing had happened.

This methodological technique would help to develop willpower, courage and determination, concentration, and dedication in the execution of the assignment.

Everyone in class must perform all exercises

In almost any group of students, an instructor would find one or more individuals trying to avoid performing specific complex or risky exercises. The individuals I have in mind are either cowardly or narcissistic. The former ones are simply afraid to do the task; the latter are reluctant to look ridiculous or awkward. There is also a third category – just lazy students. None of these personalities is desirable in our line of business. Moreover, some such students would often try to assure the instructor that they would work by themselves and would demonstrate the results next time. Beware, as a rule, this never happens.

From the beginning of the session, the teacher should consider a rigid rule – to avoid introducing a more complex exercise until everyone in the group performs the previous one sufficiently. Initially, it sure would take valuable time out of a lesson, but the instructor should insist on the execution of an exercise "now" by everyone. One should help the lagging students in all possible ways to get it done even if the rest of the group is just waiting. The student's reward will come in the form of supporting reaction of the peers and the instructor's encouragement.

Every so often, one comes across a freakish student with a bad temper. This kind of behavior is potentially damaging for a future actor when becoming a part of a production. The instructor must restrain such conduct from the start. The perseverance of the teacher in a case like this would ensure success.

The teacher needs to know each student well – individuality, health problems (if any) his/her particular interest in the arts. If there are health problems, the instructor might decide to free a student from performing certain exercises. If a student has talent but has a health problem, it is not a reason to remove him or her from the program.

Thus, apply this methodological technique sternly to those capricious. However, make careful considerations for those students who have a reasonable excuse.

Repetition of exercises until performed correctly by the entire class

Like the previous, the instructor should keep this methodological technique in mind continuously. Because of the differences in capabilities, talent level, the level of concentration, etc. between students in a group, the instructor would always face a situation when some students grasp the technique faster than the others do. The general rule is to continue repetitions until everyone in class performs it correctly. One should not necessarily announce this rule to the group. Perhaps the students that usually hold the class should remain unidentified. It would become evident for everyone without this. However, announced by the instructor, it might cause a mental blockade in some students.

If a part of the group repeatedly causes the process to slow down, the instructor might want to review the tasks and, for a while, make the exercises a bit easier to perform from the first attempt. As these students would catch up with the group, one can make the exercises more challenging again. In the majority of such cases, the problem is with the student's imagination. The instructor should help these students and watch how effectively they use their visualization to build the pattern first in their minds.

Furthermore, one should always remember that the execution of the movement pattern must be unique to each student and avoid misinterpreting such individual performance as an error.

Complexity of tasks

At the beginning of the semester, the instructor should carefully assess the level of the group's abilities. This determination is essential to deciding on the complexity of tasks and the pace of learning offered to this particular group.

The rule of thumb is - a task should be simple enough to execute for the entire group from the first or second attempt. However, the instructor should be aware that overly simple tasks would cause the students to lose interest in training soon, and accordingly, their attention would diminish.

On the other hand, if the task is too complicated for the majority of the group, it would discourage many participants, and it would tire them ahead of schedule. As every new group is unique, the instructor should decide on the level of the complexity that would be appropriate for this particular group very soon after the beginning of the semester. As the program progresses, this criterion might be adjusted from time to time.

Fourfold repetition of exercises when introduced

Certain exercises in the program are the subject of the fourfold repetition when introduced. More than others, it concerns Coordination exercises. Make sure a pattern verbally explained by the instructor executed four times in a row. The experience shows that this technique ensures the correct execution in the majority of cases.

During the first repetition out of four, usually, a very rough image of the exercise produced; in the second repetition – initial technique defined and a pattern created; in the third repetition, the pattern complemented with details; and in the fourth repetition, the pattern performed in a complete form. Even so, the fourth repetition is still lacking in free expression and accuracy.

By steadily applying this methodological technique, one would gradually create a habit of putting together all the body resources and the mind to execute a new pattern on the fourth repetition. Of course, the pattern itself has to be of a reasonable size. Usually, it is a pattern consisted of four simple motions; or one that fits within one bar of music.

Our experience demonstrates that by performing less than four repetitions, the students more likely would not be successful in the completion of the exercise. More than four at a time would make the additional repetitions a bit tedious and a waste of time. The drill of concentration would discontinue right there, as, after the fourth repetition, the pattern would be executed automatically. Remember, our goal is to develop the student's abilities, and the pattern, which we ask to execute, is merely a medium for that and not a goal.

If the entire group does not perform a new exercise correctly after the initial four repetitions, the instructor should offer another repetition and repeat it four times. The students lagging should be encouraged.

Besides the advantages described above, this methodological technique is akin to preparation for a role. In working on a bit in production, the actor in the first repetition seeks a correct action; in the second – the action defined; in the third – the actor searches for accessories or details. In the fourth repetition, the actor finally performs organically.

Explanation of the purpose of each exercise

It is important to let the students know the purpose of each exercise offered in the program. That would help to make the training to become conscious and purposeful. The students should understand which exercise develops what qualities and how this would help them in the future in professional work in theater, film, or TV. The instructor should give the examples and should answer any questions aroused. It is always more intriguing to provide examples from personal experience, but any lively illustration would do the job.

We suggest reserving an explanation at the time exercise moves to the final form. When starting a new exercise, explain just a basic technique. For complex exercises, do not give out the purpose of each part and sometimes even the exercise title. Only after the basic pattern contained and the students have an impression of the entire exercise should the instructor tell the group about the effect of this exercise on the quality of movement. In case the practice develops a specific skill, the instructor should explain this and state the circumstances this skill might find application in the production.

Correction of errors in process of exercises performance

One should announce and corrected the errors, usually after the exercise is finished. However, correct small errors while the students are performing the exercise. That would save an instructor a lot of time. However, the comments must be short and to the point, as the lengthy explanations would break the concentration. It would be appropriate to specify to whom this comment referred so that the rest of the class would carry out the task without paying attention to the feedback.

In case the correction or comment concerns the majority of the group, the instructor should make it known to the students by using words like "attention" or "continue the exercise, but..." etc. This methodological technique used only when there is a certainty that the basic pattern already performed semi-automatically. Otherwise, by doing this, the instructor might destroy the scheme and even cause the exercise to a halt, which would be damaging to the process.

To use this technique successfully, the instructor should establish suitable short commands and phrases that would help fix an error quickly and, at the same time, would not break the rhythm of the exercise. As these commands pronounced over the musical accompaniment, the instructor would have to force his voice to make the command clear and audible. Also, the accompanist should be aware of this technique and, perhaps, reduce the volume during a comment.

Besides saving time and reducing the number of repetitions, this methodological technique is an excellent source to train multi-planar attention, selective attention, and coordination in students.

Introduction of unexpected tasks and commands in process of the exercise performance

After the previous methodological technique put into practice successfully, the instructor can begin using surprised commands during the execution of exercises. These commands would request the students to change physical behavior to different degrees. The command should be unexpected but easy to obey. It could be a change of direction of walking or a change of tempo, termination of a part of the pattern while the rest of the exercise continues, etc. For instance, the teacher instructed the students to walk forward in quarter-notes. Unexpectedly, the instructor commands the group in the process of the activity, "walk backward." Another example, the students were told to perform an exercise with both arms at the same time. In the process of it, the instructor announces, "Continue with the right arm only!" In any case, the commands must be clear and loud enough for everyone to hear.

After this technique used in class for the first time, it would be appropriate to explain the group that such a method helps to drill quick responses and that it mobilizes the entire nervous system. The instructor should also advise that he will repeat surprised commands like this in most of the lessons from that point on.

This methodological technique substantially raises the emotional level of the lesson. However, the instructor should be careful in creating changes. Finding the appropriate time in a lesson and within an exercise for this kind of training is the solution. Usually, a good time for this technique is when a feeling of an emotional level's fading arises.

Use of preliminary exercises before learning complicated combination

A good portion of patterns and skills in the Essential Stage Movement program is too complicated to master at once, as a whole. Others are just dangerous to perform right away. In cases like this, the instructor should use so-called "preparatory" exercises. In this textbook, preparatory exercises that need to precede the main exercise described in detail. Sometimes we call them "stages." Using preliminary exercises consists of breaking the skill (or pattern) in several parts, each presenting the student with a simple exercise that is instantly achievable. And then, the parts should be put together. For various exercises, it is either in a particular order (one following another) or performed simultaneously with different parts of the body to create the final version of the exercise.

Some intricate patterns demand multiple preparatory exercises, and as they are impossible to execute within one lesson. The instructor should plan to introduce these in a logical order in several consecutive lessons.

For tasks associated with risk in execution (mostly stunts), the instructor should explain beforehand what the job is undertaking and what are the stages. Only after that, offer the first preparatory exercise. This approach would mobilize the students for careful and serious consideration. Practice Preliminary exercises for stunts until performed perfectly well as the safety and the health of the students depend on it.

A choreographer or a theater director who arranges a stunt in production is responsible for the safety of the actors. When dealing with actors of different backgrounds and attentiveness, preliminary exercises are essential. A specialist in the field must develop such exercises. For theater directors, it is better to abandon a stunt in the production than to risk unsafe performance. One must keep in mind that a rehearsal is different from the stage performance in the sense that there are additional stimuli that occupy the actor performing the stunt.

Reduction of explanation as progress is obvious

Many exercises in the Essential Stage Movement course repeatedly performed in numerous lessons. For instance, the same set of Warm-up exercises are offered in twelve to fifteen classes without substantial variations. Certain complex exercises developed over several consecutive lessons are repeated in the following sessions in different variations. That would require describing the exercise every time it offered for performance to secure its proper execution.

Well, our next methodological technique's objective is to reduce the explanation of the exercise intentionally and gradually as it progresses through the learning process. After an exercise becomes familiar, the instructor should just briefly remind its task or objective, making these comments even shorter each time and finally announcing the title only.

It saves time and trains the student's memory and imagination. Besides, the lengthy descriptions wear the student out and dissipate his attention.

Another positive effect of this technique is that it helps to maintain the action-oriented tempo-rhythm of the lesson.

Withdrawal of exercise shortly after completion of final stage

Present complex exercises that take several lessons to accomplish in stages. Some consist of five to six stages from the beginning of learning to the final form of the exercise. Once the entire group satisfactory performs the exercise, it becomes a training tool of a particular habit or skill. In this training, the instructor would continuously change the circumstances, tempo, and amplitudes to make it continually challenging for the students.

However, finally, the time comes when all the means of complications are exhausted. It is a good time to withdraw this exercise from the training because unchallenged unemotional repetitions can only harm.

Unexpected return to abandoned exercise

We suggest offering to students an exercise that was completed and abandoned unexpectedly after awhile with original or even new circumstances. That would make the old task a fair training material once more. To offer an abandoned exercise, the instructor should choose a proper moment when the students most likely have forgotten about it. It would usually raise the emotional level of the lesson while serving as an excellent tool to drill a particular habit or skill. This skill would be invaluable to future actors who might be involved in a repertory style theater where the plays performed in a planned rotating order.

Use this methodological technique in such a way that the students must execute an exercise in its entirety offered suddenly. Give them no time for preparatory stages, as you did initially. If the first performance is mediocre, it must be repeated several times or until executed as well as once before.

We suggest using this methodological technique frequently, especially with the exercises that drill the essential psycho-physical qualities.

Diversity of tempos and rhythms in exercise and lesson

We already discussed the assortment of tasks in a lesson when analyzing the major principles of our method. Having a variety of different styles, tempo-rhythms, and amplitudes in a single lesson would benefit the training a great deal. However, even within a single exercise, we should strive whenever it is possible to introduce diversity as well.

Quite a few exercises in the Essential Stage Movement program suggest and allow such diversity. The instructor should seek any opportunity to diversify these exercises by changing tempo-rhythms and even styles. For example, part of the exercise performed in two-quarter time and another part in three-quarter time; or a part of the exercise, the students have to move in quarters, and to complete the same movements in eight notes in another part, etc.

At first, notify the students of these changes before the exercise begins. Later in the process, the instructor can introduce the changes as a surprise. One way or another, this methodological technique trains the ability to switch from one mode of movement to another swiftly without breaking its continuity. Eventually, this will grow into a skill that would help the actor making smooth transitions from one "action" to another in production.

Intentional short intermissions in class

It is correct that one must count every minute rationed for learning and that wasting time is a mistake. Also, since every lesson has its tempo-rhythm, it is a misdeed to break it. However, we are dealing with physical activities (sometimes intense), and there are some moments in the lesson when the students need a short break to relieve the tension. These episodes are hard to predict, so the instructor should be sensitive in detecting such occurrences. Once identified, the instructor should casually continue the lesson, but instead of offering a new task, he/she should ask a question, start a conversation, or even tell a joke. The best time to have such an interval is between the blocks or different themes of which a lesson consists.

Use these intervals for a brief discussion of progress in class, important information associated with the subject, an announcement of an event related to the program, etc. The message must be spontaneous (or sound as such) and short so that students do not get too much involved with it. Stage Movement is a practical discipline, so the student should spend most of the time allotted for physical training. We should remember that the stage movement teacher is also a mentor, and these intermissions are a suitable excuse to talk about something else but the exercises. However, a general discussion would not be appropriate. The instructor should somehow connect the conversation with the previous exercise and give the students an example or some other valuable information.

This methodological technique brings liveliness to the lesson and, at the same time, provides a short recess before the next theme or exercise.

Avoiding physical overload in a lesson

We should always keep in mind that the goal of stage movement training is not to develop sufficient muscles or to refine particular movement patterns. Our goal is to maximize the number of psycho-physical qualities that would enable the actor to express any emotion and thought that stems from his soul. It is also to make these abilities so steadfast that they transform into habits and skills. It makes the training of the actor different from the training of the athlete, bodybuilder, and even a dancer.

One should pay special attention to the prevention of physical overload in the lesson. For that reason, the exercises, especially strenuous, must be limited to several repetitions. As Strength and Endurance are among the abilities developed in this class, it is more beneficial to do it gradually, in small doses, and over a period. A boot-camp environment would not help to raise an artist. The students must combine rigorous training with a clear understanding of the reason they are doing all this.

The instructor should have enough experience and knowledge to detect the exact moment when to stop the load and switch to another task that would involve different groups of muscles.

Use the diversity of exercises, the change of tempo-rhythms, and the logical composition of the lesson in general to avoid the physical overload in a lesson. The lesson should always start with warm-up exercises, and the load must gradually increase until the lesson reaches its climax. After that, there should be a brief period of soft exercises, and for the conclusion – a fast-tempo exercise (usually running) to reactivate the cardiovascular apparatus.

Specificity of given circumstances in exercises involving acting

As we discussed before, one should use acting techniques in stage movement class with extra caution. The instructor should be aware of how his students taught by the acting teacher to avoid contradiction and confusion. One should be careful to impose on students within the movement program his/her idea of acting techniques. It is a delicate matter, and the best way to avoid confusion is to use whatever technique the students already accomplished in their acting class.

It is particularly important for the movement instructors, which are not very familiar with acting. Remember, a dangerous notion that everyone knows what acting is all about is still in existence among pedagogues of different theatrical disciplines. In truth, even professional actors do not necessarily know how to teach acting to others. Only people trained on how to teach acting as a particular discipline or those who have extensive experience in doing this are trustworthy to judge what's right and what's wrong in stage presentation.

That is why in the exercises that include elements of acting (even the simplest ones,) the instructor should know how to present the students with given circumstances. To be on a safe side, one should offer only very particular circumstances, as any general circumstances would provoke "acting in general" and what is even worth a cliché or a rubber stamp. K. Stanislavsky wrote, "A cliché fills up any empty spot in a role not occupied with a live feeling."

Use this methodological technique as a guide for a stage movement teacher to remain ethical and not to correct students' acting unless one detects an obvious overacting. Even then, the instructor should only comment but avoid trying to fix the error. Instead, it would be appropriate to make sure the students understand the specific given circumstances suggested by the instructor for these exercises or etude.

Switching partners

Switching partners in the paired exercises is always a challenge, as it means that the student must adjust to a new tempo-rhythm in the execution process. The ability to adapt quickly to various partners is essential for the actor, especially when working "crowd" scenes. Also, occasionally the actor must perform with a "double" due to the illness of the chief performer and such. Therefore, drill this ability periodically in the movement class. The instructor should use any suitable occasion for this. For instance, with every new repetition of a paired exercise, the entire group should switch partners.

We consider the level of training high when this factor does not affect the performance in paired exercises anymore.

Exercises with an imaginary partner

Use this methodological technique in paired exercises when an odd number of students attend. A student without a partner would have to execute all the motions as if he does have a partner. Instead of just staying and relaxing, a student can still practice the pattern without a real partner. When he/she gets one as a consequence of switching partners, the exercise scheme is already familiar.

This technique has its fundamental purpose – it makes the student use his imagination to recreate not just his movements, but also the movements of his imaginary partner, which, in a way, doubles the effort. Therefore, it is advisable to have every student in class occasionally perform exercises alone, with an imaginary partner. This technique has yet another application: it teaches the actor how to rehearse a scene in the secure atmosphere of his room by imagining the partner and his actions.

This technique would develop the ability of the actor to recreate the scene in his mind, just sitting in the chair or lying in bed.

However, the instructor should terminate any attempt to "show off" to attract the attention of peers, unless the given circumstances call for it.

Performing exercises with the right as well as with left limbs of the body

The majority of people in the world are right-handers. Left-handedness is relatively uncommon; in reality, only seven to ten percent of the adult population is left-handed. It is one of the reasons we begin moving forward or backward in the performing arts, mostly with the right foot. We strongly believe that the actors should be able to perform the movements of everyday activities with the right part of the body and with the left part with almost the same level of dexterity.

By tradition, we suggest performing many exercises in this program with the right foot on the music's downbeat or with the right arm only. Some of these exercises are a combination of arms movements and walking—others associated with moving to the right, etc. Our experience proves that having the students perform such exercises in both directions or perform them regularly with right and left hand or foot just as important. One should offer to perform in reverse practically every exercise comprehended to a final level.

Besides the uniform development of different parts of the brain, this technique would advance the actor's critical quality: to be able (if there is a need) to perform the same movement pattern in both directions. The conventionality of theater reveals such a need almost constantly.

Maintaining professional ethics and aesthetics in class

It is wise to use the stage movement class, among other important things, for ongoing education of ethics and aesthetics. Do it in every suitable moment of the lesson and in every possible way. Regarding ethics and aesthetics, the instructor should be a model - getting to class on time, dressing appropriately, behaving with grace and dignity, being respectful of students, and demanding respect for the teacher and theater arts in general.

The instructor should disallow himself to ridicule the students, or to show dislike for a student in any form or shape. By adhering to all these rules, the instructor secures the right to demand similar behavior in students. We recommend pointing discussing any manifestation of disrespect or disobedience, any evidence of bad taste in dressing or physical behavior. This can be done either in front of the classmates or outside of the class, depending on severity.

The process of esthetic education should begin literally from the first lesson and continue throughout the entire program. Develop, train, and nurture the sense of beauty with every possible tool, including the exercises themselves, the musical accompaniment, the clothing worn in class, the relationships between the students, etc. Not for a moment should we forget that these are future artists who intend to carry esthetics to the people from the stage, a movie, or a TV screen. This part of education is no less important than the training of faculties, habits, and skills.

* * *

Other Methodological techniques are of limited use and belong to particular exercises. These additional techniques are described in individual paragraphs attached to the exercises and called *Methodological guidelines*.

It is obvious now that Stage Movement Instructor is a distinctive and multifaceted profession. Also, it is a unique profession. A respectable stage movement teacher must know a great deal in so many different areas of the arts and of the sciences to successfully develop psycho-physical abilities in future actors. However, no one is born a Stage Movement Instructor. Moreover, nobody perhaps dreams of becoming one. Young people dream of becoming actors, directors, and playwrights. Therefore, in our opinion (supported by personal experience), people become acting teachers, speech teachers, or movement instructors not because they always wanted to, but because at a particular stage of their artistic career, they feel a calling.

Unfortunately, there is still a common misconception that "those who can – do, those who can't – teach." The teacher is a very sophisticated, intellectual, and multifaceted occupation. Teacher of stage movement is hardly an exception. Of course, there are teachers, and there are teachers. One who previously learned a series of exercises as a student and soon after began teaching these exercises to other people is not a teacher yet. This individual can become one, but only after he or she recognizes that it is a distinct profession and one ought to master it thoroughly. Besides, this profession requires unique qualities and specific talents. Only those who have it might become good teachers.

The qualities required for this occupation are, essentially, sophisticated artistic taste and high theater ethics. Then, an instructor should develop excellent professional qualities, such as knowledge of the subject, the ability to conduct the class or a communication gift, and the knowledge of pedagogical psychology. In addition to the general requirements that are common for a teacher of any discipline, the stage movement instructor must have certain specific qualities. Knowledge of arts in general and theater arts, in particular, would be essential, as would a vivid imagination and understanding of the related disciplines.

As mentioned before, a functional movement teacher must be familiar with the acting technique, the theater's history, and the basics of music and dance. Ideally, the instructor should have decent acting skills, so that his demonstrations of "how not to," and occasionally "how-to," would be impressive and artistic. That would diversify the lessons and make the teacher be artistically on the same level as his students. The instructor must be proficient in all the exercises included in the program and capable perhaps occasionally to "surprise" his students with an excellent demonstration of a small portion of an exercise.

A skilled instructor must conduct constant research regarding this subject and take part in all possible discussions and disputes concerning the development of the matter in his school, in the community, nationally, and internationally.

Stage movement instructor, in many ways, is akin to stage director. He or she must visualize the objective for a particular group of students, must sense each student's capacity, and must be able, as mentioned before, to arrange each lesson regarding tempo-rhythm and the level of physical stress. An individual specializing in the teaching stage movement should be able to perform all kinds of choreographic work in productions in the school or the community theaters, as he might be the only specialist of expressive movement in the entire district. Such activity must be a subject to seek in the theaters, and it would raise the credibility of the instructor in the eyes of his students.

There are still some teachers around who try to build authority in a class by telling students about personal experiences and successes in the performing, by generally speaking about the arts, the objectives in theater education, and about how the future actor must be physically expressive. Such lessons become boring soon, and the benefit of such lessons is minimal. In his book, Ivan Koch wrote, "The drive to achieve a goal always mobilizes human being and does it better than extensive explanations of the fact that one must perform the exercise as energetic as possible."[2]

Mr. Koch also used to repeat more than once, that if the student does not perform a task correctly, it is not the student's fault, but the instructor's. We always tend to find an excuse for our students' poor performance. However, the truth is, good students, appear from a good instructor.

The basis of the pedagogue's success is in his ability to teach professionally and be sincere, honest, and benevolent with the students. That does not exclude being strict with them. The instructor should connect with students, not just in the classroom, but also out of it. However, the instructor should always maintain a distinction between the class, where they work together, and the outside of the class, where the instructor might be a senior friend and an advisor.

CHAPTER SIXTEEN

MANAGING EDUCATIONAL PROCESS

A great deal of the successful application of the Essential Stage Movement program depends on the teacher's experience and the skills. As we stated before, stage movement is an auxiliary subject, which in the amalgamation with other disciplines helps shape the professional actor. As such, one should teach it in close collaboration with these disciplines. The stage movement instructors must be proficient in leading aspects of these disciplines to use their skills within the demands of the profession.

However, the decisive feature of a stage movement instructor is an in-depth knowledge of the subject. This knowledge would allow a movement teacher to assist the student in developing all the necessary Faculties, Habits, and Skills. Besides the familiarity with this subject, the movement instructor should obtain basic knowledge and skills in such subject matters as Human Anatomy, Physiology, and Psychology. One should be literate in music, familiar with Folk, Modern, Ballroom, and Classical Dance, acquainted with Acrobatics, and knowledgeable in Acting as a profession.

Working methodically with young people who prepare themselves for a performer's profession, the teacher must be well educated in Theatre history and must possess an impeccable artistic taste. It is a huge responsibility to tell an impressionable young person authoritatively what to consider right and what to believe is wrong in the arts. It is not a secret that, at times, one careless word might alter the mind of an aspiring artist in the wrong way. We ought to remember also that a stage movement teacher, like any teacher of just about any discipline, is also a mentor and a role model for the pupils. A good teacher is one, from whom students would seek advice in creative and even everyday life issues.

A determined stage movement teacher continuously strives to improve the skills in the area of instructions and related topics. The involvement in school projects as a choreographer or a consultant on particular movement sequences would allow a teacher to work with students outside the class setting and to demonstrate in practice how the skills learned in class utilized in a situation of production.

A stage movement instructor must possess some artistic skills to be fascinating and convincing in the description of tasks and in communicating with students and possible guests of the class. It is understandable that the teacher should know all the exercises as well as methodological principles and techniques perfectly well and should be able to execute any of them if needed. Some of the exercises in the Essential Stage Movement do need a demonstration, and the teacher must be prepared to display them if necessary.

A person who takes upon him/herself a great responsibility to teach a practical discipline in theater arts must fully understand the nature of the performing process and, if possible, to have an actor's experience. Also, a stage movement instructor should have some skills of a theatrical director as well. We tend to think of a stage movement program and of every individual lesson in the program as a sort of theatrical production with all the elements one should contain. There must be the subject matter, the logic, the beginning, the end, the climax, the tempo-rhythm, etc. It is up to the instructor's talent and imagination to assemble the entire program and every lesson in a way that would be meaningful, exciting, educating, and entertaining all at the same time. The teacher must be ready and able to communicate on a professional level with the fellow instructors of other professional disciplines in the school, to understand the problems encountered and to adjust his or her instructions to the collective goal in developing a group and an individual student.

However, to successfully implement all the knowledge and skills mentioned above, the instructor should also enjoy teaching people and possess enough patience to last as long as needed to develop all the necessary Faculties, Habits, and Skills in the students.

The outcome of the training is what creates a lasting reputation for the instructor. In the case of movement training, colleagues – the teachers of related disciplines - can detect the progress. It can also be a director who works with the group in the practical application of their skills. The students themselves would rarely appreciate the training upon completion. It is only years later that they would acknowledge it after numerous occasions applying skills acquired in class. After comparing their abilities with those of fellow actors educated in other schools, they would discover that they own the skills received from their movement instructor through strict and vigorous training.

In a wide variety of existing methods and techniques, it is common to come across an instructor, which can organize the process and maintain good discipline and respect for the subject. However, the teachings have little to do with the future profession. Such training turns into a meaningless waste of the students' time and energy with no necessary skills obtained in the end; the reputation of such a pedagogue is minimal, notwithstanding apparent safety.

Some instructors in an attempt to substitute the lack of scientific, institutionalized methodology fill in the lessons in stage movement with general discussions of the importance of physical expressiveness for the actor. The instructors of this trend would hand out numerous examples of the achievements of actors who correctly used their gestures and bodies in creating characters, etc. They leave the majority of their students with a sense of confusion and disappointment. It is only apparent that a lecture cannot substitute practical exercise in developing psycho-physical skills.

The instructor of the Essential Stage Movement doesn't need to dress for the class in a proper uniform because he or she does not demonstrate the movements in class. That would only confuse the students. However, the instructor should wear regular attire complying with age, sex, and build. It would be a good sign of professionalism for one to adjust attire deliberately in preparation for the work just before the beginning of the lesson. For men, it would be taking off the coat, or loosen up a necktie, for women – removing a scarf or substituting high heel shoes with more comfortable ones. Such behavior without further explanation would demonstrate the instructor's readiness for serious work.

The secret of pedagogical success is the ability to teach professional skills and to communicate the instructions in a sincere, truthful, and benevolent way. However, that does not mean that the teacher should not be strict and demanding.

The instructor should ensure that the students always prepared for the Stage Movement class, both physically and mentally. The requirement for uniforms is different with various instructors. Still, the attire should be comfortable enough to enable the student to bend knees and arms freely and to move the body in any direction without difficulty. On the other hand, the uniform must be simple enough to make the body movements observable to the instructor and peers. Fancy blouses, skirts, and wide trousers would be unacceptable for a stage movement lesson. Jewelry of any kind, including wristwatches, could become an obstacle for many exercises; shoes must be light with no or a small heel for both men and women. The ideal shoes for stage movement class still are jazz shoes.

Once established, it is only rational to maintain the dress code. In case a student is not entirely prepared for the class, he/she should not be allowed to participate but should observe the lesson instead and to make notes about every new task given on this day. It is enough to allow one student to participate without the proper attire and open a door for all kinds of excuses and grievances.

One should make clear at the beginning of the program that as there is no homework ever in movement class, the students must do the work "here and now," and that giving a 100% of energy and attention expected from everyone. However, when working with young people, be prepared for a situation when, for one reason or another, a student would not perform with full dedication. In every such case, the instructor should determine the cause for the ineffective behavior, and if it is justifiable, the student should observe the lesson rather than participate in it. The reason is, such action might become a discouraging example for the entire group.

In this effect, it is important to determine any serious illnesses or disabilities beforehand that can prevent a student from executing any of the exercises in the program. By neglecting this, a situation may arise when it would be too late to remove a student from the program. Giving permanent indulgence to such a student might negatively affect the entire process.

To get the best results in developing Faculties, Habits, and Skills using the Essential Stage Movement program, the instructor should thoroughly plan the program by having in mind a particular group of students. Consider every aspect of this group. For instance, consider the participants' age, as the attention span of younger people is shorter. Furthermore, younger students tend to get tired sooner, thus losing their interest faster. We do not recommend having formal class in stage movement with students younger than sixteen years. For such youngsters, let say, middle school students, the selected exercises from this textbook can be included in a general theater program to break a routine or to make the acting class a bit more physical. Without a doubt, the warm-up part of the class must precede any physical exercises.

The instructor should fully understand the goal and the capacities of a particular school, department, or program. What level of a theater program is this group? What other disciplines did students learn at the same time? How many hours allocated for stage movement? Do students take Dance classes simultaneously? If not, did they take any dance classes before?

We strongly recommend including the Essential Stage Movement in the first year of the Acting program. As some exercises described in this text in their primary stages are quite simple, the more advanced students might be discouraged at first, even though soon enough, they will discover that the program gets more challenging. However, what we do not recommend is to combine in a single group the students with different advancements in Acting, Dance, and Movement. Our experience shows that the results with a group like this are least productive. Unfortunately, small Drama Departments have no choice but to offer a class in Movement or Speech to any student majoring in Theatre and sometimes even to any student who wants to take it. Often suffering are those students who came to acquire the acting profession.

A critical aspect of planning the course is the amount of time allocated for it. If one chooses to present all the exercises described in the text, it would be sufficient for two full semesters of continuous lessons or approximately sixty lessons one hour and 15 minutes each. However, our experience shows that the best way to use this program is to select enough exercises for one semester (about 30– 32 lessons). Plan the rest of the material, including more complicated stages of certain exercises, for the next semester. To fulfill the program, add the elements of the Hand-to-hand Combat and Period Movement. This way, the second semester would turn into a more practical utilization of movement patterns into skits and etudes.

Whether arranging an entire semester or a lesson, particular Methodological Principles and Methodological Techniques described in Chapter 15 of this book should guide this project. Among others are: maintaining the lesson's tempo-rhythm, repeating exercises until performed by the entire group, and the complexity of tasks, etc.

Every lesson should consist of eight to ten sequences, or episodes, lasting anything from five to ten minutes. Commit every such episode to the purposeful development of a particular faculty, habit or skill, or a combination of them. For that reason, the practical part of this textbook presented in chapters, each representing a group of exercises designed to develop a particular quality.

Before the classes began, the instructor's mission would be to construct an effective program, varied in tempo rhythm, refreshing, challenging, and fulfilling. This task calls for serious planning. Nevertheless, even a thorough preparation would leave plenty of space for quick adjustments and sometimes for considerable changes during the lesson. Be prepared for this, just as the actor ought to be ready for improvisation in a stage situation. For creative artists, the educational process should be no less creative and flexible. For this, the instructor must be able to operate all the tools of the Essential Stage Movement with ease – from simple exercises to major methodological principles and various techniques.

To help an instructor to understand better how this program works, we are offering below a typical plot for several lessons on various levels of the process. As we stated before, the instructor should develop the actual content of every lesson. The content would depend on many factors the teacher must consider. We present below the samples of five lessons. This presentation is based on the conditions that the subject taught within a semester, 30 to 32, one-hour-and-fifteen-minute lessons, twice a week.

LESSON ONE

1. ***Opening exercises*** (see Chapter 4.)
  This is the first lesson in the Essential Stage Movement. The instructor should begin it with an explanation of the objectives and essential requirements of the class and the future work. The instructor should introduce the accompanist (if there is one) to the students and explain the role of this person in the learning process. One should make sure everybody is ready and able to execute the physical exercises. After this short introduction, the instructor should begin with *Exercise 1*, "Walking" and finish it in its complete form in this lesson.
  Continue with *Exercise 2*, "Walking on Tiptoes," then *Exercise 3*, "Walking on Tiptoes, Knees Up," then *Exercise 4*, Skipping," and then *Exercise 5*, "Running."
  This part of the class, along with the Introduction, should take 10 to 12 minutes.

2. ***Warm-up Exercises*** (see Chapter 4.)
  It is rational to keep the students in the formation of the previous exercise, which was a circle, to save valuable time. Just ask them to face the center and to get ready for the *Exercise 17*, "Squatting." After this move to *Exercise 20*, "Bending Forward," than to *Exercise 21*, "Rotating Upper Body," then to *Exercise 22*, "Bending Over," then to *Exercise 23*, "Bending Backwards," and then offer the *Exercise 30*, "Spring."

Please note that some Warm-up exercises described in Chapter 4 skipped in this lesson. We intentionally avoid overloading students with new terminology, patterns, and tasks.

As the explanation of the new exercises initially takes considerable time, this episode of the lesson should last about 10 to 12 minutes.

3. *Rhythmicity* (see Chapter 5.)

Begin with changing to a "crowd" formation (explaining it.) Then tell the importance of developing Rhythmicity for the actor.

Move to *Exercise 64*, "Quarters, Halves, Whole Notes" and finish it in this lesson; then move to *Exercise 65*, "Four Quarters, Two Halves" and complete all the stages within this lesson. As these exercises are quite unusual, the instructor should move slowly from one stage of the exercise to the next, making sure the students perform every task precisely and accurately. See that every student in the group makes no mistakes in imitating the rhythmical pattern to avoid problems in the forthcoming, more complicated exercises of this kind.

This episode of Lesson 1 should take anything from 9 to 10 minutes.

4. *Posture and Gait* (see Chapter 6.)

The instructor should explain the reason this group of exercises included in the Essential Stage Movement program. Present *Exercise 79*, "Regular Walk" to the students and concentrate on Stage 1 of the exercise; move slowly from one task to the next. Remember, this is the *initial* presentation of the concept of correct posture and correct gait. Spell it out in all the details. Repeat the exercise as many times as needed to make every student perform it sufficiently.

This episode should take no more than 9 or 10 minutes of the lesson.

5. ***Awareness and Movement Coordination*** (see Chapter 7.)

The instructor should explain the role of this group of exercises in the program and its verbal form of introduction. Make clear that the visualization will precede the physical execution of the exercise in all exercises of this kind.

Offer *Exercise 88,* "Arms Coordination #1" and move slowly from Stage 1 to Stage 2, and then to Stage 3 of this exercise, thus presenting it all in one lesson. You would have to repeat each stage of the exercise several times until every student would do it right and in time with the music. It would take 12 to 14 minutes, as this is quite a unique exercise to do.

6. ***Expressive Hand*** (see Chapter 12.)

The instructor should explain the importance of flexible and expressive hands in the acting profession. Offer *Exercise, 153* "The Tardy Hand" and follow it up to the stage when the exercise performed with both arms sideways at the same time. Repeat it several times and make sure the students understood the concept of "tardy hand."

Move on to *Exercise 154,* "The Fish." Finish all the variations of this exercise and move to the next *Exercise 155,* "The Claws." Make the students complete all the variations of this exercise as well.

This episode of the lesson would take 12 to 14 minutes because all the exercises in this lesson are a novelty, and a detailed explanation takes time. Later, in the following lessons, it would take less time to describe the exercise and to correct some errors. Finally, the time will come when the students perform the exercise only by the instructor's announcement.

7. ***Concluding Exercise***

For the conclusion of this first lesson, do *Exercise 5,* "Running" introduced already in the Opening Exercises segment at the beginning of the lesson. After the students run for 30– 40 seconds, switch running to walking and, gradually slowing the tempo, make the group stop at the end of the music.

Explain to the students that the first lesson was not very difficult because it was just the beginning and that the exercises will become increasingly more complicated in the future.

This final episode would take 3 to 4 minutes of the lesson.

The instructor should manage the time allotted for the lesson and try to adhere to the plan as firmly as possible. With all this, however, do not interrupt or abandon none of the exercises without some resolution.

LESSON SEVEN

1.   *Opening Exercises* (see Chapter 4.)

Make sure by this time in the program that all the exercises described in the Opening Exercises part of Chapter 4 comprehended and performed with music as one continuous piece of work. It should lead the students from "walking" to "walking on tip-toes," then to "walking on tip-toes with knees up to the chest," to "skipping," and then to "running" and "walking" again. So, the instructor should use *Exercise 6* (complex exercise) and watch that the students carefully follow the transitions from one mode of moving to another; see that the students perform all the elements in time with music and keep walking with the left foot on a downbeat. Remind the students to breathe rhythmically and to save energy by making only the motions necessary for a particular mode of movement.

By this time, the students must learn how to stop at the end of the Opening Exercise together with the music and stand a few seconds motionless, indicating the finale. This episode should take only 2 minutes of the lesson.

2.   *Breathing Exercises* (see Chapter 4.)

Use *Exercise 9*, "Running, reciting logical text" as breathing exercise in this lesson.

Right after the conclusion of the previous exercise, instruct the students to recite Multiplication tables for "three" standing in place. See that the text pronounced clearly and in time with the music. By this time in the program, the students must be able to control their breathing and to practice the ability to regulate breathing while speaking.

This part of the lesson should take one minute.

3. *Concentration Exercises* (see Chapter 4.)

Preserve a circle formation and offer the students to execute *Exercise 14*, "Three steps forward, one step sideways, and one step backward." See that the students maintain equal distances in the process. Repeat the exercise one or two more times if necessary. Depending on the number of repetitions, this part of the lesson would take 1 to 2 minutes.

4. *Warm-up Exercises* (see Chapter 4.)

Use the circle formation and make the students perform the following exercises successively from the Warm-up chapter of the book:

Exercise 17 – Squatting.
Exercise 18 – Squatting, knees together.
Exercise 20 – Bending forward.
Exercise 21 – Rotating upper body.
Exercise 22 – Bending over.
Exercise 23 – Bending backward.
Exercise 24 – Bending sideways.
Exercise 25 – Bend/unbend legs.
Exercise 26 – Arch body up.
Exercise 27 – Lie down, sit up.
Exercise 28 – Legs apart, legs together.
Exercise 30 – Springing while sitting down.
Exercise 29 – Arching body.
Exercise 32 – Spring.

Right after the Spring exercise, instruct the group to stay with right (or left) shoulder towards the center of the circle, walk in a circle in quarters, then run for about 20 to 30 seconds, then walk again and stop in time with the music.

The Warm-up part of this lesson should take about 12 minutes.

5. *Rhythmicity* (see Chapter 5.)

Carry out with *Exercise 71*, "Echo." Remind the students that whenever the eighth-note beats appear in a sample, they must respond by running with light steps. If one or two students make mistakes reproducing a sample, make the accompanist repeat the same test, and make sure this time everyone performed it correctly.

Ask the accompanist to play several sets of Echoes, each consisting of 8 to 10 samples; after each set completed, stop the group, instruct the students to make an about-turn, and continue with another collection of Echo samples. The accompanist should vary the samples to present different rhythmical patterns.

Repeat the exercise Echo several times until you feel that the interest in the exercise begins to decline.

Go to the *Exercise 72*, "Conducting March" and work on Stage 1 of this exercise. Make sure the students indicate the downbeat of each bar of the music with sharp movements of their hands and maintain the attention of the invisible "band" with their palms open. Repeat the exercise several times, slightly changing the tempo with each repetition.

This episode of the lesson should take 4 to 5 minutes.

6. *Posture and Gait* (see Chapter 6.)

Continue working on *Exercise 7*, "Regular Walk" and concentrate on Stage 1, 2, and 3 of the exercise. Try to achieve the correct posture and a smooth and continuous gait while they walk in quarter-notes. Use surprised commands to change the direction of the walking. Repeat the exercise several times in various combinations and tempos.

Go to *Exercise 80*, "Regular walk with arms' positions." As this is the first time the exercise offered, explain it, and make the students perform the various positions of arms. Demonstrate these positions if necessary; then use these positions in combination with walking in quarters forward and backward.

The instructor should remember that introducing various positions of arms in combination with walking is just another means to drill correct posture and gait, so pay attention to the way the students develop these essential skills. Repeat the exercise several times and drill the correct posture and proper gait.

Go to Stage 4 of *Exercise 79*, "Regular walk." Train the students in walking in halves, and then combine the walking in halves with surprised commands; first, to change the direction of walking, and then to change the position of arms while walking. Finally, offer the exercise in which you would combine the changes in the manner of walking with the changes in the position of arms – all this using surprised commands.

Now introduce the *Exercise 81*, "Regular walk in a curve," and train the gait and posture in combination with these new motions in several repetitions. And now, combine all the changes in arms' positions and changes of directions with regular walking in quarters and halves, and drill the posture and gait for one or two minutes more. Altogether, this episode of the lesson should take anything from 10 to 12 minutes.

7. *Awareness and Motor Coordination* (see Chapter 7.)

Conduct the *Exercise 91*, "Coordination #3" and follow the usual order of presenting movement coordination exercises. First, let the students execute four movements with the right arm and repeat it four times; then, let them do the exercise with the left arm only. Finally, make them perform the exercise with both arms at the same time standing in place.

Combine this exercise with walking forward in quarters and watch that the students perform the movements of the arms and the correct gait properly.

Now continue with the same exercise and suggest that the students walk forward in half-notes but keep moving the arms in quarters at the same time. It is a challenging task, so the instructor might ask to repeat the exercise several times until everyone performs it satisfactory.

Let the students repeat the exercise but instruct them to walk in halves continuously but move the arms assertively, as they did before. Then continue developing this exercise and suggest that the students would walk forward for one bar in quarters, then for the next bar in halves, and continue alternating these two modes. Repeat the exercise with surprised commands changing the direction of walking from forward to backward and reverse. Repeat it and improvise your commands changing the direction of walking and the rhythm of moving.

This episode should last anything from 7 to 9 minutes.

8. *Expressive Hand* (see Chapter 12.)
Begin this part of the lesson with *Exercise 155*, "The Claws." Repeat the exercise several times with different variations.
To continue developing expressive hand in this lesson, use *Exercise 15*, "The Snake," and follow this with *Exercise 153*, "The Tardy Hand."

After that, conduct *Exercise 157*, "Right Angle," Then, let the students perform *Exercise 158*, "The Gears." After repeating the initial version, keep working on this exercise in this lesson. Suggest that the students begin the exercise positioning their arms to the left of the body and perform it by gradually moving their arms to the right and then back to the beginning position.

Following The Gears, make the students perform Stage 1 and then Stage 2 of *Exercise 159*, "The Fan."

Introduce in this lesson the new hands, *Exercise 160*, "Make Waves." Repeat Version 1 of the exercise several times.

This episode should take 9 to 11 minutes of the lesson.

9. *Balance* (see Chapter 10.)
Conduct the *Exercise 112*, "The Heron" in combination with the exercise "The Fan." Follow it with *Exercise 111*, "The Goalkeeper," then offer to perform *Exercise 114*, "Jumping Jack," and make them repeat it eight times, moving forward on the right foot, then eight times on the

left foot. Repeat this exercise with different variations moving forward and backward, using the right foot, and then left foot for support.

Introduce a new exercise in balance, *Exercise 118,* "Stretching Arm, Leg," and make the students perform Version 1 of the exercise.

Now introduce another new exercise in balance, *Exercise 120,* "Step over the Chair." Let the group repeat the exercise several times and then offer to perform *Exercise 117,* "The Cork Opener," first rotating to the left, and then in reverse. This episode of the lesson should take anything from 10 to 12 minutes.

10. *Acrobatics* (see Chapter 11.)

Continue working on the "Shoulder Stand" (*Exercise 124*). Try to achieve balanced and smooth transitions and synchronization of motions with the music.

Next, go to *Exercise 125,* "The Bridge." Remind the students to tilt their heads back so they can see the ground. Make sure they band all away so that the arms and legs are straight.

Move up to *Exercise 126,* "The Frog." In this lesson, let the students walk forward in quarters in the "frog" position several times, and then let them jump forward in this position. See that the students maintain balance throughout the entire exercise.

Next exercise in Acrobatics is "Forward Roll" (*Exercise 127.*) As it is only the second lesson since this exercise introduced, explain in detail the technique and, if needed, let the student perform the stunt one by one, so that you can check the precision of the movements.

Acrobatics should last about 7 to 8 minutes in this lesson.

11. *Concluding Exercise*

Conclude this lesson with "Running" in a circle. Start this part of the lesson immediately after the last exercise in Acrobatics and let the students run for 30 to 40 seconds in a fast tempo.

Stop the running abruptly and make the students recite Multiplication tables for "two" standing in place. See that they manage to regulate their breathing while reciting the tables. By the end of the recitation, the voices must sound natural and clear.

This episode of the lesson should take 2 or 3 minutes.

LESSON FIFTEEN

1.   *Opening Exercise* (Chapter 4.)

Students must perform the final version of the Opening Exercise with the running part lasting longer than usual.

2.   *Breathing Exercise* (Chapter 4.)

Stop the group and let the students recite odd numbers from "one" and up taking a breath between the bars.

3.   *Concentration Exercise* (Chapter 4.)

Apply *Exercise 16* to prepare the group for the major part of the lesson. Make sure the landing after the jumps performed noiselessly.

4.   *Warm-up Exercises* (Chapter 4.)

In this lesson, introduce the group to the new set of Warm-up exercises – the Exercises with an ordinary chair. As these exercises are in some way unusual for the students, it would take some time to explain each exercise.

> *Exercise 42* – Backward Bend
> *Exercise 43* – Sideways Bend
> *Exercise 44* – Forward Bend
> *Exercise 45* – Leg over Seat
> *Exercise 46* – Chair Lifts
> *Exercise 47* – Bend/Unbend Legs
> *Exercise 48* – Sit-ups
> *Exercise 49* – Step up - Step down

Notice, some exercises avoided. Introduce the rest of the exercises with a chair in the following lesson.

5.   *Rhythmicity* (Chapter 5.)
        Develop *Exercise 71*, "Echo" further and offer Stage 3 of it, thus introducing the terms "legato" and "staccato."
        Continue with *Exercise 72*, "Conducting March." Work first on Stage 1 of the exercise, then move to Stage 2 and repeat the exercise several times.
        The next exercise is "Conducting ¾-time" (Exercise 73) Let the students perform Part 2 and Part 3 of the exercise.
        Continue with Exercise 74, "Conducting 4/4-time." Repeat Stage 1 and Stage 2 and Stage 3 of the exercise, but concentrate the attention on Stage 4 of the exercise and let the students perform it several times or until you notice a significant improvement. After that, introduce Stage 5, "Conducting a Band," and work on it for several minutes.

6.   *Posture and Gait* (Chapter 6.)
        As you introduced the exercise "Hamlet" (*Exercise 87*) in the previous lesson, continue it, adding Stage 3 of the exercise. After getting satisfactory results, move to Stage 4 of the exercise and finish this part of the exercise in the current lesson. However, try not to overdo it because Stage 4 is extensive and needs more time to master. Do it in the next lesson.

7.   *Speech-Motor Coordination* (Chapter 8.)
        Continue working on the exercise "Little Miss Muffet" (*Exercise 100)*. Repeat Stage 1 of the exercise to make sure the students still remember the patterns for both arms. Then repeat the poem once or twice in time with music and standing in place. Finally, let the students perform the movements, walk and recite the poem at the same time; in other words, perform Stage 4 of the exercise. Drill speech-movement coordination further by changing tempo, by giving surprised commands, by making the students move in half-notes instead of quarters.

8.   ***Expressive Hand*** (Chapter 12.)

To drill the expressive hand, offer the following exercises in this lesson:

> *Exercise 153* – "The Tardy Hand."
>
> *Exercise 158* – "The Gears," Version 2.
>
> *Exercise 160* – "Make Waves," repeat Version 3, 4, and 5.
>
> *Exercise 161* – "The Kitten."

Repeat Stages 1 and 2 and introduce stages 3 and 4 of the exercise.

> *Exercise 162*, "The Bowl." Introduce this new exercise

and let the students perform it with the right hand, then with the left hand, and then with both hands at the same time. As the movements for this exercise are stylized, the students would better understand the pattern with some demonstration.

9.   ***Balance*** (Chapter 10.)

Drill balance with the following exercises:

> *Exercise 113* – "The Barrier Gate," do both versions again and then offer given circumstances for a skit performance.
>
> *Exercise 112* – "The Heron," repeat it several times in different variations.
>
> *Exercise 118* – "Stretching Arm and Leg."
>
> *Exercise 120* – "Step over the Chair."
>
> *Exercise 117* – "The Cork Opener."

10. ***Acrobatics*** (Chapter 11.)

Practice the Forward roll further in all possible combinations: *Exercise 129*, "Three consecutive Forward Rolls," then *Exercise 130* "Forward Roll in Slow Motion," and then *Exercise 131* "Three Forward Rolls, change direction." Go to the next exercise, a combination of the "Bridge" and "Shoulder Stand." Let the students perform the combination in time with music in a pattern created by the instructor.

11. *Concluding Exercise*

   Make the students run around the room in a circle for 40 to 50 minutes; change the tempo of running several times. Immediately after "running" exercise, make the students recite "Little Miss Muffet" standing in the spot and see that they take a breath at the right moment so that their breathing is regular by the end of the poem.

LESSON TWENTY-FIVE

1.   *Opening Exercise* (Chapter 4.)
   Do the final version of the Opening Exercise.

2.   *Warm-up Exercises* (Chapter 4.)
   Apply a full set of Warm-up Exercises II (advanced collection) with no or very short intervals in between the exercises.
   Complete the Warm-up part of this lesson with walking, then running, and then walking again. Stop the group and let the students recite "Humpty-Dumpty" to regulate the breathing.

3.   *Rhythmicity* (Chapter 5.)
   To start this part of the lesson, let the students "Conduct Waltz" (*Exercise 73*) standing in place.
   Next, instruct the group to perform Stage 2 of this exercise once and then offer them to perform Stage 3.

4.   *Posture and Gait* (Chapter 6.)
   Work on the final version of exercise "Hamlet" (*Exercise 87.)* Introduce surprise changes in the musical accompaniment, perform the exercise beginning with the right foot, then with the left, change some given circumstances, etc.

5.   *Speech-Motor Coordination* (Chapter 8.)
   Work on the final version of the exercise "Little Miss Muffet" (*Exercise 100*) and let the students perform one of the sets of given circumstances previously established.

Repeat the exercise one more time and suggest that students create their own set of circumstances. Remind them that they still must perform the exercise in sync with the music and that the movement pattern remains the same for everyone.

Continue training Speech-Motor Coordination with the *Exercise 104,* "The West was Getting out of Gold" and repeat Stage 3 of the exercise once by reciting the poem and walking; for the second repetition include arms' movements.

Now, the instructor should explain the poem's concept in detail and then let the students perform Stage 4 (final) of the exercise. In this lesson, let the students first recite the poem standing in place and consider all the given circumstances and the actions. Only after achieving some satisfactory results in the recitation allow the group to perform the exercise along with arms' movements.

6. **Singing-Motor Coordination** (Chapter 9.)

Conduct the exercise "Mary had a Little Lamb" (*Exercise 105*) and let the students repeat Stage 4 of it. Next, perform Stage 5 of the exercise.

Begin a new *Exercise 108,* "Old Macdonald had a Farm." Introduce Stage 1 of the exercise and practice until performed sufficiently. Next, move to Stage 2 and later to Stage 3 of the exercise.

Go to the next exercise, which is "Canon One" (*Exercise 106*), and repeat Stage 2 of the exercise several times. Pay attention to the turns and the final position.

Move to Stage 3 and introduce the music of "Frère Jacques," then let the students perform the basic pattern with this music. Next, make the students learn and memorize the song; let them sing the song several times standing in place. Now instruct the students to put together the singing and the motor part of the exercise.

7. **Expressive Hand** (Chapter 12.)

Exercise 165, "The Prayer" (final version), should be performed in this part of the lesson. Work on Stage 5, then on Stage 6 of the exercise, trying to get a smooth and balanced performance.

Next, introduce the music written specifically for this exercise, make the students listen to it, and notice the peculiarities and dynamics in it. After this, tell the students about the circumstances for this exercise, let them visualize them, and add their details while standing in place.

Let the students perform the entire exercise (Stage 7, final) with the music using the visualizations they created.

Go to *Exercise 171,* "The Goblet." Repeat the first four parts of the exercise introduced in the previous lesson. Next, introduce parts 5, 6, 7, and 8 of the exercise and put together the entire task. Repeat it several times, correcting the errors in transitions and the main pattern.

8. **Balance** (Chapter 10.)
Let the students perform the following exercises in Balance:

    Exercise 121 – "Semi-Squat on One Foot."
    Exercise 119 – "Sit next to Knees."
    Exercise 115 – "Tight Rope."

9. **Acrobatics** (Chapter 11.)
Begin the Acrobatic episode of the lesson with *Exercise 135* "Two Backward Rolls" and let the students perform the two rolls consecutively in time with the music.

Continue working on the Forward Roll in several combinations with Backbend, Shoulder Stand, and the Backward Roll. Let the students perform Exercise 139 "Backward Roll, Forward Roll, Shoulder Stand."

Introduce the new exercise "Head Stand" (*Exercise 152.*) Make sure the students understood the concept of this exercise: maintain the triangle at all times to support the body in this stunt. Try to get satisfactory results in this lesson, as by this time, your students should be able to do it after several attempts.

10. *Concluding Exercise*

Make the group conclude this lesson by running in a circle for 50 seconds to one minute with a full version of *Exercise 105* "Mary Had a Little Lamb" following the running. Ensure the students finished the exercise in a pose and held it for several moments to indicate the end of the episode and the conclusion of the lesson.

FINAL (TEST) LESSON

1.   Opening Exercise
Let the students perform the final version of Opening Exercise.

2. Warm-up Exercises
Apply a full version of Warm-up exercises I (Collection of exercises on the floor) from Chapter 4. Note, the warm-up part of this lesson is part of the final test, and the demonstration of rhythmical and economic performance should be expected and appreciated.

Conclude this part of the lesson with walking, then running, and walking again to take the breathing to regular mode.

3. Rhythmicity
As the first exercise in Rhythmicity offer "Walk in a circle and conduct 4/4-time music" (*Exercise 72*, Stage 2.)

Understand, as this is the Final Lesson, the instructor should only announce the exercise without any explanation and reminder. By this time in the process, the students must understand all the commands and freely respond to all of them.

Continue with this exercise and let the students walk forward for the first eight bars of music, then make an about-turn and continue walking in the same direction but backward. They should conduct an imaginary band at the same time.

The next variation of this exercise would be performing the task "conducting a marching band" with some given circumstances, which the instructor should announce right before the beginning of the skit. Furthermore, surprise the students with the new musical piece for this version of the exercise, the one they never heard before.

4. Posture and Gait

Let the students perform the final version of the exercise "Hamlet" (Chapter 6, *Exercise 87*) with all the given circumstances established previously. If there are guests or faculty members in attendance who are not familiar with the exercises, announce the given circumstances shortly before the exercise begins.

Repeat this exercise once or twice, and change the circumstances slightly with each repetition. It would be appropriate also to let the students perform the exercise in reverse.

5. Speech-Motor Coordination

Offer the students to perform a completely new exercise for Motor Coordination. The order of techniques and the method should be familiar to them, but the motions should be unique. The idea is to test the group for the ability to perform all the tasks from the first attempt.

Continue developing the exercise and combine it with walking in quarters, then in halves, and then in the whole-notes. Next, let the students perform different variations of this exercise, walking forward, backward, walking in various tempos and rhythms.

Continue, add to this exercise reciting the poem "Humpty-Dumpty," first in combination with plain steps in quarters, and the second time with given circumstances and unexpected commands.

Next, let the students perform the final version of exercise "The West was getting out of Gold." To freshen up the memory, allow them to perform it the first time with steps and arms' movements only. On the second repetition, suggest performing the entire exercise with all the circumstances and actions developed previously.

6. Singing-Motor Coordination

Let the students perform the final stage of Exercise 105, "Mary had a Little Lamb." Next, announce a new set of given circumstances to the students for this exercise and let them perform it once or twice.

The second repetition would make the exercise more challenging by introducing clapping hands on a particular beat of the music.

Continue with exercise "The Bricks" (*Exercise 102*) and let the student perform two or three different versions of the exercise with numbers, names, colors, etc.

Next, demonstrate exercise "Canon One" (*Exercise 106.*) Begin with Stage 3 of the exercise and let the student do it once to refresh their memory. Afterward, allow them to perform the task with different challenges, such as interrupting the music while the exercise is in progress.

7. Acrobatics

Announce a completely new combination of different stunts accomplished previously; explain in detail all the technical tasks such as the duration of each stunt, the transitions from one to another, the peculiarities, etc. You might want to repeat the task twice (second time a shorter version) because the combination must be performed sufficiently in the first attempt. Do not make this combination too complicated, as this might discourage the students.

Note, this exercise supposed to demonstrate the ability of your students to visualize the series of tasks, to memorize the order of motions, and to find adjustments in the process of performing the tasks.

Repeat the combination two or three times after that to give the group a chance to improve their performances.

8. Novelty Exercise

Pick up an exercise from this textbook, or one created by you, and offer it as Novelty Exercise that the students would have to learn "here and now." Use the methodological Principles and Techniques of the Essential Stage Movement and develop this exercise from the beginning to specific, determined by you, level.

The tasks should be challenging but not too complicated to perform from the first or second attempt. The final version should have some artistic values but not necessarily include given circumstances and actions.

This exercise would demonstrate your students' ability to learn a new pattern quickly and tenaciously, something they acquired during the entire semester.

9. Expressive Hand

Let the students perform the final version of the exercise "The Goblet" (*Exercise 171*) first paying attention only to the technical execution of the motions, and the second time with all the circumstances and the actions established previously. As before, the instructor might want to explain the guests a short description of the given circumstances.

Repeat this exercise, if needed, one more time with the given circumstances slightly changed.

10. Exercise "Echo" (Chapter 5, Rhythmicity.)

Present this exercise separately to test this special skill. The accompanist should have a set of samples specially prepared for the Final lesson and representing a wide variety of tempos, dynamics, and other specific qualities of music.

Offer the first set of samples in 4/4-time with one bar played at a time; the second set should represent samples lasting two bars each.

11. Canon II (Exercise 107, Chapter 9.)

Let the students perform the Stage 3 of the exercise with steps only.

Next, make them perform this exercise with the music "Battle Hymn of the Republic" without singing yet (Stage 4 of the exercise.)

Finally, instruct the students to perform the entire exercise with the given circumstances announced for the first time. Also, (if possible) introduce a new rendition of the song, perhaps played by a band (recorded). However, the students should listen to this variation first before the exercise begins.

Continue working with exercise "Canon II" and let the students perform it with the music "Oh, Susanna." It is important to observe how the students would use one movement pattern to perform such polarized tempo-rhythms.

Use the same pattern yet again and suggest the students use a "Tango" with these movements.

12. **The Prayer** (*Exercise 165*, Chapter 12.)

Instruct the students to perform "The Prayer," first paying attention to the movements and trying to perform the pattern as accurately as possible. Announce a set of given circumstances and let the students complete the exercise considering these circumstances.

Let the students repeat the exercise one more time and offer to come up with individual circumstances and actions. Never mind this time that the exercise performed as a group.

13. **Old MacDonald** (Exercise 108.)

Ask the group to perform Stage 4 of the exercise first and concentrate on the pattern's techniques.

Repeat the exercise with a set of given circumstances.

Let the students perform the exercise as a Canon, by numbers, singing, and moving at the same time.

14. *Concluding Exercise*

As usual, conclude the Final Lesson with walking, then running, and then walking again. In the end, express your gratitude to the students for good work done in this lesson and the entire semester.

APPENDIX

MUSIC SCORES

1.

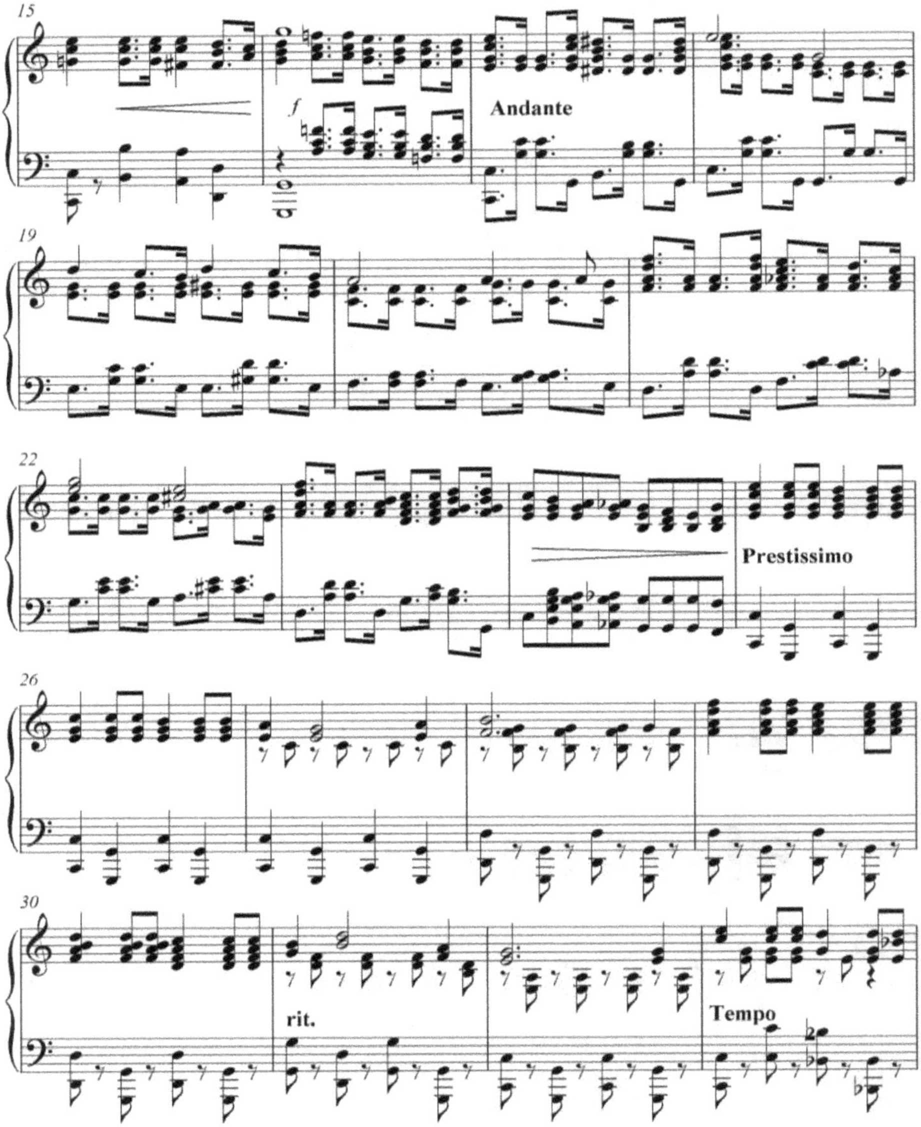
15
f
Andante
19
22
Prestissimo
26
30
rit.
Tempo

2.

3.

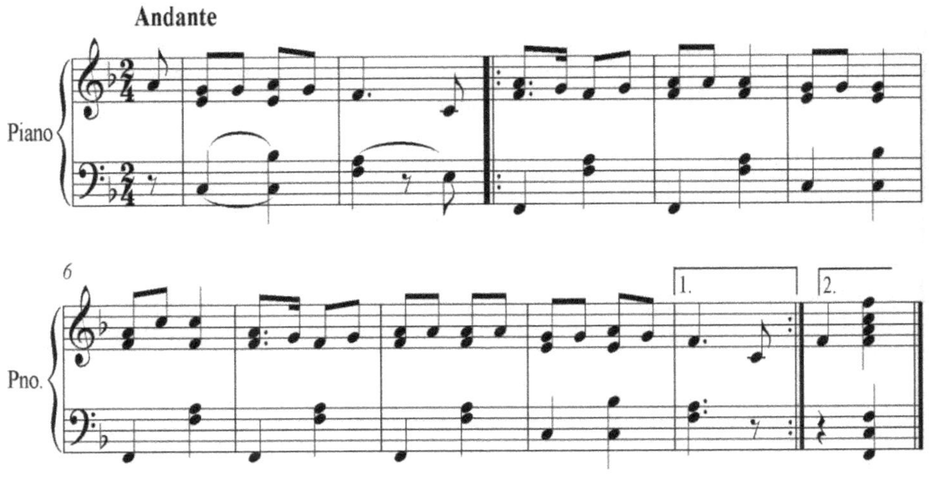

4.

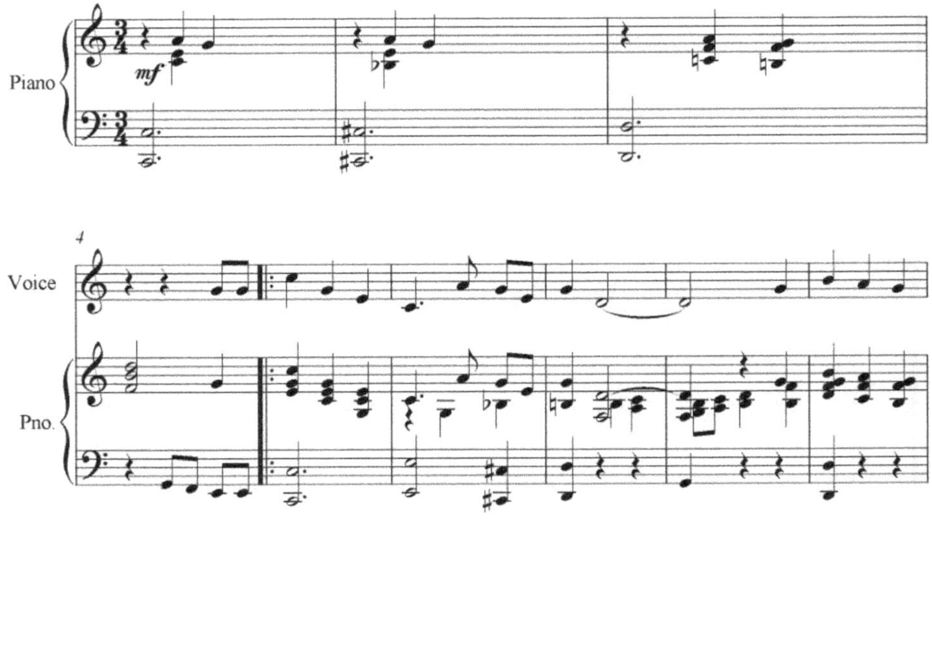

5.

6.

7.

8.

9.

10.

11.

12.

13.

14.

15.

16.

17.

18.

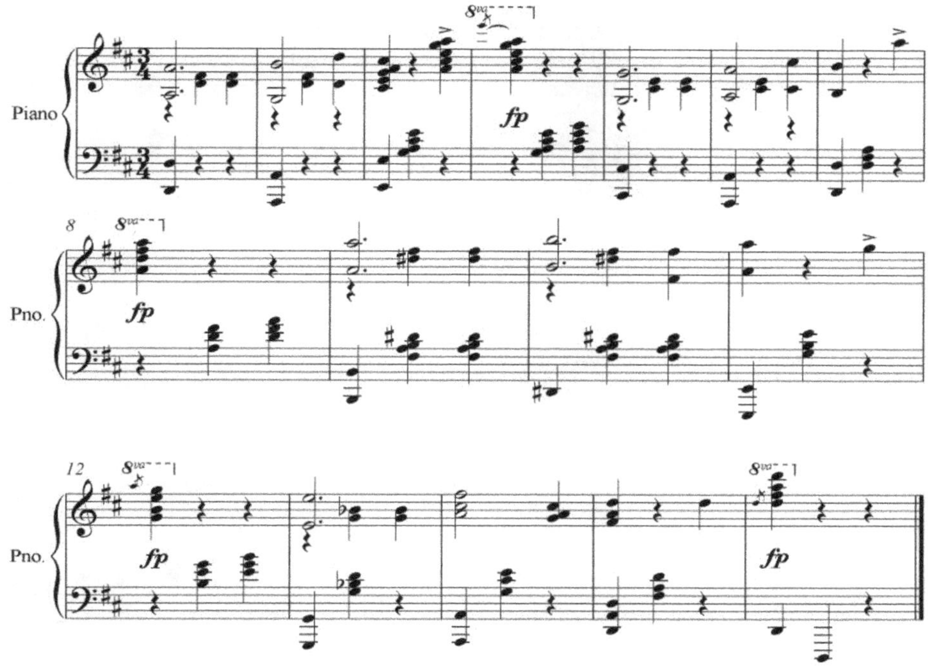

19.

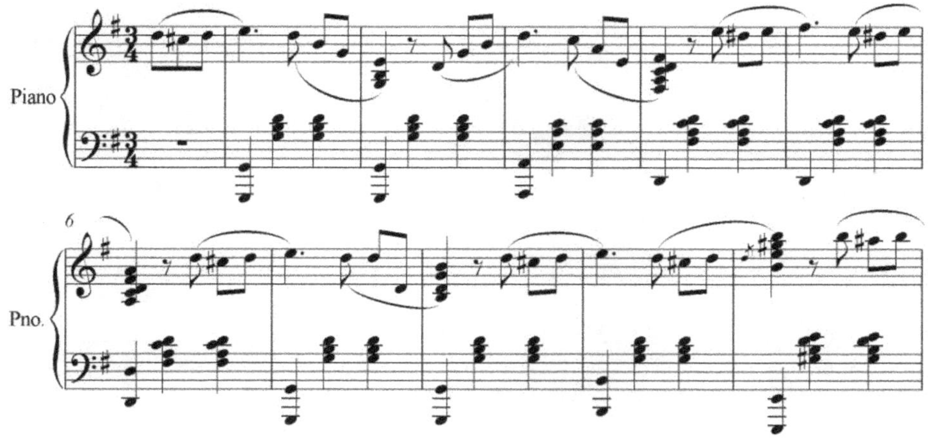

20.

21.

22.

23.

24.

25.

26.

27.

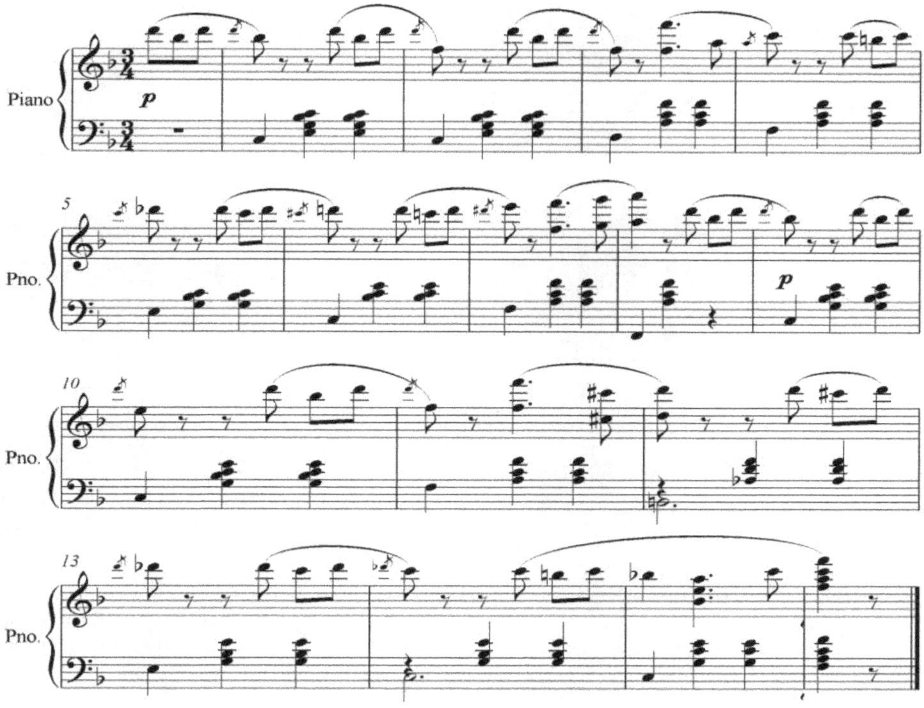

28.

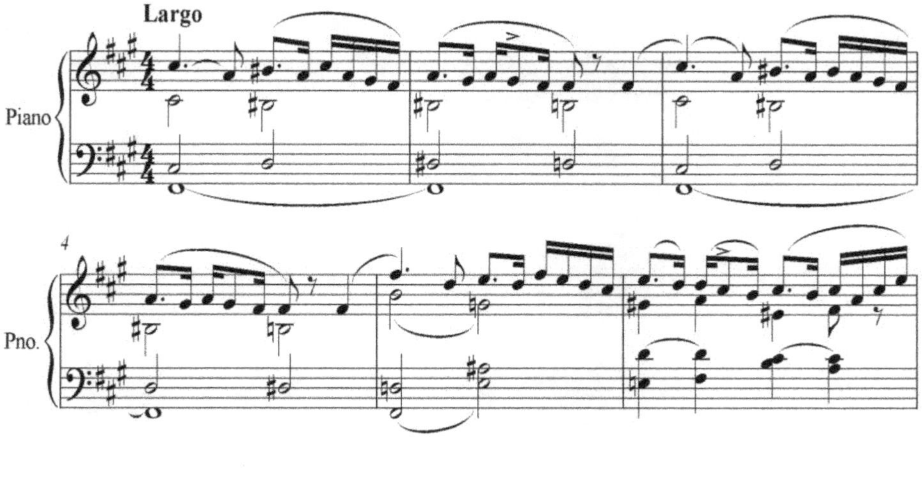

29.

30.

NOTES

Chapter One

1. Here and elsewhere, translation of K. Stanislavsky is mine. E. Rozinsky.
2. Ted Shawn, *Every Little Movement, a Book about Delsarte* (New York: Dance Horizons, Inc., 1963), 11.
3. Prince Sergey Volkonsky, *Expressive Man* (Saint Petersburg: Sirius, 1913), 20.
4. Emile Jaques-Dalcroze, Translated from the French by Harold F. Rubenstein, *Rhythm, Music, and Education* (London: The Dalcroze Society, 1921) 39.
5. Same, Page 27.
6. Same, Page 37.
7. Same, Page 102.
8. The word "synthetic" here is used as derived from *synthesis*, a complex whole formed by combining (Webster's Encyclopedic Unabridged Dictionary.)
9. Translation from the Russian is mine. E. Rozinsky.
10. Konstantin Stanislavsky, *Sobranie sochinenii*, 8 vols. (Moscow: Iskusstvo, 1954 – 1961), Volume III, 32-33.
11. I. S. Ivanov, E. S. Shishmariova. *Educating Actor's Movement* (Moscow: Khudozhestvenaia Literature, 1937) 5.
12. The word "plastic" is used in the meaning of "having the power of artistic expression" (Webster's Encyclopedic Unabridged Dictionary.)
13. Bella Merlin, *Beyond Stanislavsky* (New York: Routledge, 2002), 9.

Chapter Two

1. Georg Wilhelm Friedrich Hegel, Aesthetics: *Vorlesungen über die Ästhetik* (Eng. trans., *Lectures on Aesthetics* (Berlin: Heinrich Gustav Hotho,1835).

2. Translation from the Russian is mine. E. Rozinsky.
3. Translation of the term from the Russian by Sharon M. Carnicke.
4. N. M. Gorchakov, *Directorial Lessons of Stanislavsky* (Moscow, Iskusstvo, 1942), 194.
5. K. S. Stanislavsky, *Articles. Speeches. Interviews. Letters.* (Moscow: Iskusstvo, 1953) 630.
6. B. E. Zakhava, *Mastership of Actor and Director* (Moscow: "Prosviaschenie", 1978), 165.
7. A. Y. Tairov, *About Theatre* (Moscow: Vserosiiskoe Teatral'noe Obshestvo, 1970), 127.
8. L. P. Novitskaia, *Lessons in Inspiration* (Moscow: VTO, 1984), 135.

Chapter Three

1. I. M. Sechenov, *Refleksy golovnogo mozga*, (*Reflexes of the Brain*) (Moscow: Academy of Science USSR, 1952) Vol. I, 9.
2. K. Stanislavsky, *Sobranie sochinenii*, 8 vols. (Moscow: Iskusstvo, 1954 – 1961), Vol. II, 374.
3. N. Bernstein, *O Lovkosti I ee Razvitii*, (*About Dexterity and its Development*) (Moscow: Fizkultura I Sport, 1991.)
4. Stanislavsky's term.
5. K. S. Stanislavsky, *Sobranie sochinenii*, 8 vols. (Moscow: Iskusstvo, 1954 – 1961), Vol. 3, 152.

Chapter Four

1. Here and thereafter, the descriptions of the exercises are presented in a fashion similar to that given by an instructor to a group of students.
2. *Time*, unlike the word *tempo* (which means speed or pace), is used in music for the metrical divisions or bar-lengths of a piece of music. These are indicated at the beginning of a work of music or at the introduction of a changed time, by two

numbers that form a *time signature*. The upper number shows how many beats there are in a bar, while the lower number shows what kind of note is it. Thus, 4/4 means that each bar consists of four quarter-notes (or crotchets) or their equivalent in notes of shorter or longer duration.

3. The *beat* or *pulse* in a piece of music is the regular rhythmic pattern of the music. Each bar should start with a strong beat (also known as *Down-Beat*) and each bar should end with a weak beat (also known as *Up-Beat*). "Up and down" describe the gestures of a conductor, whose preparatory up-beat is of even greater importance to players than his down-beat.

4. A *measure*, or a *bar*, is music written between the vertical bar-lines on the stave to mark the metrical units of a piece of music.

Chapter Five

1. All musical terms are traditionally of Italian origin.

Chapter Six

1. K. Stanislavsky, *Sobranie sochinenii*, 8 vols. (Moscow: Iskusstvo, 1954 – 1961), Vol. III, 49.
2. K. Stanislavsky, Rabota Aktera nad soboij, (Actor's prepares) (Moscow: Iskusstvo, 1955), 52.
3. In this text, all Stanislavsky's terms are given in the interpretation by Sharon M. Carnicke.

Chapter Eight

1. K. Stanislavsky, *Sobranie sochinenii*, 8 vols. (Moscow: Iskusstvo, 1954 – 1961), Vol. II, 84.

Chapter Nine

1. One foot in front of the other, heel touches the middle of the other foot, toes apart 90 degrees.

2. This exercise and other similar exercises of Chapter Nine are called *"Canon"* in the musical meaning of this word, which is a musical composition in which the melody is imitated exactly and completely by the successive voices.

Chapter Eleven

1. K. C. Stanislavsky, *Rabota Aktera nad soboij*, (Moscow: Iskusstvo, 1955), Vol. III, 34.
2. A term for continuous various jumps following one another at the end of the circus show.

Chapter Twelve

1. S. M. Mikhoels, *Editorials, Discussions, Lectures* (Moscow: Iskusstvo, 1965)

Chapter Fifteen

1. Ivan Kokh, *Principles of Stage Movement* (Leningrad: Iskusstvo, 19700, 464.

www.ingramcontent.com/pod-product-compliance
Lightning Source LLC
Chambersburg PA
CBHW031228090426
42742CB00007B/117